SAA-C03: AWS Certified Solutions Architect Associate

Study Guide with Practice Questions and Labs

Fourth Edition

www.ipspecialist.net

Document Control

Proposal Name	:	AWS Certified Solutions Architect Associate
Document Edition	:	Fourth Edition
Document Volume	:	Volume 3
Document Release Date	:	25th March 2023
Reference	:	SAA-C03

Feedback:
If you have any comments regarding the quality of this book, or otherwise alter it to better suit your needs, you can contact us through email at info@ipspecialist.net
Please make sure to include the book's title and ISBN in your message.

About IPSpecialist

IPSPECIALIST LTD. IS COMMITTED TO EXCELLENCE AND DEDICATED TO YOUR SUCCESS.

Our philosophy is to treat our customers like family. We want you to succeed and are willing to do everything possible to help you make it happen. We have the proof to back up our claims. We strive to accelerate billions of careers with great courses, accessibility, and affordability. We believe that continuous learning and knowledge evolution are the most important things to keep re-skilling and up-skilling the world.

Planning and creating a specific goal is where IPSpecialist helps. We can create a career track that suits your visions as well as develop the competencies you need to become a professional Network Engineer. Based on the career track you choose, we can also assist you with the execution and evaluation of your proficiency level, as they are customized to fit your specific goals.

We help you STAND OUT from the crowd through our detailed IP training content packages.

Course Features:

- ❖ Self-Paced Learning
  - Learn at your own pace and in your own time
- ❖ Covers Complete Exam Blueprint
  - Prep for the exam with confidence
- ❖ Case Study Based Learning
  - Relate the content with real-life scenarios
- ❖ Subscriptions that Suits You
  - Get more and pay less with IPS subscriptions
- ❖ Career Advisory Services
  - Let the industry experts plan your career journey
- ❖ Virtual Labs to test your skills
  - With IPS vRacks, you can evaluate your exam preparations
- ❖ Practice Questions
  - Practice questions to measure your preparation standards
- ❖ On Request Digital Certification
  - On request digital certification from IPSpecialist LTD.

About the Authors:

This book has been compiled with the help of multiple professional engineers. These engineers specialize in different fields e.g., Networking, Security, Cloud, Big Data, IoT, etc. Each engineer develops content in its specialized field that is compiled to form a comprehensive certification guide.

About the Technical Reviewers:

Nouman Ahmed Khan

AWS-Architect, CCDE, CCIEX5 (RandS, SP, Security, DC, Wireless), CISSP, CISA, CISM is a Solution Architect working with a major telecommunication provider in Qatar. He works with enterprises, mega-projects, and service providers to help them select the best-fit technology solutions. He also works closely as a consultant to understand customer business processes and helps select an appropriate technology strategy to support business goals. He has more than 18 years of experience working in Pakistan/Middle-East and UK. He holds a Bachelor of Engineering Degree from NED University, Pakistan, and M.Sc. in Computer Networks from the UK.

Abubakar Saeed

Abubakar Saeed has more than twenty-five years of experience, Managing, Consulting, Designing, and implementing large-scale technology projects, extensive experience heading ISP operations, solutions integration, heading Product Development, Presales, and Solution Design. Emphasizing adhering to Project timelines and delivering as per customer expectations, he always leads the project in the right direction with his innovative ideas and excellent management.

Dr. Fahad Abdali

Dr. Fahad Abdali is a seasoned leader with extensive experience managing and growing software development teams in high-growth start-ups. He is a business entrepreneur with more than 18 years of experience in management and marketing. He holds a Bachelor's Degree from NED University of Engineering and Technology and a Doctor of Philosophy (Ph.D.) from the University of Karachi.

Mehwish Jawed

Mehwish Jawed is working as a Senior Research Analyst. She holds a Master's and Bachelors of Engineering degree in Telecommunication Engineering from NED University of Engineering and Technology. She also worked under the supervision of HEC Approved supervisor. She has more than three published papers, including both conference and journal papers. She has a great knowledge of TWDM Passive Optical Network (PON). She also worked as a Project Engineer, Robotic Trainer in a private institute and has research skills in the field of communication networks. She has both technical knowledge and industry-sounding information, which she utilizes effectively when needed. She also has expertise in cloud platforms, such as AWS, GCP, Oracle, and Microsoft Azure.

Syeda Fariha Ashrafi

Syeda Fariha Ashrafi is working as a technical content developer. She has completed bachelor's degree in Telecommunication Engineering from NED University of Engineering and Technology. She has also completed the CCNA (Routing and Switching) course. During her bachelor's program, she has worked on the project "Smart metering using PLC (Power Line Communication).

Free Resources

For Free Resources: Please visit our website and register to access your desired Resources Or contact us at: helpdesk@ipspecialist.net

Career Report: This report is a step-by-step guide for a novice who wants to develop his/her career in the field of computer networks. It answers the following queries:

- What are the current scenarios and future prospects?
- Is this industry moving toward saturation, or are new opportunities knocking at the door?
- What will the monetary benefits be?
- Why get certified?
- How to plan, and when will I complete the certifications if I start today?
- Is there any career track that I can follow to accomplish the specialization level?

Furthermore, this guide provides a comprehensive career path towards being a specialist in networking and highlights the tracks needed to obtain certification.

IPS Personalized Technical Support for Customers: Good customer service means helping customers efficiently, and in a friendly manner. It is essential to be able to handle issues for customers and do your best to ensure they are satisfied. Providing good service is one of the most important things that can set our business apart from others.

Excellent customer service will attract more customers and attain maximum customer retention.

IPS offers personalized TECH support to its customers to provide better value for money. If you have any queries related to technology and labs, you can simply ask our technical team for assistance via Live Chat or Email.

2023 BONUS MATERIAL! FREE SURPRISE VOUCHER

1. Get **500** UNIQUE Practice Questions (online) to simulate the real exam.

AND

2. Get FREE **Exam Cram Notes** (online access)

Get the Coupon Code from the **References** Section

Our Products

Study Guides
IPSpecialist Study Guides are the ideal guides to developing the hands-on skills necessary to pass the exam. Our workbooks cover the official exam blueprint and explain the technology with real-life case study-based labs. The content covered in each workbook consists of individually focused technology topics presented in an easy-to-follow, goal-oriented, step-by-step approach. Every scenario features detailed breakdowns and thorough verifications to help you completely understand the task and associated technology.

We extensively used mind maps in our workbooks to visually explain the technology. Our workbooks have become a widely used tool to learn and remember information effectively.

Practice Questions
IP Specialists' Practice Questions are dedicatedly designed from a certification exam perspective. The collection of these questions from our Study Guides is prepared to keep the exam blueprint in mind, covering not only important but necessary topics. It is an ideal document to practice and revise your certification.

Exam Cram
Our Exam Cram notes are a concise bundling of condensed notes of the complete exam blueprint. It is an ideal and handy document to help you remember the most important technology concepts related to the certification exam.

Hands-on Labs
IPSpecialist Hands-on Labs are the fastest and easiest way to learn real-world use cases. These labs are carefully designed to prepare you for the certification exams and your next job role. Whether you are starting to learn a technology and solving a real-world scenario, our labs will help you learn the core concepts in no time.

IPSpecialist self-paced labs were designed by subject matter experts and provide an opportunity to use products in a variety of pre-designed scenarios and common use cases, giving you hands-on practice in a simulated environment to help you gain confidence. You have the flexibility to choose from topics and products about which you want to learn more.

Companion Guide

Companion Guides are portable desk guides for the IPSpecialist course materials that users (students, professionals, and experts) can access at any time and from any location. Companion Guides are intended to supplement online course material by assisting users in concentrating on key ideas and planning their study time for quizzes and examinations.

Content at a glance

Table of Contents

AWS Cloud Certifications

AWS Certifications are industry-recognized credentials that validate your technical cloud skills and expertise while assisting your career growth. These are the most valuable IT certifications right now since AWS has established an overwhelming lead in the public cloud market. Even with several tough competitors such as Microsoft Azure, Google Cloud Engine, and Rackspace, AWS is by far the dominant public cloud platform today, with an astounding collection of proprietary services that continues to grow.

The two key reasons as to why AWS certifications are prevailing in the current cloud-oriented job market are as follows:

- There is a dire need for skilled cloud engineers, developers, and architects – the current shortage of experts is expected to continue into the near future
- AWS certifications stand out for their thoroughness, rigor, consistency, and appropriateness for critical cloud engineering positions

Value of AWS Certifications

AWS places equal emphasis on sound conceptual knowledge of its entire platform and hands-on experience with the AWS infrastructure and its many unique and complex components and services.

For Individuals
- Demonstrate your expertise in designing, deploying, and operating highly available, cost-effective, and secured applications on AWS
- Gain recognition and visibility for your proven skills and proficiency with AWS
- Earn tangible benefits such as access to the AWS Certified LinkedIn Community, invites to AWS Certification Appreciation Receptions and Lounges, AWS Certification Practice Exam Voucher, Digital Badge for certification validation, AWS Certified Logo usage, access to AWS Certified Store
- Foster credibility with your employers and peers

For Employers

- Identify skilled professionals to lead IT initiatives with AWS technologies
- Reduce risks and costs to implement your workloads and projects on the AWS platform
- Increase customer satisfaction

Types of Certification

Role-based Certification:

- *Foundational* - Validates overall understanding of the AWS Cloud. Prerequisite to achieving the Specialty certification or an optional start toward the Associate certification
- *Associate* - Technical role-based certifications. No pre-requisite
- *Professional* - The highest level of technical role-based certification. Relevant Associate certification required

Specialty Certification:

- Validates advanced skills in specific technical areas

- Requires one active role-based certification

Certification Roadmap

AWS Certified Cloud Practitioner is a new entry-level certification. Furthermore, there are five different AWS certification offerings in three different tracks. These include Solutions Architect, Developer, and SysOps Administrator. AWS also offers two specialty certifications in technical areas: Big Data and Advanced Networking.

AWS Certified Solutions Architect Associate

People who work as solutions architects should take the AWS Certified Solutions Architect - Associate (SAA-C03) exam. A candidate's ability to use AWS technologies to create solutions based on the AWS Well-Architected Framework is verified by the test.

The test confirms a candidate's capacity to carry out the following duties:

- Create solutions that use AWS services to address both present-day business demands and anticipated future requirements.
- Create cost-effective, resilient, high-performing, and safe architectures;
- Evaluate current solutions and identify ways to make them better.

Intended Audience

Candidates may be business analysts, project managers, chief experience officers, AWS Academy students, and other IT-related professionals. They may serve in sales, marketing, finance, and legal roles.

About AWS – Certified Solutions Architect Associate Exam

Exam Questions	Case study, short answer, repeated answer, MCQs
Number of Questions	100-120
Time to Complete	150 minutes
Exam Fee	165 USD

Recommended AWS Knowledge

- 1 year of hands-on experience designing available, cost-effective, fault-tolerant, and scalable distributed systems on AWS
- Hands-on experience using compute, networking, storage, and database AWS services
- Hands-on experience with AWS deployment and management services
- Ability to identify and define technical requirements for an AWS-based application
- Ability to identify which AWS services meet a given technical requirement
- Knowledge of recommended best practices for building secure and reliable applications on the AWS platform
- An understanding of the basic architectural principles of building in the AWS Cloud
- An understanding of the AWS global infrastructure

- An understanding of network technologies as they relate to AWS
- An understanding of security features and tools that AWS provides and how they relate to traditional services

All the required information is included in this study guide.

	Domain	Percentage
Domain 1	Design Secure Architectures	30%
Domain 2	Design Resilient Architectures	26%
Domain 3	Design High-Performing Architectures	24%
Domain 4	Design Cost-Optimized Architectures	20%
Total		100%

Domain 1: Design Secure Architectures
- Design secure access to AWS resources.
- Design secure workloads and applications.
- Determine appropriate data security controls

Domain 2: Design Resilient Architectures
- Design scalable and loosely coupled architectures.
- Design highly available and/or fault-tolerant architectures

Domain 3: Design High-Performing Architectures
- Determine high-performing and/or scalable storage solutions.
- Design high-performing and elastic compute solutions.
- Determine high-performing database solutions.
- Determine high-performing and/or scalable network architectures.
- Determine high-performing data ingestion and transformation solutions.

Domain 4: Design Cost-Optimized Architectures
- Design cost-optimized storage solutions.
- Design cost-optimized compute solutions.
- Design cost-optimized database solutions
- Design cost-optimized network architectures.

Chapter 08: High Availability (HA) Architecture

Introduction

In this chapter, we will discuss load balancing, types of load balancing, auto scaling, and auto scaling options, as these are the building blocks of a High Availability (HA) architecture. We will focus on what HA architecture is and why it is necessary. We will learn how to add resilience and fault tolerance to an architecture.

Load Balancers

Access to many services, such as Amazon EC2 instances, that provide a consistent experience for end users is advantageous in cloud computing. A method for ensuring consistency and efficiently distributing request load among numerous servers. A load balancer is a technique that distributes or balances traffic across several EC2 instances automatically. You can manage your virtual load balancers on Amazon and use the AWS cloud service called Elastic Load Balancer, which provides a managed load balancer for you.

You may distribute traffic over a set of Amazon EC2 instances in a single or several Availability Zones with Elastic Load Balancer, allowing you to achieve high availability for your applications. Elastic Load Balancer scales to the vast majority of workloads automatically. Hypertext Transfer Protocol (HTTP), Transmission Control Protocol (TCP), Hypertext Transfer Protocol Secure (HTTPS), Secure Socket Layer (SSL), and routing to Amazon EC2 instances are all supported by Elastic Load Balancer. A CNAME record maps a domain name or a subdomain name to a CNAME. You can create a CNAME record to point a specified subdomain name to a CNAME. By default, Application Load Balancer (ALB) provides domain names to allow external access.. It also supports both internal application-facing and Internet-facing load balancers. To ensure that the traffic is not routed to unhealthy and failing instances, Elastic Load Balancing (ELB) supports health checks for Amazon EC2 instances. Elastic Load Balancer can automatically scale by collected metrics.

Advantages of using Elastic Load Balancer

Because ELB (Elastic Load Balancer) is a managed service that automatically scales in and out to satisfy the demand for high availability within the area as a service and increase application traffic, it has various advantages. Elastic Load Balancer distributes traffic across healthy instances to ensure that your apps are available in many locations. Elastic Load Balancer automatically scales Amazon EC2 instances behind the load balancer with auto scaling service. Elastic Load Balancing is secure. Elastic Load Balancer supports SSL termination and integrated certificate management. Customers can enable Elastic Load Balancing within a single or multiple Availability Zones for more consistent application performance.

> **EXAM TIP:** Elastic Load Balancer is a highly available service that may be used to help develop highly available systems.

Types of Load Balancers
There are three different types of Load Balancers in AWS;

- Application Load Balancer
- Network Load Balancer (Beyond the scope of this course)
- Classic Load Balancer

Application Load Balancer

The Application Load Balancer is an AWS ELB that allows a developer to transport inbound traffic to AWS apps. The Application Load Balancer is ideally suited for HTTP and HTTPS traffic load balancing. It is application-aware and runs at layer 7. Advanced request routing allows you to send a specific request to specific web servers.

The Application Load Balancer inspects packets and sets up HTTP and HTTPS header access. It distributes load to the target efficiently based on the flow of HTTP messages. You can do the following with an Application Load Balancer:

- Content-Based Routing
  An Application Load Balancer lets you define rules for routing traffic to different target groups. The target groups are usually services in architecture.
- Container Support
  On an EC2 instance, Application Load Balancer enables you to balance the load across multiple ports. This functionality is targeted for containers that are integrated with Amazon ECS.
- Application Monitoring
  You can monitor and associate health checks per target group with an Application Load Balancer.

Network Load Balancer

A Network Load Balancer is ideally suited for Load Balancing of Transfer Control Protocol (TCP) traffic where exceptional performance is required. Network Load Balancer operates at the connection level (Layer 4) and can handle millions of requests per second while maintaining ultra-low latencies. It is a high-performance material.

Classic Load Balancer

The legacy Elastic Load Balancer is known as the Classic Load Balancer. You can employ layer 7-specific capabilities like X-forwarded and sticky sessions to load balance HTTP/HTTPS apps. For applications that rely solely on the TCP protocol, stringent Layer 4 load balancing can also be used.

In comparison to an Application Load Balancer, a Classic Load Balancer provides the following advantages:

- Support for EC2 Classic instances
- Support for TCP and SSL listeners
- Support for sticky sessions using cookies that are generated by applications

---

EXAM TIP: To offer a single and stable entry point, AWS advises referring to a load balancer by its Domain Name System (DNS) name rather than the IP address of the load balancer.

Internal Load Balancer

It is commonly used in a multi-tier application to load balance traffic between layers, such as when an Internet-facing load balancer receives and balances traffic to the web or presentation tier's Amazon EC2 instances and sends its request to the application tier's load balancer. Internal load balancers can direct traffic to Amazon EC2 instances in private VPCs. An internal (or private) load balancer is used where private IPs are needed at the frontend only.

HTTPS Load Balancer

Load Balancers can be created using the SSL/TLS (Transport Layer Security) protocol encrypted connections, also known as SSL offload. You can encrypt the traffic between the client that initiates the HTTPS session and your load balancer and for the connection between your back-end instances and your load balancer. Elastic Load Balancer provides pre-defined SSL negotiation configuration security policies that are used to negotiate connections between the load balancer and the client. You must install an SSL certificate to use SSL on the load balancer, which is used to terminate the connection and decrypt the request before sending a request to the back-end Amazon EC2 instance from the client. It is optional to enable authentication on your back-end instances. Elastic Load Balancing does not support SNI (Server Name Indication) on your Load Balancer. This means that you will need to add SAN (Subject Alternative Name) for each website if you want to host more than one website on a fleet of Amazon EC2 instances, with a single SSL certificate behind the Elastic Load Balancing to avoid site users seeing a warning message when the site is accessed.

Listeners

Every Load Balancer has multiple *listeners* configured. It is a process that checks connection requests, such as a CNAME configured to record the name of the Load Balancer. Every listener is configured with the port (Client to Load Balancer) and protocol for the back-end and a protocol and a port for a front-end (load balancer to Amazon EC2 instance) connection. The following protocols are supported by Elastic Load Balancing;

- HTTP
- HTTPS
- TCP
- SSL

Configuration Elastic Load Balancing

You can configure the Load Balancer's server aspects with Elastic Load Balancer, including idle connection timeout, connection draining, cross-zone load balancing, sticky sessions, proxy protocol, and health checks. You can modify configuration settings using either Command Line Interface (CLI) or AWS Management Console.

Idle Connection Timeout

For every request that the client makes through the load balancer, there are two connections maintained by the load balancer. One is with the client, and the other is with the back-end instances. The load balancer manages an idle timeout for each connection triggered when data is not sent over the connection for a specified period. When the idle timeout period has elapsed, the connection closes by the load balancer if data has not been sent or received.

> **EXAM TIP:** Elastic Load Balancer sets an idle timeout for 60 seconds by default. Ensure that the value set for keep-alive time is higher than the idle timeout settings on your load balancer to make sure that the load balancer is responsible for closing the connection to your back-end instances.

Load Balancer Errors

The ELB (Classic Load Balancer) will react with a 504 error if your application stops responding. This indicates that the program is experiencing problems, which could be at the Web server or database layer. Determine where the application is failing and, if possible, scale it up or down.

Sticky sessions

By default, Load Balancer directs each request to the registered instance with the smallest load. You can use the sticky session feature, also known as session affinity, which allows the load balancer to associate the user's session with a certain instance. It also ensures that the user's requests are sent to the same instance during the session.

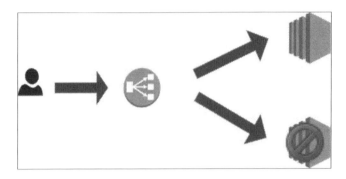

Figure 8-01: Sticky Sessions Enabled

Health checks

Health checks are supported by Elastic Load Balancing to test the status of Amazon EC2 instances behind an Elastic Load Balancing load balancer. At the time of health check, the status of the instance that is healthy is *InService*, and the health status of any instance unhealthy is *out of service*. To determine the health of an instant Load Balancer, perform health checks on all registered instances. You can set a threshold for multiple consecutive health check page failures before an instance is found unhealthy.

> **EXAM TIP:** A single load balancer can hold up to 25 certificates. If you want to use more than 25 certificates you have to select more than one load balancer.

This is a very frequent exam topic. Consider the scenario in Figure 8-01; we have a user trying to access a website placed behind a load balancer. And because sticky sessions are enabled, one user's session is stuck with a Target group or, in the case of a CLB, to a specific EC2 instance. In the exam, you may be asked what you can do as an Admin to distribute traffic to the other target group. The answer is simple, you go in and disable sticky sessions. Or the case could be the opposite; that is why a user is not bound to a specific EC2 instance, so you will need to enable sticky sessions.

Cross Zone Load Balancing

Cross-zone load balancing enables your CLB to distribute requests evenly across the registered instances in all enabled availability zones. Application load balancers use this by default. It will be easier to understand the idea if we discuss an example that will give you an idea of what it will be like in the exam.

Example

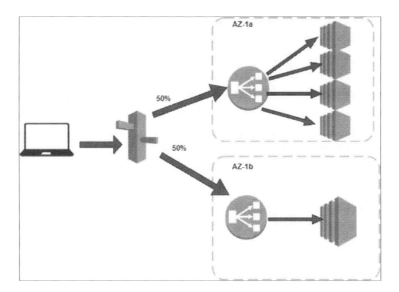

Figure 8-02: Cross Zone Load Balancing Disabled

Consider the scenario in Figure 8-02; Route 53 is being used as the DNS provider, splitting the traffic 50-50 to two different availability zones. In both AZs, we have CLBs. In AZ 1a, we have 4 EC2 instances; in 1b, we only have 1 EC2 instance. Since cross-zone load balancing is not enabled, the load balancer is unable to route requests to other availability zones, so AZ 1a will receive 50% of the traffic, and it will be distributed in 4 instances, while in AZ 1b, the 50% will be routed to the single instance. Each instance in AZ 1a will receive 12.5% traffic, while the instance in AZ 1b will have to serve 50% traffic. This is not even, and the purpose of load balancing failed here; if cross-zone load balancing were enabled, each instance in both AZs would have received 20% traffic because load balancers would be able to route the traffic across availability zones, as depicted in Figure 8-03.

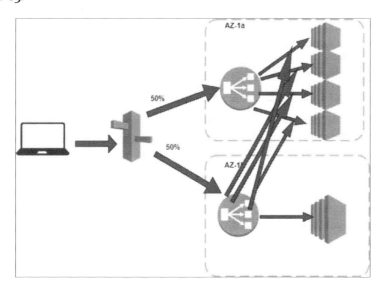

Figure 8-03: Cross Zone Load Balancing Enabled

A common exam scenario is that you have instances in two AZs behind load balancers. Still, instances in one AZ are receiving traffic while the other AZ is not receiving any traffic at all. You should be able to answer it because Route 53 is sending 100% traffic to one AZ, and cross-zone load balancing is not enabled.

Path-based Routing

You may need to forward requests based on the URL path. To do so, you can create a listener with rules. This is called path-based routing or path patterns. If micro-services are being used, path-based routing can be used to route traffic to multiple back-end services.

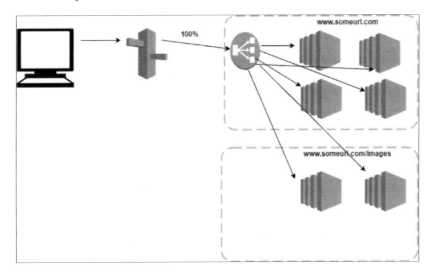

Figure 8-04: Path-based Routing

Here is an example of path-based routing in Figure 8-04. Route 53 sends 100% of user requests to a single load balancer, and path patterns are enabled, so all the requests to www.someurl.com are routed to the instances in AZ 1a, and the requests for imaged rendering are forwarded to AZ 1b. This is how path patterns work, and you might see some scenario questions in the exam about enabling and disabling path-based routing.

Lab 8-01: Load Balancers and Health Checks

Step 1. Log in to AWS and go to EC2 under Compute

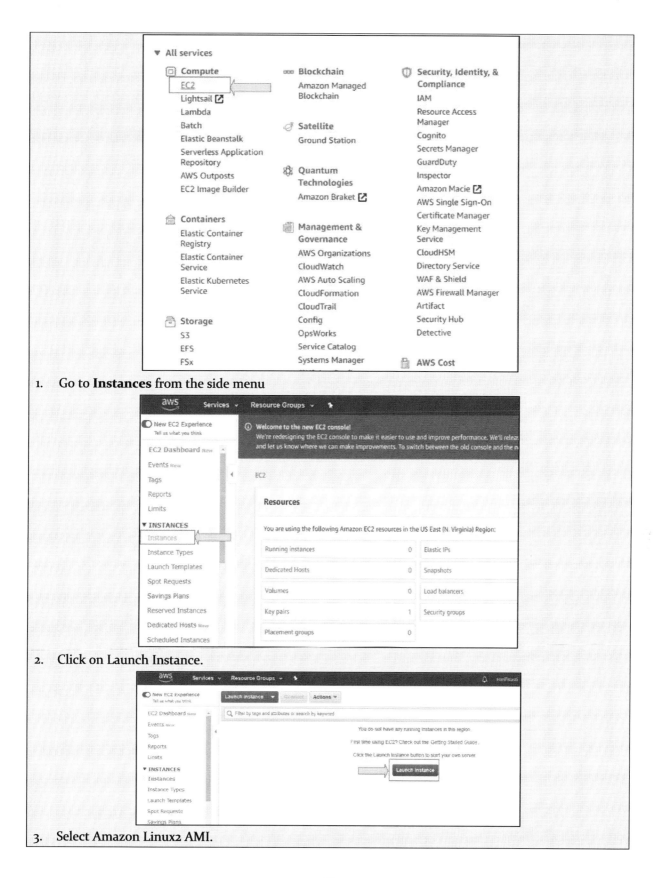

1. Go to **Instances** from the side menu

2. Click on Launch Instance.

3. Select Amazon Linux2 AMI.

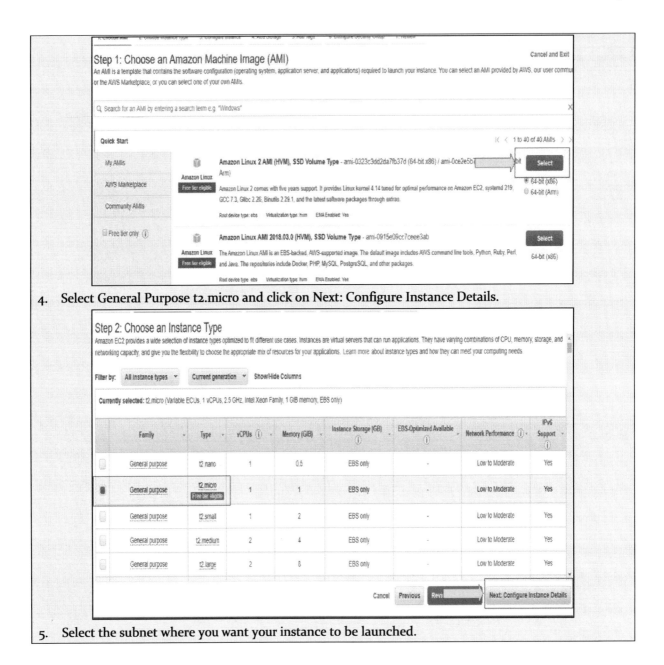

4. Select General Purpose t2.micro and click on Next: Configure Instance Details.

5. Select the subnet where you want your instance to be launched.

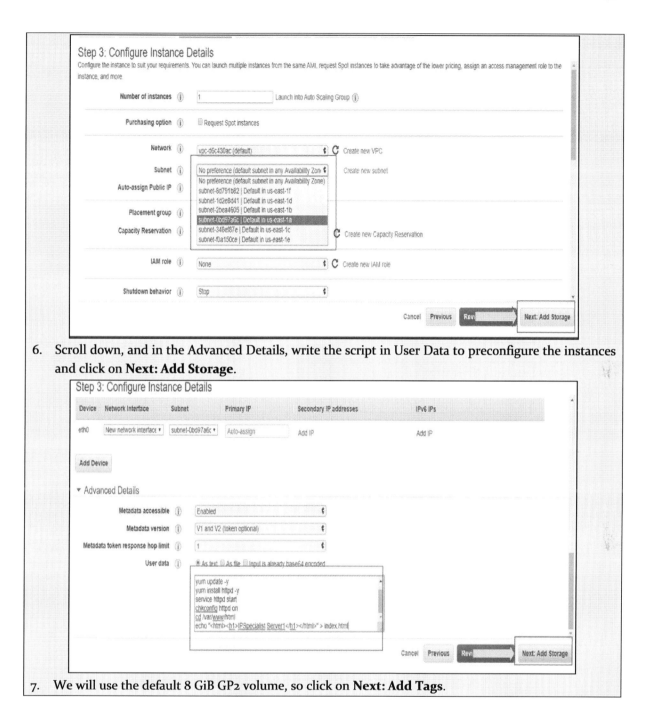

6. Scroll down, and in the Advanced Details, write the script in User Data to preconfigure the instances and click on **Next: Add Storage**.

7. We will use the default 8 GiB GP2 volume, so click on **Next: Add Tags**.

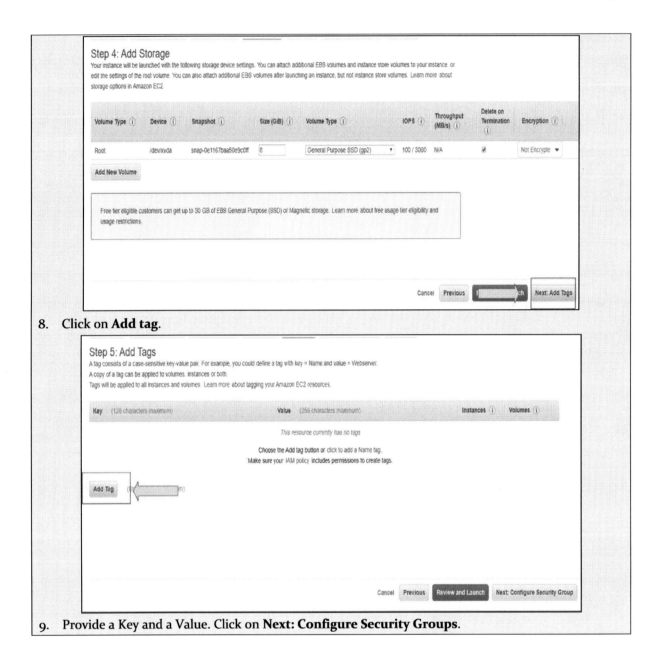

8. Click on **Add tag**.

9. Provide a Key and a Value. Click on **Next: Configure Security Groups**.

10. Create a new security group and open SSH and HTTP ports. Click on **Review and Launch**.

11. Review the instance details and click **Launch**.

12. Create a new key pair to access **EC2 instances** and download the key pair.

13. Click on Launch Instance.

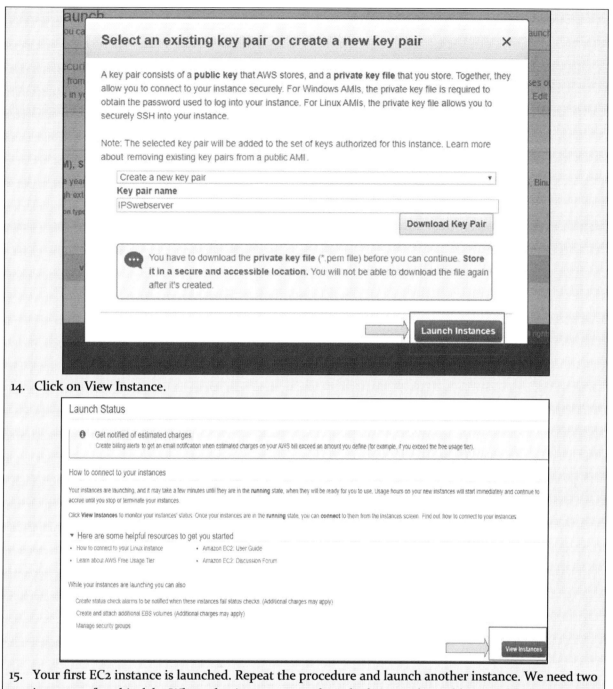

14. Click on View Instance.

15. Your first EC2 instance is launched. Repeat the procedure and launch another instance. We need two instances for this lab. When the instances are launched, copy the public IP address from the description tab.

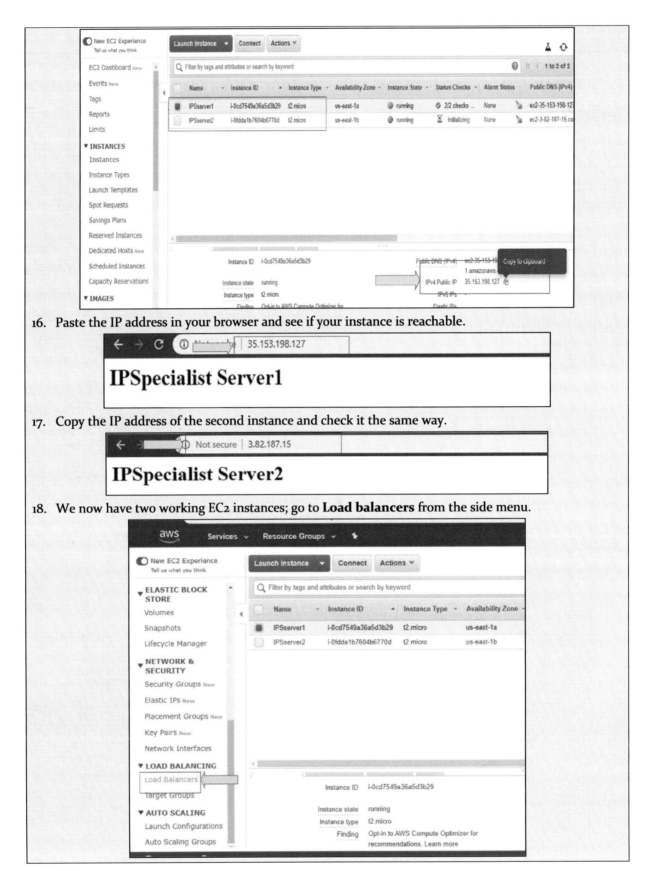

16. Paste the IP address in your browser and see if your instance is reachable.

IPSpecialist Server1

17. Copy the IP address of the second instance and check it the same way.

IPSpecialist Server2

18. We now have two working EC2 instances; go to **Load balancers** from the side menu.

19. Click on Create Load Balancer.

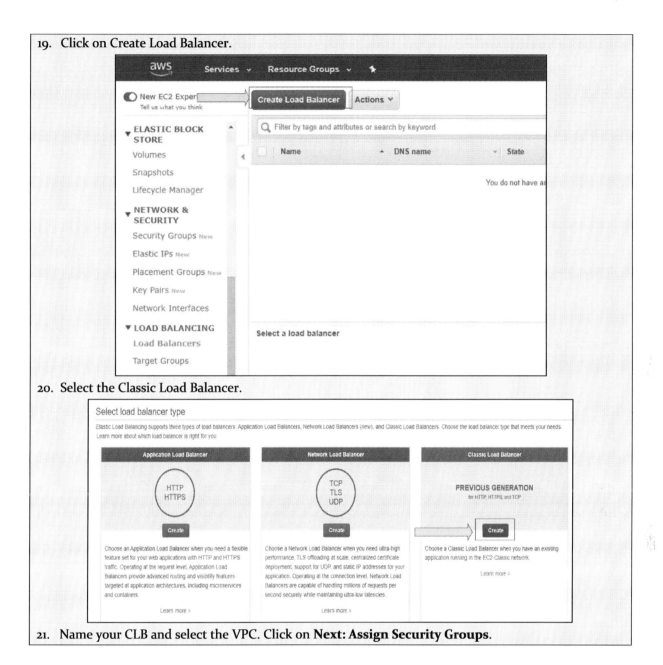

20. Select the Classic Load Balancer.

21. Name your CLB and select the VPC. Click on **Next: Assign Security Groups**.

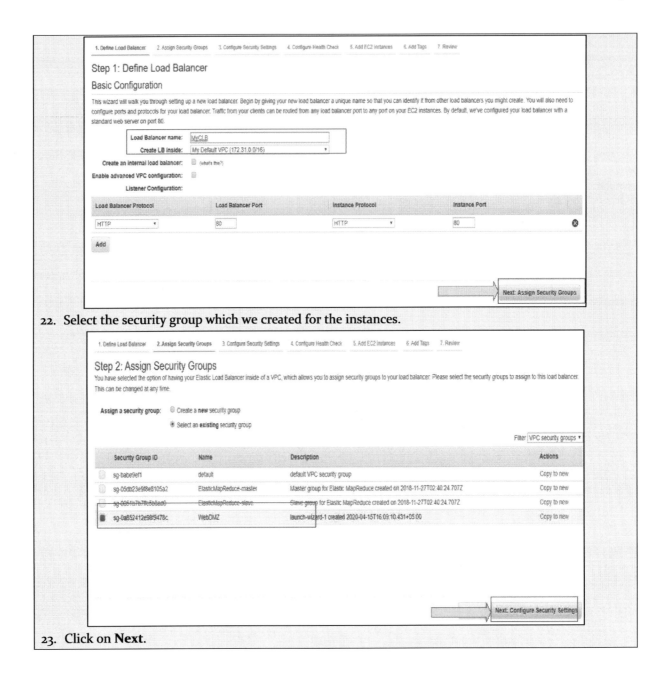

22. Select the security group which we created for the instances.

23. Click on **Next**.

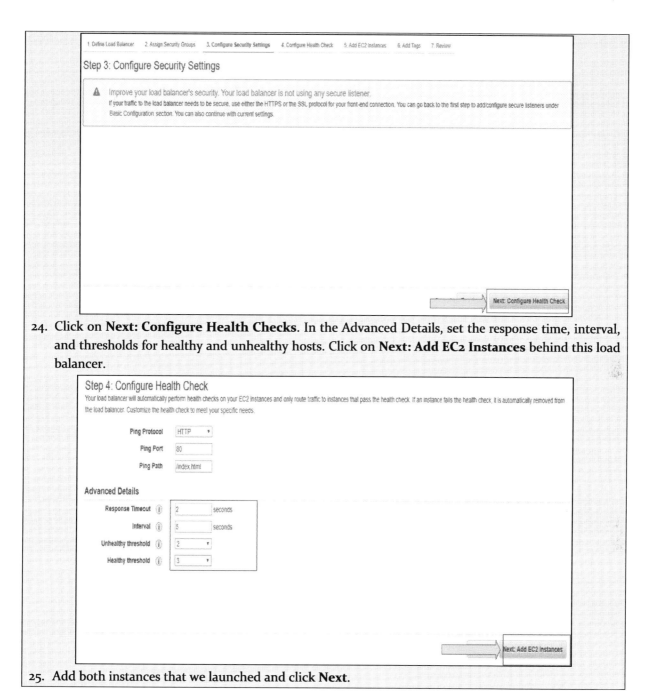

24. Click on **Next: Configure Health Checks**. In the Advanced Details, set the response time, interval, and thresholds for healthy and unhealthy hosts. Click on **Next: Add EC2 Instances** behind this load balancer.

25. Add both instances that we launched and click **Next**.

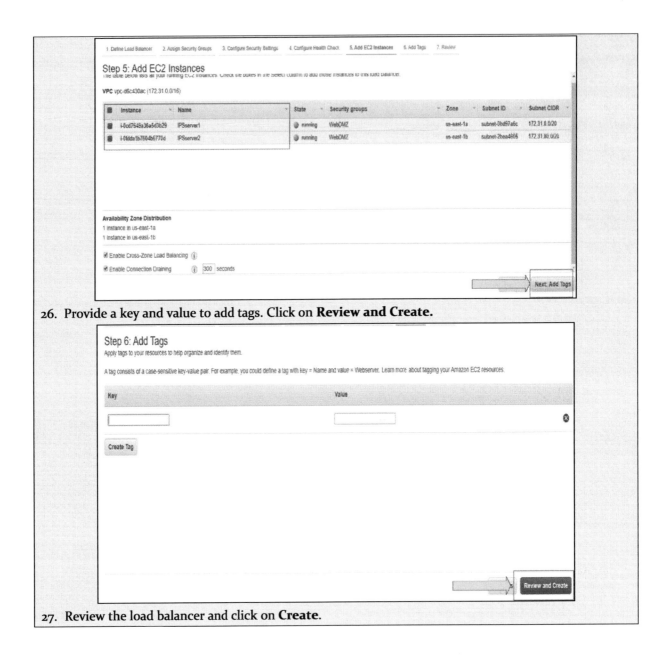

26. Provide a key and value to add tags. Click on **Review and Create.**

27. Review the load balancer and click on **Create.**

28. The load balancer has been successfully created.

29. Select the load balancer and check the status of your instances. You might see OutofService because the health check has not passed yet. Wait for a while; the status will change to InService.

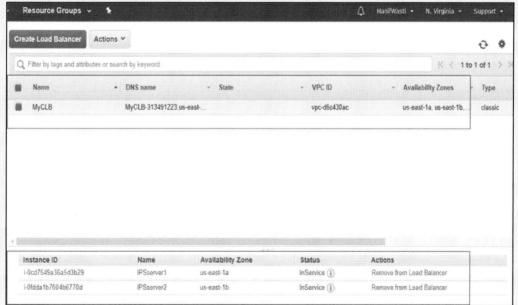

30. Select a load balancer and copy the DNS name from the description box to access the instances behind the load balancer.

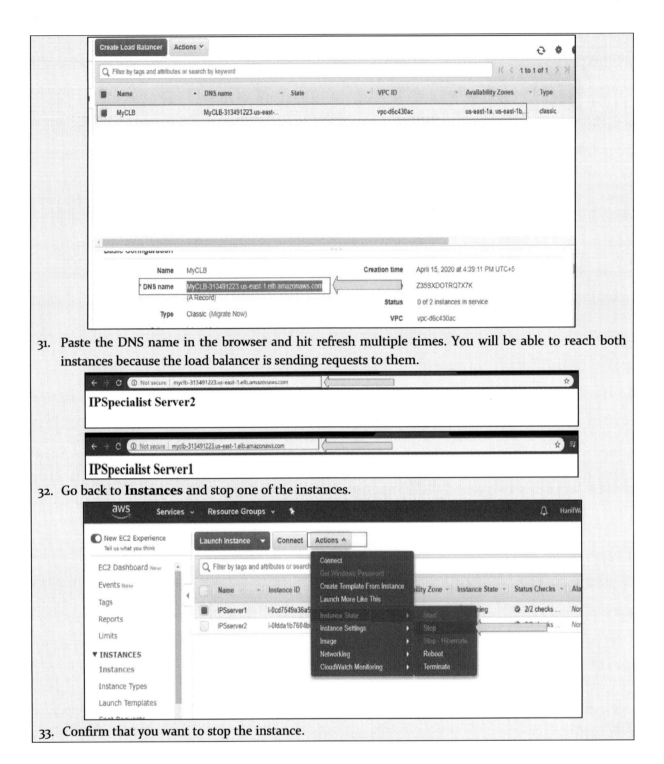

31. Paste the DNS name in the browser and hit refresh multiple times. You will be able to reach both instances because the load balancer is sending requests to them.

32. Go back to **Instances** and stop one of the instances.

33. Confirm that you want to stop the instance.

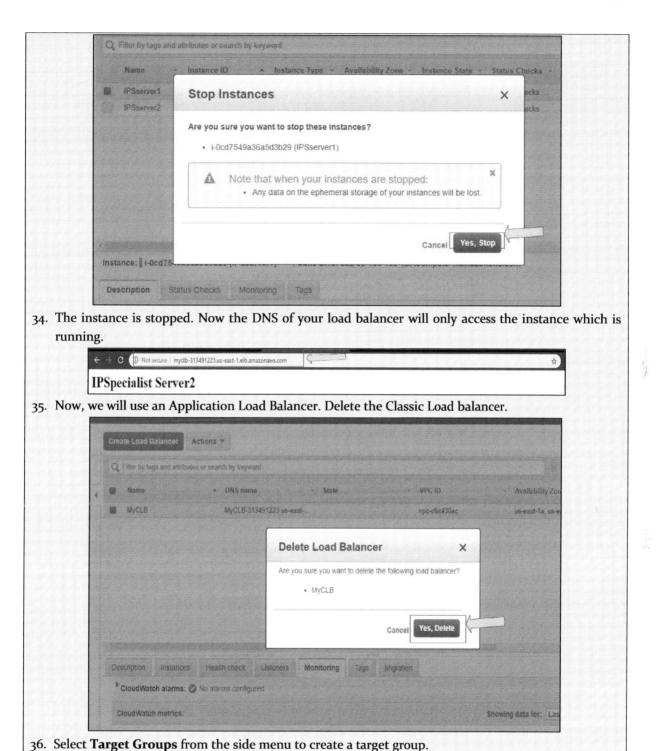

34. The instance is stopped. Now the DNS of your load balancer will only access the instance which is running.

IPSpecialist Server2

35. Now, we will use an Application Load Balancer. Delete the Classic Load balancer.

36. Select **Target Groups** from the side menu to create a target group.

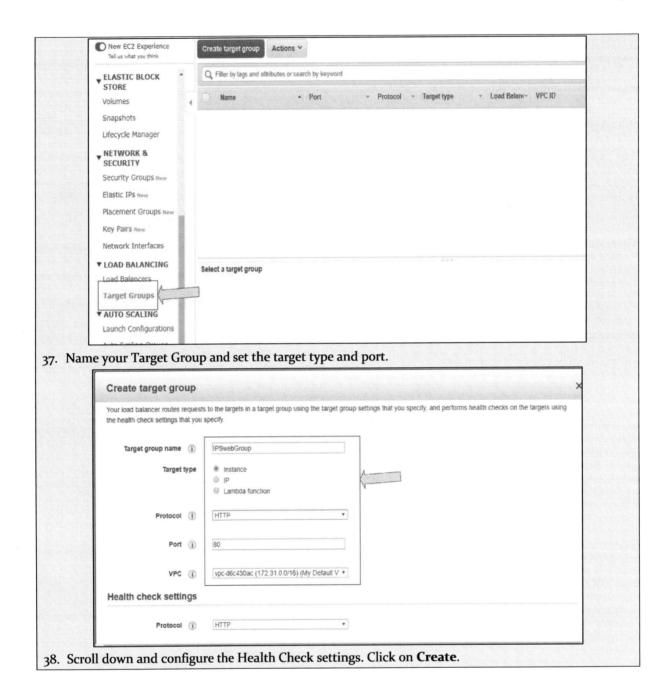

37. Name your Target Group and set the target type and port.

38. Scroll down and configure the Health Check settings. Click on **Create**.

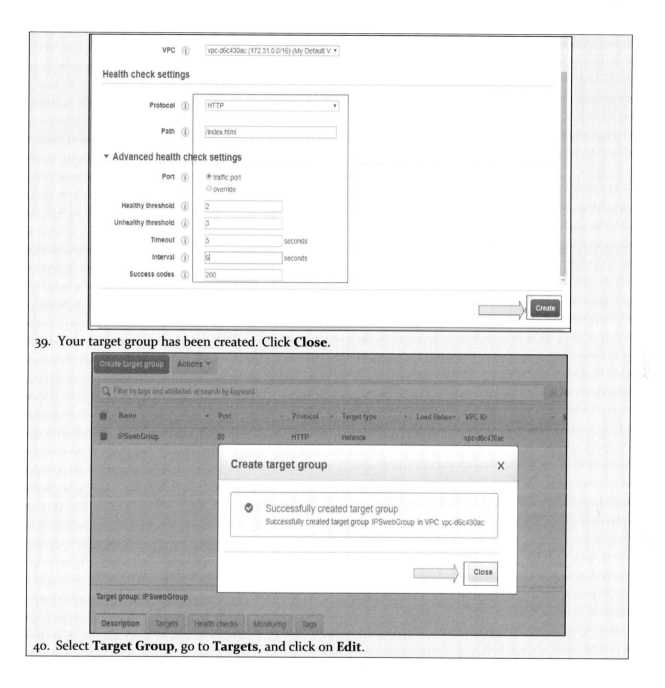

39. Your target group has been created. Click **Close**.

40. Select **Target Group**, go to **Targets**, and click on **Edit**.

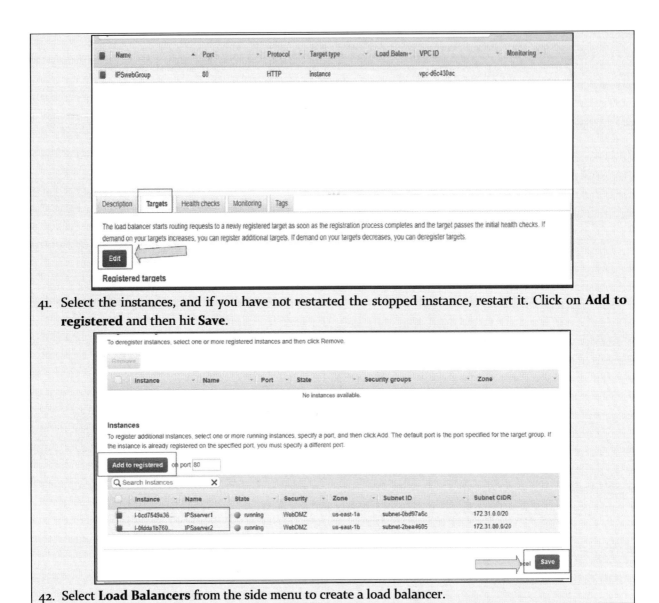

41. Select the instances, and if you have not restarted the stopped instance, restart it. Click on **Add to registered** and then hit **Save**.

42. Select **Load Balancers** from the side menu to create a load balancer.

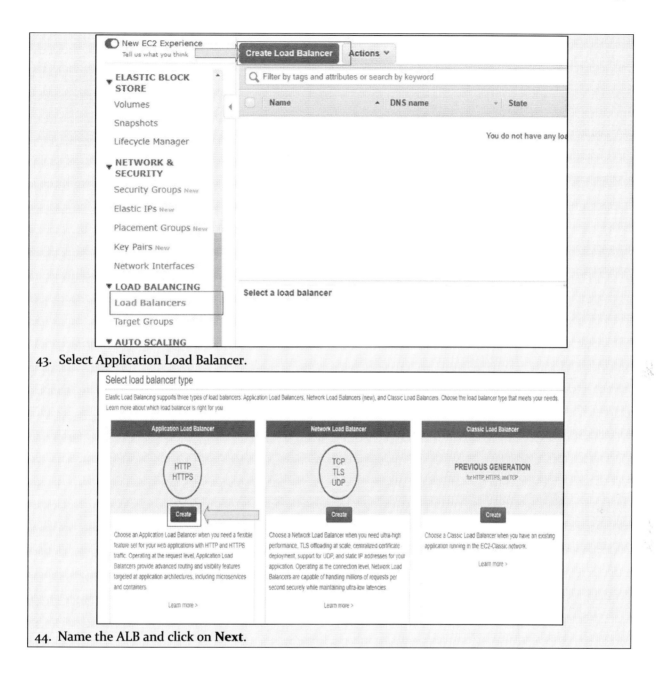

43. Select Application Load Balancer.

44. Name the ALB and click on **Next**.

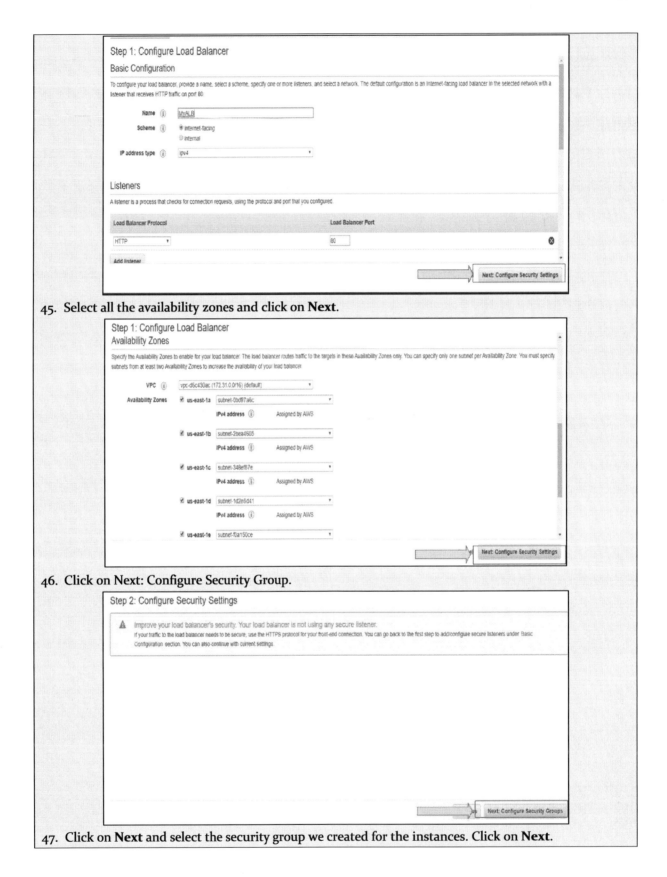

45. Select all the availability zones and click on **Next**.

46. Click on Next: Configure Security Group.

47. Click on **Next** and select the security group we created for the instances. Click on **Next**.

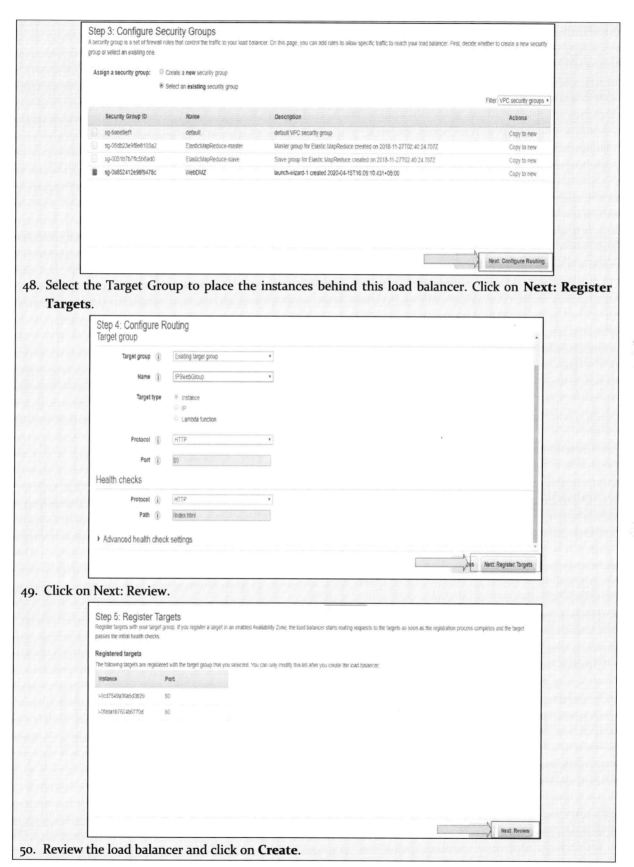

48. Select the Target Group to place the instances behind this load balancer. Click on **Next: Register Targets**.

49. Click on Next: Review.

50. Review the load balancer and click on **Create**.

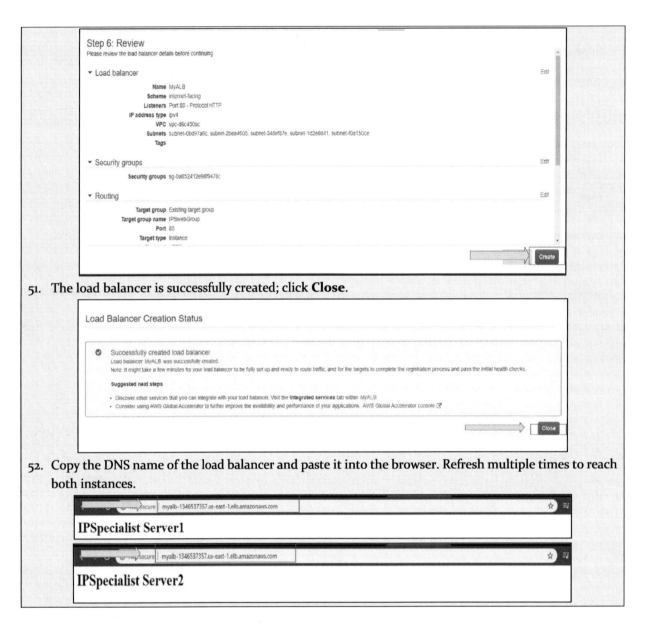

51. The load balancer is successfully created; click **Close**.

52. Copy the DNS name of the load balancer and paste it into the browser. Refresh multiple times to reach both instances.

What Are Launch Templates and Launch Configurations?

Launch Template

A launch template specifies all of the needed settings that go into building out an EC2 instance. It is a collection of settings you can configure so you do not have to walk through the EC2 wizard repeatedly.

Template vs. Configuration

Template	Configuration
• **More than just auto scaling**	• Only for auto scaling
• **Supports versioning**	• Immutable
• **More granularity**	• Limited Configuration options
• **AWS recommended**	• Not recommended by AWS

Exam TIP:
- Launch Templates - The most up to date and flexible way to create a template.
- User-data is included in the template or configuration.

Auto Scaling

Now that you have understood the working of a load balancer and its importance in the architecture, it is time to learn auto scaling, its components, and its types. It is crucial to understand the importance of auto scaling both professionally and for the exam. So let's understand what it is.

Components of Auto Scaling

Auto scaling consists of three components: groups, configuration templates, and scaling options. We will discuss each component so that you understand it better.

Groups

An Auto Scaling Group (ASG) is the logical grouping of EC2 instances. The purpose of groups is automatic scaling and management. With an auto scaling group, you can also enable Amazon EC2 auto scaling features such as health check replacements and scaling policies. The core functionality of the Amazon EC2 Auto Scaling service is maintaining the number of instances in an auto scaling group and automatic scaling.

Configuration Templates

ASGs use a configuration template to launch EC2 instances. In a configuration template, you can specify information such as the AMI ID, key pair, security groups, and block device mapping for your instance. Once a launch configuration is created, it cannot be modified. If you want to change the launch configuration for an ASG, you must create a new configuration template and update your ASG with it.

Scaling Options

With scaling options, you get several ways to scale your ASGs. For example, you can schedule a group to scale or specify a condition to scale your group, also called dynamic scaling. There are five different scaling options:

- Maintain current instance level at all times
  You can configure your ASG to maintain a specified number of running instances. To maintain that capacity, the auto scaling service uses periodic health checks, unhealthy instances are terminated, and new instances are launched.
- Scale manually
  It is the most basic way to scale resources, where you specify only the minimum, maximum, or desired capacity of your ASG.
- Scale based on a schedule
  Scaling actions are performed as a function of time and date.
- Scale based on demand
  You can use scaling policies by defining scaling parameters, a more advanced way of scaling resources.
- Use predictive scaling

Amazon EC2 scaling can be combined with AWS auto scaling to scale resources across multiple services. AWS auto scaling combines predictive and dynamic scaling and maintains optimal availability.

Auto Scaling Policies

Step Scaling

You select the scaling metrics and threshold values for the CloudWatch alarms that start the scaling process when using step scaling and simple scaling. You specify the scaling of your Auto Scaling group when a threshold is violated for a predetermined number of evaluation periods.

Instance Warm-Up and Cooldown

Warm-Up

Stop Instances from being placed behind the load balancer, failing the health check, and being terminated

Cooldown

Pauses auto scaling for a set amount of time. Helps to avoid runaway scaling events.

Avoid Thrashing

You want to create instances quickly and spin them down slowly.

Scaling Types

Reactive Scaling

You are playing catchup. Once the load is there, you measure it and then determine if you need to create more resources.

Scheduled Scaling

If you have a predictable workload, create a scaling event to prepare your resources before they are actually needed.

Predictive Scaling

AWS uses its machine learning algorithms to determine when you will need to scale. They are re-evaluated every 24 hours to create a forecast for the next 48.

Exam TIP:
- Scale in conservatively - Once the instance is up, slowly roll them back when not needed.
- Provisioning - Keep an eye in provisioning times. Bake those AMIs to minimize it.
- Costs - Use EC2 RIs for the minimum count of EC2 instances.

Lab 8-02: Auto Scaling Groups

1. Log in to AWS and go to EC2 under Compute.

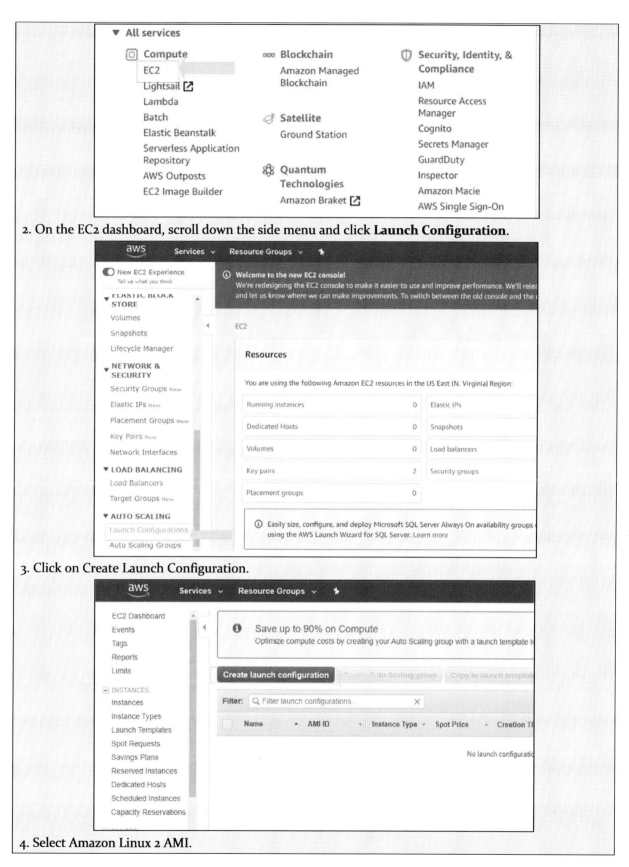

2. On the EC2 dashboard, scroll down the side menu and click **Launch Configuration**.

3. Click on Create Launch Configuration.

4. Select Amazon Linux 2 AMI.

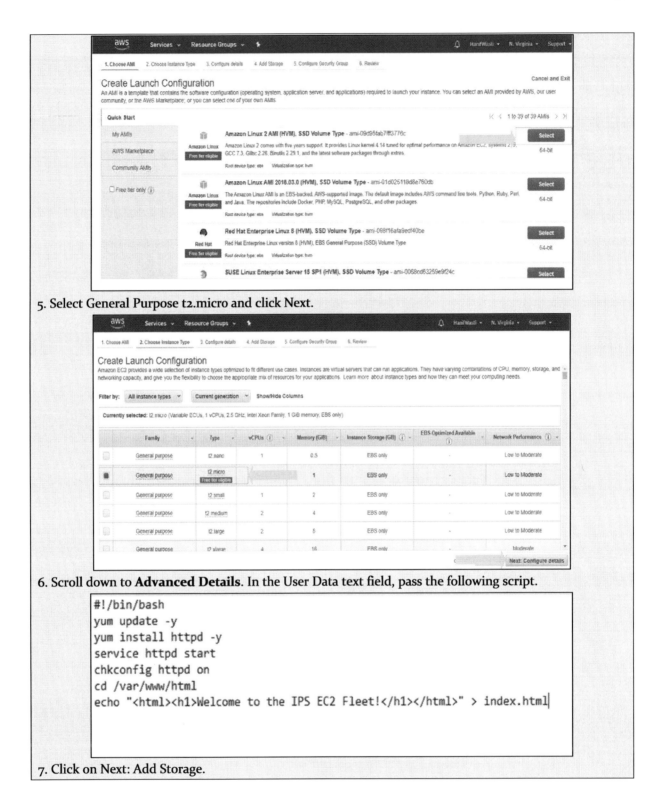

5. Select General Purpose t2.micro and click Next.

6. Scroll down to **Advanced Details**. In the User Data text field, pass the following script.

```
#!/bin/bash
yum update -y
yum install httpd -y
service httpd start
chkconfig httpd on
cd /var/www/html
echo "<html><h1>Welcome to the IPS EC2 Fleet!</h1></html>" > index.html
```

7. Click on Next: Add Storage.

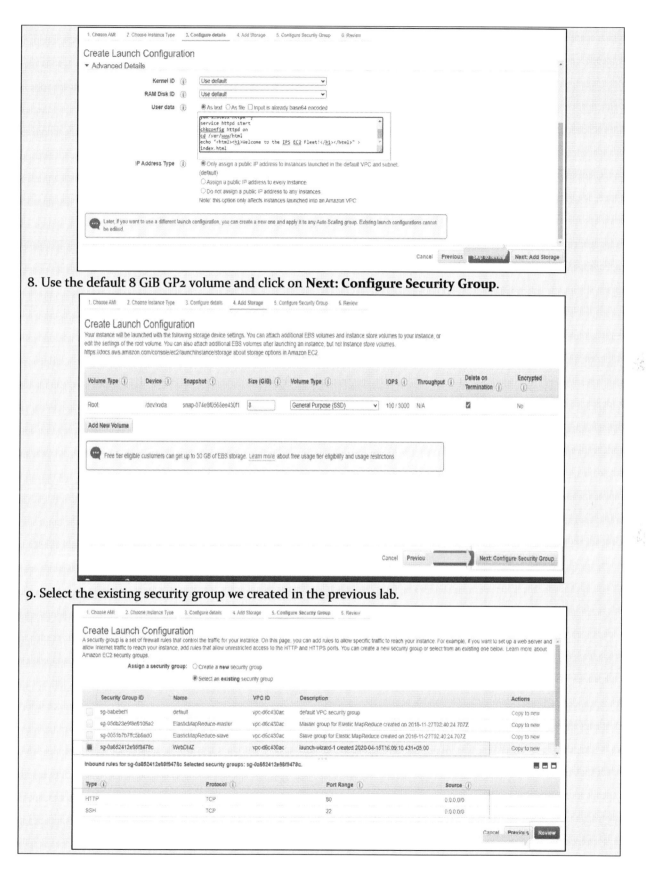

8. Use the default 8 GiB GP2 volume and click on **Next: Configure Security Group**.

9. Select the existing security group we created in the previous lab.

10. Click on Create Launch Configuration.

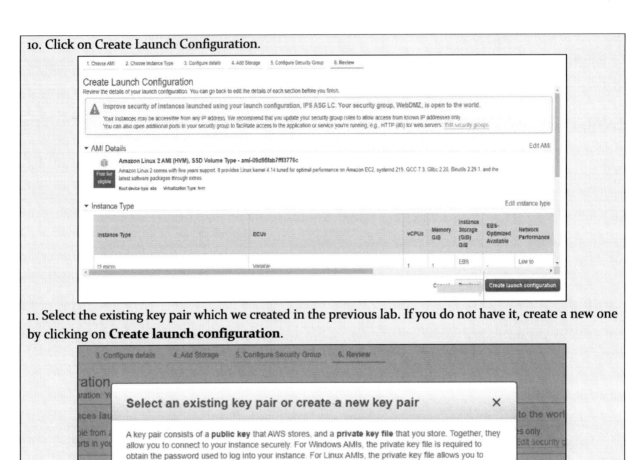

11. Select the existing key pair which we created in the previous lab. If you do not have it, create a new one by clicking on **Create launch configuration**.

12. Launch Configuration has been created. Now, click on Create an Auto Scaling Group using this launch configuration.

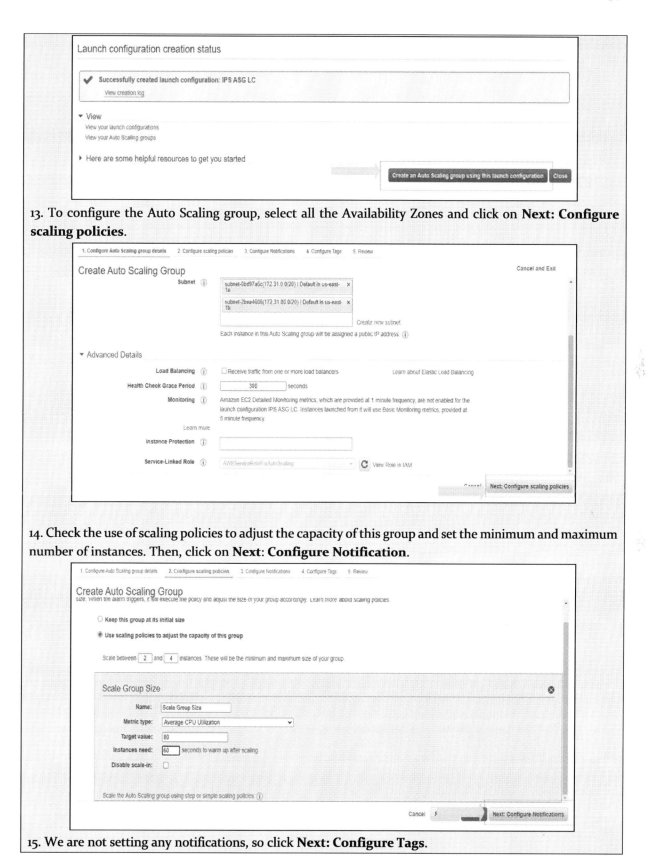

13. To configure the Auto Scaling group, select all the Availability Zones and click on **Next: Configure scaling policies**.

14. Check the use of scaling policies to adjust the capacity of this group and set the minimum and maximum number of instances. Then, click on **Next: Configure Notification**.

15. We are not setting any notifications, so click **Next: Configure Tags**.

16. Give a name and value to add tags to identify the instances. Click **Review**.

17. Review the Auto Scaling Group and click **Create**.

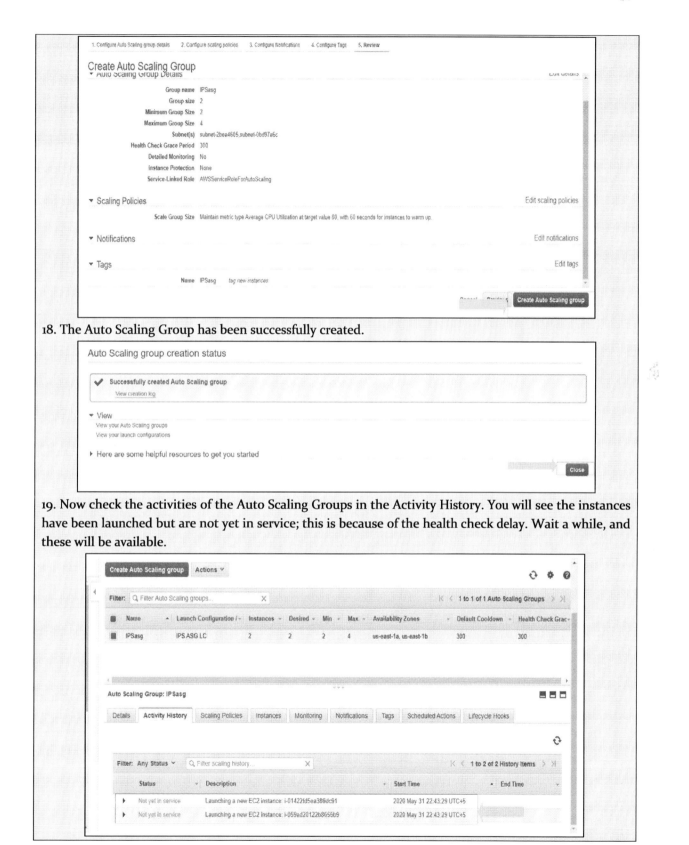

18. The Auto Scaling Group has been successfully created.

19. Now check the activities of the Auto Scaling Groups in the Activity History. You will see the instances have been launched but are not yet in service; this is because of the health check delay. Wait a while, and these will be available.

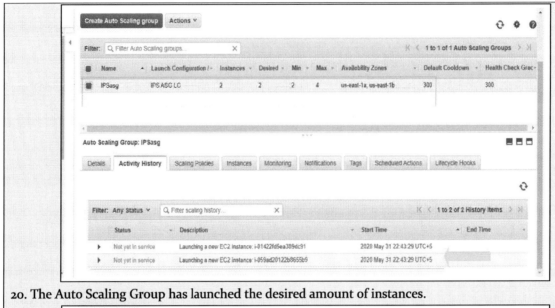

20. The Auto Scaling Group has launched the desired amount of instances.

21. Go to instances and terminate an instance to see what Auto Scaling Group will do.

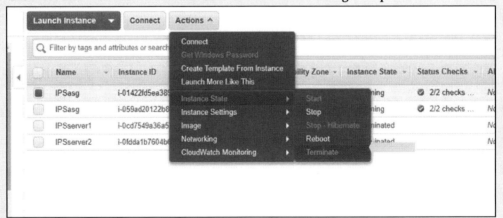

22. You will see that the instance is terminated, and only one instance is running.

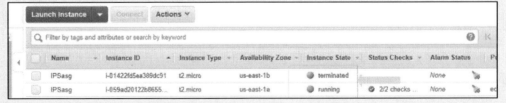

23. Refresh the page after a while, and you will see a new instance running because the ASG has detected the termination.

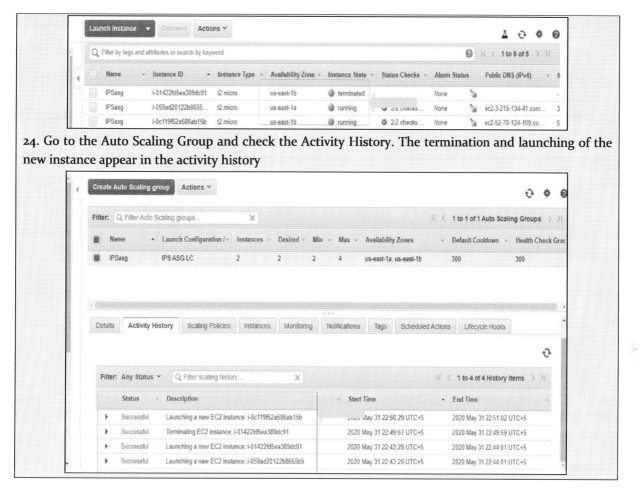

24. Go to the Auto Scaling Group and check the Activity History. The termination and launching of the new instance appear in the activity history

HA Architecture

High Availability (HA) architecture has become a core requirement nowadays. You will see a lot of scenario questions in the exams about such architecture. Understanding and implementing it practically is a skill that employers search for. So let's understand what it actually is.

The first thing to remember is the quote of CTO AWS, Warner Vogels, "Everything fails, all the time." When building an architecture or developing a solution, you must plan for failure because, eventually, you will have to deal with the failure, so always plan ahead. A good example of planning for failure is Netflix's simian army; it injects failure into its production systems so that it can be sure about the system's working during the disaster. Let's take a look at an example of HA.

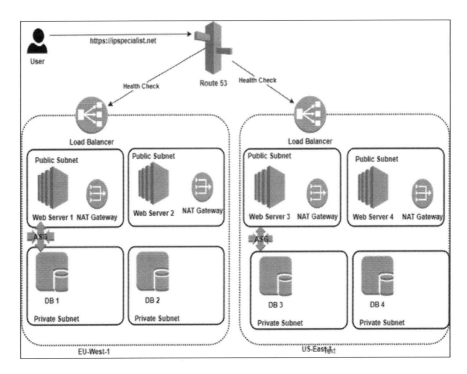

Figure 8-05: HA Architecture

Figure 8-05 depicts a high-availability architecture. Users are requesting ipspecialist.net, which is hosted on Route 53. Route 53 sends the request to EU west-1 as a European user. In the region, we have our web servers and NAT gateways in public subnets 1 and 2 such that each subnet is a different AZ. We also have private subnets where databases are kept, and we have auto scaling groups between them. So if the databases perform some heavy task, then auto scaling will help by adding to the capacity.

Similarly, it will also help handle requests in public subnets. The same infrastructure is replicated in another region, which is US East 1, so you can failover. Route 53 keeps performing health checks to ensure availability. This is a really good example of HA architecture.

HA Best Practices
So far, we have learned what a high-availability architecture is and how it works. The key points to keep in mind are as follows:

Always Design for Failure

We have discussed this point before - when designing infrastructure, remember that if everything fails, you should add features to deal with when a failure occurs.

Multiple AZs and Regions

As discussed in the HA example picture, using multiple AZs and regions is better for fault tolerance and load distribution; it will also help in failover.

Multi-AZ and Read Replica for RDS

Keep in mind the differences between RDS Multi-AZ and Read Replicas. Multi-AZ is for disaster recovery, while read replicas improve performance.

Scale Out and Scale Up

Scaling out refers to the use of auto scaling groups where more EC2 instances are added when needed; scaling up is when we increase the resources inside an EC2 instance, such as you scale up a T2.micro instance to T2.xlarge; you increase the amount of RAM and processing here.

Always Consider Cost

Cost-effectiveness is mandatory. When designing a solution, you must ensure you are not paying extra. Whatever resources you are using should be justifiable and be used completely.

CloudFormation

Developers and system administrators can use the AWS CloudFormation service. It allows them to create a group of related AWS resources and provision them in an arranged and predictable manner. AWS CloudFormation service is free; the resources that it provisions are not.

Lab 8-03: Building a Fault-Tolerant WordPress Site Using CloudFormation

Scenario: Let's assume you are a web developer in an organization. Your organization wants you to develop different static websites, such as fashion blog websites, food recipe websites, sports news websites, etc. They want to use the WordPress framework to build these static websites and want them all to be fault-tolerant. How would you automate this work?

Solution: The solution is simple. You use AWS CloudFormation resources to build your fault-tolerant WordPress websites within minutes. You should not manually configure and launch EC2 and RDS instances. You should not manually create an S3 storage bucket, as CloudFormation will create all your required resources to create a WordPress environment within AWS.

Follow the given steps to build a fault-tolerant WordPress site using CloudFormation.

1. Log in to the AWS Console.
2. Click on **Services.**
3. Scroll down to Management & Governance. Select Cloud Formation.

4. If you have never used CloudFormation, you will get a screen like the following.

5. From the options given on the main dashboard, click on **Create stack**.

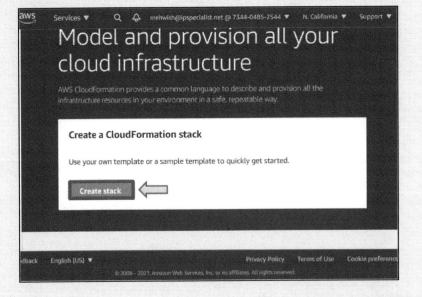

6. Select Use a Sample template.

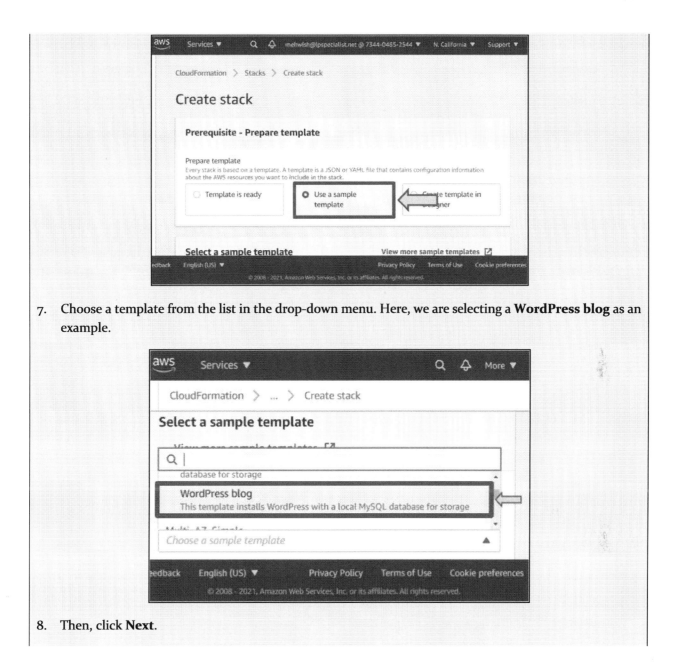

7. Choose a template from the list in the drop-down menu. Here, we are selecting a **WordPress blog** as an example.

8. Then, click **Next**.

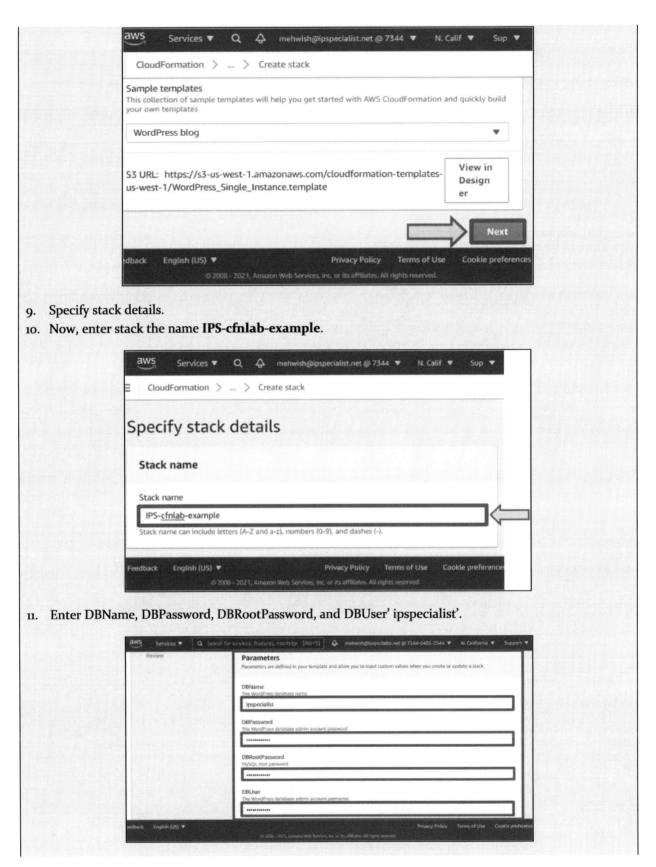

9. Specify stack details.
10. Now, enter stack the name **IPS-cfnlab-example**.

11. Enter DBName, DBPassword, DBRootPassword, and DBUser' ipspecialist'.

12. Select webserver (EC2) instance type **t2.micro**.

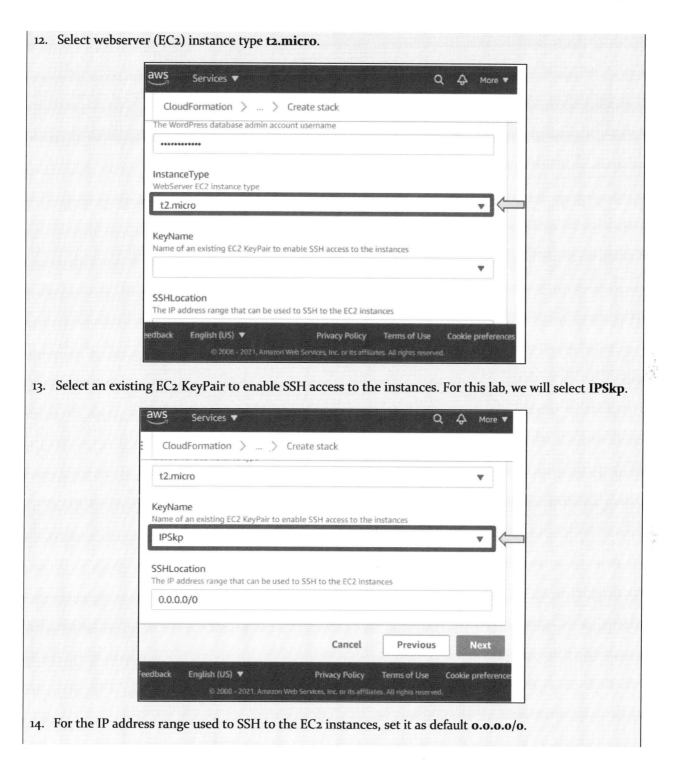

13. Select an existing EC2 KeyPair to enable SSH access to the instances. For this lab, we will select **IPSkp**.

14. For the IP address range used to SSH to the EC2 instances, set it as default **0.0.0.0/0**.

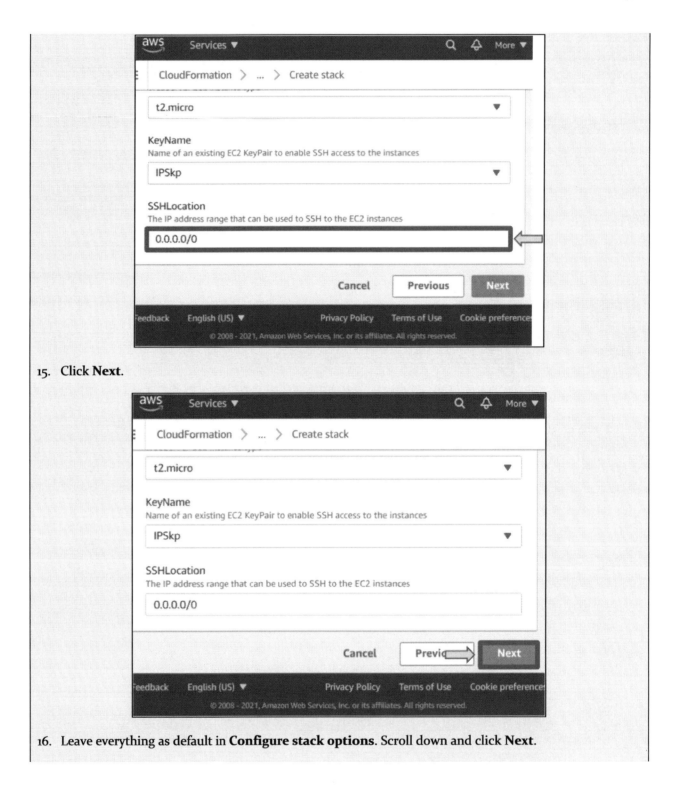

15. Click **Next**.

16. Leave everything as default in **Configure stack options**. Scroll down and click **Next**.

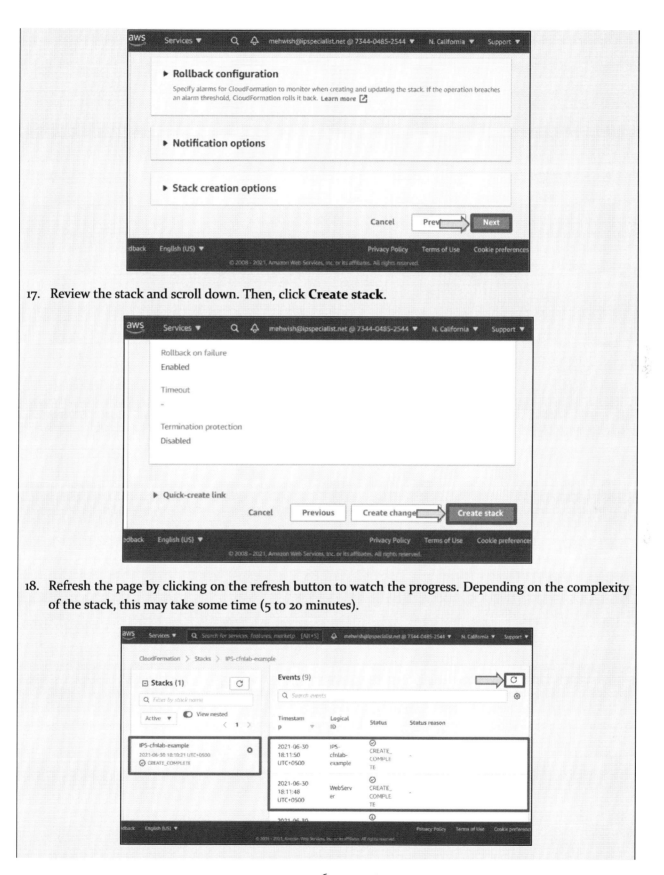

17. Review the stack and scroll down. Then, click **Create stack**.

18. Refresh the page by clicking on the refresh button to watch the progress. Depending on the complexity of the stack, this may take some time (5 to 20 minutes).

19. Once the stack has been created, select the **Outputs** tab. You will be able to see your website URL address.

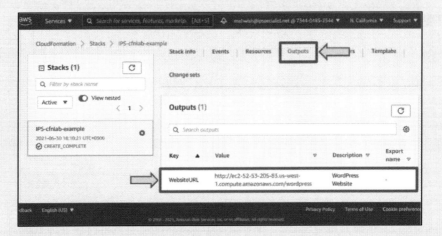

20. This is the Website URL of your WordPress site. Click on it to be directed to your WordPress site.

Note: You can also delete the entire CloudFormation Stack and its provisioned resources anytime.

21. Select **IPS-example**. Then click on the **Delete** button.

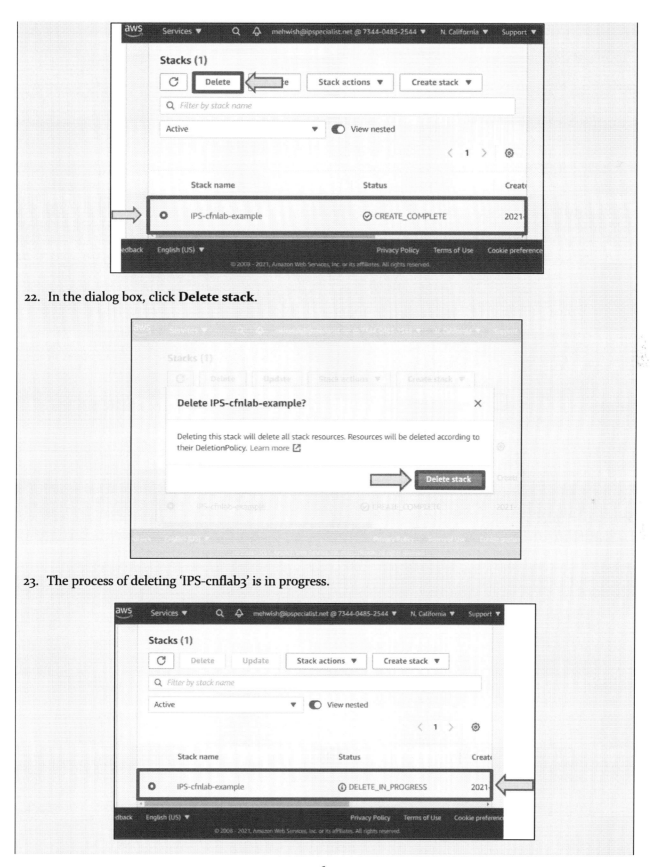

22. In the dialog box, click **Delete stack**.

23. The process of deleting 'IPS-cnflab3' is in progress.

24. Click on the refresh button, and you will see that the 'IPS-cfnlab-example' stack name has been removed.

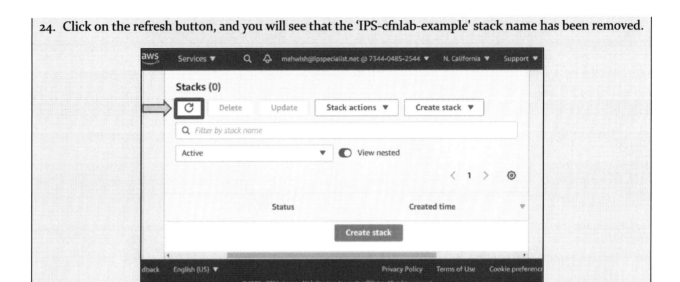

Lab 8-04: Getting Started with AWS CloudFormation

Scenario: Assume you are a DevOps engineer in an organization. Your task is to continue make changes with technology and platform improvements to create an excellent experience for customers. For this, you need a tool that will automate all of the work that you manually do, such as launching and configuring EC2 instances or creating S3 storage buckets. Which tool would be best to automate your work?

Solution: The solution is simple. You use the AWS CloudFormation service to automate all the work. In CloudFormation, you run a template of JSON or YAML to deploy the entire frontend and backend stack into the AWS environment.

There are three sections in this lab. The first section is to make a stack. The section is used to update the stack. The deleted stack is the third and final section. This is illustrated in the figure below.

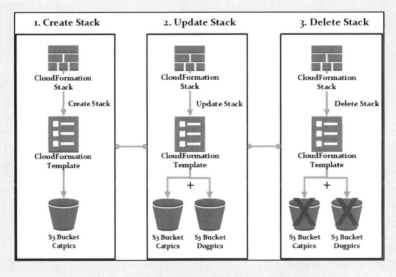

Figure 8-06: CloudFormation Lab Sections

Before starting the lab, you must first understand the CloudFormation templates. The templates are pieces of code. This CloudFormation is used to create or update a stack. Let's consider a template as code. It is a way of specifying resources declaratively, and it is written in either the JSON or the YAML format.

1. Download template files from the GitHub Repository provided in the link below:

https://github.com/12920/IPSLabResources/blob/main/Course-Certified-Solutions-Architect-Associate tree/master/labs/getting_started_with_cfn

2. After downloading the templates file, open **templatesstructure.json** on the code editor.
3. This is a CloudFormation template, and it has nine sections. Not all of these sections are required. This is an example of a template written in JSON.

```
{} templatestructure.json  ×

C: > Users > Mohammad Usman Khan > Desktop > getting_started_with_cfn > {} templatestructure.json > ...
 1   {
 2       "AWSTemplateFormatVersion" : "2010-09-09",
 3
 4       "Description" : "this template does XXXX",
 5
 6       "Metadata" : {
 7
 8       },
 9
10       "Parameters" : {
11
12       },
13
14       "Mappings" : {
15
16       },
17
18       "Conditions" : {
19
20       },
21
22       "Transform" : {
23
24       },
25
26       "Resources" : {
27
28       },
29
30       "Outputs" : {
31
32       }
```

4. There is an equivalent YAML version at template structure.yaml.

69

```
! templatestructure.yaml  X

C: > Users > Mohammad Usman Khan > Desktop > getting_started_with_cfn > ! templatestructure.yaml
1    ---
2    AWSTemplateFormatVersion: "2010-09-09"
3
4    Description:
5      this template does XXXX
6
7    Metadata:
8      template metadata
9
10   Parameters:
11     set of parameters
12
13   Mappings:
14     set of mappings
15
16   Conditions:
17     set of conditions
18
19   Transform:
20     set of transforms
21
22   Resources:
23     set of resources
24
25   Outputs:
26     set of outputs
```

5. Note that the patterns are the same. Both files contain nine sections.
6. In this lab, a JSON format template is used.
7. The first section of a CloudFormation template is the 'format' version. This is optional. However, if the template format changes, it is difficult to future-proof the product.

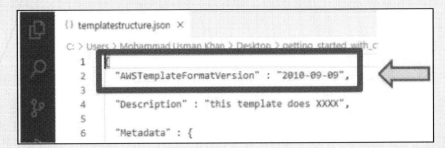

8. The next section is 'Description.' This is where you can describe the template.

```
1    {
2      "AWSTemplateFormatVersion" : "2010-09-09",
3
4      "Description" : "this template does XXXX",
5
6      "Metadata" : {
```

9. The 'metadata' section is a multi-purpose section. It can be used for something simple, like controlling how the template looks when creating a stack.

```
{} templatestructure.json  ×
C: > Users > Mohammad Usman Khan > Desktop > getting_started_
  1   {
  2       "AWSTemplateFormatVersion" : "2010-09-09",
  3
  4       "Description" : "this template does XXXX",
  5
  6       "Metadata" : {
  7
  8       },
  9
```

10. The 'parameter' section is where you can define the information that you want the template to ask for.

```
  4       "Description" : "this template does XXXX",
  5
  6       "Metadata" : {
  7
  8       },
  9
  10      "Parameters" : {
  11
  12      },
  13
```

11. The next section is 'Mappings,' which allows you to include data that can be used conditionally.

```
  5
  6       "Metadata" : {
  7
  8       },
  9
  10      "Parameters" : {
  11
  12      },
  13
  14      "Mappings" : {
  15
  16      },
  17
```

12. The 'Conditions' section controls whether specific resource properties are assigned based on several values.

```
  13
  14      "Mappings" : {
  15
  16      },
  17
  18      "Conditions" : {
  19
  20      },
  21
```

13. The transformation section is something that is usually used for serverless applications.

```
17
18      "Conditions" : {
19
20      },
21
22      "Transform" : {
23
24      },
25
```

14. The 'outputs' are another optional part of the template that allows you to return values once the stack is completed.

```
25
26      "Resources" : {
27
28      },
29
30      "Outputs" : {
31
32      }
```

15. Now, the resources section is the last part of a CloudFormation template. It is a very important part of the CloudFormation template.

```
23
24      },
25
26      "Resources" : {
27
28      },
29
30      "Outputs" : {
```

16. The template that is used in this lab is 'createstack.json.' This template only has a resource section used; all of the other sections are optional.

```
{} createstack.json ×
C: > Users > Mohammad Usman Khan > Desktop >
1    {
2
3        "Resources": {
4
5          "catpics": {
6            "Type": "AWS::S3::Bucket"
7          }
8
9        }
10
11   }
```

Follow the given steps to create the AWS CloudFormation stack.

1. Log in to the AWS Console.
2. Click on **Services**.
3. Scroll down to Management & Governance. Select Cloud Formation.

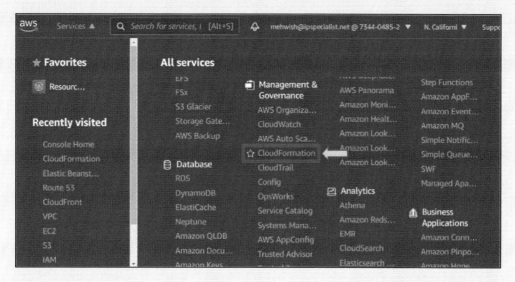

Create a CloudFormation Stack

4. If you have never used CloudFormation, you will get a screen like the following.

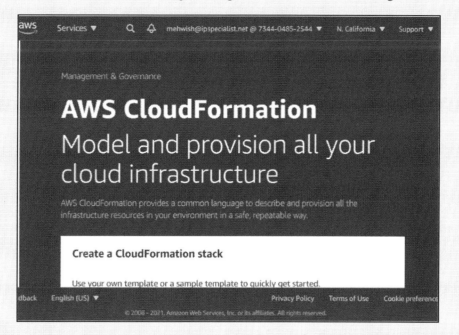

5. Click on the **Create stack** button.

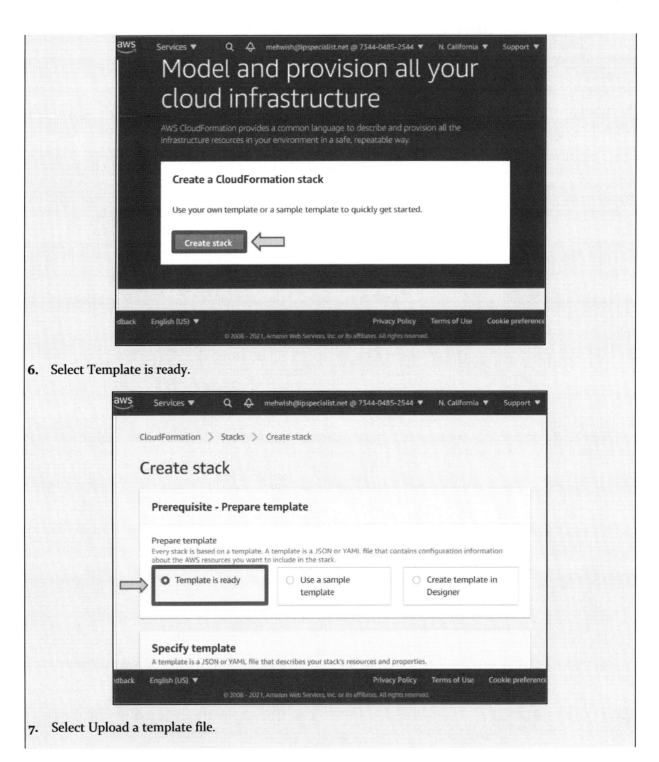

6. Select Template is ready.

7. Select Upload a template file.

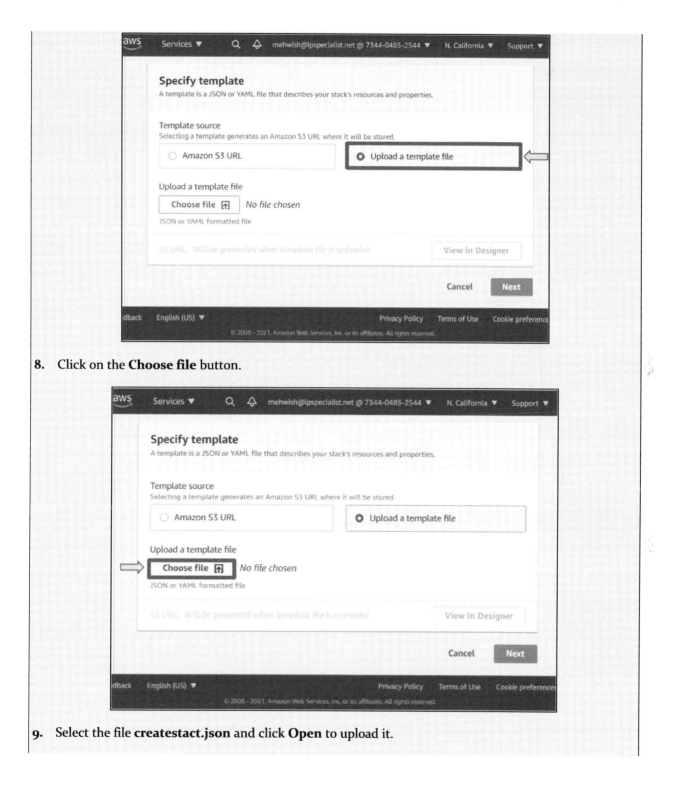

8. Click on the **Choose file** button.

9. Select the file **createstact.json** and click **Open** to upload it.

10. Then click on the **Next** button.

11. Name the stack **IPS-cfnlab**.

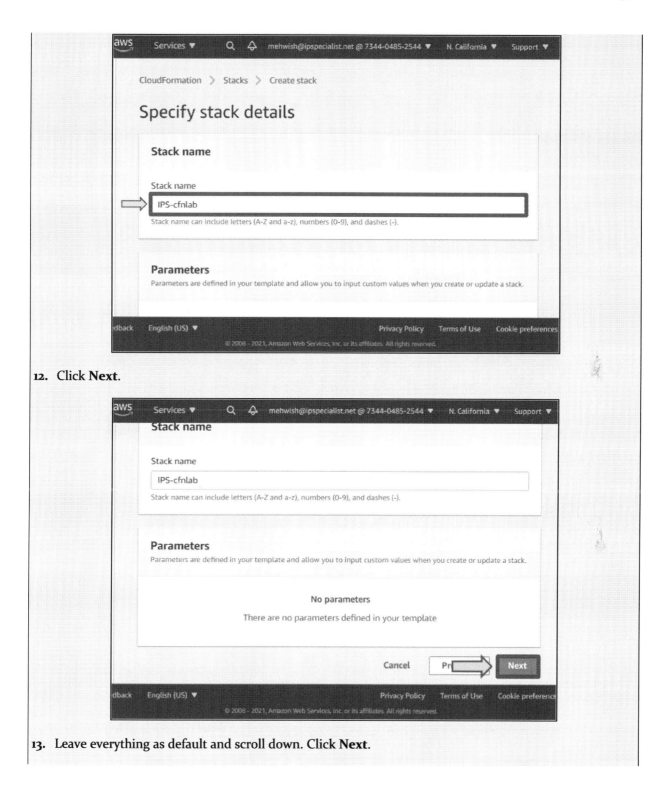

12. Click **Next**.

13. Leave everything as default and scroll down. Click **Next**.

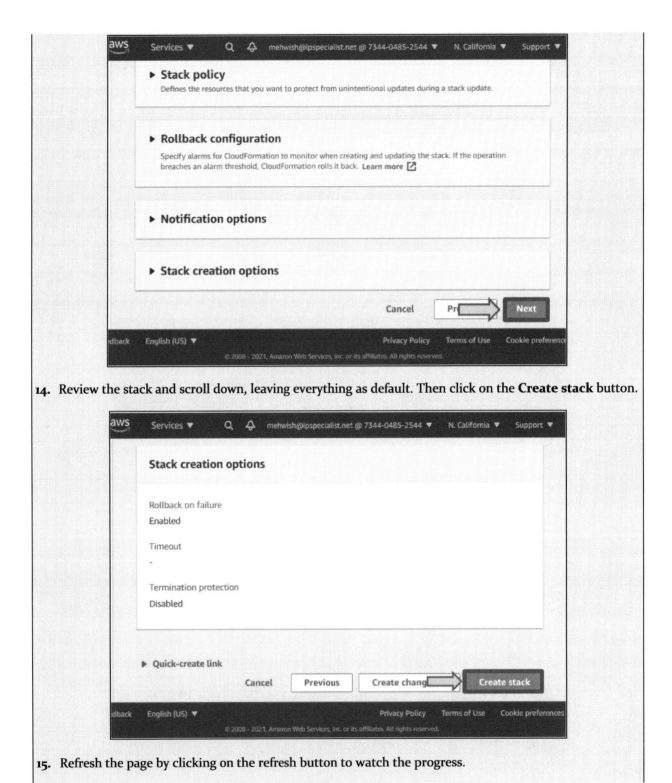

14. Review the stack and scroll down, leaving everything as default. Then click on the **Create stack** button.

15. Refresh the page by clicking on the refresh button to watch the progress.

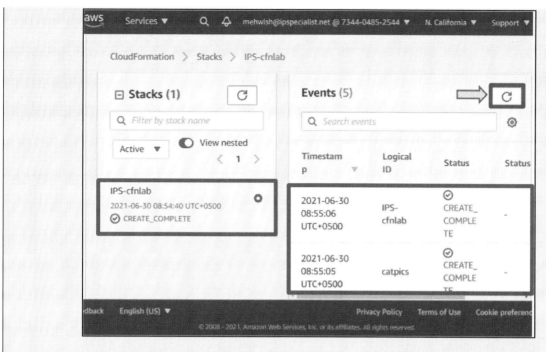

16. Now go to **S3**. As we did not specify the name in the '.json' file for this bucket, AWS names it with the <STACK_NAME>-<LOGICAL_VOLUME_NAME>-<RANDOM_STRING> format. In this case will be; '*IPS-cfnlab-catpics*'-*<RANDOM_STRING>*.

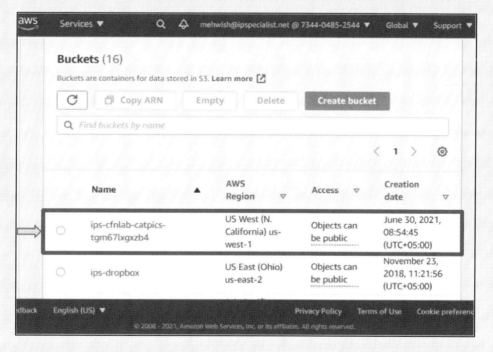

Update the CloudFormation Stack

Update # 1

14. Go to the CloudFormation dashboard by clicking on **Stacks**.

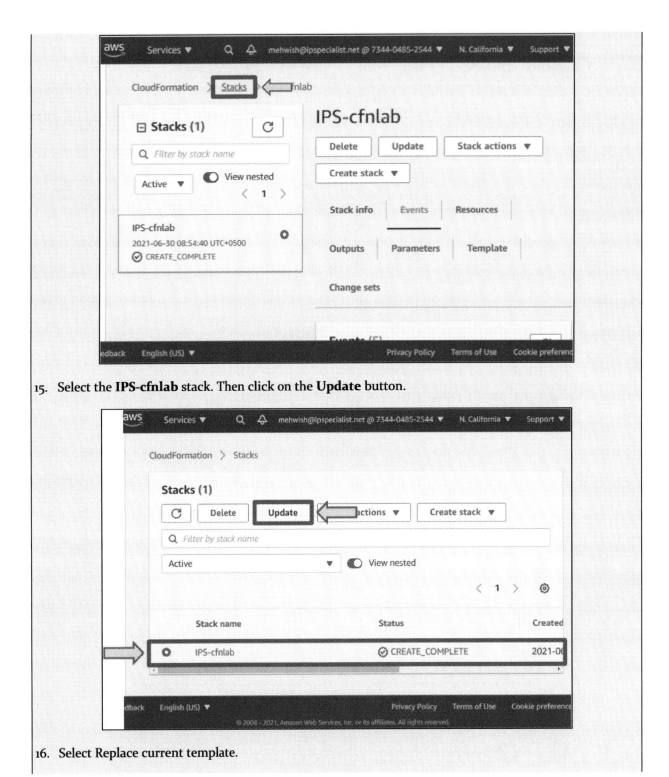

15. Select the **IPS-cfnlab** stack. Then click on the **Update** button.

16. Select Replace current template.

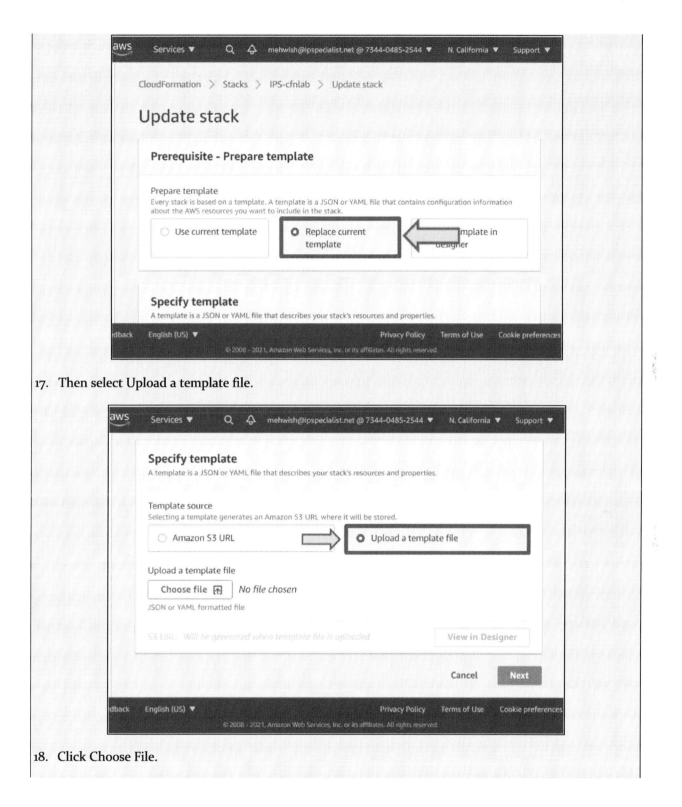

17. Then select Upload a template file.

18. Click Choose File.

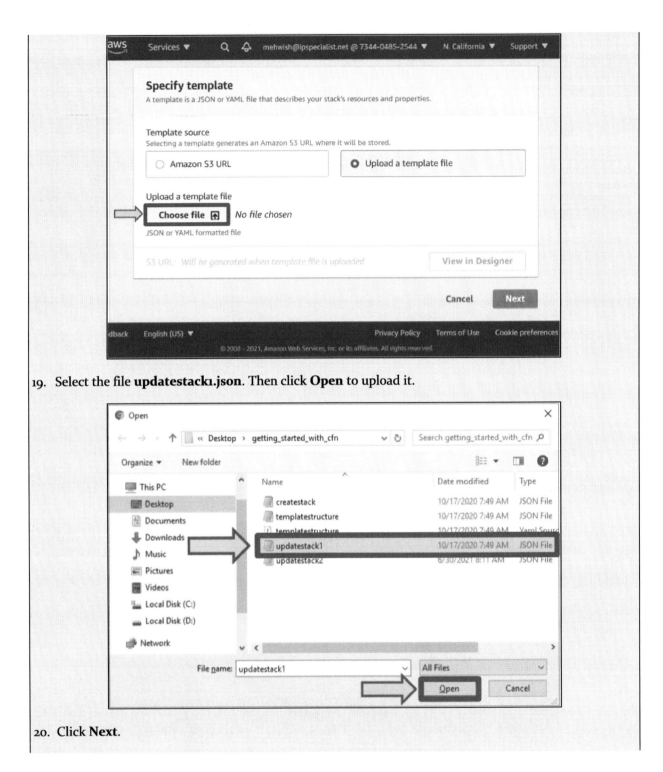

19. Select the file **updatestack1.json**. Then click **Open** to upload it.

20. Click **Next**.

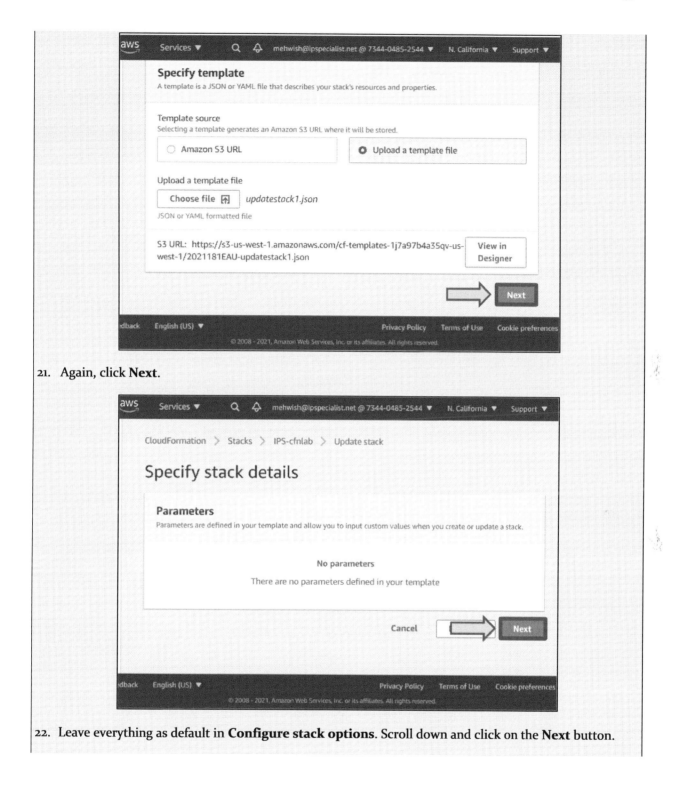

21. Again, click **Next**.

22. Leave everything as default in **Configure stack options**. Scroll down and click on the **Next** button.

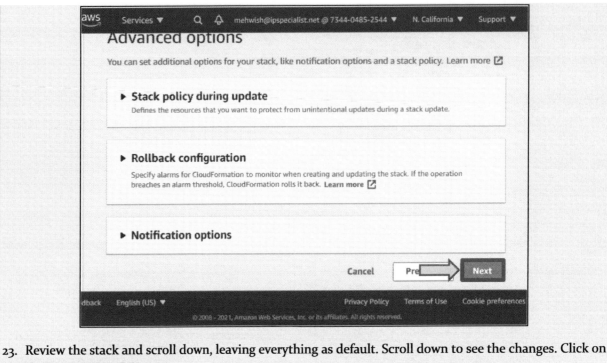

23. Review the stack and scroll down, leaving everything as default. Scroll down to see the changes. Click on the **Update Stack** button.

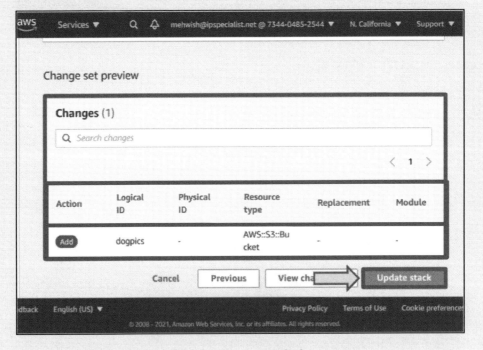

24. Refresh the page by clicking on the refresh button to watch the progress.

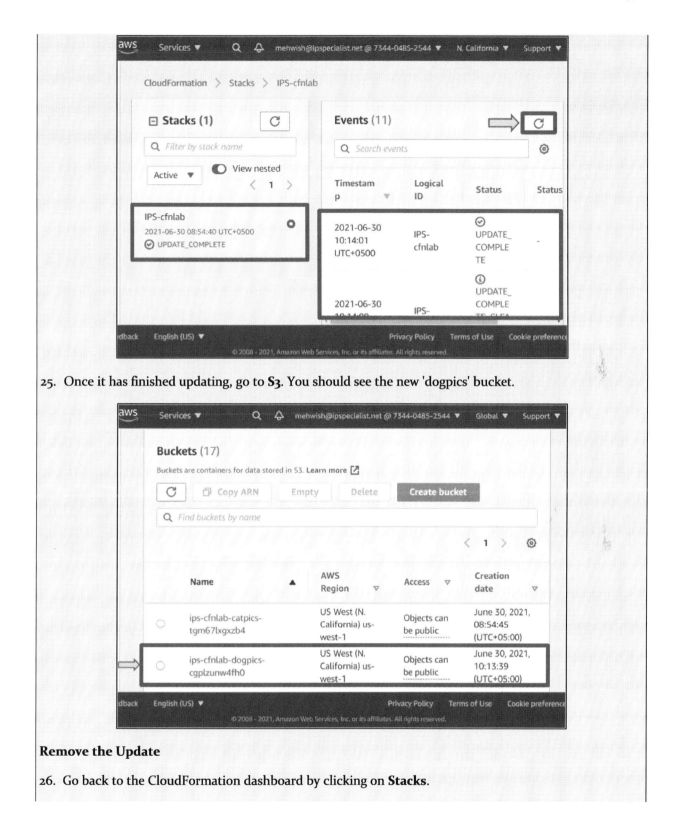

25. Once it has finished updating, go to **S3**. You should see the new 'dogpics' bucket.

Remove the Update

26. Go back to the CloudFormation dashboard by clicking on **Stacks**.

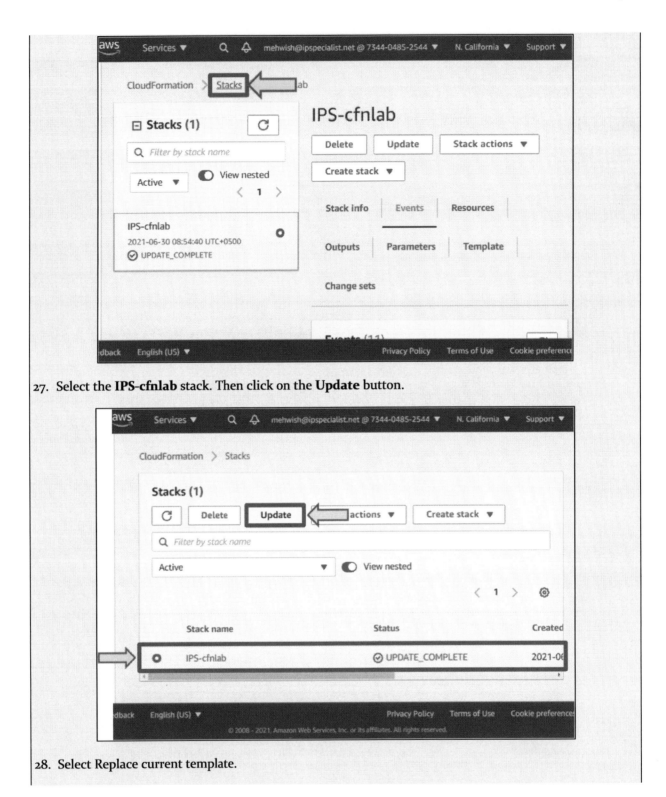

27. Select the **IPS-cfnlab** stack. Then click on the **Update** button.

28. Select Replace current template.

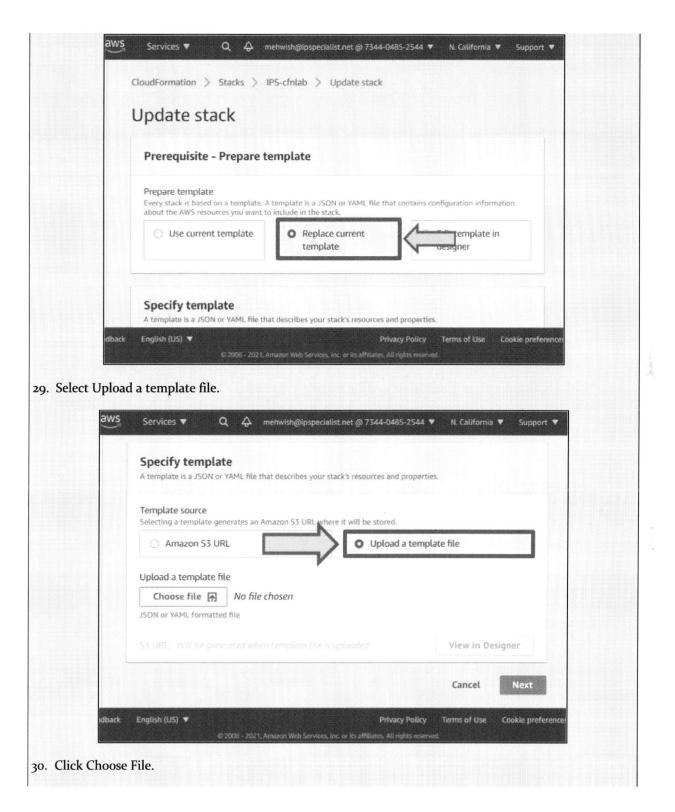

29. Select Upload a template file.

30. Click Choose File.

31. Select the file **createstack.json** again. Then click **Open** to upload it.

32. Click **Next**.

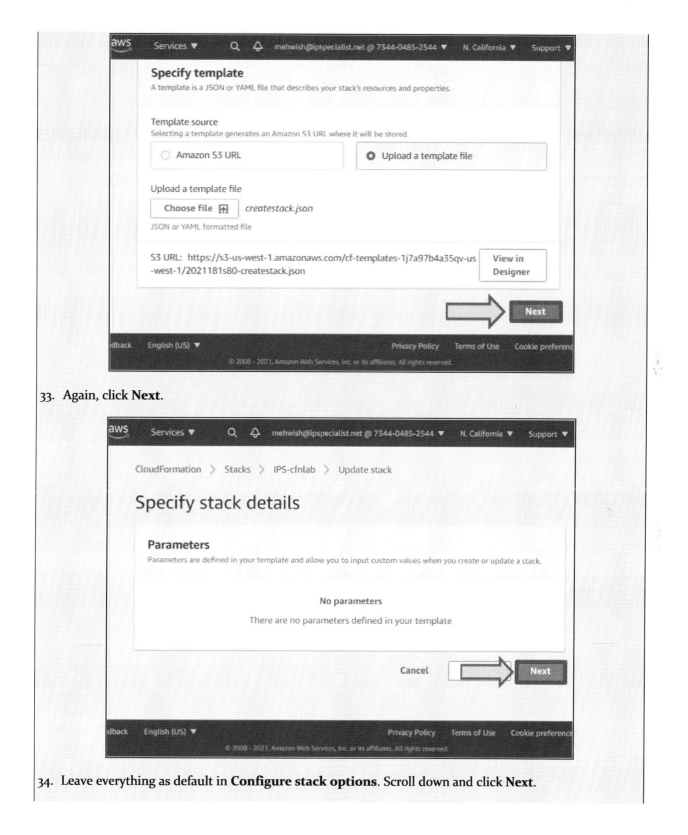

33. Again, click **Next**.

34. Leave everything as default in **Configure stack options**. Scroll down and click **Next**.

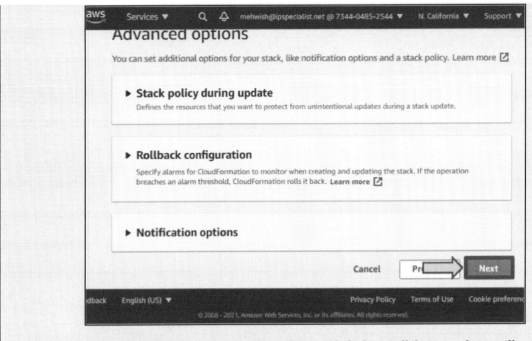

35. Review the stack and scroll down, leaving everything as default. Scroll down, and you will see the changes. Click on the **Create stack** button.

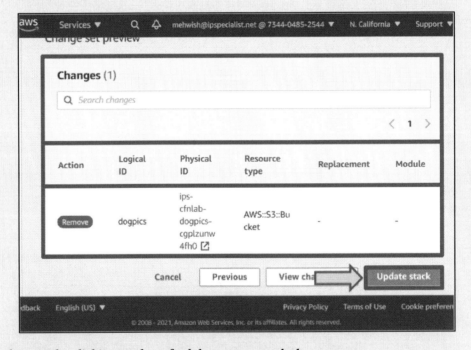

36. Refresh the page by clicking on the refresh button to watch the progress.

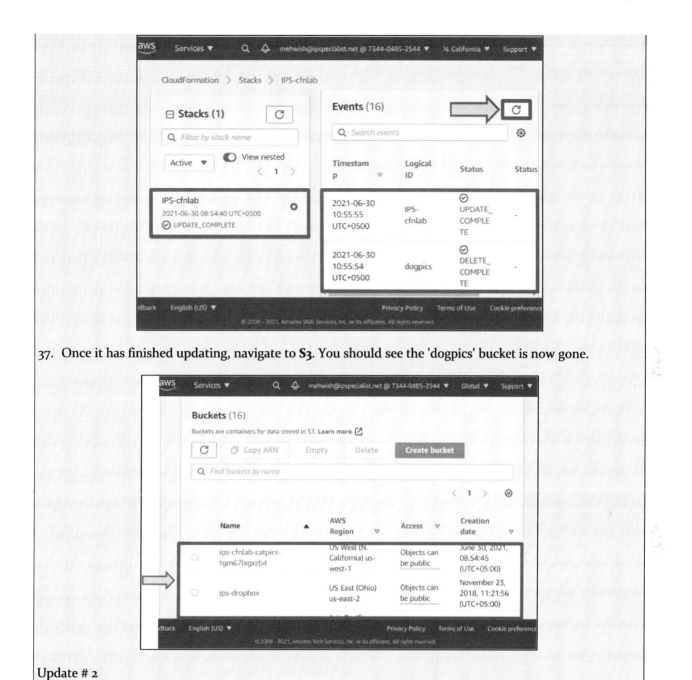

37. Once it has finished updating, navigate to **S3**. You should see the 'dogpics' bucket is now gone.

Update # 2

38. Open the **updatestack2.json** file in the code editor.

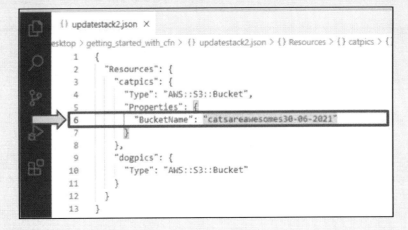

39. Change 123 characters in 'catsareawesome123' to something unique: e.g., your birthday and today's date.

40. Save the file.

41. Now, go back into the CloudFormation dashboard by clicking on **Stacks**.

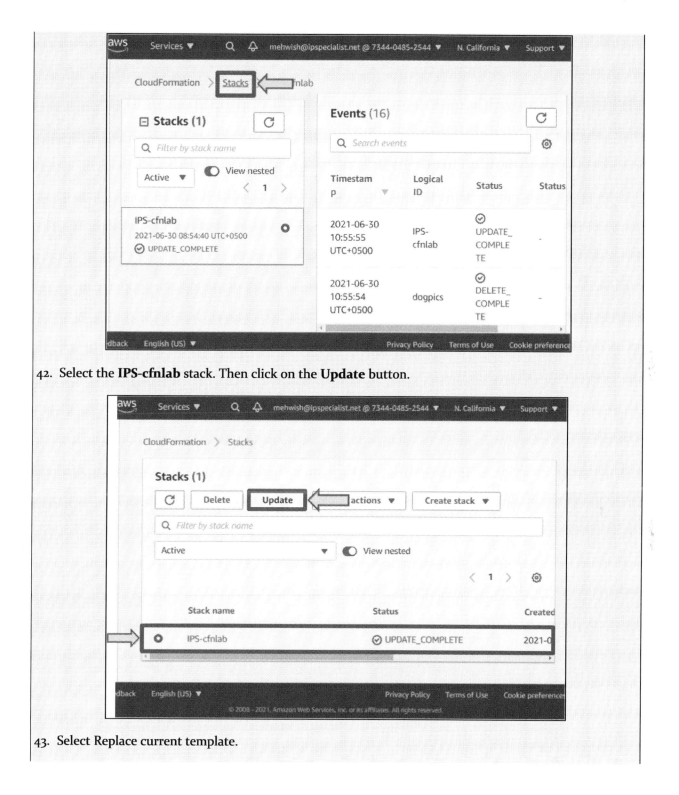

42. Select the **IPS-cfnlab** stack. Then click on the **Update** button.

43. Select Replace current template.

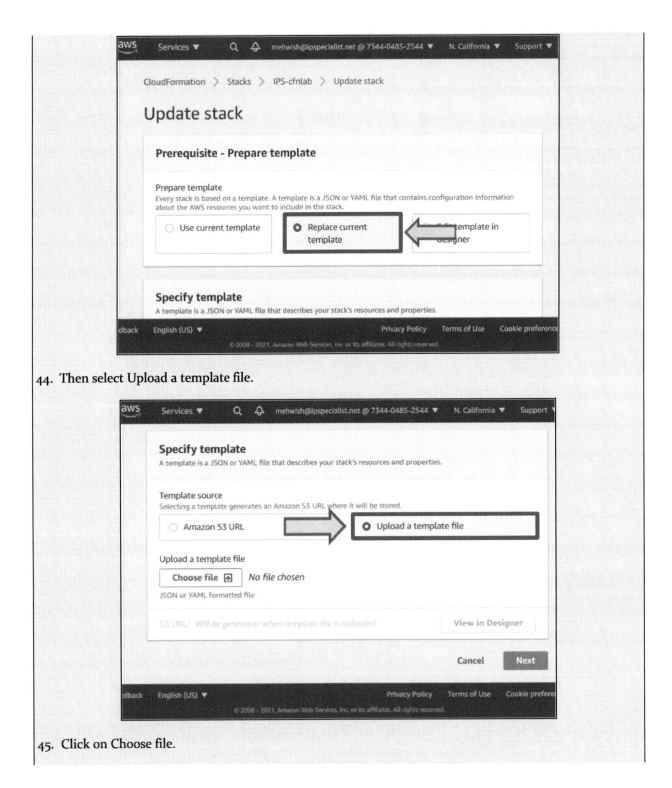

44. Then select Upload a template file.

45. Click on Choose file.

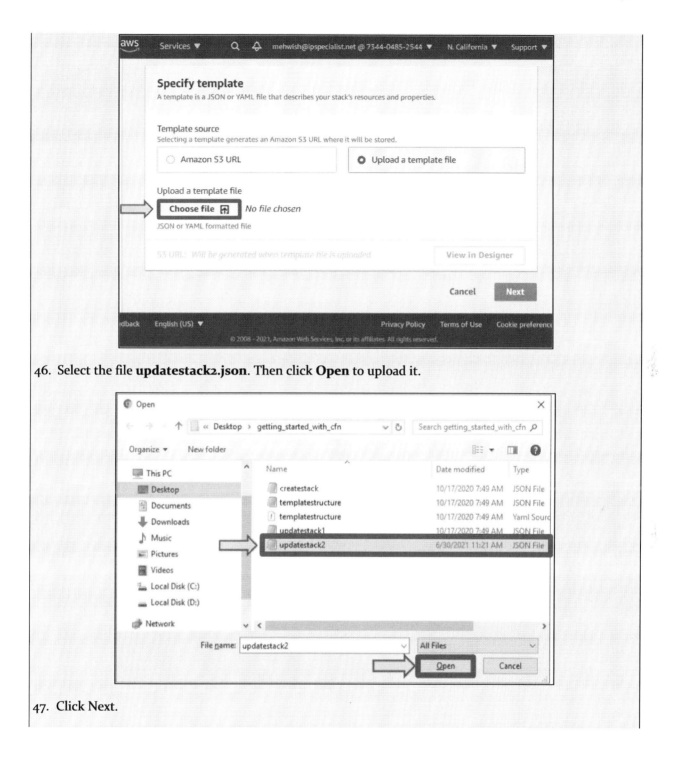

46. Select the file **updatestack2.json**. Then click **Open** to upload it.

47. Click Next.

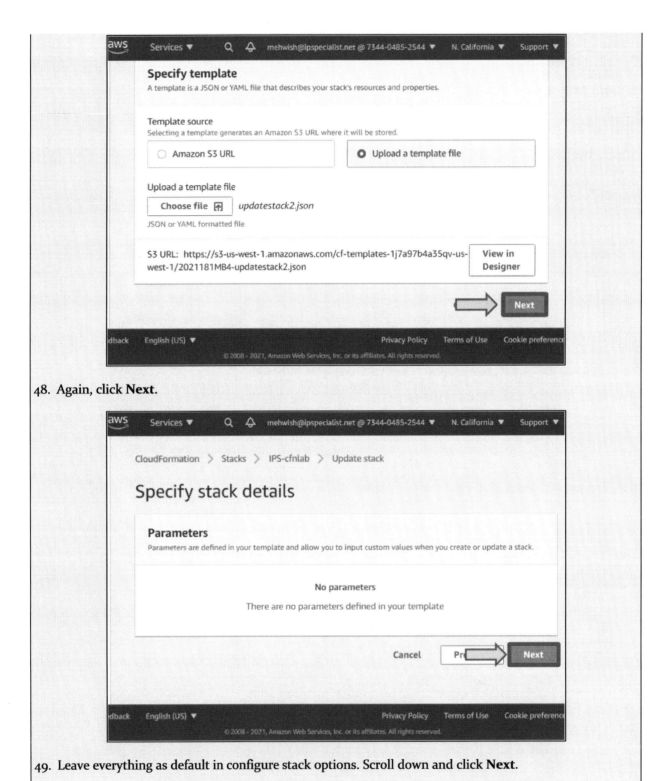

48. Again, click **Next**.

49. Leave everything as default in configure stack options. Scroll down and click **Next**.

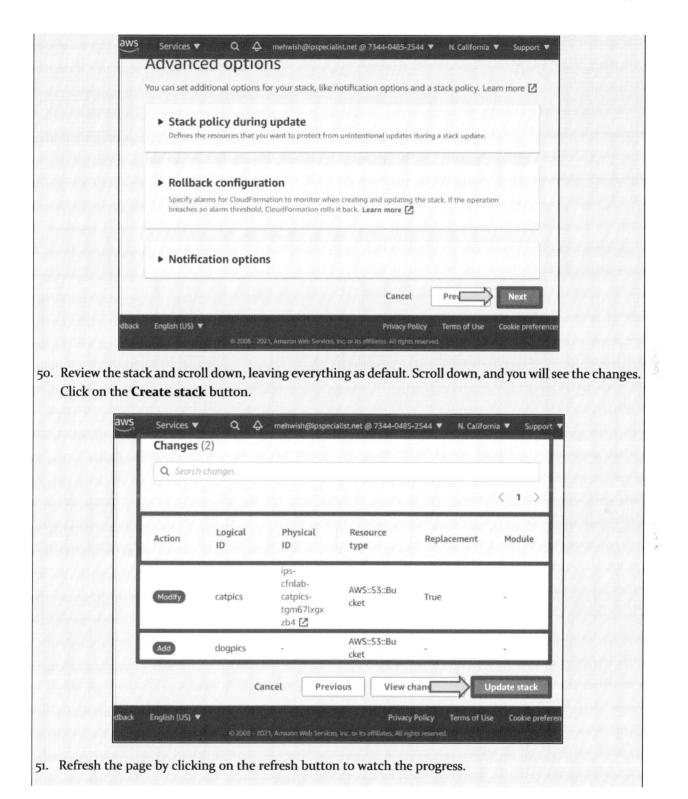

50. Review the stack and scroll down, leaving everything as default. Scroll down, and you will see the changes. Click on the **Create stack** button.

51. Refresh the page by clicking on the refresh button to watch the progress.

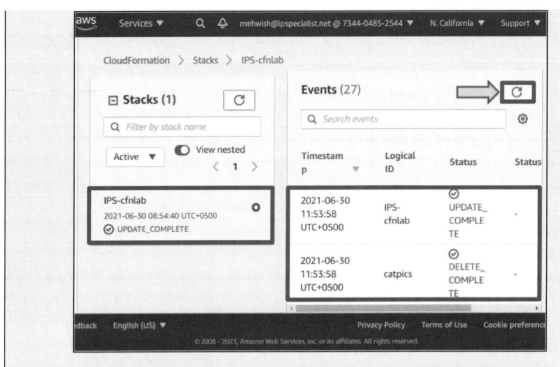

52. Once it has finished updating, go to **S3**. You should see two changes; the 'dogpics' bucket is back, and the bucket name is updated to the new value.

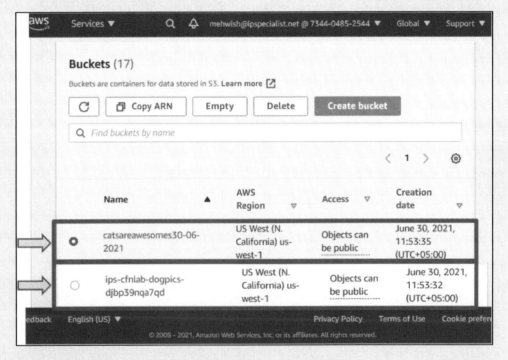

Add CloudFormation Stacks

53. Now create a new stack with 'updatestack2.json.'
54. Go to the CloudFormation dashboard by clicking on **Stacks**.

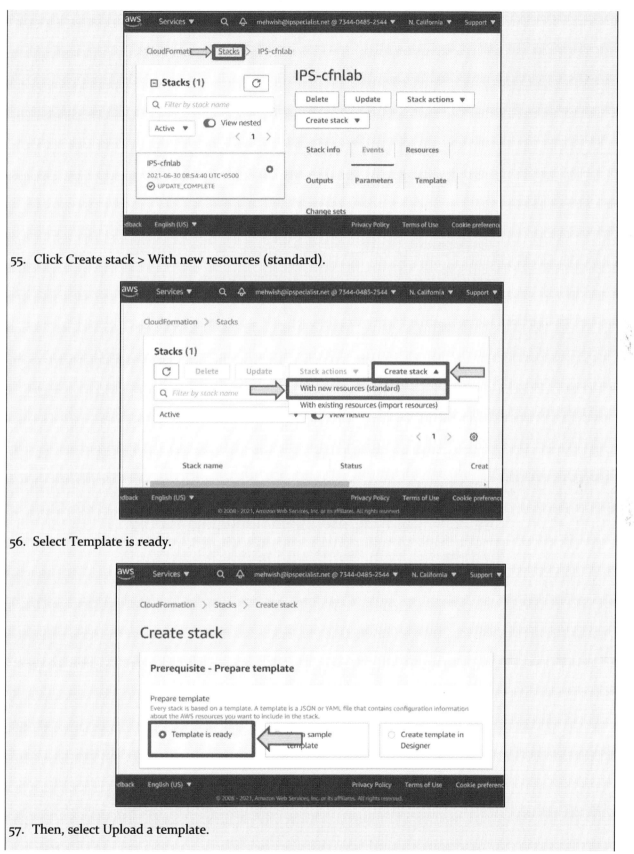

55. Click Create stack > With new resources (standard).

56. Select Template is ready.

57. Then, select Upload a template.

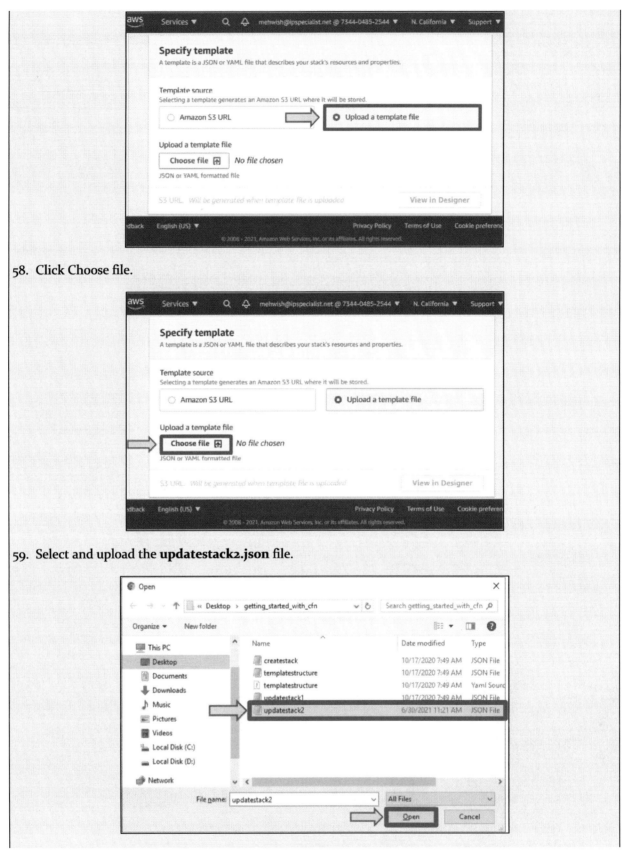

58. Click Choose file.

59. Select and upload the **updatestack2.json** file.

60. Click **Next**.

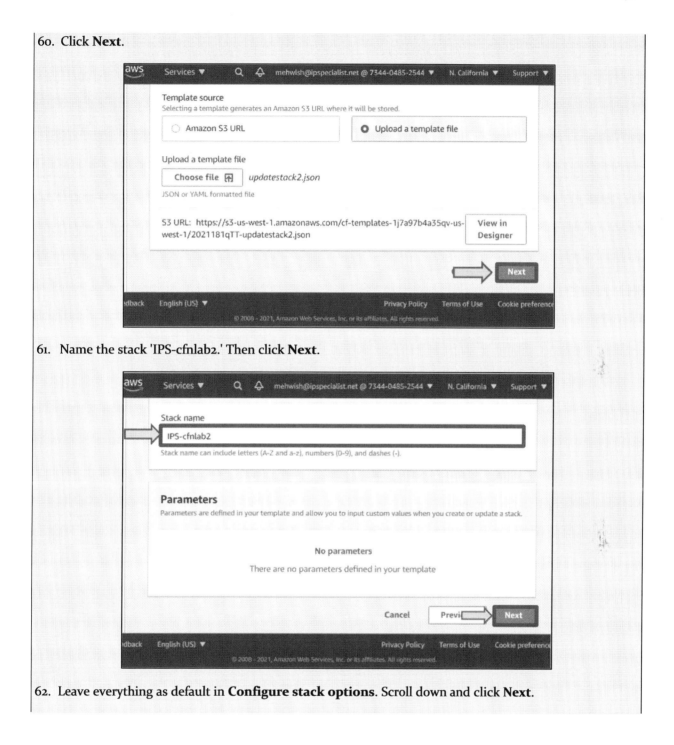

61. Name the stack 'IPS-cfnlab2.' Then click **Next**.

62. Leave everything as default in **Configure stack options**. Scroll down and click **Next**.

63. Review the stack. Scroll down and click on the **Create stack** button.

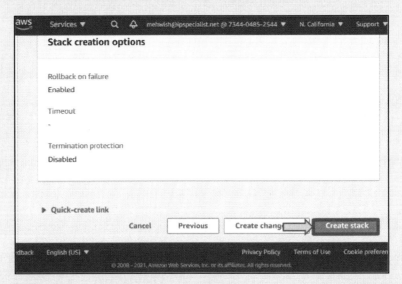

64. Refresh the page to watch the progress.

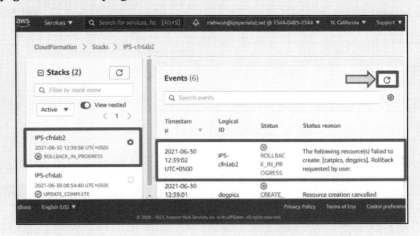

65. Note that the process eventually fails; you cannot have another S3 bucket with the same name.
66. Now create a stack with **updatestack1.json**.
67. Navigate to the CloudFormation dashboard by clicking on **Stacks**.

68. Click Create stack > With new resources (standard).

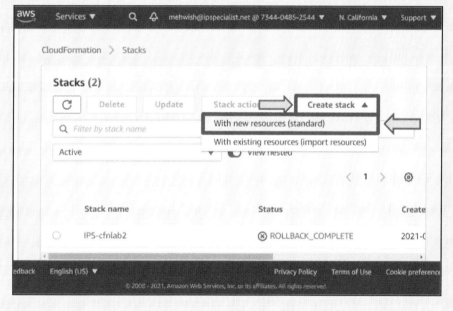

69. Select Template is ready.

103

70. Then select Upload a template.

71. Click Choose File.

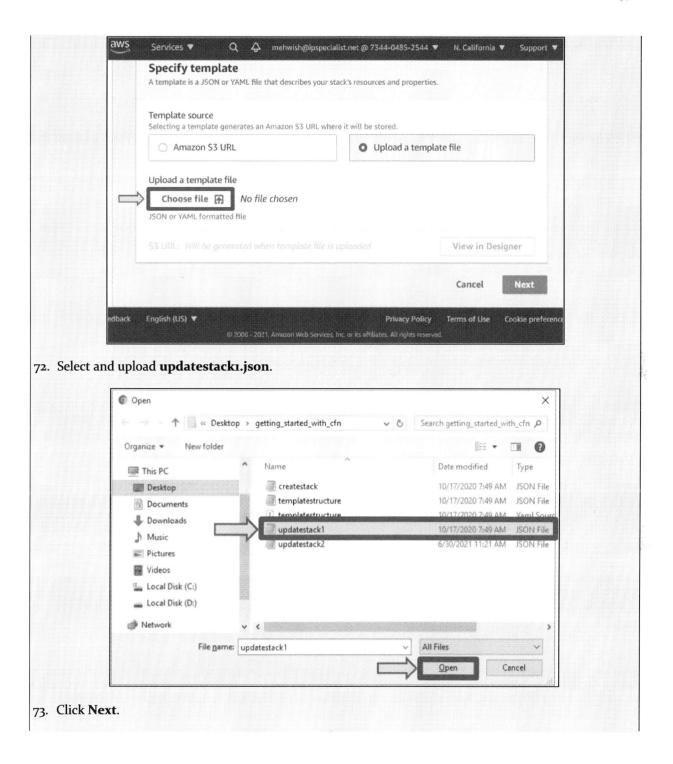

72. Select and upload **updatestack1.json**.

73. Click **Next**.

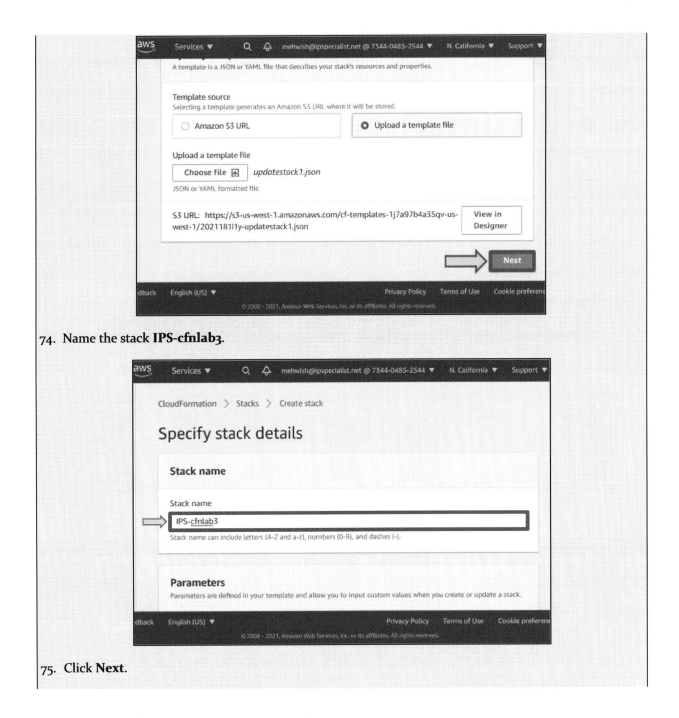

74. Name the stack **IPS-cfnlab3**.

75. Click **Next**.

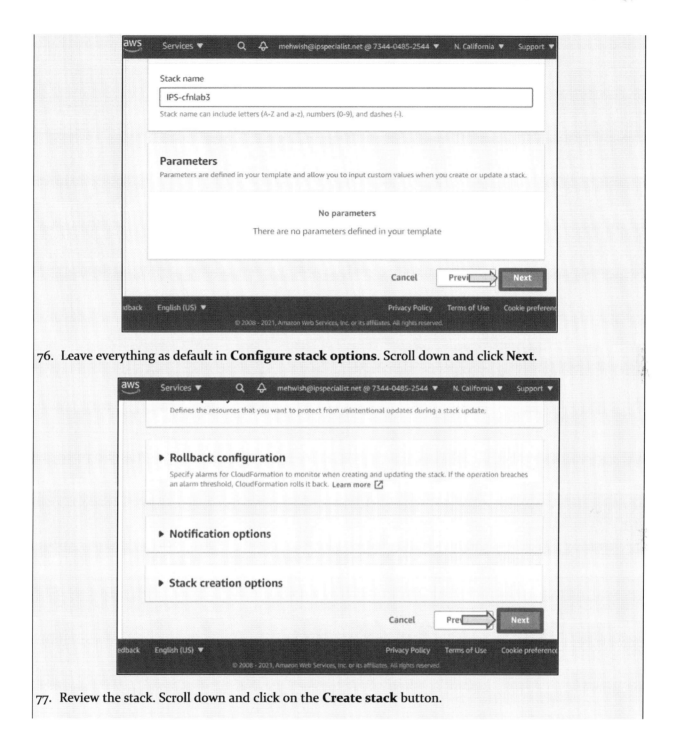

76. Leave everything as default in **Configure stack options**. Scroll down and click **Next**.

77. Review the stack. Scroll down and click on the **Create stack** button.

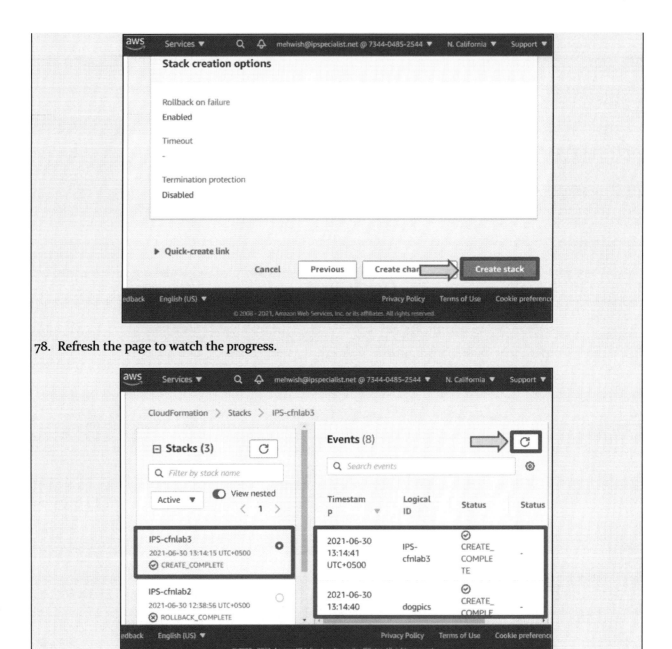

78. Refresh the page to watch the progress.

79. Once it is complete, go to the **S3**, where you should see two new buckets: IPS-cfnlab3-catpics-<RANDOM_STRING> and IPS-cfnlab3-dogpics-<RANDON_SRING>.

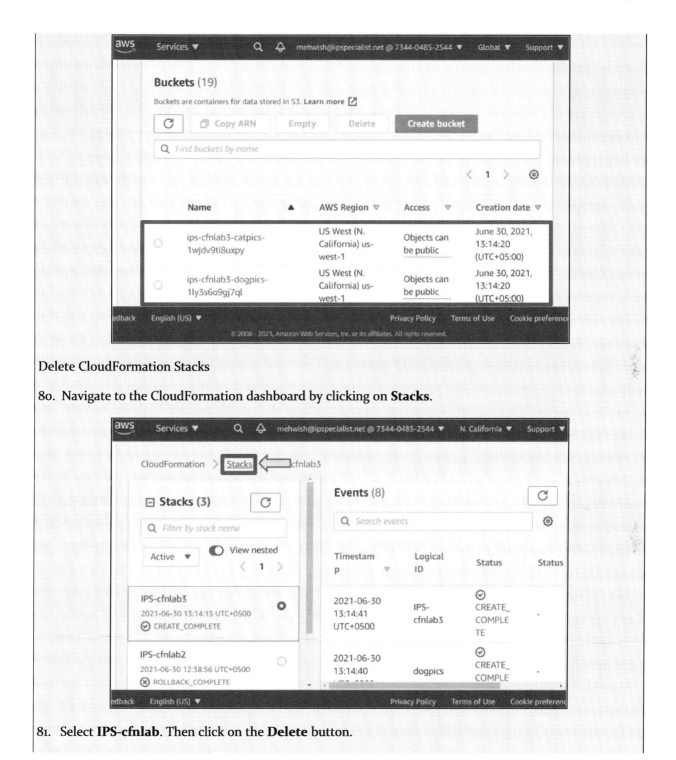

Delete CloudFormation Stacks

80. Navigate to the CloudFormation dashboard by clicking on **Stacks**.

81. Select **IPS-cfnlab**. Then click on the **Delete** button.

82. In the dialog box, click **Delete stack**.

83. Select **IPS-cfnlab2**. Then click on the **Delete** button.

84. In the dialog box, click **Delete stack**.

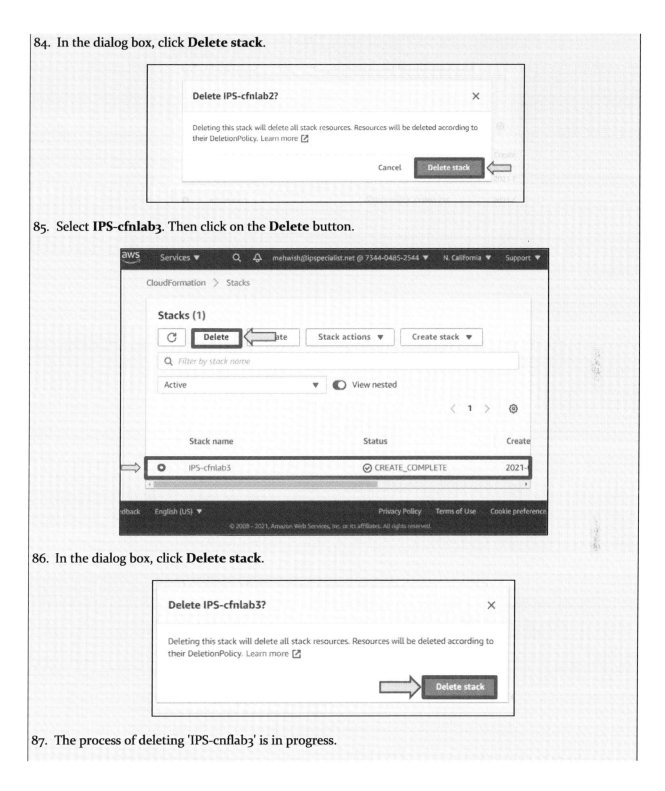

85. Select **IPS-cfnlab3**. Then click on the **Delete** button.

86. In the dialog box, click **Delete stack**.

87. The process of deleting 'IPS-cnflab3' is in progress.

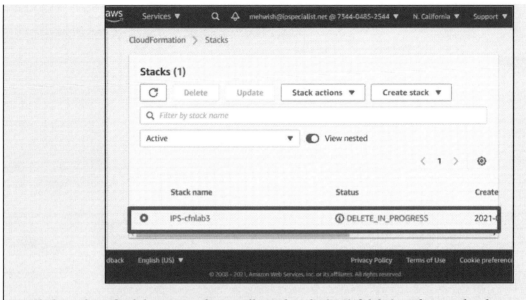

88. Click on the refresh button, and you will see that the 'IPS'cfnlab3' stack name has been removed.

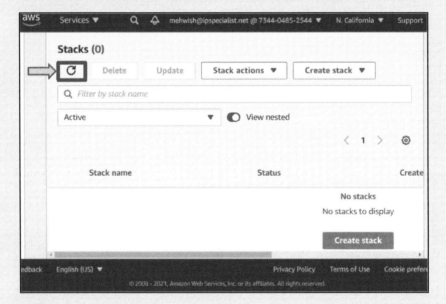

89. Once it is all done, navigate to S3. You should see all the 'IPS-cfnlab' buckets are gone, as well as the 'catsareawesome' bucket.

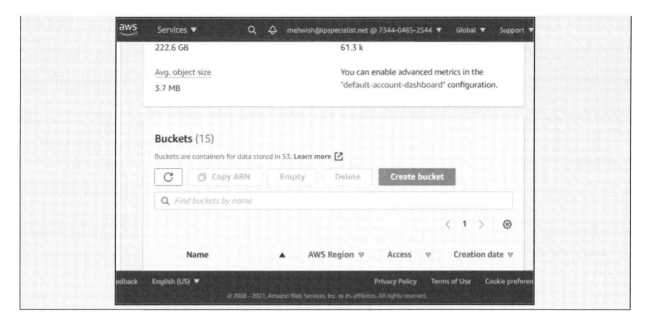

AWS Quick Starts

AWS Quick Starts is a simple and quick way to get started if you are new to AWS and want to deploy any technology onto the AWS cloud. Quick Starts are automated reference deployments, such as templates, created by AWS solutions architects and partners to aid you in deploying popular solutions of major technologies on AWS cloud while following AWS best practices for security and high availability.

Each Quick Starts deploys the AWS compute, network, storage, and other services required to install a given workload on AWS, then configures and operates them. You can set up your test or production environment in a few simple steps and begin using it immediately. Quick Starts saves time by automating hundreds of laborious installation and configuration tasks with a single click.

Quick Starts include:

1. A reference architecture for the deployment.
2. AWS CloudFormation templates (JSON or YAML scripts) that automate and configure the deployment.
3. A deployment guide explains the architecture and implementation in detail and provides instructions for customizing the deployment.

Demo 8-01: AWS Quick Starts Dashboard

1. Browse to https://aws.amazon.com/quickstart/?solutions-all.sort-by=item.additionalFields.sortDate&solutions-all.sort-order=desc&awsf.filter-tech-category=*all&awsf.filter-industry=*all&awsf.filter-content-type=*all

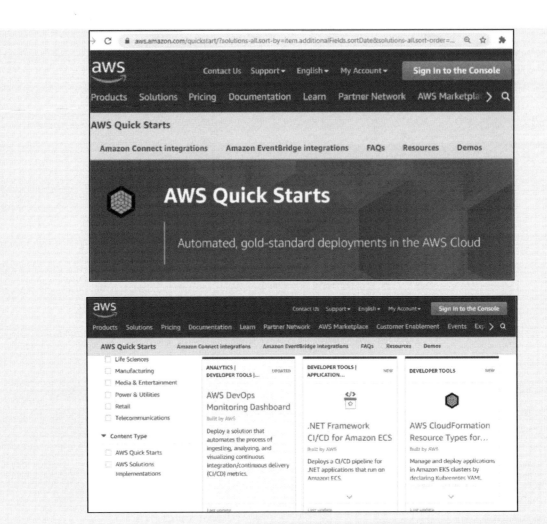

2. You will see a list of popular deployment models. Select the solution you need to deploy by clicking 'View guide.' For this example, we will deploy a SharePoint server.

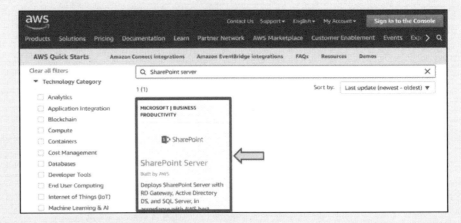

3. You will see a complete guide to the deployment solution you selected. After reading the guide, click **Launch Quick Starts**. This will open up the AWS console and launch AWS CloudFormation, which can be used to set up your SharePoint infrastructure without manually configuring the resources.

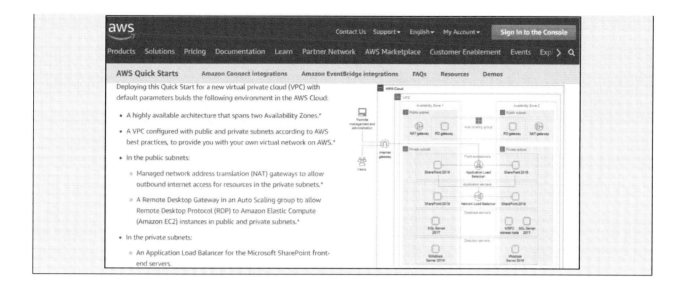

 EXAM TIP:

1. Quick Starts is a way of completely scripting your cloud environment.

2. Quick Starts is a bunch of CloudFormation templates already built by AWS Solutions Architects, allowing you to quickly create complex environments.

AWS On-Premises Strategies

The On-Premises Strategies that are used with AWS are as follows:

- ***Database Migration Service (DMS):*** The AWS Database Migration Service (DMS) is a web service that allows you to move data from one datastore to another. Endpoints are the names for these two data storage. You can migrate data across endpoints that utilize the same database engine from one Oracle database to another Oracle database. You may also migrate data between source and target endpoints that utilize different database engines, such as Oracle, to PostgreSQL. The only condition for using AWS DMS is that one of your endpoints has to be hosted on an AWS service. Moving from one on-premises database to another is impossible using AWS DMS.

- ***Server Migration Service (SMS):*** Your on-premises servers can be incrementally replicated in AWS using the AWS Server Migration Service (SMS). The AWS Server Migration Service automates the migration of VMware vSphere, Microsoft Hyper-V/SCVMM, and Azure virtual machines from your on-premises environment to the AWS Cloud. AWS SMS replicates your server VMs in the cloud as Amazon Machine Images (AMIs) that may be deployed on Amazon EC2. You can quickly test and update your cloud-based images using AMIs before deploying them in production. It can be used as a backup tool, as part of a multi-site plan on-premises and off-premises, and as part of a Disaster Recovery (DR) strategy.

- ***AWS Application Discovery Service***: AWS Application Discovery Service helps enterprise customers plan migration projects by gathering information about their on-premises data centers. You install the

AWS Application Discovery Agentless Connector as a virtual appliance on VMware vCenter. It will then build server utilization and dependency maps of your on-premises environment. The collected data is retained in encrypted format in an AWS Application Discovery Service data store. You can export this data as a CSV file and use it to estimate the Total Cost of Ownership (TCO) of running on AWS and planning your migration to AWS. This data is also available in AWS Migration Hub, where you can migrate the discovered servers and track their progress as they get migrated to AWS.

- ***VM Import/Export***: VM Import/Export makes it simple to move virtual machine images from your existing environment to Amazon EC2 instances and back. By integrating your virtual machines into Amazon EC2 as ready-to-use instances, you can leverage your current investments in virtual machines that you've made to fulfill your IT security, configuration management, and compliance requirements. You may also export imported instances to your on-premises virtualization architecture, allowing you to distribute workloads around your network. Beyond the regular usage charges for Amazon EC2 and Amazon S3, VM Import/Export is provided at no additional cost. It can be used to set up a disaster recovery strategy on AWS or to use AWS as a backup site.

- ***Download Amazon Linux 2 as an ISO***: AWS allows you to download Amazon Linux 2 as an ISO. It works with all major virtualization providers such as VMware, Hyper V, KBM, Virtual Box, Oracle hypervisor technology, etc. Hence, you can take your little piece of EC2 and run it on-premises in your own data centers.

EXAM TIP: You need to be aware of what high-level AWS services you can use on-premises for the exam:

1. Database Migration Service (DMS)
2. Server Migration Service (SMS)
3. AWS Application Discovery Service
4. VM Import/Export
5. Download Amazon Linux 2 as an ISO

AWS Transfer Family

AWS Transfer Family allows you to easily move files in and out of S3 or EFS using Secure File Transfer Protocol, SFTP, FTPS, or FTP.

How Does It Transfer?
Transfer Family supports SFTP and FTPS from outside of your AWS environment into S3 and into EFS, but it only supports FTP transfer internally, inside of your VPC, and that is for security reasons because FTP is not secure.

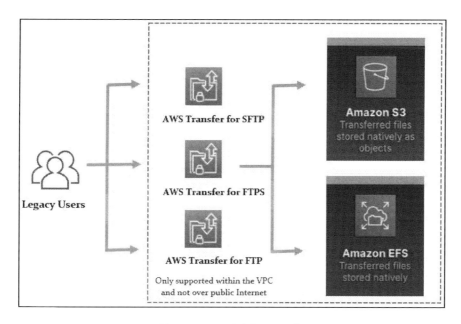

Figure 8-07: AWS Transfer

Moving to the Cloud with Migration Hub

Server Migration Service

AWS Server Migration Service (AWS SMS) automates the migration of your on-premises VMware vSphere, Microsoft Hyper-V/SCVMM, and Azure virtual machines to the AWS Cloud. AWS SMS incrementally replicates your server VMs as cloud-hosted Amazon Machine Images (AMIs) ready for deployment on Amazon EC2. Working with AMIs, you can easily test and update your cloud-based images before deploying them in production.

By using AWS SMS to manage your server migrations, you can:

- Simplify the cloud migration process.
- Orchestrate multi-server migrations.
- Test server migrations incrementally.
- Support the most widely used operating systems.
- Minimize downtime.

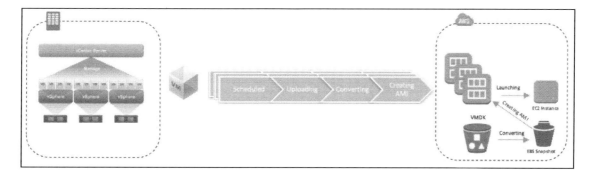

Figure 8-08: Server Migration Service

Database Migration Service

AWS Database Migration Service (AWS DMS) is a cloud service that makes it easy to migrate relational databases, data warehouses, NoSQL databases, and other types of data stores. You can use AWS DMS to migrate your data into the AWS Cloud or between combinations of cloud and on-premises setups.

With AWS DMS, you can perform one-time migrations and replicate ongoing changes to keep sources and targets in sync. If you want to migrate to a different database engine, you can use the AWS Schema Conversion Tool (AWS SCT) to translate your database schema to the new platform. You then use AWS DMS to migrate the data. Because AWS DMS is a part of the AWS Cloud, you get the cost efficiency, speed to market, security, and flexibility that AWS services offer.

At a basic level, AWS DMS is a server in the AWS Cloud that runs replication software. You create a source and target connection to tell AWS DMS where to extract from and load to. Then you schedule a task that runs on this server to move your data. AWS DMS creates the tables and associated primary keys if they don't exist on the target. You can create the target tables yourself if you prefer. Or you can use AWS Schema Conversion Tool (AWS SCT) to create some or all of the target tables, indexes, views, triggers, and so on.

The following diagram illustrates the AWS DMS replication process.

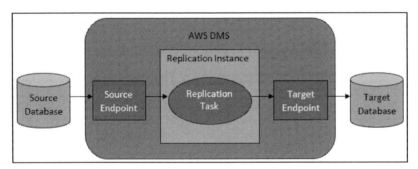

Figure 1-09: Database Migration Service

Mind Map

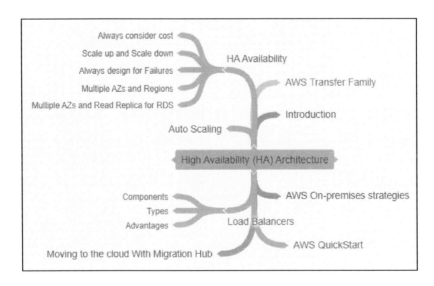

Figure 8-10: Chapter Mind Map

Practice Questions

1. Which type of load balancer is used when extreme performance is required?
   a) Application
   b) Network
   c) Classic

2. Which type of load balancer is often used in a multi-tier application to load balance between tiers of the application?
   a) Classic
   b) Network
   c) Internal
   d) Application

3. Which of the following protocols are not supported by Application Load Balancers listeners? (Choose multiple)
   a) TLS
   b) HTTPS
   c) UDP
   d) HTTPS

4. You can use SDKs to configure load balancer
   a) True
   b) False

5. If the data is not sent or received over a specified time period, the load balancer closes the connection, this is called _____
   a) Path based routing
   b) Idle connection timeout
   c) Listener error
   d) Health check failure

6. Sticky session feature is also known as
   a) X-forwarding
   b) Content based routing
   c) Session affinity
   d) Idle connection

7. To test the status of EC2 instances placed behind an ELB, we can use
   a) Health checks
   b) Listeners
   c) Idle connection timeout

d) X-forward

8. Auto scaling can launch instances using
   a) Scaling options
   b) Configuration templates
   c) Groups
   d) Health checks

9. Netflix Simian Army is a great example of planning for failure
   a) True
   b) False

10. Multi AZ is for disaster recovery while read replicas improve performance
    a) True
    b) False

11. Which is the comprehensive way of scripting cloud environments in AWS?
    a) CloudFront
    b) CloudFormation
    c) CloudProgramming
    d) CloudStack

12. Which one of the following is a branch of CloudFormation where templates are already built by AWS Solution Architects?
    a) AWS Quick Start
    b) AWS S3
    c) AWS EC2
    d) AWS SageMaker

13. Which AWS service can you quickly deploy and manage applications in the cloud without worrying about the infrastructure?

    a) Quick Start
    b) AWS CloudFormation
    c) AWS EC2
    d) AWS Elastic Beanstalk

14. Which AWS on-premises strategy allows you to move data from one datastore to another?

    a) Server Migration Service
    b) VM Import/Export
    c) Database Migration Service
    d) AWS Application Discovery Service

15. Which AWS on-premises strategy supports incremental replication of your on-premises server into AWS?

    a) Server Migration Service
    b) VM Import/Export
    c) Database Migration Service
    d) AWS Application Discovery Service

16. Which of the following gathers and provides data to help enterprise clients better understand the configuration, usage, and behavior of servers in their IT systems?
    a) AWS VPC
    b) AWS EC2
    c) AWS PrivateLink
    d) AWS Application Discovery Service

17. Which of the following uses JSON or YAML format files to describe the collection of AWS resources (known as a stack)?

    a) AWS Transit Gateway
    b) AWS CloudFormation
    c) AWS VPN CloudHub
    d) AWS EC2

18. Fault tolerance can be achieved by introducing redundancy into your system. True or False?

    a) False
    b) True

19. Which of the following can be used to achieve high availability or fault-tolerance?

    a) Auto Scaling
    b) Read Replicas
    c) Read Access Memory
    d) EC2 hibernate

20. Which AWS service is used to deploy non-web applications?

    a) AWS PrivateLink
    b) AWS Transit Gateway
    c) AWS VPN CloudHub
    d) AWS Elastic Beanstalk

Chapter 09: Applications Introduction

Introduction

There are several services available under the Application and Mobile Services section of the Amazon web services Management Console. Application services include Amazon Simple Queue Service (SQS), Amazon Simple Workflow Service (SWF), Amazon AppStream, Amazon Elastic Transcoder, Amazon Simple Email Service (SES), Amazon CloudSearch, and Amazon API Gateway. Mobile services include Amazon Cognito, Amazon Simple Notification Service (SNS), AWS Device Farm, and Amazon Mobile Analytics. This chapter focuses on the core services required to be familiar with to pass the exam.

Decoupling Workflows

Tight Coupling
Tightly coupled applications consist of parallel processes that are dependent on each other to carry out the calculation. Unlike a loosely coupled computation, all processes of a tightly coupled simulation iterate together and require communication with one another.

Loose coupling
A loosely coupled workload entails processing a large number of smaller jobs. Generally, the smaller job runs on one node, either consuming one process or multiple processes with shared memory parallelization (SMP) for parallelization within that node..

Upcoming Services

Simple Queue Service (SQS)

You can decouple and grow serverless applications, distributed systems, and microservices with SQS, a fully managed message queuing service.

Simple Notification Service (SNS)

For both application-to-application (A2A) and application-to-person (A2P) communication, SNS is a fully managed messaging service.

API Gateway

Developers can quickly and easily construct, publish, maintain, monitor, and protect APIs at any size with API Gateway, a fully managed service.

> EXAM TIP: Every level of an application should be loosely coupled.

Simple Queue Service (SQS)

Amazon SQS (the first AWS service) is a web service that gives you access to a message queue that can store messages while waiting for a computer to process them.

It is a distributed queue system that enables web service applications to quickly and reliably queue messages that one component in the application generates to be consumed by another component. A queue is a temporary repository for messages that are awaiting processing.

In short, SQS is the queuing system; it is a way of storing messages independently from your EC2 instances. You can use Amazon's simple queue services to transfer any volume of data, at any level of throughput, without misplacing messages or requiring other services to be continuously available.

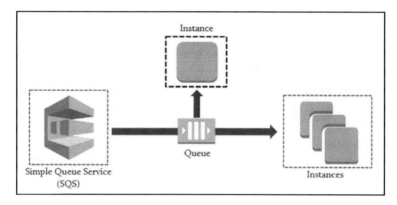

Figure 9-01: Simple Queue Service (SQS)

Example: Meme Website

One example of SQS is shown in Figure 9-02. The picture is called "Meme Website." To build a meme website, a person must upload a picture to a website called a meme website. This can be d one by visiting "memegenerator.com."." The user first must upload this image to S3, which will trigger a "Lambda" function, as shown in Figure 9-02. The Lambda function is an ultimate abstraction layer that manages and provisions the server. If a user wants to write sometime on that image like "Welcome To IPSpecialist," then the Lambda function takes that S3 image and stores the text in "SQS." EC2 instances or a fleet of EC2 instances will pull the message from the queue. EC2 instances intercept that text message and create a meme with images consisting of "Welcome To IPSpecialist." This image will then be stored in an S3 bucket.

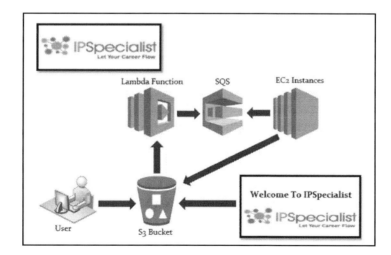

Figure 9-02: Meme Website

The main advantage of this setup is that if you lose an EC2 instance while trying to create the meme, the message will become available again in the queue. Another EC2 instance can go in, then create that meme. So the information will not be lost.

SQS is a way of storing messages independently. If one of the EC2 instances is lost and can no longer process the message, then another EC2 instance will come along and take that message.

Example: Travel Website

An example of a travel website is shown in Figure 9-03. A user wants to use a travel website. They want some deals on flights and hotels as well. For this purpose, the user will go to the EC2 web server and store some information. The EC2 web server will pass that information to an SQS queue. If there are some application servers or a fleet of servers in the background, then each server will do the configuration to get that message and look for different airlines, as shown in the figure. The server will give suitable flights and hotels for that date. The EC2 instance will collect this information. It will pass back to the web server, which will pass back to the end user.

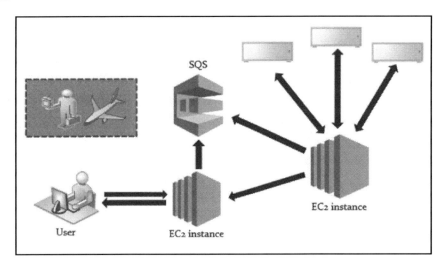

Figure 9-03: Travel Website

The main advantage of this setup is that if you lose an individual EC2 instance, you will not lose the information. Another EC2 instance will pull the message from the queue and return it to the user.

Advantages of SQS

The following are some advantages of Amazon SQS.

Decoupling of Components

Using Amazon SQS, you can decouple the components of applications so they run independently, easing message management between the components.

Fail-Safe Queue

Any component of a distributed application can store messages in a fail-safe queue.

Store Messages in any Format

Message can contain up to 256KB of text in any format. Any component can later retrieve programmatically using Amazon SQS API.

> EXAM TIP: Messages are 256KB in size or less. Message can be kept in the queue from 1 minute to 14 days; the default retention period is four days.

> **Note:** If you want to store the message that contains above 256KB of text, then this message will not be stored in SQS. The message will be stored in the S3 bucket.

Understanding of SQS

In SQS, the queue acts as a buffer between the component producing and saving the data and the component receiving the data for processing. This means the queue resolves issues if the producer produces work faster than the consumer can process or if the producer or consumer is only intermittently connected to the network.

Visibility Timeout – The amount of time the message is invisible in the SQS queue after a reader picks up that message. This can be understood better with the example shown in Figure 9-02, where the user stores the image in S3 and creates a text stored in the SQS queue. The EC2 instance picks it up and writes the text through an image. The visibility timeout is the length of time the message will be. The message is invisible in the queue until the EC2 instance has processed the job. The message will be deleted from the queue if the job is processed before the visibility timeout expires. If the job is not processed within that time, the message will become visible again, and another reader will process it. This could result in the same message being delivered twice.

The visibility timeout maximum is 12 hours.

> EXAM TIP: Amazon SQS long polling is a way to retrieve messages from SQS queues. While the regular short polling returns immediately even if the message queue is being polled as empty, long polling does not return a response until a message arrives in the message queue or the long poll times out.

Types of Queue

There are two types of the queue:

1. **Standard Queue** – Standard queue happens when we create a queue by default.
2. **FIFO Queue** – FIFO is the "First In, First Out" queue.

Standard Queues

Amazon SQS offers a standard queue as the default queue type. A standard queue allows us to have a nearly unlimited number of transactions per second. A standard queue guarantees that a message is delivered at least once.

Sometimes (because of the highly-distributed architecture that allows high throughput), more than one copy of the message may be delivered out of order. However, the standard queue best-effort order ensures that messages are generally delivered in the same order as they are sent.

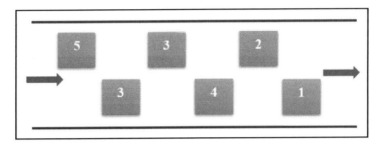

Figure 9-04: Standard Queue

FIFO Queues

The FIFO queue complements the standard queue.

The most important features of this queue type are FIFO and exactly-once processing.

The order in which messages are sent and received is strictly preserved. A message is delivered once and remains available until the consumer processes and deletes it; duplicates are not introduced into the queue.

FIFO queues also support message groups that allow multiple ordered message groups within a single queue. FIFO queues are not as fast as standard queues. These queues are limited to 300 transactions per second (TPS); however, it has all the capabilities of the standard queue.

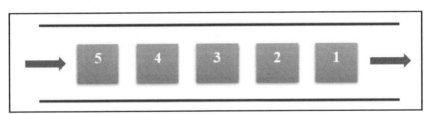

Figure 9-05: FIFO Queue

EXAM TIP: There is no guarantee with standard queues. Your application needs to be able to cope with two things:

1. The message is being delivered out of order.
2. Multiple copies of the same messages are being delivered twice.

In the FIFO queue, the order is strictly maintained and the message is delivered only once.

Messaging with SQS

SQS
SQS is a messaging queue that allows asynchronous processing of work. One resource will write a message to an SQS queue, and then another resource will retrieve that message from SQS.

Important settings

Delivery Delay

Default is 0. It can be set up to 15 minutes.

Message Size

Messages can be up to 256 KB of text in any format.

Encryption

Messages are encrypted in transit by default, but you can add them at rest.

Message Retention

With a range of 1 minute to 14 days, the default setting is 4 days.

Long vs. Short

Long polling is not the default, but it should be.

Queue Depth

This can be a trigger for auto scaling.

Sidelining Messages with Dead-Letter Queues

Dead-letter queues (DLQ), which other queues (source queues) can target for messages that can't be effectively processed (consumed), are supported by Amazon SQS. Dead-letter queues allow you to isolate unconsumed messages to ascertain why their processing fails, which helps debug your application or messaging system.

 EXAM TIP: DLQs are the best Slide lines.
- DLQs are just SQS queues that are set to receive the reject messages.
- Same Retention Window - Messages will be held up to 14 days.
- Usable with SNS - you can create SQS DLQ for SNS topics.

Ordered Messages with SQS FIFO

SQS Message Ordering

Standard

- Best-effort ordering
- Duplicat messages.
- Nearly unlimited transactions per second.

FIFO

- Guaranteed ordering
- No message duplication

- 300 messages per second

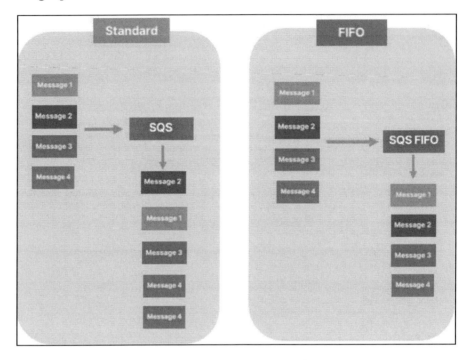

Figure 9-06: SQS Message Ordering

Exam TIP:
- Performance - FIFO queues do not have the same level of performance.
- You can order messages with SQS standards.
- Message Group ID - this ensures messages are processed one by one.
- Cost - It costs more since AWS must spend compute power to reduplicate messages.

Simple WorkFlow Service (SWF)

Amazon Simple WorkFlow Service is a web service that makes coordinating work across distributed application components easy. Amazon SWF enables an application for a wide range of use cases, including media processing, web application back-ends, business process workflow, and analytics pipelines, to be designed as coordination of tasks.

A task represents the invocation of various processing steps in an application that can be performed by executable code, web service calls, human action, and scripts. Amazon SWF gives you the full authority to achieve and coordinate tasks without being concerned about basic complications such as tracking their progress and maintaining their state.

The worker and the decider can run on cloud infrastructures, such as Amazon EC2, or machines behind firewalls. Amazon SWF breaks the interaction between workers and the decider. It allows the decider to get consistent views into the process of the task and to initiate new tasks in an ongoing manner.

> EXAM TIP: Simple WorkFlow Service (SWF) combines your digital environment with the manual tasks and human beings.

SWF Actors

Simple WorkFlow Service actors are composed of:

WorkFlow Starters

It is an application that can initiate or start a workflow. It could be your e-commerce website following the placement of an order or a mobile app searching for bus times.

Deciders

It controls the flow of the activity task in the workflow execution. A decider decides what to do next if something has finished or failed in a workflow.

Activity Worker

These are the workers that go in and carry out the activity task.

Difference between SQS and SWF

Simple Queue Service (SQS)	Simple WorkFlow Service (SWF)
SQS has a retention period of up to 14 days	With SWF, WorkFlow execution can last up to 1 year
It offers a message-oriented API	It presents a task-oriented API
With SQS, there is a need to handle duplicated messages and may also need to ensure that a message is processed only once	It ensures that the task is assigned only once and is never duplicated
With SQS, you need to implement your application-level tracking, especially when applications use multiple queues	It keeps track of all the tasks and events in an application

Table 9-01: SQS vs. SWF

Simple Notification Service (SNS)

Amazon Simple Notification Service is a web service that makes it simple to set up, operate, and grant notifications from the cloud. It gives developers a highly scalable, flexible, and cost-effective efficiency in sending messages from an application and instantly delivering them to subscribers or other applications.

Push Notifications

Simple Notification Service (SNS) allows push notifications. You can use these notifications for Apple, Google, Fire OS, and Windows devices, as well as Android devices in China with Baidu Cloud Push. In short, it allows making push notifications to the mobile device.

SQS Integration

Besides pushing cloud notifications directly to mobile devices, Amazon SNS can also deliver notifications by SMS text message or email to Amazon SQS queues or any HTTP endpoint. It is a way of pushing out information to mobile devices, text messages, etc.

Topic

Simple Notification Service allows us to group multiple recipients using topics. A topic is an "access point" for allowing recipients to dynamically subscribe for identical copies of the same notification. For example, when you set a billing alert, it is a topic. There are some subscribers within the topic.

One topic can support deliveries to multiple endpoint types. For example, you can group iOS, Android, and SMS recipients. When you publish once to a topic, SNS delivers appropriately formatted copies of your message to each subscriber.

SNS Availability

All messages published to Amazon SNS are stored redundantly across multiple availability zones to prevent the message from being lost.

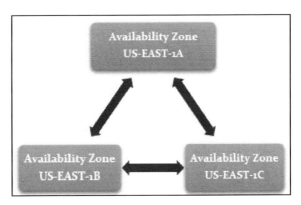

Figure 9-07: SNS Availability

Benefits of SNS

Some of the main benefits of SNS are as follows:

- It gives instantaneous, push-based delivery (push service) - There is no pulling
- It gives simple API and easy integration with applications
- You can get flexible message delivery over multiple transport protocols
- It is inexpensive; it is a pay-as-you-go model with no up-front costs
- Its Web-based AWS Management Console offers the simplicity of a point-and-click interface

Delivering Messages with SNS

SNS is a push-based messaging service. The subscribed endpoints will get messages in a proactive manner from it. This can be applied to alert a person or a system.

SNS Settings

Subscribers

Kinesis Data Firehose, SQS, Lambda, email, HTTPs, SMS, platform application endpoint.

Message Size

Messages can be up to 256 KB of text in any format.

DLQ Support

It is possible to keep undeliverable messages in an SQS DLQ.

FIFO or Standard

FIFO only supports SQS as a subscriber.

Encryption

By default, messages are encrypted in transit, but at-rest encryption can be added.

Access Policy

Similar to S3, a resource policy can be introduced to a subject.

 EXAM TIP: SNS and CloudWatch are the easiest way to alert you that something happened.

Difference between SQS and SNS

Both SQS and SNS are messaging services in AWS.

SQS – Simple Queue Service is a pull-based service. It is a way of storing messages independently from your EC2 instances.

SNS – Simple Notification Service is a push service. You can push messages out to different devices via text or notification.

Elastic Transcoder

The elastic transcoder is a media transcoder in the cloud. It allows the conversion of media files from their source format into different formats that will play on smartphones, tablets, PC, etc. It is a way of transcoding video to multiple different devices. Elastic Load Balancer is a highly available service that may be used to help develop highly available systems.

The way it works is that you pay based on the minutes you transcode and the resolution at which you transcode.

How to use Elastic Transcoder

Let's consider the example shown in Figure 9-08. You have an "S3 bucket" that stores your recorded video in this example. You go on to the website that you have implemented. You then upload that recorded video and store that in "S3". The video triggers the "Lambda Function," which will look at that video, take all the metadata, and send it to the "Elastic Transcoder." The transcoder will transcode that video. It functions in a very high resolution and stores the transcoded video in another "S3 bucket."

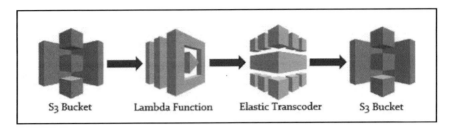

Figure 9-08: Working of Elastic Transcoder

> **EXAM TIP:** Elastic Transcoder is a cloud-based media transcoder. It enables the conversion of media files from their original format to formats that can be played on smartphones, tablets, PCs, and other devices.

Amazon API Gateway

Amazon API Gateway is short for Application Programming Interface. It is a fully managed service that makes it easy for developers to publish, maintain, monitor, and secure APIs at any scale.

You can create an API that acts as a front door for applications to access data, business logic, or functionality from your back-end services, such as an Amazon Elastic Compute Cloud (Amazon EC2) application, AWS Lambda code, or any web application, with just a few clicks in the AWS Management Console.

> **EXAM TIP:** Amazon API Gateway is a doorway into your AWS environment. Typically, it will use in communication with an EC2 instance, Lambda function, or other things.

Workings of API Gateway

The picture, as shown in Figure 9-09, explains the working of Amazon API Gateway. There are multiple users that make a call to API Gateway. API Gateway is the front end or the front door to the whole AWS environment. Depending on the users' call, the API gateway passes the call to the Lambda function, or it could be passed through to an EC2 instance or could also write something to Dynamo DB.

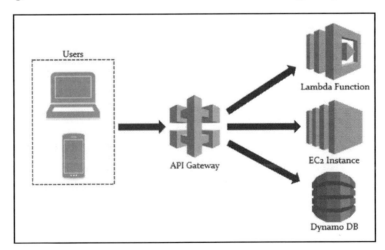

Figure 9-09: Working of API Gateway

What can API Gateway do?

In terms of its function, it can do the following things:

- Amazon API Gateway can expose HTTPS endpoints to define a RESTful API
- It can severlessly connect to services like Lambda, Dynamo DB, etc.
- It can send each API endpoint to a different target
- It runs efficiently at a very low cost
- It scales effortlessly and automatically. There is no need to worry about the auto scaling group or anything like that. It automatically scales along with your traffic
- You can track and control usage by using an API key
- You can throttle requests to prevent attacks
- You can also connect CloudWatch to log requests for monitoring
- You can also maintain multiple API versions (like test/dev API, production API, etc.)

API Gateway Configuration

The configuration of the Amazon API Gateway can be done by using the following steps:

- Define an API (or a Container)
- Define resources and nest resources within it by using URL paths
- For each resource:
  - You need to select the supported HTTP method (GET, POST, or any other supported HTTP method)
  - Set up your security
  - Choose your target (such as EC2 instance, Lambda, Dynamo DB, etc.)
  - Set request and respond transformations as well

API Gateway Deployments

The following are the steps used for the deployment of API Gateway.

- You can deploy API Gateway to a stage
- Use API Gateway domain by default (its Domain Name)
- You can also use the custom domain name
- It also supports the AWS Certified Manager for free SSL or TLS certificates

Note: You can use HTTPS with API Gateway, so you can get SSL or TLS certificates for free if you have been using a certificate manager to register your SSL certificates.

API Gateway Caching

API Gateway caching is a very important topic that you need to understand for the exam. API Gateway caching is a way to cache your endpoint's response. With caching, you can reduce the number of calls made to your endpoint and also improve the latency of the requests to your API.

API Gateway caches replies from your endpoint for the specified Time-To-Live (TTL) period in seconds when you activate caching for the stage. Instead of accessing your endpoint, API Gateway responds to the request by pulling up the endpoint answer from the cache.

Workings of API Gateway Caching

The working of API Gateway Caching is shown in Figures 9-10 (a, b). There are two users, "A" and "B." User "A" initiates the requests to API Gateway. It then forwards requests (GET requests) to the Lambda function. The lambda function responds to that request. User "B" sends the same request, and API Gateway has cached that now. It does not forward requests to the Lambda function. It sits in the cache and returns the response to user "B."

For user A:

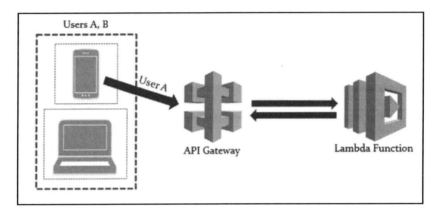

Figure 9-10(a): Working of API Gateway Caching w.r.t "User A"

For user B:

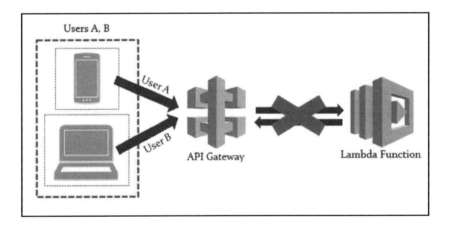

Figure 9-10(b): Working of API Gateway Caching w.r.t "User B"

EXAM TIP: API Gateway has caching capabilities to increase performance. You can cache common requests. The request is cached for the length of time you specify, and it is always in seconds.

Fronting Applications with API Gateway

API Gateway

With the help of the fully managed Amazon API Gateway service, you can quickly publish, create, maintain, monitor, and secure your API. You can use it to create a secure "front door" for your application.

Features

Security

Using this service, you may quickly secure your endpoints by connecting a web application firewall (WAF).

Stop Abuse

Users may quickly build DDoS mitigation and rate restriction to prevent endpoint abuse.

Ease of Use

API Gateway is simple to get started with. Easily build out the calls that will kill off other AWS services in your account.

 Exam TIP:
- API Gateway is a secure and safe front door for your application.
- DDoS - You can front API Gateway with a web application firewall (WAF).
- Versioning - API Gateway supports versioning of your API.
- Using an API gateway stops you from baking credentials into your code.

Same Origin Policy

In terms of API Gateway, cross-origin resource sharing is very important. To understand the cross-origin resource sharing, the same origin policy must be understood.

In computing, the same-origin policy is an important concept in the web application security model. Under the policy, a web browser permits scripts contained in a first web page to access data in a second web page, but only if both web pages have the same origin or domain name. So, one page can talk to another page, provided the first page has the same domain name. This is called the same origin policy.

The same Origin Policy is used to stop malicious websites from attacking other websites sometimes, called Cross-Site Scripting (XSS) attacks. The two things that are done to prevent Cross-Site scripting are:

- Enforced by web browsers
- Ignored by tools like PostMan and curl

Both things are done to prevent Cross-Site Scripting. For this reason, there are different domain names on Amazon.

Cross-Origin Resource Sharing (CORS)

The way to allow different AWS components to talk to each other is by using CORS. CORS stands for Cross-Origin Resource Sharing. CORS is one way the server at the other end (not the client code in the browser) can use the same-origin policy.

Cross-Origin Resource Sharing (CORS) is a mechanism that allows restricted resources (e.g., fonts) on a web page to be requested from another domain outside the domain from which the first resource was served.

EXAM TIP: CORS is a way for a web page in one domain to talk to a web page in another domain and request resources from it.

Working of CORS

Cross-Origin Resource Sharing can work as follows:

- The browser makes an HTTP OPTIONS call for a URL (OPTIONS is an HTTP method like GET, PUT, POST, etc.)

The server returns the response that says:

"These other domains are approved to GET this URL." Or, you may get an error message: "Origin Policy cannot be read at the remote resource?". You need to enable CORS on API Gateway when you see this error message.

> EXAM TIP: When using Javascript/AJAX that uses multiple domains with API Gateway, ensure that you have enabled CORS on API Gateway.
>
> CORS is enforced by the client (your browser).

Amazon Kinesis

Through this platform, you can gather, process, analyze the data, and process the streaming of data cost-effectively.

Streaming Data

Streaming data is data generated continuously by thousands of data sources, typically sent in the data records simultaneously and in small sizes (order of Kilobytes).

Some examples of streaming data are:

Purchase from an online store (such as amazon.com) – When you purchase a book or anything else, you will get the transaction ID, device description, unique ID of an individual item, etc. This is the actual data that is generated when you are purchasing something from an online store.

Stock Prices – Stock prices can be in Microsoft, Amazon, etc. The stock price continuously changes all the time. As soon as there is a change in the stock price, it is then streamed into something that needs processing.

Game Data – Data that is generated from gaming, like what is the particular level, etc.

Social Network Data – An example of this is Twitter. Twitter continuously generates data in terms of tweets, re-tweets, comments, etc.

Geospatial Data – An example of this is Uber. When you are catching an Uber, where you are on the map is always streamed into a central source server so Uber can go through and calculate the fastest way to get from your source to your destination. In this case, Uber will also get some traffic from other data sources.

IoT Sensor Data – IoT devices can generate different types of data, which could be streamed into a central source by the IoT sensor.

Amazon Kinesis

Amazon Kinesis is a platform on AWS to send your streaming data to. Amazon Kinesis makes it easy to load and analyze streaming data and allows you to build custom applications for your business needs.

> 💡 **EXAM TIP:** Amazon Kinesis is a service that processes, collects, and analyzes real-time and streaming data. It is a place to send all of your streaming data.

Types of Amazon Kinesis

There are three services for real-time streaming of data provided by Amazon Kinesis:

- Amazon Kinesis Streams
- Amazon Kinesis Firehose
- Amazon Kinesis Analytics

Each service can handle unlimited data streaming.

Figure 9-11: Types of Amazon Kinesis

Amazon Kinesis Streams

As discussed earlier, Amazon Kinesis collects and processes a large stream of data in real-time. Essentially, you create a data processing that reads the data from Amazon Kinesis Stream as a data record. The process records can then be sent to the dashboard. They are used to generate alerts and dynamically change the pricing or can be used to change the advertising strategy dynamically.

There are some common use cases for Kinesis Stream. The first one is fast logging; other than that, data intake processing is fast in Kinesis Stream. In this, you can have your application push data directly into the stream, which could be an application or system log. Another scenario is real-time metrics and reporting. In this, you can use the data collected in your stream for analysis and reporting in real-time. The data processing application works on metrics and reporting for logs as the data streaming waits to receive patches of the data. Kinesis Streams can also be used for real-time data analytics and complex stream processing that involves many Kinesis Streams inserting the data from one stream to another using different Kinesis Stream applications.

Benefits of Amazon Kinesis Streams

- Real-time aggregation of data
- It loads the aggregate data into a data warehouse or map-reduce clusters. It means loading the data into Redshift or EMR
- Kinesis Stream is also durable and elastic

- Multiple applications can read data from the stream at the same time. The process can be run in parallel, performing different functions on the same data

Kinesis Data Streams

The architectural diagram of Kinesis Data Streams is shown in Figure 9-12. There are several devices like mobiles for using "Uber," laptops for using "Twitter," EC2 instances for monitoring "Stock Prices," and IoT sensors for monitoring data coming from "IoT devices." These all are data producers. The data producer continuously pushes the data into the Kinesis data stream and the consumer processes the data in real-time. The Kinesis stream is a place to store data. By default, it can store data for 24 hours. However, it can store for up to seven days. All this data is contained in "Shards," which are uniquely identified groups of a data record within a stream. These shards are available for different purposes (e.g., for social media data, geospatial data, stock prices, etc.). The data consumer (EC2 instances) analyzes the data stored inside the shards. The data consumer may run an algorithm to analyze these data. Once the EC2 instances (data consumers) analyze the data, they can store it in several different places using an AWS service, such as Amazon DynamoDB, Amazon S3, Amazon Elastic MapReduce, and Amazon RedShift.

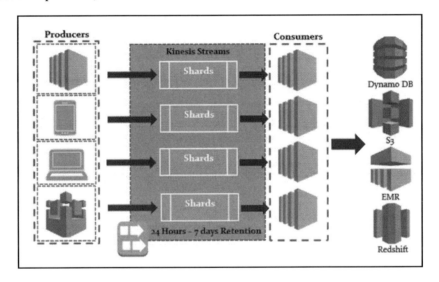

Figure 9-12: Amazon Kinesis Streams

> 💡 EXAM TIP: Amazon Kinesis Streams allows us to persistently store data for 24 hours to seven days. Data consumer goes through the data and, after analyzation, can store analytics where EC2 instance can access.

Kinesis Stream Core Concepts

Shards

Amazon Kinesis Stream consists of shards. Shards are uniquely identified groups of a data record within a stream. A Stream is made up of one or more than one shards, each of which provides a fixed amount of capacity. Each shard is capable of supporting up to 5 transactions per second for reading, up to a maximum data read rate of 2 MB per second, and up to 1,000 records per second for writes, which include a maximum total data write rate of 1 MB per second (including partition keys). The capacity of the single shard is 1MB per second of data input.

The capacity of your stream's data is a function of the wide variety of shards you specify for the stream. The entire capacity of the stream is the addition of the capacities of its shards. If your data charge increases, you could boom or lower the number of shards allocated to your stream.

 EXAM TIP: When you put your data into Kinesis Streams, it is stored in individual shards.

Amazon Kinesis Firehose

Amazon Kinesis Firehose is a fully managed service that collects and loads streaming data in near real-time into S3, Redshift, and Elasticsearch Cluster. Kinesis Firehose is highly available and durable. The data is replicated across AWS regions. Firehose is a fully managed service that can automatically scale to meet your throughput requirements; it requires no administration. This service also handles sharding and Monitoring. Firehose can process the data by reducing the amount of storage in S3 if that is the destination of your data. It will help you in reducing the cost. With firehose, you can also encrypt the data before it is loaded. You can create a Firehose delivery scheme in the Management Console or use the API.

Consider the example in Figures 9-13 (a, b, and c). There are data producers regarding EC2 instances, smartphones, laptops, and IoT. The produced data is sent to Kinesis Firehose. Inside Kinesis Firehose, there is no persistent storage. The data has to be analyzed as it comes in. Inside Kinesis Firehose, the Lambda function is present. As soon as the data comes in, it triggers a lambda function. The lambda function runs a particular set of codes for that data. Then, save the output in a place like Amazon S3.

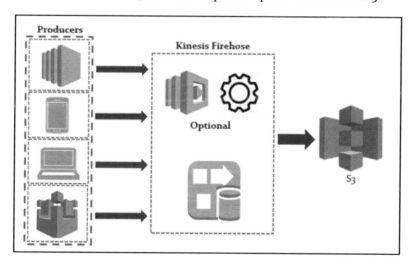

Figure 9-13(a): Amazon Kinesis Firehose with S3

The output can also be stored in Amazon Redshift. But, it first comes through S3 and then imports that data into Amazon Redshift.

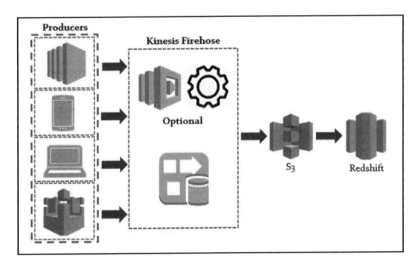

Figure 9-13(b): Amazon Kinesis Firehose with Redshift

The output can also be stored in Elasticsearch Cluster.

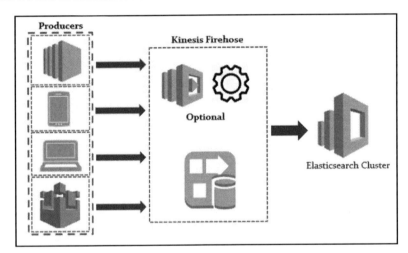

Figure 9-13(c): Amazon Kinesis Firehose with Elasticsearch Cluster

> **EXAM TIP:** It is very important to understand the difference between Kinesis Streams and Kinesis Firehose for the exam.
>
> Kinesis Streams has shards, and your data has persistence. By default, it is stored for 24 hours. Whereas in Kinesis Firehose, there is no data persistence. The data should be analyzed when it comes to the Kinesis Firehose.

Amazon Kinesis Analytics

Amazon Kinesis Analytics is used when you need to process streaming data and do not want to learn any other programming language. You use standard SQL to build the streaming application. It automatically scales your throughput according to the rate of your data.

An example of Amazon Kinesis Analytics is shown in Figure 9-14. There are data producers regarding EC2 instances, smartphones, laptops, and IoT. Kinesis Analytics works with Kinesis Streams and with Kinesis Firehose. The produced data is sent to Kinesis Firehose. Firehose analyzes the data when it comes in. Then, this data is stored in either S3, Redshift, or Elasticsearch Cluster.

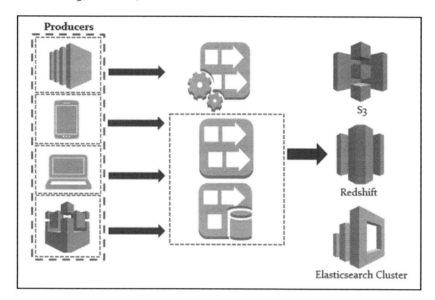

Figure 9-14: Amazon Kinesis Analytics

EXAM TIP: When you want to analyze the data inside the Kinesis, you can use Kinesis Analytics. It analyses the data inside Kinesis Streams and Kinesis Firehose both.

Web Identity Federation and Cognito

Web Identity Federation
Web Identity Federation provides access to your users over AWS resources after successfully authenticating them from a web-based identity provider such as Google, Facebook, and Amazon.

After the successful authentication from a Web ID provider, the user receives an authentication code from the Web ID provider, which they can use for temporary AWS security credentials allowing them to assume an IAM role, allowing access to AWS resources.

EXAM TIP: Federation allows users to authenticate with a Web Identity Provider (Google, Facebook, or Amazon).

Amazon Cognito
Amazon Cognito is an AWS service that enables the Web Identity Federation with the following features:

- Sign-up and Sign–in to your applications
- You can add access for guest users
- It acts as an Identity Broker between your applications and Web ID providers, so you do not need to provide any additional code to sign in to social media platforms or other places as well

- It synchronizes user data across multiple devices

Amazon Cognito is recommended for all mobile applications that run on AWS service.

EXAM TIP: Amazon Cognito is the recommended approach for Web Identity Federation using social media accounts like Facebook.

Amazon Cognito Use Cases

An application of Amazon Cognito is shown in Figure 9-15. A website that consists of Lambda function, Dynamo DB, and S3. A user wants to use these resources. For this, the user needs to go and authenticate with Facebook. Facebook will give the user an authentication token. This authentication token will be sent to Amazon Cognito. Cognito will respond and grant access to the AWS environment depending on what level of access that user is permitted to. After this, the user can execute Lambda functions, store data in Dynamo DB tables, store images in S3, etc. The user can easily access the AWS environment.

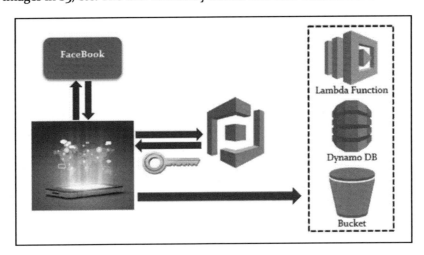

Figure 9-15: Application of Amazon Cognito

Cognito Brokers between the app and Facebook or Google provide temporary credentials that map to an IAM role allowing access to the required resources.

The application does not need to embed or store AWS credentials locally on the device, giving users a seamless experience across all mobile devices.

EXAM TIP: Amazon Cognito is an Identity Broker that handles interaction between applications and Web ID providers (there is no need to write your code to do this).

Cognito User Pools

Cognito User Pools are user directories used to manage sign-up and sign-in functionality for mobile and web applications. Users can sign-in directly to the User Pool, which means username and password are stored within Cognito itself, or they can use a third-party identity broker like Facebook, Amazon, or Google. Cognito

acts as an Identity Broker between the identity provider and AWS. A successful authentication generates a JSON Web Token (JWT).

Cognito Identity Pools

Cognito Identity Pools are enabled to provide temporary AWS credentials to access AWS services like S3 or Dynamo DB. Identity Pools are all about authorization access to AWS resources.

> EXAM TIP: Cognito User Pools are all about the actual users (user registration, authentication, and account recovery).

Cognito Identity Pool grants the IAM role and authorizes access to AWS resources.

Workings of Amazon Cognito

A real-time example of Amazon Cognito is shown in Figure 9-16. There is a user who wants to connect to a website. For this, the user will log in to their Facebook account. Once Facebook has authenticated its account as genuine (valid username and password), Facebook will pass back an authentication token to Cognito. Cognito will convert the authentication token to JSON Web Tokens (JWTs). Users will then send that JWT token to an Identity Pool; the identity pool will grant users AWS credentials in the form of an IAM role. Users can now access AWS resources like Dynamo DB, Lambda, S3, etc.

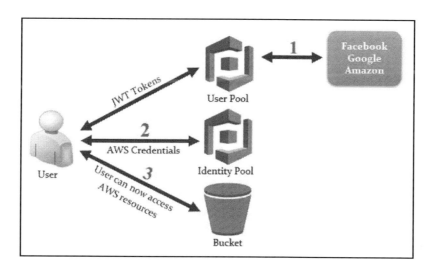

Figure 9-16: Working of Amazon Cognito

Cognito Synchronization

Cognito tracks the association between the user identity and the devices they sign-in from. To provide a seamless user experience for your application, Cognito uses Push Synchronization to push updates and synchronizes user data across multiple devices.

Amazon SNS sends a silent push notification to all the devices associated with the given user identity whenever data stored in the cloud changes.

Push Synchronization using SNS

An example of this is shown in Figure 9-17. The user wants to update their email address, change the password, or make some app changes. In this case, Cognito will send a Simple Notification Service Silent Push Notification. The notification will be sent out to the user's laptop, mobile phone, or tablet. All these devices will be synchronized with the new data.

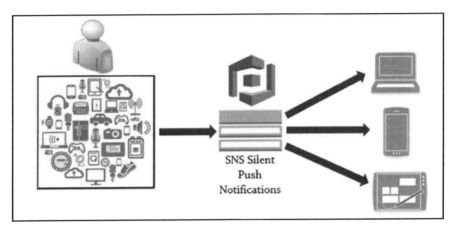

Figure 9-17: Push Synchronization using SNS

Event Processing Patterns

Introduction

Applications are separated into smaller, independent building components in modern cloud architecture, making them easier to design, deploy, and manage. Many solution architects create event-driven systems in which one or more AWS services respond to events caused by other AWS services by automatically performing tasks. This architectural pattern can improve the reusability, interoperability, and scalable

Event-Driven Architecture

Publish/Subscribe or PUB/SUB Messaging

Publish/Subscribe or PUB/SUB messaging provides instant event notifications for these kinds of distributed applications. The pub/sub model allows messages to be broadcast asynchronously to different parts of a system.

- **SNS Message**

SNS message provides a mechanism to broadcast asynchronous event notifications and endpoints, allowing other AWS services to connect to the topic to send and receive those messages.

- **Publisher**

To broadcast a message, a component called a publisher pushes a message to the topic. The publisher can be your application or one of many AWS services to publish messages to SNS topics. The publisher does not need to know who is using the broadcasting information.

- **Subscribers**

Subscribers to the message subject often have distinct functions and can do different things with the message simultaneously. Subscribers do not need to know who sent the message.

 EXAM TIP: You want to understand the PUB/SUB pattern, and SNS facilitates that.

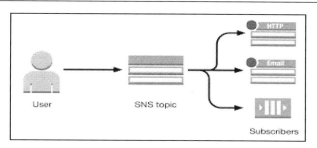

Figure 9-18: PUB/SUB Messaging

Dead-Letter Queue (DLQ)

DLQ is analogous to a dead letter office, a facility within a postal system where undeliverable mail is processed.

Sometimes messages are inspected for potential redelivery or will stay unclaimed forever.

Services in AWS That Use Dead-Letter Queues

- **SNS**

The dead letter queue is an SQS queue to which messages published to a topic can be sent in case those messages cannot be delivered to a subscribed endpoint messages that cannot be delivered due to client errors or server errors are held in the dead letter queue for further analysis or reprocessing.

- **SQS**

When a source queue has a re-drive policy with a max receive a count of five and the consumer of the source queue receives a message six times without ever deleting it, SQS will move the message to the dead letter queue.

- **Lambda**

In Lambda, dead letter queues store the messages that resulted in failed asynchronous executions of your Lambda function and execution, resulting in errors for several reasons.

Note: Your code might raise an exception, timeout, or run out of memory. The runtime executing your code might encounter an error and stop. Your function might hit its concurrency limit and be throttled. Regardless of the archetype, when this kind of error occurs, your code might have run completely partially or not at all. Lambda tries Twice to run the function if it returns an error before sending it to the dead letter queue.

How DLQs Work

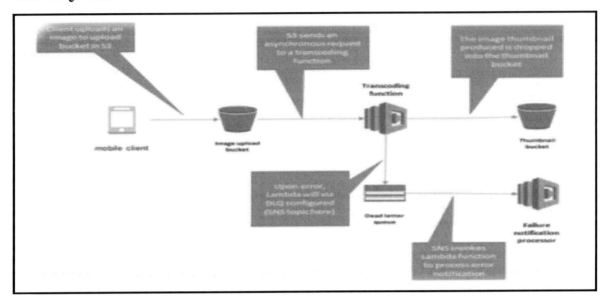

Figure 9-19: Working of DLQ

> **EXAM TIP:** You should understand which AWS services support DLQ. These include SNS, SQS, and Lambda.

Fanout Pattern

The fanout pattern is when a publisher delivers an SNS message to a topic first, then replicates and pushes that message to numerous SQS queues rather than connecting directly with the SQS queues. For the new order, all SQS queues that are subscribing to that topic will receive identical notifications.

Another way to use this fanout pattern is to replicate data sent to your production environment. With your test environment, you can subscribe to another queue on the same topic for new incoming orders. Then, by attaching this new queue to your test environment, you could continue to improve and test your application using the same data sent to your production environment.

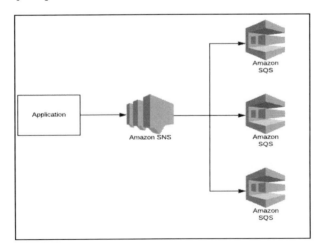

Figure 9-20: Fan out Pattern

S3 Event Notification

The S3 event notification functionality allows you to be notified when specific events in your bucket occur; alerts can be sent to SQS queues, SNS topics, or Lambda functions. For example, if objects are uploaded to a bucket, a message will be sent to multiple subscribers or destinations simultaneously. You can also filter what objects you want to receive notifications about. For example, you can limit notifications to just PNG files or by specifying a wild card.

Note: Sometimes, you will miss a notification here or there to get around this. You will want to enable versioning to ensure you get a notification for every success.

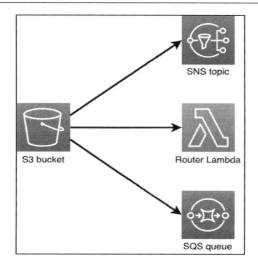

Figure 9-21: S3 Event Notification

Amazon OpenSearch Service

Introduction

OpenSearch is a distributed, community-driven, Apache 2.0-licensed, 100% open-source search and analytics suite used for a broad set of use cases like real-time application monitoring, log analytics, and website search. OpenSearch provides a highly scalable system for providing fast access and response to large volumes of data with an integrated visualization tool, OpenSearch Dashboards that makes it easy for users to explore their data. The Apache Lucene search library powers openSearch, and it supports a number of search and analytics capabilities such as k-nearest neighbors (KNN) search, SQL, Anomaly Detection, Machine Learning Commons, Trace Analytics, full-text search, and more.

Features

Advanced Security

Offers encryption, authentication, authorization, and auditing features. They include integrations with Active Directory, LDAP, SAML, Kerberos, JSON web tokens, and more. OpenSearch also provides fine-grained role-based access control to indices, documents and fields.

Built-in Search Capabilities

Offers a number of features to help you customize your search experience such as Full-text querying, Autocomplete, Scroll Search, customizable scoring and ranking, and more.

SQL Query Syntax

Provides the familiar SQL query syntax. Use aggregations, group by, and where clauses to investigate your data. Read data as JSON documents or CSV tables so you have the flexibility to use the format that works best for you.

Data Prepper

Data Prepper is a server-side data collector capable of filtering, enriching, transforming, normalizing, and aggregating data for downstream analytics and visualization. Data Prepper lets users build custom pipelines to improve the operational view of applications.

Trace Analytics

Trace Analytics provides a way to ingest and visualize OpenTelemetry data in OpenSearch. This data can help you find and fix performance problems in distributed applications.

Application Analytics

Use application analytics to create custom observability applications to view the availability status of your systems, where you can combine log events with trace and metric data into a single view of overall system health. This lets you quickly pivot between logs, traces, and metrics to dig into the source of any issues.

k-NN search

Using Machine Learning, run the nearest neighbor search algorithm on billions of documents across thousands of dimensions with the same ease as running any regular OpenSearch query. Use aggregations and filter clauses to further refine similarity search operations. k-NN similarity search powers use cases such as product recommendations, fraud detection, image and video search, related document search, and more.

OpenSearch license

All of the software in the OpenSearch project is released under the Apache License, Version 2.0 (ALv2). ALv2 grants well-understood and permissive usage rights that match the freedoms people expect with open source software: freedoms such as being able use, modify, extend, monetize, and resell the open source software where and how they want. For OpenSearch, we believe this license will enable broad adoption and contributions benefiting all members of the community. We have also published permissive usage guidelines for the OpenSearch trademark, so you can use the name to promote your offerings.

Amazon Kinesis Client Library (KCL)

Introduction

One of the methods of developing custom consumer applications that can process data from KDS data streams is to use the Kinesis Client Library (KCL).

KCL helps you consume and process data from a Kinesis data stream by taking care of many of the complex tasks associated with distributed computing. These include load balancing across multiple consumer

application instances, responding to application instance failures, checking processed records, and reacting to resharding.

The KCL is different from the Kinesis Data Streams APIs that are available in the AWS SDKs. The Kinesis Data Streams APIs help you manage many aspects of Kinesis Data Streams, including creating streams, resharding, and putting and getting records. The KCL provides a layer of abstraction around all these subtasks, specifically so that you can focus on your consumer application's custom data processing logic.

Features

The KCL acts as an intermediary between your record processing logic and Kinesis Data Streams. The KCL performs the following tasks:

- Connects to the data stream
- Enumerates the shards within the data stream
- Uses leases to coordinate shard associations with its workers
- Instantiates a record processor for every shard it manages
- Pulls data records from the data stream
- Pushes the records to the corresponding record processor
- Checkpoints processed records
- Balances shard-worker associations (leases) when the worker instance count changes or when the data stream is resharded (shards are split or merged)

KCL Concepts

KCL consumer application

An application that is custom-built using KCL and designed to read and process records from data streams.

Consumer application instance

KCL consumer applications are typically distributed, with one or more application instances running simultaneously to coordinate on failures and dynamically load balance data record processing.

Worker

A high-level class that a KCL consumer application instance uses to start processing data.

Lease

Data that defines the binding between a worker and a shard. Distributed KCL consumer applications use leases to partition data record processing across a fleet of workers. Each shard of data records is bound to a particular worker by a lease identified by the leaseKey variable at any given time.

Lease table

A unique Amazon DynamoDB table that is used to keep track of the shards in a KDS data stream that is being leased and processed by the workers of the KCL consumer application. The lease table must remain in sync (within a worker and across all workers) with the latest shard information from the data stream while the KCL consumer application is running.

Record processor

The logic defines how your KCL consumer application processes the data it gets from the data streams. At runtime, a KCL consumer application instance instantiates a worker, and this worker instantiates one record processor for every shard to which it holds a lease.

Lease Table

For each Amazon Kinesis Data Streams application, KCL uses a unique lease table (stored in an Amazon DynamoDB table) to keep track of the shards in a KDS data stream that are being leased and processed by the workers of the KCL consumer application.

You can view the lease table using the Amazon DynamoDB console while the consumer application is running.

If the lease table for your KCL consumer application does not exist when the application starts up, one of the workers creates the lease table for this application.

AWS Lake Formation

Introduction

AWS Lake Formation is a service that makes it easy to set up a secure data lake in days. A data lake is a centralized, curated, and secured repository that stores all your data in its original form and prepared for analysis.

How it works

AWS Lake Formation easily creates secure data lakes, making data available for wide-ranging analytics.

Figure 9-22: AWS Lake Formation Working

Use cases

Build your data lake in days

Quickly import data from all your data sources, and then describe and manage them in a centralized data catalog.

Secure and govern your data lake at scale

Scale permissions more easily with fine-grained security capabilities, including row- and cell-level permissions and tag-based access control.

Enable self-service analytics across your organization

Centrally manage access to available datasets and apply fine-grained permissions for all data users.

Build data mesh with minimal data movement

Deploy a data mesh or data fabric, or simplify cross-account data sharing in your organization.

Features

Build data lakes quickly

Import data from databases already in AWS

Once you specify where your existing databases are and provide your access credentials, AWS Lake Formation reads the data and its metadata (schema) to understand the contents of the data source. It then imports the data to your new data lake and records the metadata in a central catalog. With Lake Formation, you can import data from MySQL, PostgreSQL, SQL Server, MariaDB, and Oracle databases running in Amazon Relational Database Service (RDS) or host in Amazon Elastic Compute Cloud (EC2). Both bulk and incremental data loading are supported.

Import data from other external sources

You can use Lake Formation to move data from on-premises databases by connecting with Java Database Connectivity (JDBC). Identify your target sources and provide access credentials in the console, and Lake Formation reads and loads your data into the data lake. To import data from databases other than the ones listed above, you can create custom ETL jobs with AWS Glue.

Import data from other AWS services

Using Lake Formation, you can also pull in semi-structured and unstructured data from other Amazon Simple Storage Service (S3) data sources. You can identify existing Amazon S3 buckets containing data to copy into your data lake. Once you specify the S3 path to register your data sources and authorize access, Lake Formation reads the data and its schema. Lake Formation can collect and organize datasets, such as logs from AWS CloudTrail, AWS CloudFront, Detailed Billing Reports, and AWS Elastic Load Balancing (ELB). Using custom jobs, you can also load your data into the data lake with Amazon Kinesis or Amazon DynamoDB.

Catalog and label your data

Lake Formation crawls and reads your data sources to extract technical metadata (such as schema definitions) and creates a searchable catalog to describe this information for users so they can discover available datasets. You can also add your own custom labels to your data (at the table and column level) to define attributes, such as "sensitive information" and "European sales data." Lake Formation provides a text-based search over this metadata, so your users can quickly find the data they need to analyze.

Transform data

Lake Formation can perform transformations on your data, such as rewriting various date formats for consistency, to ensure that the data is stored in an analytics-friendly fashion. Lake Formation creates transformation templates and schedules jobs to prepare your data for analysis. For better performance, your

data is transformed with AWS Glue and written in columnar formats, such as Parquet and ORC. Less data needs to be read for analysis when data is organized into columns as opposed to scanning entire rows. You can create custom transformation jobs with AWS Glue and Apache Spark to suit your specific requirements.

Clean and deduplicate data

Lake Formation helps clean and prepare your data for analysis by providing a Machine Learning (ML) Transform called FindMatches for deduplication and finding matching records. For example, use FindMatches to find duplicate records in your database of restaurants, such as when one record lists "Joe's Pizza" at "121 Main St." and another shows "Joseph's Pizzeria" at "121 Main." You don't need to know anything about ML to do this. FindMatches will simply ask you to label sets of records as either "matching" or "not matching." The system will then learn your criteria for calling a pair of records a match and will build an ML Transform that you can use to find duplicate records within a database or match records across two databases.

Optimize partitions

Lake Formation also optimizes the partitioning of data in Amazon S3 to improve performance and reduce costs. Raw data that is loaded may be in partitions that are too small (requiring extra reads) or too large (reading more data than needed.) Lake Formation organizes your data by size, time period, and/or relevant keys. This enables both fast scans and parallel, distributed reads for the most commonly used queries.

Row and Cell-level security

Lake Formation provides data filters that allow you to restrict access to a combination of columns and rows. Use row and cell-level security to protect sensitive data like Personal Identifiable Information (PII).

Simplify security management

Enforce encryption

Lake Formation uses the encryption capabilities of Amazon S3 for data in your data lake. This approach provides automatic server-side encryption with keys managed by the AWS Key Management Service (KMS). S3 encrypts data in transit when replicating across Regions and lets you use separate accounts for source and destination Regions to protect against malicious insider deletions. These encryption capabilities provide a secure foundation for all data in your data lake.

Define and manage access controls

Lake Formation provides a single place to manage access controls for data in your data lake. You can define security policies that restrict access to data at the database, table, column, row, and cell levels. These policies apply to AWS Identity and Access Management (IAM) users and roles and to users and groups when federating through an external identity provider. You can use fine-grained controls to access data secured by Lake Formation within Amazon Redshift Spectrum, Amazon Athena, AWS Glue ETL, and Amazon EMR for Apache Spark.

Implement audit logging

Lake Formation provides comprehensive audit logs with CloudTrail to monitor access and show compliance with centrally defined policies. You can audit data access history across analytics and ML services that read the data in your data lake via Lake Formation. This lets you see which users or roles have attempted to access what data, with which services, and when. You can access audit logs the same way as any other CloudTrail logs using the CloudTrail APIs and console.

Governed tables

Use ACID (atomic, consistent, isolated, and durable) transactions to allow multiple users and jobs to reliably and consistently insert data across multiple tables on Amazon S3. Transactions for Governed Tables automatically manage conflicts and errors and ensure consistent views for all users. You can query Governed Tables using Amazon Redshift, Amazon Athena, and AWS Glue transactions.

Provide self-service access to data

Label your data with business metadata

With Lake Formation, you can designate data owners, such as data stewards and business units, by adding a field in table properties as custom attributes. Your owners can augment the technical metadata with business metadata that further defines appropriate uses for the data. You can specify appropriate use cases and label the sensitivity of your data for enforcement by using Lake Formation security and access controls.

Enable self-service access

Lake Formation facilitates requesting and vending access to datasets to give your users self-service access to the data lake for a variety of analytics use cases. You can specify, grant, and revoke permissions on tables defined in the central data catalog. The same data catalog is available for multiple accounts, groups, and services.

Discover relevant data for analysis

With Lake Formation, your users enjoy online, text-based search and filtering of datasets recorded in the central data catalog. They can search for relevant data by name, contents, sensitivity, or any other custom labels you have defined.

Combine analytics approaches for more insights

With Lake Formation, you can give your analytics users the ability to directly query datasets with Athena for SQL, Redshift for data warehousing, AWS Glue for data integration and preparation, and EMR for Apache Spark-based big data processing and ML (Zeppelin notebooks). Once you point these services to Lake Formation, the datasets available are shown in the catalog, and access controls are enforced consistently, allowing your users to readily combine analytics approaches on the same data.

Pricing

AWS Lake Formation provides database, table, column, and tag-based access controls and cross-account sharing at no charge. Governed Tables provide ACID transactions as a fully managed service that enables you to reliably update multiple tables while maintaining a consistent view for all users. Managing concurrent transactions and being able to travel back to the previous version of the table requires storing metadata about each transaction. Lake Formation charges a fee for transaction requests and for metadata storage. In addition, to providing a consistent view of data and enforcing row and cell-level security the Lake Formation Storage API scans data in Amazon S3 and applies row and cell filters before returning results to applications. There is a fee for this filtering.

Application Integration

Amazon MQ

Introduction

Amazon MQ is a managed message broker service for Apache ActiveMQ and RabbitMQ that streamlines the setup, operation, and management of message brokers on AWS. With a few steps, Amazon MQ can provision your message broker with support for software version upgrades.

How it works

Message brokers allow software systems that often use different programming languages on various platforms to communicate and exchange information. Amazon MQ is a managed message broker service for Apache ActiveMQ and RabbitMQ that streamlines the setup, operation, and management of message brokers on AWS. With a few steps, Amazon MQ can provision your message broker with support for software version upgrades.

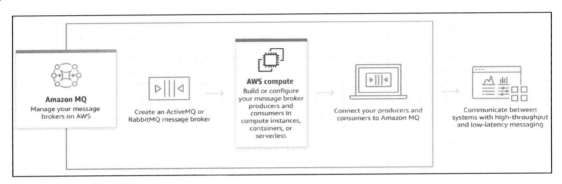

Figure 9-23: Amazon MQ Working

Features

Amazon MQ

Managed Service

With Amazon MQ, you can use the AWS Management Console, AWS CloudFormation, the Command Line Interface (CLI), or simple API calls to launch a production-ready message broker in minutes. Amazon MQ manages administrative tasks such as hardware provisioning, broker setup, software upgrades, and failure detection and recovery.

Security

Amazon MQ provides encryption of your messages at rest and in transit. It's easy to ensure that your messages are securely stored in an encrypted format. Connections to the broker use SSL, and access can be restricted to a private endpoint within your Amazon VPC, which allows you to isolate your broker in your own virtual network.

Amazon MQ is integrated with AWS Identity and Access Management (IAM) and provides you the ability to control the actions that your IAM users and groups can take on specific Amazon MQ brokers. Authentication from applications to the broker itself is provided using the username and password-based authentication and optionally using LDAP (Lightweight Directory Access Protocol) for ActiveMQ brokers.

Monitoring

Amazon MQ is integrated with Amazon CloudWatch and AWS CloudTrail. With CloudWatch, you can monitor metrics on your brokers, queues, and topics. For example, you can monitor the depth of your queues and generate alarms if messages aren't getting through. Using CloudTrail, you can log, continuously monitor, and retain Amazon MQ API calls.

Broker Instance Types

Amazon MQ currently supports seven broker instance types: mq.t2.micro, mq.t3.micro, mq.m4.large, mq.m5.large, mq.m5.xlarge, mq.m5.2xlarge, and mq.m5.4xlarge, which provide varying combinations of CPU, memory, and network performance. The mq.t3.micro instances are designed for initial product evaluation, and the mq.m5.large instance is for default production usage. Amazon MQ also supports both single-instance brokers, suitable for evaluation and testing, and replicated highly available deployment modes recommended for production.

Pay-as-you-go Pricing

Amazon MQ provides cost-efficient and flexible capacity, and there is no minimum fee. You pay for the number of hours your broker instance runs and the storage you use monthly. It is easy and inexpensive to create new brokers for additional capacity.

Get Started for Free

The AWS Free Tier includes up to 750 hours of a single-instance mq.t2.micro or mq.t3.micro broker, and up to 5GB of Amazon EFS storage per month for an ActiveMQ broker or 20GB of Amazon EBS for a RabbitMQ broker, for one year.

RabbitMQ

High Availability, Throughput, and Message Durability

Amazon MQ runs on the same highly reliable infrastructure used by other Amazon Web Services. Amazon MQ for RabbitMQ clusters, backed by Amazon EBS, uses multi-AZ replication for high-availability and message durability. Data transfer for replication is included at no additional cost. Clusters are created behind a single endpoint for high availability, simple management, and easy connection from your application.

Message Routing

Messages in RabbitMQ brokers are routed through exchanges before arriving at queues. RabbitMQ features several built-in exchange types for the typical routing logic.

Broad Client Language Support

Develop using your favorite programming languages, including Python, .NET, PHP, Python, JavaScript, Ruby, Java, and Go

ActiveMQ

High Availability, Throughput, and Message Durability

Amazon MQ runs on the same highly reliable infrastructure that other Amazon Web Services use. Amazon MQ for ActiveMQ provides durability-optimized brokers backed by Amazon Elastic File System (Amazon EFS) to support high availability and message durability. Durability-optimized brokers, backed by Amazon

Elastic File System (Amazon EFS), store messages redundantly across multiple Availability Zones (AZs), and active-standby brokers automatically failover to a standby instance if a broker or AZ fails, so you can continue sending and receiving messages. Connecting brokers into a network provide active-active availability with almost instant fail-over. Amazon MQ also supports creating throughput-optimized message brokers backed by Amazon Elastic Block Store (EBS), perfect for use cases that require high throughputs such as high-volume order processing, stock trading, text processing, and many more. Throughput optimized message brokers reduce the number of brokers required and the cost of operating high-volume applications using Amazon MQ.

Industry-standard APIs and Protocols

ActiveMQ supports a wide range of clients, including Java Message Service (JMS) 1.1, .NET Message Service (NMS), and a range of other languages, including Node.js, Go, Python, Ruby, and C++. ActiveMQ also supports wire-level protocols, including AMQP, STOMP, OpenWire, WebSocket, and MQTT. This compatibility with industry standards facilitates migration from existing message brokers, enables interoperability between vendors, and helps you avoid vendor dependency.

JMS Messaging Features

ActiveMQ provides all the standard JMS features, including point-to-point (message queues), publish-subscribe (topics), request/reply, persistent and non-persistent modes, JMS transactions, and distributed (XA) transactions. In addition to basic queues and topics, ActiveMQ also supports more complex patterns such as composite destinations (producers can send the same message to multiple destinations, useful for real-time analytics) and virtual destinations (publishers broadcast messages via a topic to a pool of receivers subscribing through queues).

Pricing

With Amazon MQ, you pay only for what you use. There are no minimum fees or upfront commitments. You pay for the time your message broker instance runs, the storage you use monthly, and standard data transfer fees. It is easy to get started with Amazon MQ for the first 12 months with the AWS Free Tier.

Broker Pricing

You pay for message broker usage on an hourly basis (billed at one-second resolution), with varying fees depending on the size of the message broker instance and whether you choose a single-instance broker, 3-node cluster, or active/standby broker.

Broker Storage Pricing

Two types of broker storage are available for Amazon MQ for ActiveMQ – durability optimized using Amazon Elastic File System (Amazon EFS), and throughput optimized using Amazon Elastic Block Store (Amazon EBS). Amazon MQ for RabbitMQ brokers all uses Amazon EBS. With Amazon MQ you pay for the average amount of monthly storage you use. This is calculated by adding up the GB used each hour and dividing by the number of hours in the month, resulting in a value in "GB-Months".

AWS Free Tier

Amazon MQ is free to try. The AWS Free Tier includes up to 750 hours of a single-instance mq.t2.micro or mq.t3.micro broker per month using either ActiveMQ or RabbitMQ. It also includes up to 5GB of durability

optimized Amazon EFS storage per month for ActiveMQ and 20GB of Amazon EBS storage for RabbitMQ, for one year. New AWS accounts receive 12 months of AWS Free Tier access.

Amazon AppFlow

Introduction

Amazon AppFlow is a fully managed integration service that enables you to securely transfer data between Software-as-a-Service (SaaS) applications like Salesforce, SAP, Zendesk, Slack, and ServiceNow, and AWS services like Amazon S3 and Amazon Redshift, in just a few clicks. With AppFlow, you can run data flows at an enterprise scale at the frequency you choose - on a schedule, in response to a business event, or on demand. You can configure data transformation capabilities like filtering and validation to generate rich, ready-to-use data as part of the flow itself, without additional steps. AppFlow automatically encrypts data in motion, allowing users to restrict data from flowing over the public Internet for SaaS applications integrated with AWS PrivateLink, reducing exposure to security threats.

Benefits

Integrate with a few clicks

Anyone can use AppFlow to integrate applications in a few minutes – no more waiting days or weeks to code custom connectors. Features like data pagination, error logging, and network connection retries are included by default so there's no coding or management. With Appflow, data flow quality is built in, and you can enrich the flow of data through mapping, merging, masking, filtering, and validation as part of the flow itself.

Transfer data at a massive scale

AppFlow easily scales up without the need to plan or provision resources, so you can move large volumes of data without breaking it down into multiple batches. AppFlow can run up to 100 GB per flow, enabling you to easily transfer millions of Salesforce records, Zendesk events, Marketo responses, or other data - all while running a single flow.

Automate data security

All data flowing through AppFlow is encrypted at rest and in transit, and you can encrypt data with AWS keys or bring your own custom keys. With AppFlow, you can use your existing Identity and Access Management (IAM) policies to enforce fine-grained permissions rather than creating new policies. For SaaS integrations with AWS PrivateLink enabled, data is default secured from the public internet.

How it works

You can use AppFlow to set up secure data flows in minutes without managing complex connectors or writing code.

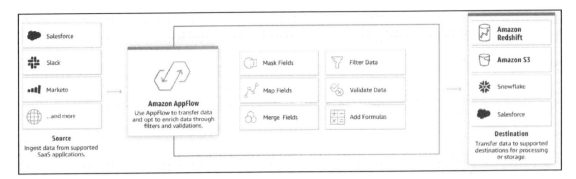

Figure 9-24: Amazon AppFlow Working

Features

Ease of Use

Point and click user interface

You can use AppFlow to set up data flows in minutes - no coding required. A point and click user interface enables you to select your data sources and destinations, configure optional transformations and validations, and run your flow without creating dependencies on technical teams.

Flexible data flow triggers

AppFlow enables you to run data flows on demand to do bulk transfers or tests, set up a routine schedule to keep data in sync, or run flows in response to business events like the creation of a sales opportunity, the status change of a support ticket, or the completion of a registration form.

Native SaaS integrations

AppFlow includes native integration with the Software-as-a-Service (SaaS) applications used daily for business operations, including Salesforce, Marketo, Slack, and more - and more integrations are planned. With AppFlow, you can easily transfer data from any supported SaaS application in just a few clicks.

Easy to use field mapping

You use the AppFlow interface to map source and destination fields together through bulk mapping, or map each field at a time. For data flows with a large number of fields, you can also upload a csv file to map many fields quickly.

Cost Savings

Pay as you go

Amazon AppFlow offers a significant cost-savings advantage compared to building connectors in-house or using other application integration services. There are no upfront charges or licensing fees to use AppFlow, and customers only pay for the number of flows they run and the volume of data processed.

Scalable

High-scale data transfer

Amazon AppFlow can run up to 100 GB of data per flow, which enables you to easily transfer millions of Salesforce records, Marketo leads or Zendesk tickets - all while running a single flow.

Enterprise grade data transformations

AppFlow enables you to perform data transformations like mapping, merging, masking, filtering, and validation as part of the flow itself, so there's no need for additional steps. For example, you can validate that data is in the right numeric format, merge first and last names, or mask credit card details.

Secure & Reliable

Data privacy defaults through PrivateLink

AWS PrivateLink simplifies the security of data shared with cloud-based applications by eliminating the exposure of data to the public Internet. For SaaS applications that have PrivateLink enabled, AppFlow automatically creates and configures private endpoints, so your data remains private by default.

Custom encryption keys

All data flowing through AppFlow is encrypted at rest and in transit, and you can encrypt data with AWS keys or bring your own custom keys.

IAM policy enforcement

With AppFlow, you can use your existing AWS identity and access management (IAM) policies to enforce fine-grained permissions and keep access consistent across your organization without creating new policies. With strictly enforced IAM policies, application administrators can safely create and manage data flows without depending on technical teams.

Built-in reliability

Amazon AppFlow is built with a highly available architecture to prevent single points of failure. Amazon AppFlow takes advantage of AWS scaling, monitoring, auditing, and billing features, so there's no need to configure these yourself.

Pricing

Amazon AppFlow offers a significant cost-savings advantage compared to building connectors in-house or using other application integration services. There are no upfront charges or fees to use AppFlow, and customers only pay for the number of flows they run and the volume of data processed.

Pricing table

You pay for every successful flow run. A flow run is a call to the source application to transfer data to a destination. Flow runs to check for new data will count towards your flow run costs, even if no new data is available in the source system for transfer.

Data processing charges

The volume of data processed in a month by Amazon AppFlow is billed per GB aggregated across all flows in an AWS account. You pay for data processing (schema mapping, field validation, filtering, masking fields, and field transformation).

Additional charges

You will be charged standard requests and storage to read and write from AWS services such as Amazon S3. AWS Key Management Service will also charge you for AppFlow's use of Customer Master Keys (CMKs) for encrypting your access tokens and data in transit. Except as otherwise noted, our prices are exclusive of applicable taxes and duties, including VAT and applicable sales tax.

Mind Map

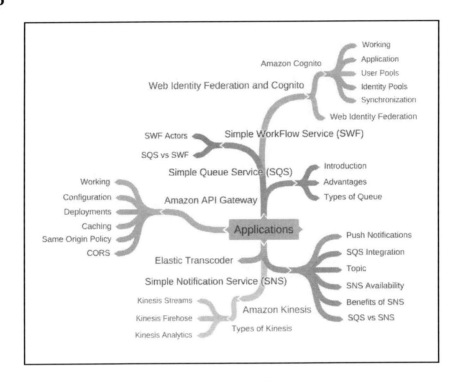

Figure 9-25: Mind Map

Practice Questions

1. Which of the following AWS application service is used to store messages and transfer any volume of data without misplacing the messages?

a) Simple Notification Service (SNS)
b) Simple Queue Service (SQS)
c) Simple WorkFlow Service (SWF)
d) Elastic Transcoder

2. Alex is working as a "Data Engineer" in an organization where he constantly requires to use AWS services and he wants to store complex data of 300KB. Which of the following service should he use to store the data?

a) Dynamo DB
b) Elasticsearch Cluster
c) Simple Queue Service (SQS)
d) S3 Bucket

3. An IT Company is using Amazon SQS queue to store data because of its guaranteed delivery of messages. By default, the company always uses the FIFO queue due to its high speed. Is this approach correct?

a) Yes

b) No

4. Which of the following AWS services combines your digital environment with manual tasks?

a) Simple Notification Service (SNS)

b) Simple Queue Service (SQS)

c) Simple WorkFlow Service (SWF)

d) All of the above

5. Which of the following is an SWF Actor?

a) Decider

b) Producer

c) Consumer

d) None of these

6. How is Simple Queue Service (SQS) different from Simple WorkFlow Service (SWF)?

a) SQS is a message-oriented API, whereas SWF is a task-oriented API

b) SQS is push-based, SWF is pull-based

c) SQS is a queuing system, SWF is a stack-based system

d) Both SQS and SWF are the same

7. Which of the following AWS service is a push-based service?

a) Simple Queue Service (SQS)

b) Simple WorkFlow Service (SWF)

c) Simple Storage Service

d) Simple Notification Service (SNS)

8. In SNS, which of the following is considered an "access point" to receiving notifications?

a) Activity Worker

b) Topic

c) Visibility Timeout

d) Push Notification

9. How is a Simple Queue Service (SQS) different from a Simple Notification Service (SNS)?

a) SQS is a message-oriented API, whereas SNS is a task-oriented API

b) SQS is a queuing system, SNS is a stack-based system

c) SQS is pull-based, SNS is push-based

d) SQS is an application service, and SNS is a mobile service

10. Which AWS services act as a media transcoder in the cloud?

a) Elasticsearch Cluster

b) Elastic Transcoder

c) API Gateway

d) Amazon Cognito

11. Which of the following AWS services acts as a front door to your AWS environment?

a) Amazon Kinesis

b) Amazon Cognito

c) Amazon API Gateway

d) Elastic Transcoder

12. What is the function of the Amazon API Gateway? (Choose 2)

a) It keeps track of and controls usage

b) It connects CloudWatch for monitoring

c) It stores messages in the queue system

d) It acts as a notification service

e) It manages the sign-in and sign-up functionality of the website

13. Which of the following can reduce the number of calls made to your endpoint and also improve the latency of the requests?

a) Streaming Data

b) Amazon Kinesis

c) API Gateway Caching

d) Cognito User Pools

14. Which of the following is used to prevent Cross-Site Scripting?

a) Same Origin Policy

b) Cognito Identity Pool

c) Cognito User Pool

d) API Gateway Caching

15. Which of the following AWS services is used to process, collect, and analyze real-time and streaming data?

a) Amazon API Gateway

b) Elastic Transcoder

c) Amazon Kinesis

d) Simple WorkFlow Service

16. Which of the following services is used for the communication between AWS components?

a) Same Origin Policy

b) Cross-Origin Resource Sharing

c) API Gateway Caching

d) Amazon Cognito

17. How many types of Amazon Kinesis are there?

a) Seven

b) Two

c) Five
d) Three

18. Which Kinesis type is used to run SQL queries of data and to store them in Amazon S3, Amazon Redshift, and Elasticsearch Cluster?
a) Amazon Kinesis Streams
b) Amazon Kinesis Firehose
c) Amazon Kinesis Analytics
d) All of the above

19. Which of the following Kinesis types allows us to persistently store data for 24 hours to seven days?
a) Amazon Kinesis Streams
b) Amazon Kinesis Firehose
c) Amazon Kinesis Analytics
d) All of the above

20. In Amazon Kinesis Streams, all the data is contained in _____.
a) Topic
b) Shards
c) Redshift
d) Elasticsearch Cluster

21. Which of the following Kinesis type is a fully-managed service used to collect and load streaming data in near real-time?
a) Amazon Kinesis Steams
b) Amazon Kinesis Firehose
c) Amazon Kinesis Analytics
d) All of the above

22. Which of the following services allows users to authenticate with a Web Identity Provider?
a) Web Identity Federation
b) Amazon Cognito
c) Amazon API Gateway
d) Amazon Kinesis

23. Which of the following services is an Identity Broker that handles interaction between applications and Web ID providers?
a) Shards
b) Amazon Cognito
c) Amazon Kinesis
d) Amazon API Gateway

24. Which of the following is responsible for user registration, authentication, and account recovery?
a) Amazon Kinesis
b) Cognito Identity Pool

c) Cognito User Pool

d) Same Origin Policy

25. Which of the following grants the IAM role and authorizes access to AWS resources?

a) Amazon Kinesis

b) Cognito Identity Pool

c) Cognito User Pool

d) Same Origin Policy

26. The pub/sub model allows messages to be _____

a) Broadcast

b) Multicast

c) Uncast

27. The PUB/SUB pattern is facilitated by _____

a) SNS

b) SQS

c) Lambda

d) SNS, SQS, and Lambda

28. The S3 event notification feature enables you to _____ notifications.

a) Receive

b) Transmit

c) Receive and Transmit

d) Interface

29. A component that broadcasts a message is called _____.

a) SNS Message

b) Subscribers

c) Publisher

30. The dead letter queue is an _____ queue.

a) SNS

b) SQS

c) Lambda

Chapter 10: Serverless Services

Introduction

In this chapter, we will study the computing service called AWS Lambda. The first section of the chapter focuses on the theoretical concepts of AWS Lambda Function; the second section consists of the practical implementation of serverless websites using API Gateway and Lambda Function. In the last section of the chapter, an "Alexa" skill will be created. In short, this chapter focuses on the serverless compute services that you must be familiar with to pass the exam.

A Brief History of Cloud

Before going into the detail of AWS Lambda, let's understand the brief history of the Cloud. Previously, almost all organizations had their data centrers for storage. Some of them used "Rackspace," for example, which is the physical hardware. It means whenever the organization works with a server or web server, it is always a physical server. If an organization requires more than one server, data center, load balancer, firewall, and Storage Area Network (SAN), it could take up to 10 days to 6 months to provision because of the hardware configuration.

Amazon Web Service launched Elastic Compute Cloud (EC2) in 2006. Using EC2, you can provision a virtual machine using a simple API core. With EC2, you could have a machine that is ready in minutes. The implementation of this cloud-based virtual machine completely changed the entire architecture. From 2006 onwards, the public cloud started becoming popular and bigger. AWS soon overtook Rackspace due to the powerful features and services of the AWS cloud.

After Amazon EC2, Infrastructure as a Service (IaaS) was launched, and cloud services moved on to Platform as a Service (PaaS). Microsoft is one example of PaaS. Amazon launched PaaS services like Elastic Beanstalk. The PaaS services allow you to upload your code, and the public cloud provider covers all the infrastructure. There is no need to worry about infrastructural functions.

After PaaS, "Containers" was introduced in 2014. "Docker" and "Amazon Kubernetes" are some examples of containers. With containers, the management of containers is the responsibility of users. After containers, the cloud moved on to serverless services. The serverless feature is responsible for the code to provide any service. You can put your code into AWS or the cloud; and all the coding executions are done automatically. You only have to pay for the execution time of the code. This is a short overview of the full evolution of the cloud.

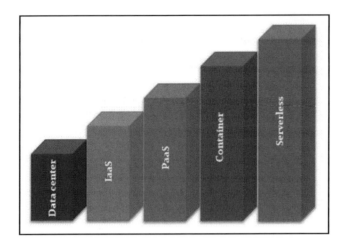

Figure 10-01: History of Cloud

In short, we have gone from the physical server inside data centers and moved towards the abstraction layer focused on the code. It brings us to the concept of the AWS Lambda Function.

AWS Lambda

What is Lambda?

AWS Lambda is the ultimate abstraction layer. Lambda is a Function as a Service (FaaS) product, which means you have a function provided with the code, and AWS executes that code. In this, unlike traditional computing, you are only billed for the number of milliseconds your code runs. Lambda runs the code in an isolated environment, which is stateless. Still, you are responsible for persistence as the environment where Lambda runs has default access to no information except incoming payload. Lambda does not maintain any data result after a function's termination, so it is your responsibility to put the result in a secure place.

AWS Lambda function can be summarized with the example shown in Figure 10-02. There are data centers, and inside these data centers, the hardware handles the assembly code or protocols in high-level languages. Then, there are operating systems running and application layers, as well as AWS APIs. AWS Lambda sits on top of all these and handles the things necessary to run code.

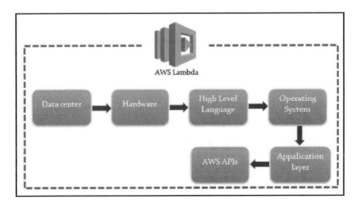

Figure 10-02: AWS Lambda Function

AWS Lambda is a compute service where you can upload your code and create lambda functions. AWS Lambda takes care of provisioning and managing the servers that you use to run the code. There is no need to worry about the operating system, patching, scaling, etc.

> **EXAM TIP**: Lambda is server-less, known as server-less AWS services; it is important to keep this in mind during the exam.

AWS Lambda Use Cases

The Lambda function can be used in several following ways.

Event-Driven Compute Service

Lambda functions can be triggered by events enabling you to build event-driven reactive systems. Lambda can be used in various scenarios, such as a Lambda function can be triggered when changes occur in your data, let's say, in an AWS DynamoDB table or your S3 bucket.

When there are multiple events to respond to, Lambda runs copies of your function in parallel to provide scaling by the workload size. Architects use the Lambda function to reduce wasted capacity. You can run Lambda functions for any application; it will scale your code with high availability.

Portions of each Lambda function are codes you want to execute, the configuration that defines how the code will execute, and event sources that detect the events and invoke your function.

Compute Service in Response to the HTTP Request

AWS Lambda can also be used as a compute service to run your code in response to HTTP requests using Amazon API Gateway, or API calls made using AWS SDKs.

AWS Lambda works in such a way that when an event happens, event data with its format is sent to the Lambda function. The function then accesses data and performs computation, optionally generating a result. As a result, it may interact with AWS services or make internet HTTP calls. Lambda functions can also generate a result in the destination or in which it needs to interact with AWS service to invoke other Lambda functions.

Example: AWS Lambda as an Event-Driven

The working of AWS Lambda with S3 is shown in Figure 10-03. A user wants to create a website the same way as discussed in chapter 9. First, the user needs to create an image and then store that image in the S3 bucket that triggers a Lambda function. Lambda function will take that image and metadata "Welcome To IPSpecialist" to put over that image. The cool thing about lambda is that the Lambda function can trigger other Lambda functions, so it can trigger another Lambda function to update the user about that image. The Lambda function can also trigger another Lambda function to store that image back in an S3 bucket. So, users can use cross-origin replication to store an image anywhere in the world.

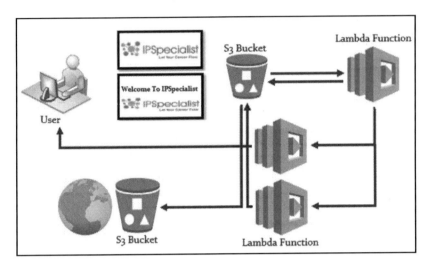

Figure 10-03: AWS Lambda as an Event-Driven

Example: AWS Lambda as a Compute Service

An example of AWS Lambda as a compute service is shown in Figure 10-04(a). There is a user who sends an HTTP request to API Gateway. API Gateway then proceeds to the Lambda function, which sends the code in response to that HTTP request. The Lambda Function then sends the code back to API Gateway, which will send it back to the user.

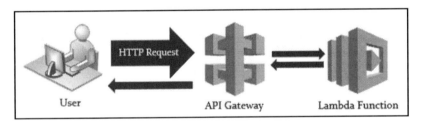

Figure 10-04(a): AWS Lambda as a Compute Service

The advantage of AWS Lambda is that it is scalable. Let's consider the example shown in Figure 10-04(b). There are now two users who send two separate HTTP requests. Both hit API Gateway, and both requests will trigger the same Lambda function with a separate run. Both are separated and isolated from each other. Both will return a response to the user.

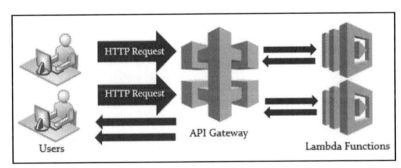

Figure 10-04(b): AWS Lambda as a Compute Service (Scalability)

So, we can say that AWS Lambda is different from auto scaling in such a way that when the user goes in, you may spread it across two web servers. For example, you have a million users hitting API Gateway at once, which will go on and trigger a million different Lambda functions. That is how AWS Lambda scales.

EXAM TIP: Lambda function can trigger other Lambda functions. Lambda functions are independent (1 event is equal to 1 function).

If one event handles the "x" number of functions, these functions trigger other functions.

Traditional vs. Serverless Architecture

It is very important to understand the difference between traditional and serverless architecture for the Certified Solutions Architect Associate exam.

Traditional Architecture

Traditional architecture in the cloud starts with a user, as shown in Figure 10-05. The user sends a request that hits Amazon Route 53 and then goes on to the Elastic Load Balancer. Load Balancer then sends it onto the web servers. These web servers communicate with back-end RDS or other database servers and send back a response to the user. In this architecture, the user relies on physical hardware, which includes virtual machines and operating systems.

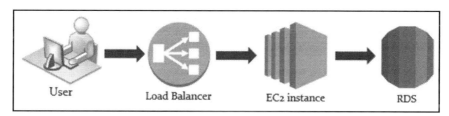

Figure 10-05: Traditional Architecture

Serverless Architecture

Serverless architecture is shown in Figure 10-06. In serverless architecture, the user sends a request to API Gateway, which then responds to AWS Lambda. AWS Lambda can communicate with databases like Dynamo DB, Amazon Aurora, or serverless Aurora. It will then send a response back to the user.

Suppose several users are hitting the API Gateway at once. Assuming you have not throttled the API Gateway. It will scale to that instantly. With serverless architecture, there is no need to worry about the auto scaling and overwhelming of EC2 instances.

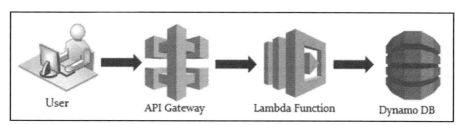

Figure 10-06: Serverless Architecture

> 💡 **EXAM TIP:** Architectures can get extremely complicated with AWS Lambda, which creates difficulties in debugging. Therefore, the AWS service "X-Ray" allows you to debug serverless applications.
>
> Traditional architecture is highly available as it can tolerate failure if you architect it correctly. But it is not as scalable as serverless architecture. Serverless architecture is considered to be the best cost-saving option.

Languages Supported by Lambda

Fundamentally, Lambda is used to execute codes. This code could be of any language that is supported by Lambda, such as:

- Node.js
- Java
- Python
- C#
- Go
- PowerShell

It is also allowed to bring libraries, artifacts, or compiled native binaries that can be executed as part of your function code package. The code you have written in any other language can also be executed by invoking that code from the supported languages in the *Lambda runtime environment*.

Lambda Pricing

AWS Lambda is priced according to two different things:

Number of Requests

AWS Lambda function is priced on the number of requests. The first one million requests are free. Then, $0.20 per 1 million requests is charged. AWS Lambda is very cheap and allows startups to scale quickly.

Duration

AWS Lambda is also priced on duration. Duration is calculated from when your code begins executing until it returns or otherwise terminates, rounded up to the nearest 100 ms. If a function runs for 200 ms or 1 minute, you are charged more for it. The price depends on the amount of memory you allocate to your function. You are charged $0.00001667 for every GB-second used.

Features of Lambda

The features of AWS Lambda are as follows:

Serverless

With AWS Lambda, there is no need for servers. You do not need system administrators, patching, operating system, anti-virus, EC2 instance crashing, etc.

Continuous Scaling

AWS Lambda is continuously scalable. When you invoke API Gateway, it will trigger a separate Lambda function.

Cheap

It allows one million requests free of cost.

 EXAM TIP: AWS Lambda is a serverless service. For the certified solutions architect associate exam, it is very important to remember the serverless service like Aurora, Dynamo DB, S3, API Gateway, etc.

EC2 is not a serverless service; it is a virtual machine.

Lambda In Action

Amazon Alexa is a cloud-based voice service that enables you to create voice experiences for people using your applications. When you deal with Alexa, it is in the form of the Amazon Echo, Echo Show, or Echo Dot. You speak to AWS Lambda or directly communicate with AWS cloud.

EXAM TIP: AWS Lambda scales out automatically. If you have five invocations, AWS Lambda scales out to five different Lambda functions executing simultaneously.

AWS Lambda can work as a global function as well. You can use Lambda to back up the S3 bucket to another S3 bucket.

Removing Servers with Fargate

Amazon Fargate

Fargate is a serverless compute engine for containers. It allows you to manage containers like Docker. Docker is the leading container technology, and Fargate works with Amazon Elastic Container Service, ECS. It scales automatically and is serverless, meaning you do not have to worry about provisioning, configuring, or scaling servers. It removes the need to interact with or even think about servers or clusters.

AWS Fargate is a technology that can be used with Amazon ECS to run containers without managing servers or clusters of Amazon EC2 instances. Fargate eliminates the need to provision, configure, and scale virtual machine clusters to run containers. It eliminates selecting server types to scale clusters or optimize cluster packing.

When using the Fargate launch type or a Fargate capacity provider to run your Amazon ECS tasks and services, you package your application in containers and specify the Operating System, CPU, and memory requirements. Then, you define networking and IAM policies to launch the application. Each Fargate task has its isolation boundary and is not shared by another task's underlying kernel, CPU resources, memory resources, or elastic network interface.

EXAM TIP: AWS Fargate is considered serverless and is used to manage containers.

Components of AWS Fargate

The various components of Fargate tasks and services and specific considerations for using Fargate with Amazon ECS are as follows.

- **Clusters**

A logical grouping of tasks or services is an Amazon ECS cluster. Clusters can be used to isolate your applications. When you run your tasks on Fargate, Fargate manages your cluster resources.

- **Task Definitions**

A task definition is a text file that describes one or more of your application's containers. It is in JSON format and can be used to describe a maximum of ten containers. The task definition serves as the application's blueprint, defining your application's various parameters. You can, for example, use it to specify operating system parameters, which containers to use, which ports to open for your application, and which data volumes to use with the containers in the task. The requirements of your specific application determine the specific parameters available for task definition.

A single task definition does not have to cover your entire application stack. Indeed, we recommend that you spread your application across multiple task definitions. You can accomplish this by grouping related containers into task definitions, each representing a single component.

- **Tasks**

Within a cluster, a task is the instantiation of a task definition. You can specify the number of tasks to run on your cluster after creating a task definition for your application in Amazon ECS. You can run a task as a stand-alone or as part of a service.

- **Services**

You can simultaneously use an Amazon ECS service to run and maintain your desired number of tasks in an Amazon ECS cluster. The Amazon ECS service scheduler launches another instance based on your task definition if any of your tasks fail or stop for any reason. It does this to replace it and thus keep the number of tasks in the service at the desired level.

Use Cases

Web apps, APIs, and Microservices

Use containers' speed and immutability to quickly build and deploy your applications, APIs, and microservices architectures. By eliminating the need to own, operate, and manage the lifespan of computational infrastructure, Fargate allows you to concentrate on what really matters: your applications.

Run and Scale Container Workloads

To operate and scale your workloads for containerized data processing, use Fargate with Amazon ECS or Amazon EKS. You may also move and operate your Amazon ECS Windows containers using Fargate without rewriting or re-architecting your legacy applications.

Support AI and ML Training Apps

Make an adaptable, portable AI and ML development environment. Gain the scalability you require with Fargate to increase server capacity without over-provisioning—for training, testing, and deploying your machine learning (ML) models.

Optimize Costs

There are no upfront costs with AWS Fargate; you simply pay for the resources you use. Use Graviton2 driven Fargate for up to 40% better price performance after further optimizing using Compute Savings Plans and Fargate Spot.

Pricing

From the moment you begin downloading your container image until the Amazon ECS Task or Amazon EKS2 Pod stops, AWS Fargate pricing is based on the vCPU, RAM, operating systems, CPU architecture, and storage1 resources used, rounded to the closest second.

Pricing for the Task or Pod is determined by the needed vCPU, memory, operating systems, CPU architecture, and storage1 resources. The five dimensions can each be set up differently.

Amazon Fargate Pricing for Amazon ECS

Customers can execute interrupt-tolerant Amazon ECS Tasks* on available capacity through Fargate Spot at up to 70% savings off the standard Fargate price. You pay the Spot fee with Fargate Spot for the duration that your Amazon ECS Tasks are active. AWS Fargate determines Fargate Spot prices, which progressively change in response to long-term patterns in the supply and demand for Fargate Spot capacity.

Fargate Ephemeral Storage Pricing for Amazon ECS

All Fargate Tasks and Pods come with 20 GB of ephemeral storage by default; you only pay for any customized extra storage.

Prices are determined by the second, with a one-minute minimum. The duration is determined, rounded to the nearest second, from the moment you begin downloading your container image (Docker pull).

Billing for Windows containers is done on a per-second basis with a 15-minute minimum.

Compute Savings Plan for Amazon ECS and Amazon EKS

If your usage of Fargate is constant, benefit from Savings Plans. In exchange for a promise to use a certain amount of computing (measured in dollars per hour) for a one- or three-year period, savings plans give savings of up to 50% on your AWS Fargate consumption.

EC2 vs. Fargate

EC2	Fargate
• **You are responsible for the underlying operating system.**	• No operating system access.
• **EC2 pricing model.**	• Pay based on resources allocated and time ran
• **Long-running containers.**	• Short-running tasks.
• **Multiple containers share the same host.**	• Isolated environments.

Fargate vs. Lambda

Fargate	Lambda
• **Select Fargate when you have more consistent workloads.**	• Great for unpredictable or inconsistent workloads.
• **Allows Dockers use across the organization and a greater level of control by developers.**	• Perfect for applications that can be expressed as a single function.

Table 10-01: Fargate vs. Lambda

Exam TIP:
- Lose the server - Fargate is a serverless compute option.
- Required Tool - ECS or EKS is a requirement. Fargate does not work by itself.
- EC2 vs. Fargate - Fargate is more expensive but easier to use.
- Fargate vs. Lambda - Fargate is for containers and applications that need to run longer. Lambda excels at short and simple functions.

EventBridge

EventBridge is all about event-driven architectures; an event is a state change. It is a serverless event bus service that allows you to link your applications to data from various sources, including Amazon's EventBridge. EventBridge sends real-time data from your applications, SaaS applications, and AWS services to AWS Lambda functions, HTTP invocation endpoints with API destinations, and event buses in other AWS accounts.

EXAM TIP: Events are state changes generated by services like AWS Config, CloudWatch, CloudTrail, etc.

EventBridge Working

EventBridge accepts an event, signals a change in the environment, and routes it to a destination using a rule. The event structure, called an event pattern or a timetable, is used to match events to targets. For example, you may create a rule that sends an event to a Lambda function when an Amazon EC2 instance goes from pending to operating.

An event bus is assigned to every event that comes to EventBridge. Because each event bus has its own rules, they can only be applied to those on that bus. You may construct custom event buses to transmit or receive events from different accounts or regions. Your account has a default event bus that accepts events from AWS services.

AWS Partners create a partner event source when they wish to transmit events to an AWS customer account. After that, the customer must link an event bus to a partner event source.

In the same manner that you would transmit event data to an AWS service or resource, EventBridge API destinations are HTTP endpoints that you may use as the target of a rule. You may utilize REST API calls to

transport events between AWS services, integrated SaaS applications, and your applications outside of AWS by utilizing API destinations. You define a connection to utilize for an API destination when you create it. Each connection specifies the permission type and parameters to use while authenticating with the API destination endpoint.

Use the input transformer to change the information before traveling to the target to customize the text from an event before passing it to EventBridge.

You can archive (or preserve) events and then play them again from the archive at a later time. Archiving is handy for testing an application because you have a collection of events to use instead of waiting for new events.

Knowing the event pattern of everyday events without producing the event might be helpful when developing serverless applications that use EventBridge. Schemas explain the event patterns and are accessible for all events created by AWS services on EventBridge. You may also develop or upload custom schemas for events that do not come from AWS services. You can obtain code bindings for common programming languages once you have a schema for an event.

You may add a custom label or tag to AWS resources to categorize them or track expenditures in EventBridge. Within EventBridge, you can govern what resources can and cannot do using tag-based policies.

To manage access to EventBridge, in addition to tag-based policies, EventBridge also offers identity-based and resource-based controls. Control the permissions of a group, position, or person with identity-based policies. Use resource-based policies to grant certain rights to each resource, such as a Lambda function or an Amazon SNS topic.

Hence, imagine services like AWS Config, CloudTrail, and CloudWatch, all generating events relating to various changes in state in your AWS account. These events can be sent to EventBridge. Within EventBridge, we can configure rules that match the events and route them to the correct target. Targets define an action that will be taken on an associated AWS service—for example, shutting down an EC2 instance that has been marked as non-compliant by AWS Config or triggering a Lambda function to take some action on your behalf in response to an event, or sending an SNS notification to notify you of an event in CloudTrail or CloudWatch.

Figure 10-07: EventBridge Working

> **EXAM TIP:** Targets can be services like Lambda, SNS, or EC2, and they respond to the event by taking some action.

Scheduled Events

EventBridge can also be used to schedule events. Hence, you can create EventBridge rules, which run on a schedule that you define. For example, once an hour or once a day, or using a cron expression, you can set a rule to run simultaneously on a specified day, week, or month. Let's assume you wanted to reboot a particular instance every month at the same time. You can do that using a scheduled event in EventBridge.

AWS can plan restarts, stop/starts, and retirements for your instances. These kinds of things do not happen very often. Suppose a planned event may affect one of your instances. In that case, AWS will send an email to the email address associated with your AWS account before the scheduled event. The email contains information on the event, such as the start and finish dates. You may be able to influence the timing of an occurrence depending on the circumstances. AWS also delivers an AWS Health event that you can track and control with Amazon CloudWatch Events.

AWS manages scheduled events; you cannot arrange events for your instances. You may see the events that AWS has planned and adjust scheduled event alerts by adding or removing tags and taking action when an instance is set to reboot, retire, or cease.

>  **EXAM TIP:** Rules match events and route them to the correct target.

Sound like CloudWatch Events

Amazon EventBridge is the recommended method of event management. The core service and API for CloudWatch Events and EventBridge are the same. However, EventBridge has extra functionality. The changes you make in CloudWatch or EventBridge will be reflected in both consoles.

Amazon CloudWatch Events was the previous name for EventBridge. In the EventBridge console, you can see the default event bus and the rules you set in CloudWatch Events. Your code will remain unchanged because EventBridge uses the same CloudWatch Events API as the CloudWatch Events API. CloudWatch Events do not receive new functionality added to EventBridge.

> **EXAM TIP:**
>
> Amazon EventBridge allows you to configure event-driven systems easily and define tasks that run on a pre-defined schedule. The same underlying technology as CloudWatch Events.

AWS EventsBridge Scenario

Let's assume that your company requires all EC2 instances to have encrypted disk volumes, and somebody has created a new EC2 instance without encrypting the attached EBS volumes. It gets detected by Config and marked as non-compliant. An event will be generated and sent to EventBridge, which triggers a rule, invoking an action to send you an email using SNS. Hence, you will be able to find out if someone has created a non-compliant EC2 instance.

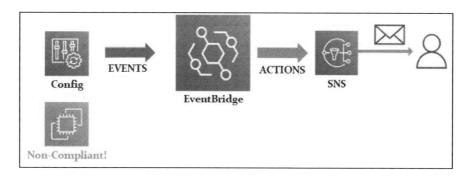

Figure 10-08: Example Scenario: Non-Compliant

Suppose CloudWatch detects that one of your EC2 instances shows CPU utilization of 99%. In that case, an event will be generated and sent to EventBridge, which triggers a rule to invoke an action to send you an email using SNS. It is all straightforward to configure because CloudWatch events, EventBridge, and SNS are well integrated. EventBridge uses the same underlying technology as CloudWatch Events.

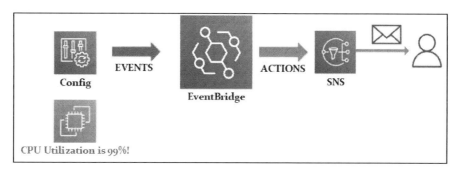

Figure 10-09: Example Scenario CUP Utilization

Features

Global Endpoints

Customers can increase the availability of their event-driven apps on AWS by using global endpoints, which is an easy and dependable method. By automatically switching their event intake to a secondary location during service failures without requiring manual intervention, the new functionality known as a global endpoint helps clients construct durable and reliable applications. Customers can reduce the amount of data that is at risk during these service interruptions by using replication, which is built-in and optional. Customers can freely set up failover criteria to control when to failover and when to send events back to the primary region using CloudWatch Alarms (through Route53 health checks).

By offering a pre-populated stack for generating a CloudWatch Alarm and Route53 Health Checks in the dashboard, we have made it simple for users to get started.

API Destinations

With the help of the new API Destinations functionality for EventBridge, developers may transmit events back to several on-premises or Software as a Service (SaaS) apps while maintaining throughput and authentication control. With just a web address, you can send events to any web-based application without having to worry about creating complex code or using the additional infrastructure. EventBridge can handle

security and delivery, and you can set rules with input transformations that will map the event's format to the receiving service's format.

Archive and Relay Events

With Event Replay, a new feature of Amazon EventBridge, you may replay previous events and route them to an event bus or a particular EventBridge rule. Developers can use this functionality to swiftly debug their apps, extend them by hydrating targets with historical events, and fix mistakes.

Schema Registry

You don't need to manually search for events and their structure because the EventBridge schema registry maintains event schema in a registry that other developers in your company can quickly search and access. To use the event as an object in your code, you may also construct code bindings for programming languages like Java, Python, or TypeScript straight in your IDE using the registry. The requirement to manually construct a schema for an event is eliminated by enabling schema discovery for an event bus, which causes the schemas of events to be automatically detected and uploaded to the registry.

All AWS services' schemas are instantly exposed in your schema registry, and when you enable schema discovery for the SaaS partner event bus, the schemas for integrated SaaS applications are also made available.

Fully Managed and Scalable Event Hubs

Applications can communicate using events with the serverless, fully managed, and scalable event bus known as Amazon EventBridge. There is no capacity to provide and no infrastructure to manage.

SaaS Integration

Depending on the events that SaaS applications produce, your AWS applications may take action. With further integrations planned, Amazon EventBridge is natively integrated with several SaaS applications from different vendors, including Datadog, OneLogin, PagerDuty, Savyint, Segment, SignalFx, SugarCRM, Symantec, Whispir, Zendesk. Your SaaS provider's authentication events just show up on your event bus; you don't need to handle any integration configuration for them.

Event Filtering

Rules can be used to filter events. Events are routed to targets for processing after a rule matches incoming events for a specific event bus. A single rule may route to a number of targets, all of which are handled concurrently. Rules enable various application components to search for and handle events that are relevant to them. By passing along only specific information or replacing it with a constant, a rule can modify an event before it is transmitted to the target. To allow different microservices or apps to select to match events based on particular filters, it is also possible to have numerous rules that match the same event.

Reliable Event Delivery

Targets can receive events from Amazon EventBridge at least once and can get retries with exponential backoff lasting up to 24 hours. Events are persistently stored across various Availability Zones (AZs), increasing your confidence that they will reach their destination. Additionally, Amazon EventBridge offers a 99.99% availability service level agreement (SLA), guaranteeing that your apps can confidently access the service.

Pricing

You pay for events added to your event bus, events consumed for schema discovery, and events replayed while using Amazon EventBridge. For regulations or event delivery, there are no extra fees. There are no upfront obligations or minimum fees. It costs nothing to publish a status change event using an AWS service.

Lab 10-01: Using Amazon EventBridge

Introduction

Amazon EventBridge

EventBridge provides real-time connectivity to AWS services, your applications, and SaaS applications without the need to write code. Pick an event source, then a target from AWS services such as Amazon SNS, Amazon Kinesis Data Firehose, and others as soon as you log in. In near-real-time utilizing Amazon EventBridge, the events will be sent to the users.

Log in to your AWS account and navigate to the Amazon EventBridge dashboard to pick an event source. If you utilize a partner app, ensure your SaaS account is set up to emit events and accept them in the Amazon EventBridge console's available event sources area. Amazon EventBridge will construct an event bus for you and route events to it automatically. Alternatively, you may instrument your application with the AWS SDK to send events to your event bus. Configure a filtering rule and a target for your events, such as a Lambda function. The events will be ingested, filtered, and sent to the chosen target in a secure and highly available manner using Amazon EventBridge.

Custom application-level events can be created and published to Amazon EventBridge using the service's APIs. You may also create scheduled events that will be created regularly and processed in any Amazon EventBridge supported targets.

Amazon Elastic Compute Cloud (EC2)

Amazon Elastic Compute Cloud (Amazon EC2) is a cloud computing service that gives the durability of computing power. It is intended to make web-scale computing more accessible to IT engineers.

Amazon EC2 offers "compute" in the cloud, much as Amazon Simple Storage Service (Amazon S3) enables "storage" in the cloud. The easy web service interface of Amazon EC2 allows you to obtain and configure capacity quickly. It lets you control your computer resources entirely and enable you to run on Amazon's tried-and-true computing infrastructure. The time to buy and boot new Amazon EC2 server instances is reduced to minutes, allowing you to scale up quickly and down capacity as your computing needs change. Amazon EC2 revolutionizes computing economics by enabling you to pay only for the resources you utilize.

Amazon CloudWatch

Amazon CloudWatch is a tracking service for Amazon Web Services (AWS) cloud services and software. Amazon CloudWatch may be used to collect and monitor data, monitor log files, and trigger alarms. Amazon CloudWatch may be used to monitor AWS resources such as Amazon EC2 instances, DynamoDB tables, RDS database instances, and custom metrics and log files created by your applications and services. Your whole system may be monitored using Amazon CloudWatch, which allows you to keep track of resource use, application performance, and operational health. These insights might help you react and keep your application working smoothly.

Amazon Simple Notification Service (SNS)

Amazon Simple Notification Service (Amazon SNS) is a cloud-based web service that makes it simple to create, manage, and deliver alerts. It gives developers a scalable, versatile, and cost-effective way to publish messages from their applications and deliver them to subscribers or other applications immediately. Programmers will be able to access web-scale computing more easily with this tool. The "publish-subscribe" (pub-sub) messaging paradigm is used by Amazon SNS, with alerts provided to clients via a "push" method that eliminates the need to check or "poll" for new information and changes regularly. Amazon SNS provides developers with a simple process to include a robust notification system in their applications. Simple APIs require minimum up-front development work, no maintenance or administrative costs, and pay-as-you-go pricing.

Problem

Assume you are a SysOps Administrator engineer in an organization. Your organization wants you to develop a solution in which all EC2 instances must have encrypted disk volumes; if any employee has created a new EC2 instance without encrypting the attached EBS volumes, it gets detected and marked as non-compliant. An event will be generated, triggering a rule which invokes an action to send you an email. Hence, you will be able to find out if somebody has created a non-compliant EC2 instance. How can this be done?

Solution

The solution is you create an SNS topic, subscribe to the topic using your email address, and confirm the subscription. Then, it would help if you created an EventBridge rule to notify of any EC2 instance state changes using SNS. After that, stop the non-compliant EC2 instance and check if you have received an email notification.

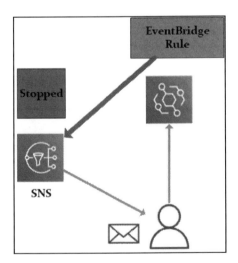

Figure 10-10: Using EventBridge

Follow the given steps to create events using Amazon EventBridge.

Before deep-diving into the lab, launch an EC2 instance.

Step 1: Create SNS Topic

1. Log in to the **AWS Console**.
2. Click on **Services**.

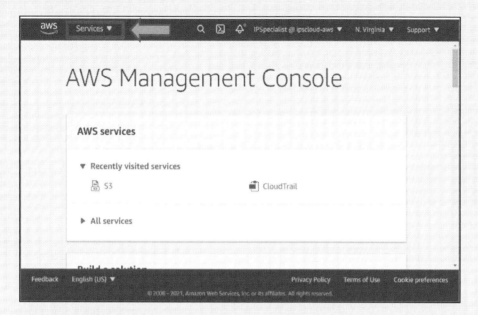

3. Select Simple Notification Service from Application Integration.

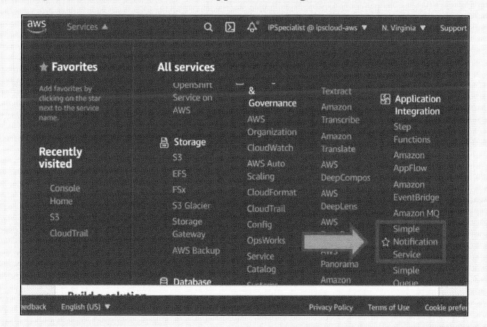

4. Create a new topic. Give a name **IPS-MyTopic**. Then, click on the **Next step** button.

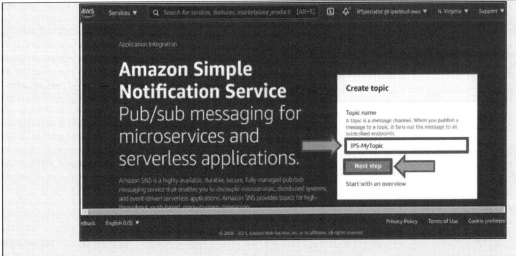

5. After that, leave everything as default. Scroll down and click on the **Create Topic** button.

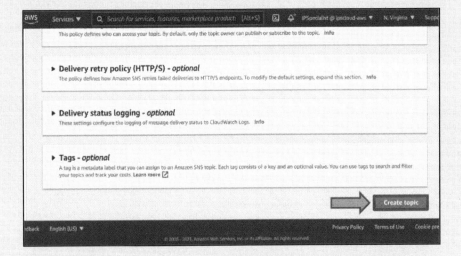

6. After creating an SNS topic, select **Subscriptions** on the left-hand side menu.

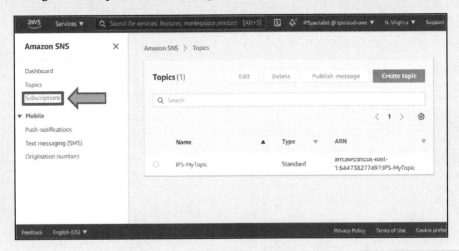

7. Click the Create Subscription button.

8. Select your **Topic ARN**.

9. In **Protocol**, select **Email**.

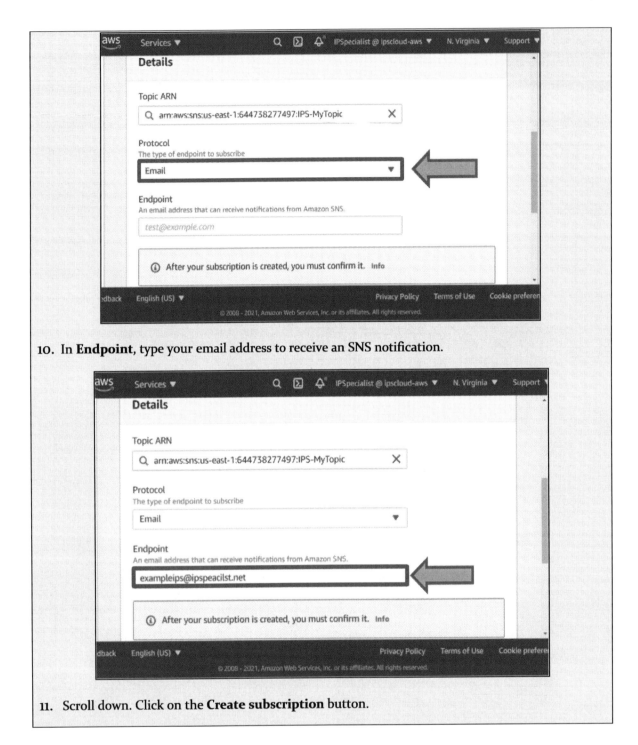

10. In **Endpoint**, type your email address to receive an SNS notification.

11. Scroll down. Click on the **Create subscription** button.

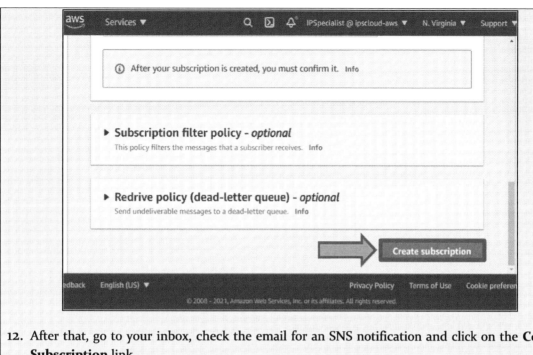

12. After that, go to your inbox, check the email for an SNS notification and click on the **Confirm Subscription** link.

13. After clicking on confirm subscription link, you should see a message like the one below.

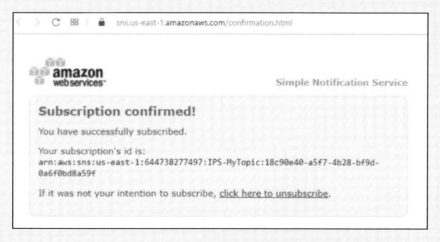

Step 2: Create EventBridge Rule

1. Click on **Services**.

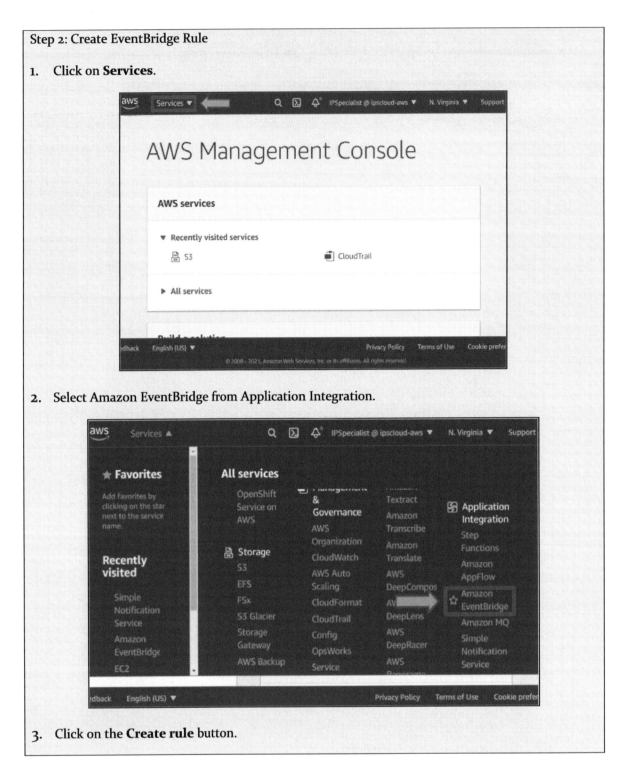

2. Select Amazon EventBridge from Application Integration.

3. Click on the **Create rule** button.

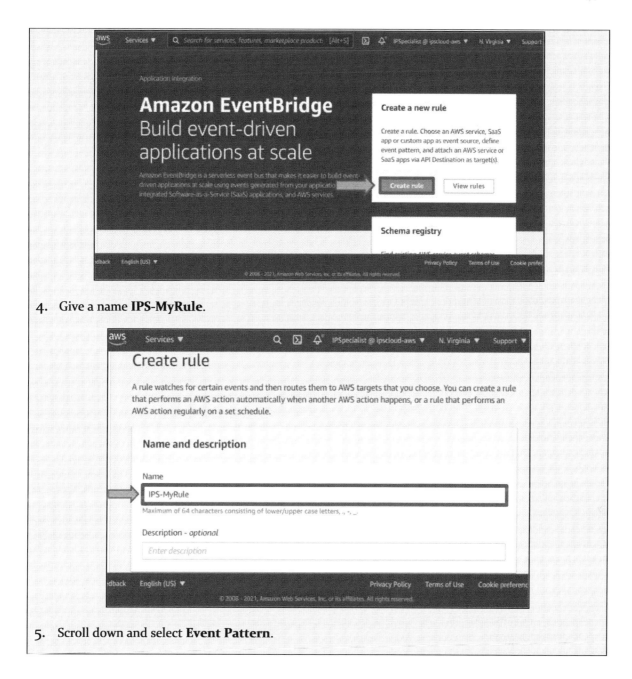

4. Give a name **IPS-MyRule**.

5. Scroll down and select **Event Pattern**.

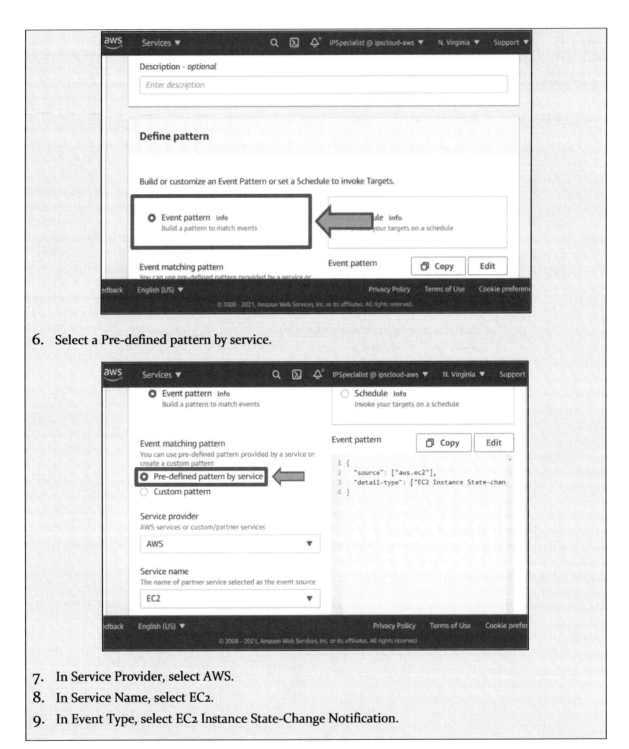

6. Select a Pre-defined pattern by service.

7. In Service Provider, select AWS.

8. In Service Name, select EC2.

9. In Event Type, select EC2 Instance State-Change Notification.

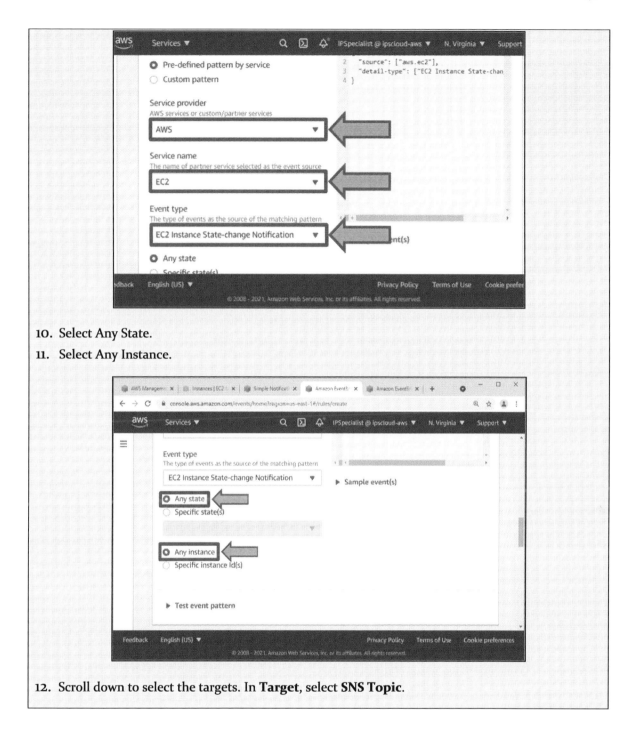

10. Select Any State.

11. Select Any Instance.

12. Scroll down to select the targets. In **Target**, select **SNS Topic**.

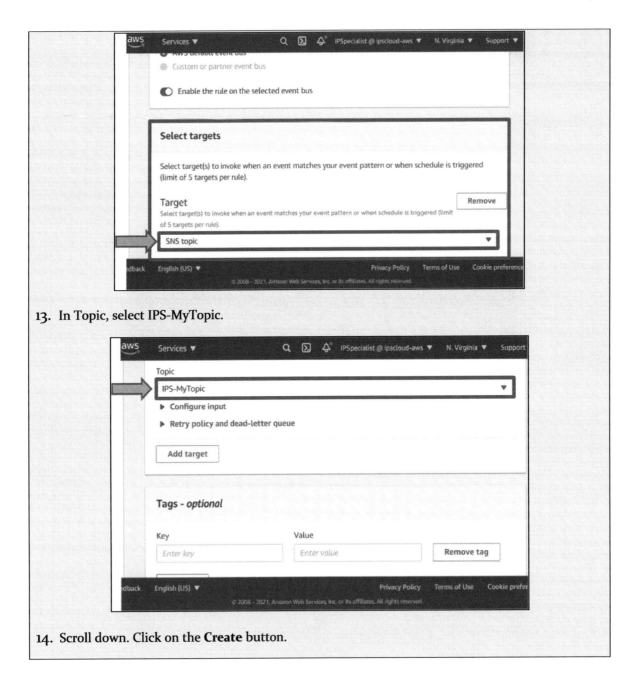

13. In Topic, select IPS-MyTopic.

14. Scroll down. Click on the **Create** button.

15. The rule has been created.

Step 3: Changing the State

1. Click on **Services**.

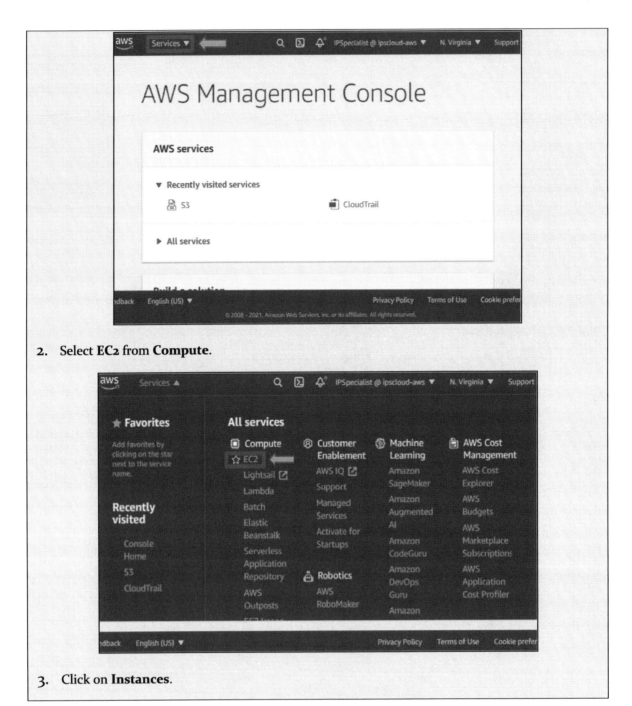

2. Select **EC2** from **Compute**.

3. Click on **Instances**.

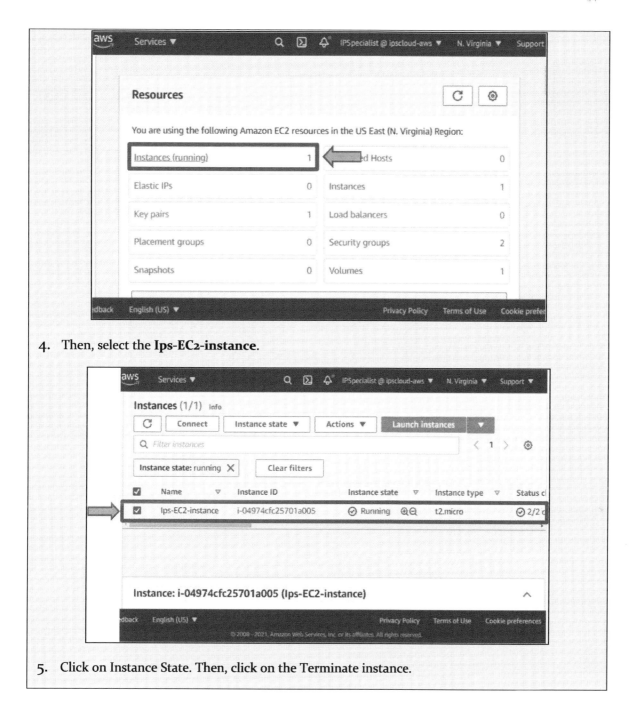

4. Then, select the **Ips-EC2-instance**.

5. Click on Instance State. Then, click on the Terminate instance.

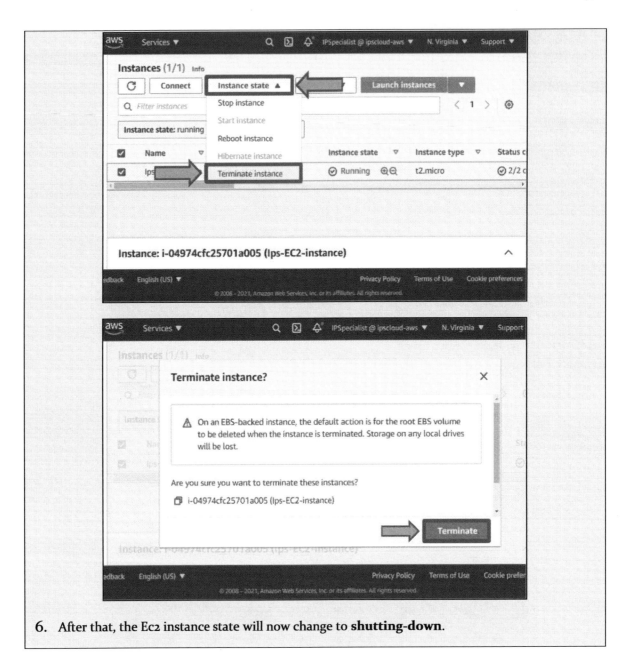

6. After that, the Ec2 instance state will now change to **shutting-down**.

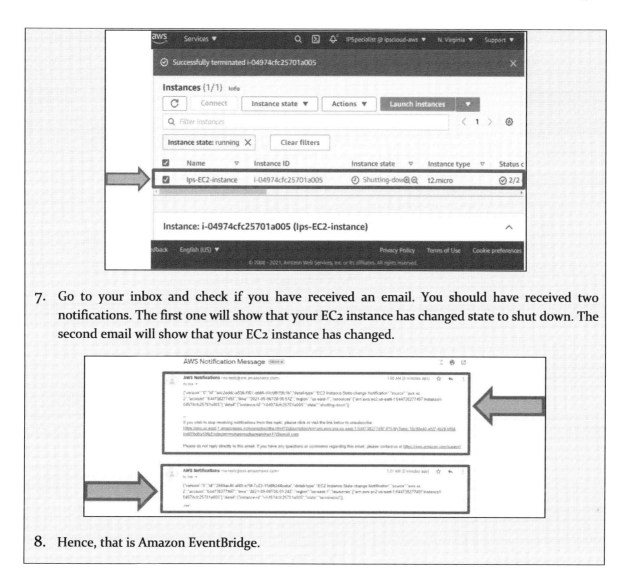

7. Go to your inbox and check if you have received an email. You should have received two notifications. The first one will show that your EC2 instance has changed state to shut down. The second email will show that your EC2 instance has changed.

8. Hence, that is Amazon EventBridge.

 EXAM TIP:

1. EventBridge receives events relating to state changes in AWS, e.g., an EC2 instance changes state or a CloudWatch alarm changes state.
2. You can use EventBridge to create rules that take actions based on the events it receives, e.g., send an SNS notification.
3. EventBridge and CloudWatch use the same underlying technology.

Introduction to Serverless Website

The structure of a serverless website is shown in Figure 10-11. A serverless website consists of a user. The user wants to go to "ips-labs.co.uk." But, there is a problem, the user does not know the IP address of that website. Here, Amazon Route 53 comes in. When the user sends a query across Route 53, it will respond with the bucket address for the website. The user goes to the S3 bucket, then to index.html. When the user views that

page, it will show the static page. So, the user will be returned to the browser. Then, a button will appear. When the user pushes that button, he will get dynamic content by request through to API Gateway. API Gateway will go to the proxy that requests a Lambda function. The Lambda function will take the data and return the result to API Gateway, which will then return the result to the user.

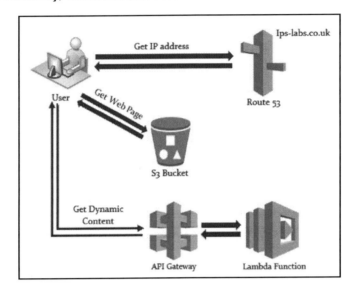

Figure 10-11: Structure of Serverless Architecture

Lab 10-02: Build A Serverless Webpage with API Gateway and AWS Lambda

Scenario: IPSpecialist wants a website to provide their students with study content. They have approached you for a solution. Also, they do not want to manage anything for this website.

Solution: In this lab, we will configure a Serverless Webpage with API Gateway and AWS Lambda.

1. Log in to AWS Management Console.
2. Go to "Services."

3. Click on **Lambda**, which is present under Compute.

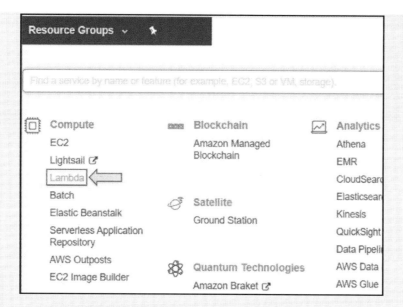

4. The screen of AWS Lambda will appear. Click on **Create function**.

5. You can make three different Lambda functions. You can use the author from scratch, you can use a blueprint, or you can use the serverless application repository.

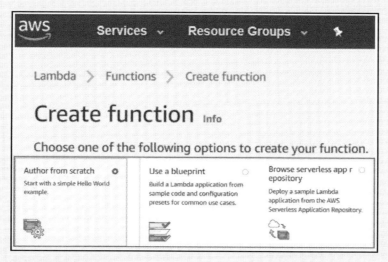

Note: Serverless Application Repository offers a bunch of applications that have already been developed and published on AWS. Blueprints are useful for creating Alexa skills. You will need to "Author from scratch" to create the Lambda function in this lab.

6. Write the function name as **IPSLambdaFunction**.

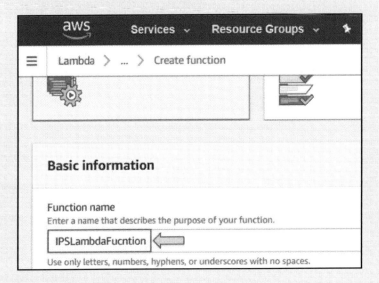

7. There are different runtime environments available, including .Net Core 2.1, Java 8, Python 2.7, Python 3.6, Python 3.7, etc.
8. Select **Python 3.6** from the given list.

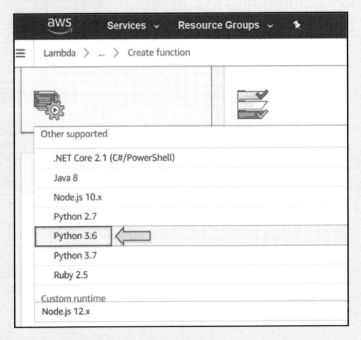

Note: You can also use other runtime environments as well.

9. Select the execution role as Create a new role from AWS policy templates.

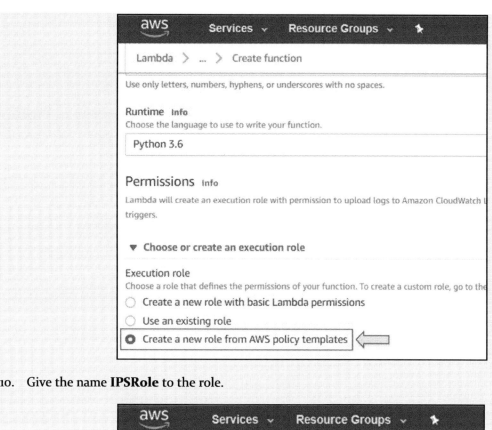

10. Give the name **IPSRole** to the role.

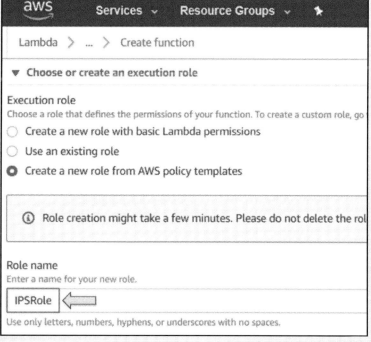

11. Choose the policy template **Simple microservice permissions** from the given list.

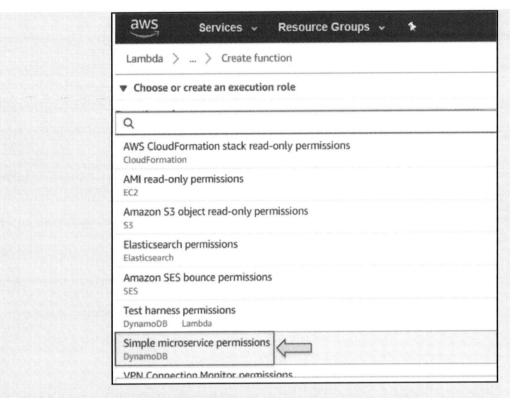

12. After that, click on **Create function**.

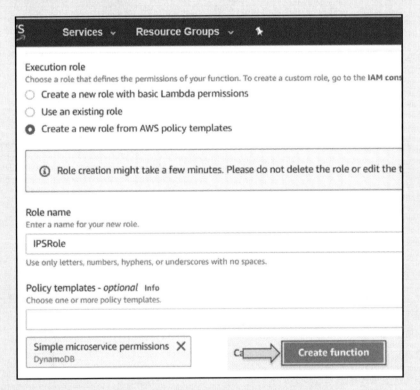

13. The notification of a successful creation of the Lambda function appears.
14. Click on + Add trigger.

Note: The configuration features include designer, function code, environment variables, tags, execution role, network, and a whole bunch of different settings.

15. The list of different triggers appears, which includes API Gateway, AWS IoT, Alexa Skill Kit, Alexa Smart Home, etc.

Note: You should remember different Lambda functions for the exam.

16. Go to the **Function code** section; the default coding for the Lambda function is shown.

Note: Function code comprises IDE (Integrated Development Environment).

17. Go to your resources section and type the following script:

def lambda_handler(event, context)

    print("In lambda handler")

    resp = {

      "statusCode": 200,

      "headers" : {

          "Access-Control-Allow-Origin": "*",

  },

  "body": "IPS Study Content"

  }

    return resp

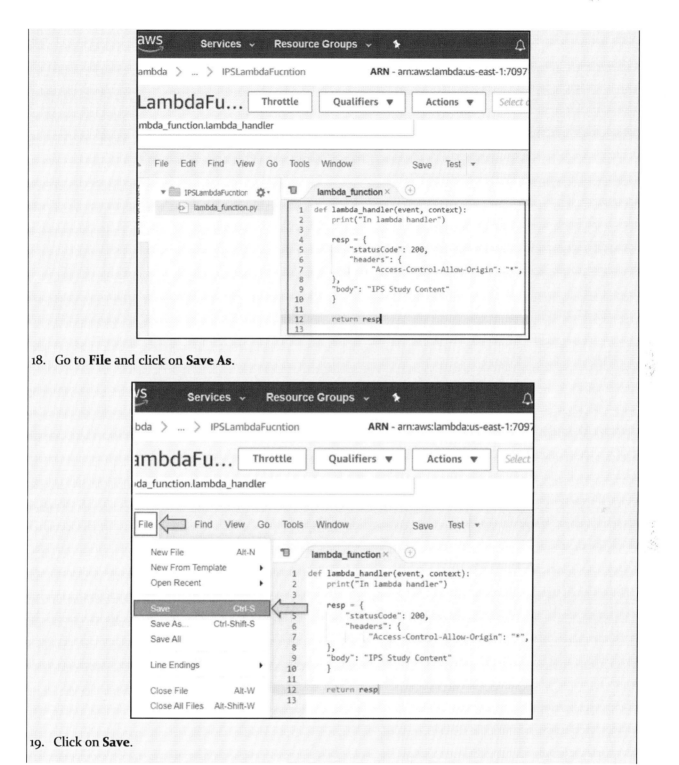

18. Go to **File** and click on **Save As**.

19. Click on **Save**.

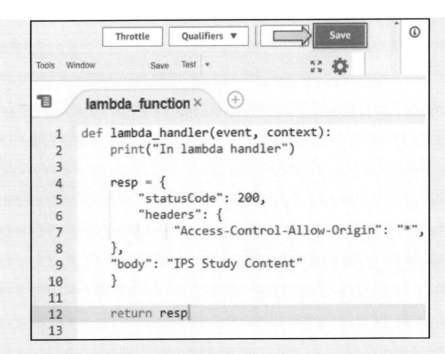

Note: This will save the IDE as well as the function.

20. After that, go to the **Basic settings**. Click on **Edit**.

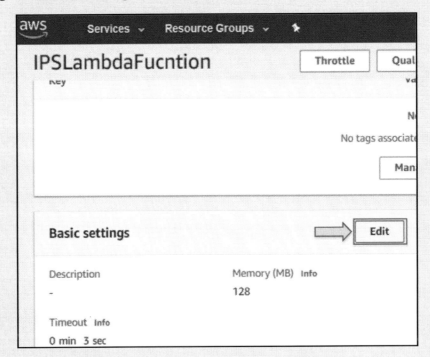

21. Name the description as **IPS Lambda Function** and allocate timeout.

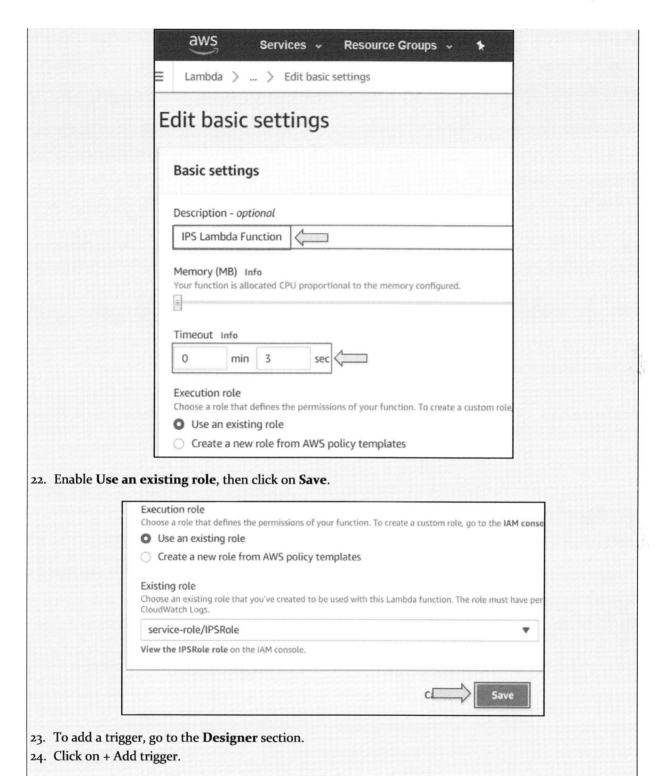

22. Enable **Use an existing role**, then click on **Save**.

23. To add a trigger, go to the **Designer** section.
24. Click on + Add trigger.

25. Click on **API Gateway**.

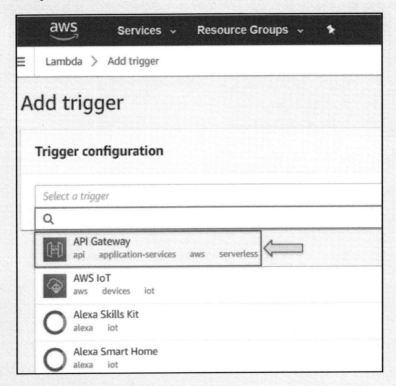

26. Select the API type as **REST API**.
27. Select **IAM** as a security mechanism for your API endpoint.

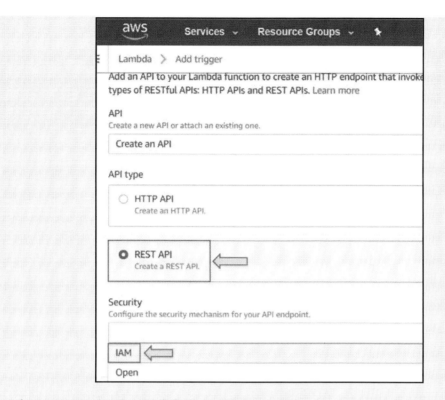

28. Leave the remaining options as default and click on **Add**.

29. The API Gateway as a trigger is shown in the figure. Click on the given link.

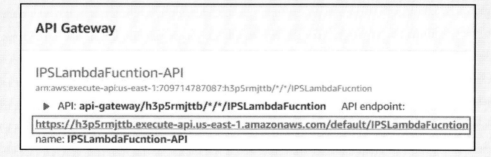

Note: This shows that the new API endpoint has been created.

30. You will get an error message.

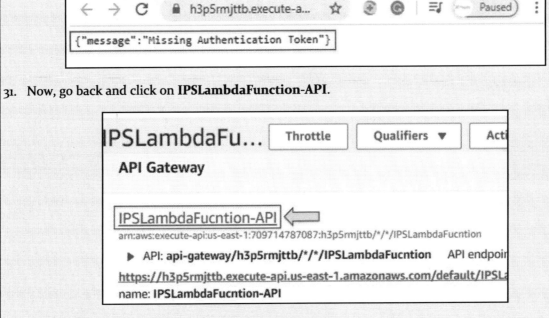

31. Now, go back and click on **IPSLambdaFunction-API**.

32. The API Gateway is shown in the form of a User Interface.

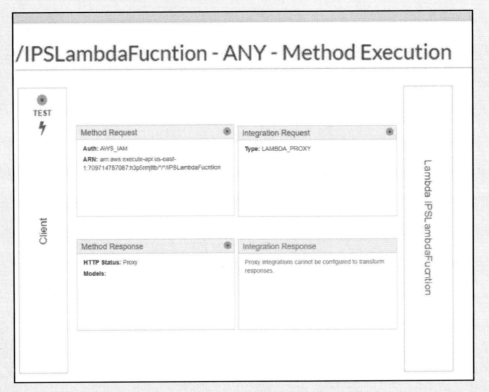

Note: The API Gateway is shown in the form of a User Interface (UI). The client is on one side, and the Lambda function is on another. The client sends a request of type "ANY." The request proxies to the lambda function, and then the lambda function responds back to the client.

33. Go to **Actions** and click on **Delete Method**.

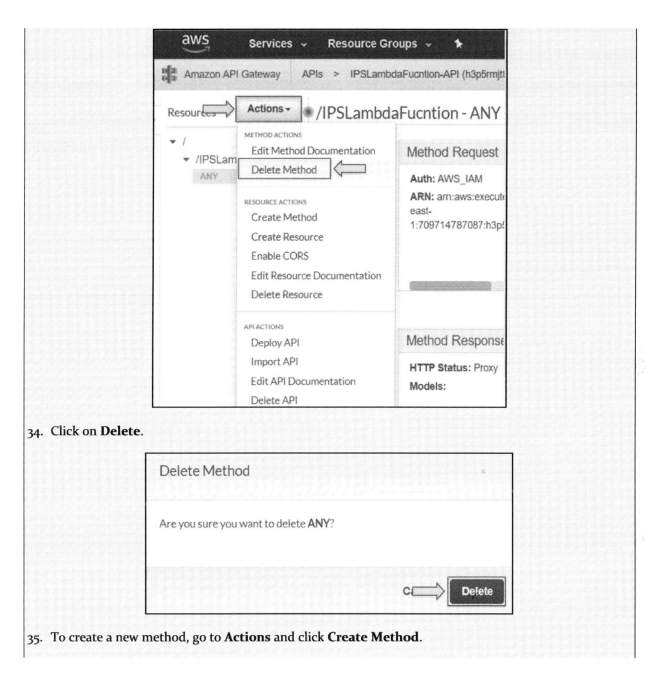

34. Click on **Delete**.

35. To create a new method, go to **Actions** and click **Create Method**.

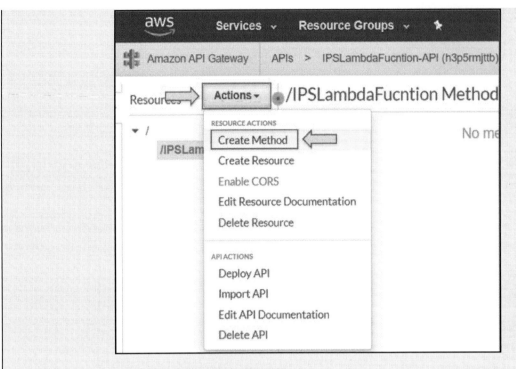

36. Select the function type **GET** from the given list.

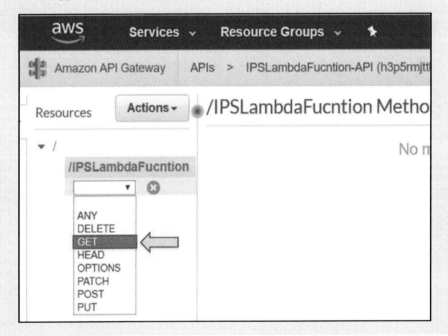

37. Select the "Integration type" as "Lambda Function."
38. Enable "Use Lambda Proxy Integration."
39. Select the N.Virginia region.
40. Give the name of Lambda Function as "IPSLambdaFunction."
41. Enable "Use Default Timeout."
42. Click on **Save**.

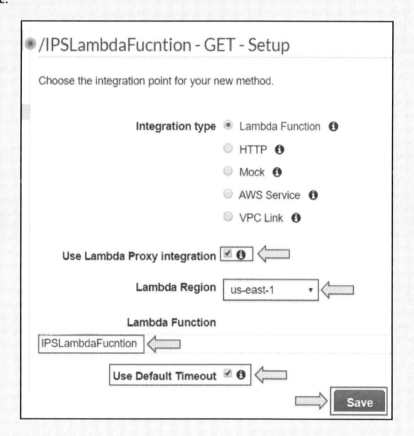

43. Click on **OK**.

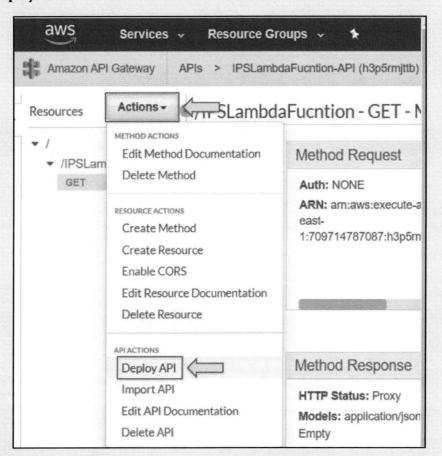

44. Now to deploy API, go to **Actions**.
45. Click on **Deploy API**.

46. Select the "Deployment stage."
47. Write the "Deployment description" as "IPS Website Deployment."
48. Click on **Deploy**.

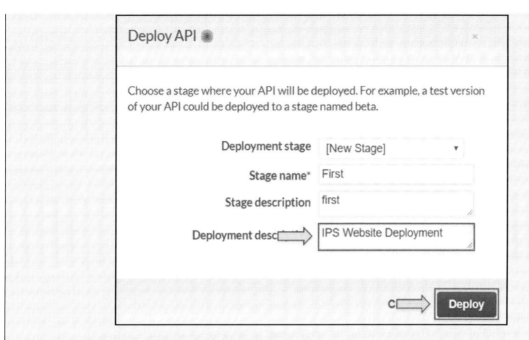

49. After the deployment of the API, click on **GET**.

50. The deployed API is shown in the figure. Click on this to invoke the URL.

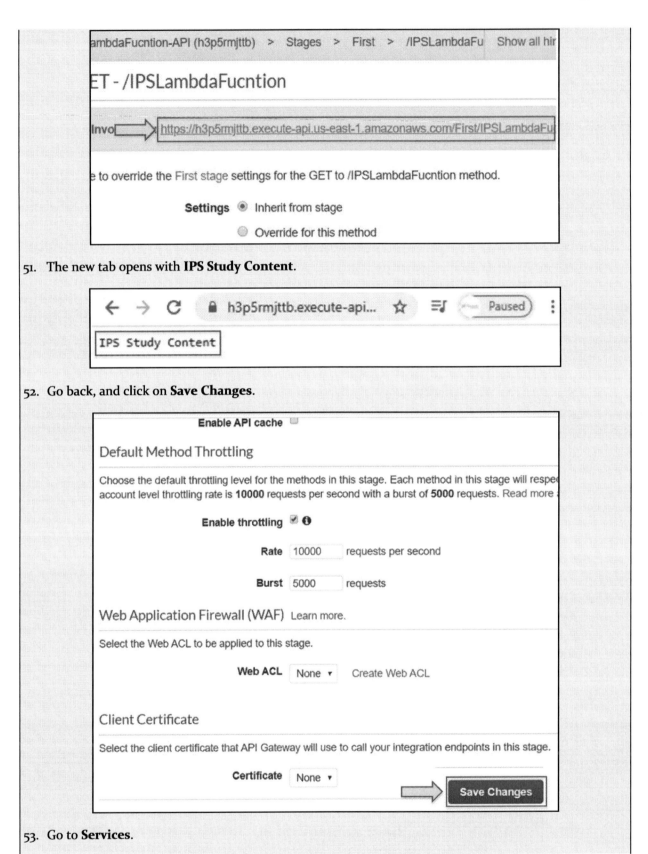

51. The new tab opens with **IPS Study Content**.

52. Go back, and click on **Save Changes**.

53. Go to **Services**.

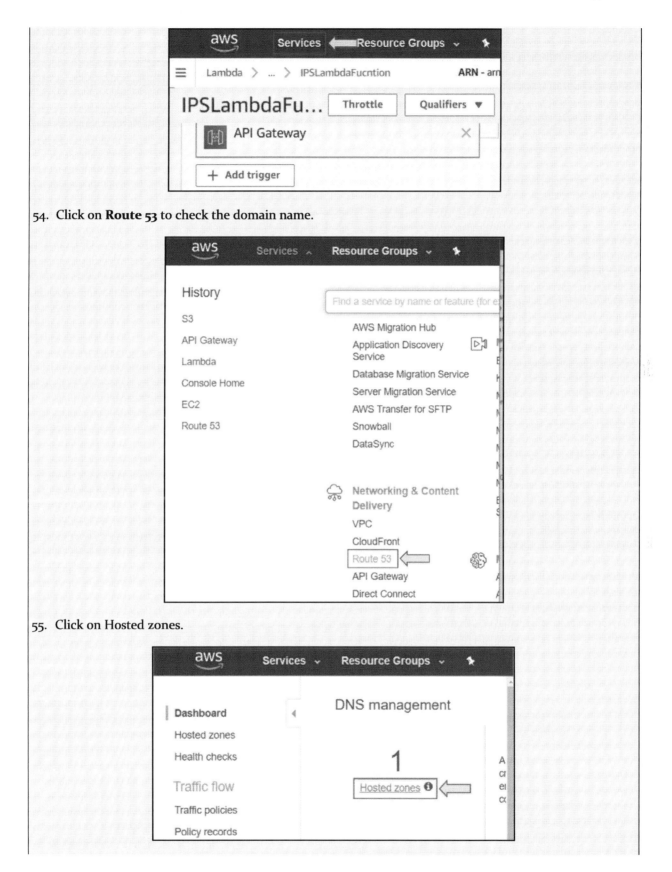

54. Click on **Route 53** to check the domain name.

55. Click on Hosted zones.

56. Click on ips-labs.co.uk.

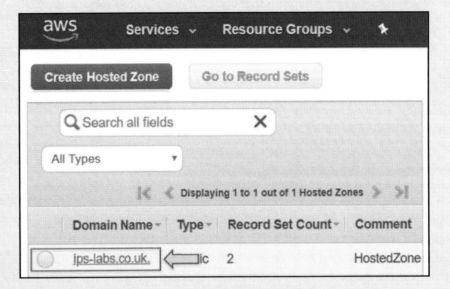

57. The registered domain name is shown with NS and SOA records.

58. Go back to **Services** and click on **S3**.

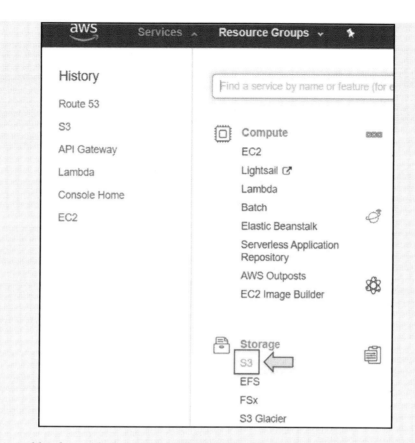

59. Select the created bucket with the name **ips-labs.co.uk**.

60. Click on **Upload**.

61. Click on **Add files**.

62. Upload the index.html and error.html files from your resources.

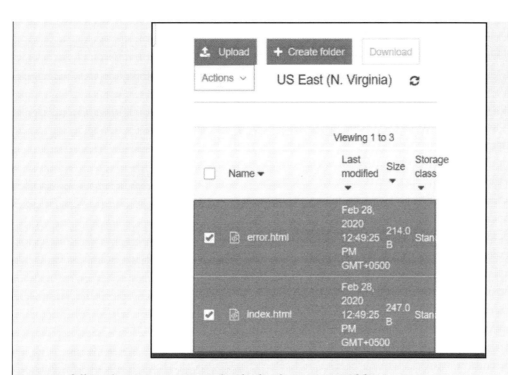

63. Now follow the given step to make the bucket access **Public**.
64. Go to **Actions** and click on **Make public**.

65. Click on **Make Public**.

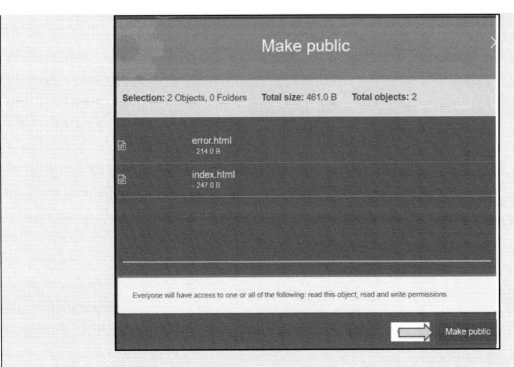

66. You will see the bucket access as **Public**.

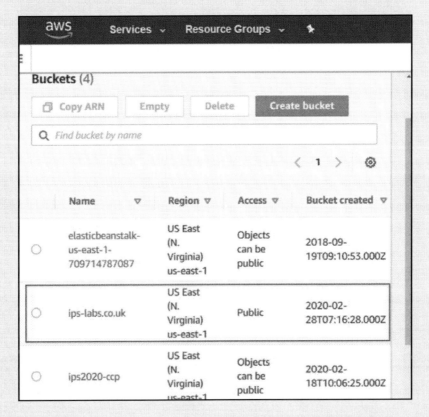

67. Click on ips-labs.co.uk.

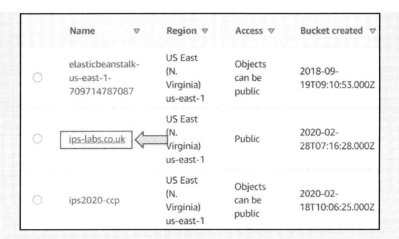

68. Click on **Properties** to configure the static website.

69. Click on Bucket hosting.

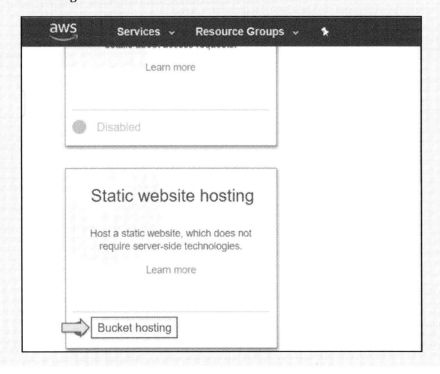

70. Write the index document as **index.html** and the error document as **error.html**.
71. Enable Bucket hosting.
72. Click on **Save**.

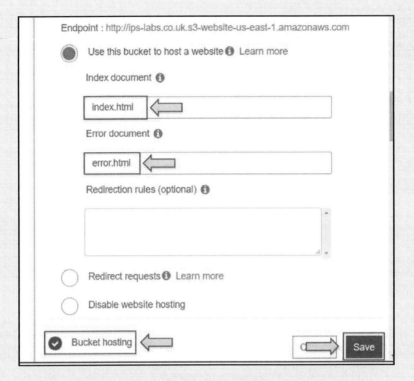

73. Go back to **Amazon S3**.

74. Click on ips-labs.co.uk.

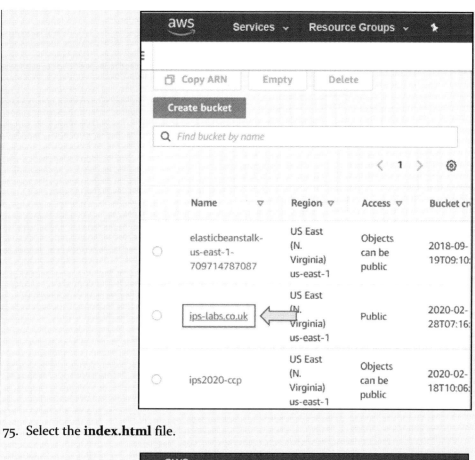

75. Select the **index.html** file.

76. Click on **Object URL**.

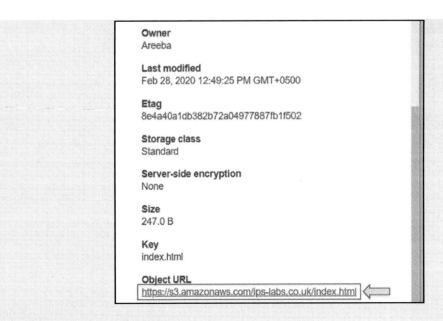

77. The loaded webpage will appear.

78. Click on **Click me**.

79. The output of the Lambda function will appear.

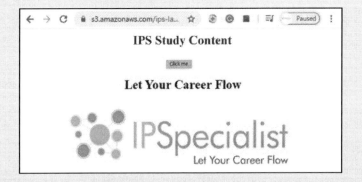

Note: When you click the **Click me** button, the output will query the API Gateway. API Gateway will pass to the Lambda function; then Lambda will send a response back to API Gateway, which is shown to the web browser.

80. Go back to **AWS Services**.

81. Click on **Route 53**.

82. Click on Hosted zones.

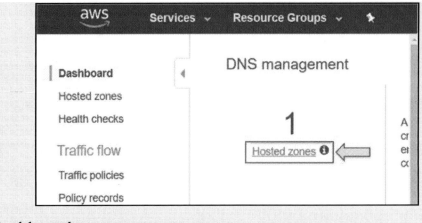

83. Click on ips-labs.co.uk.

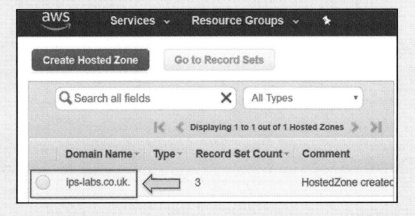

84. Click on Create Record Set.

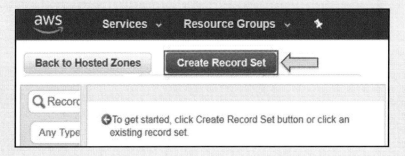

85. Use the default domain name.
86. Enable **Alias**.
87. Select Alias Target.

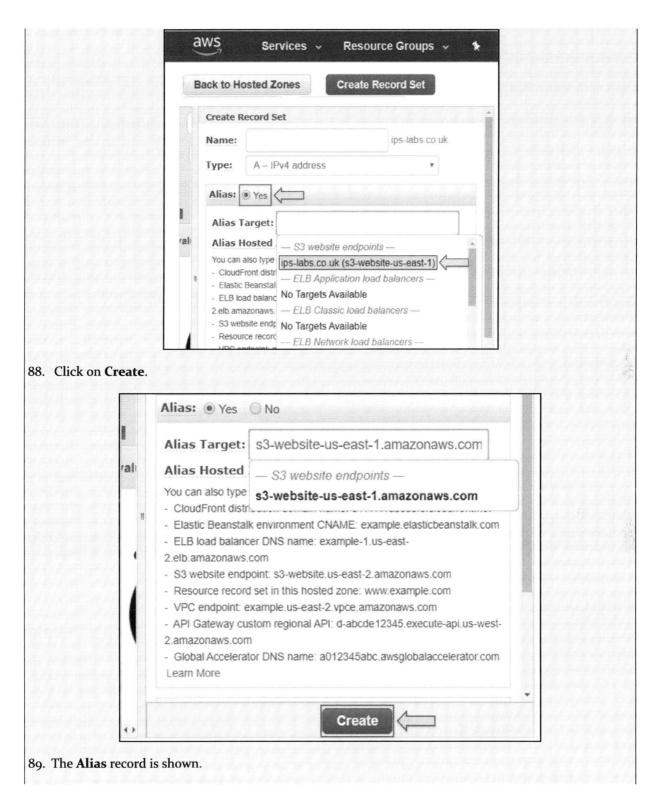

88. Click on **Create**.

89. The **Alias** record is shown.

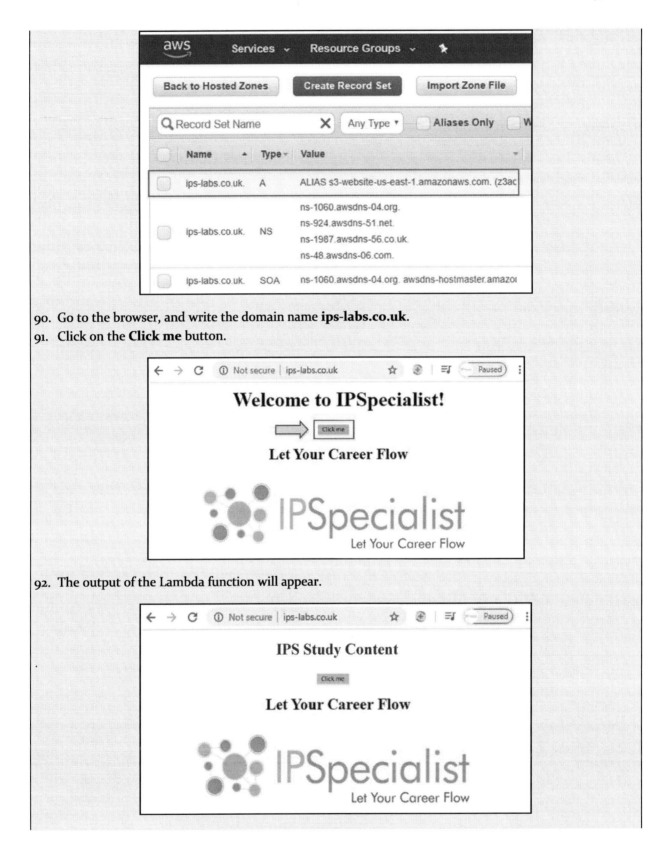

90. Go to the browser, and write the domain name **ips-labs.co.uk**.
91. Click on the **Click me** button.

92. The output of the Lambda function will appear.

> **Note:** When you click on **Click me**, the command starts talking to the API gateway, which communicates with Lambda and passes the response back to the API gateway. This will display the response to the web browser.

> EXAM TIP: In a simple routing policy, you can have only one record with multiple IP addresses. If you specify multiple values in a record, Route 53 returns all the values to the user randomly.

An Introduction to Alexa

Alexa is a service of AWS Lambda. This feature can be used in constructing skilled architecture. In skill architecture, a user first asks questions, and skill matches the intent of the question. The skill will then send the intent to the AWS Lambda function. The Lambda function will take the data and return a relevant response..

An example of Amazon Echo is shown in Figure 10-12(a). Amazon Echo is the AWS Lambda service and provides a way of directly talking to the cloud and having the cloud respond back to you.

Figure 10-12(a): Example of Alexa - Amazon Echo

Another example is shown in Figure 10-12(b). In iPhones, the voice search is called "Siri." So, you have an iPhone, which is a physical device, and when you are talking to the iPhone, you are talking to "Sri." Similarly, Alexa is the voice service for the Amazon Echo. Amazon Echo is the hardware, and when you are talking to that echo device, you are communicating with Amazon Alexa service.

Figure 10-12(b): Example of Alexa

Uses of Alexa Service

The use of the Alexa service is shown in Figure 10-13. There are hardware devices present in the form of Raspberry Pi, Amazon Echo, and Fire TV. This hardware enables devices to have the Alexa service enabled. This device uses various technologies, like automatic speech recognization, natural language understanding, and speech-to-text. These hardware devices allow us to create different skills.

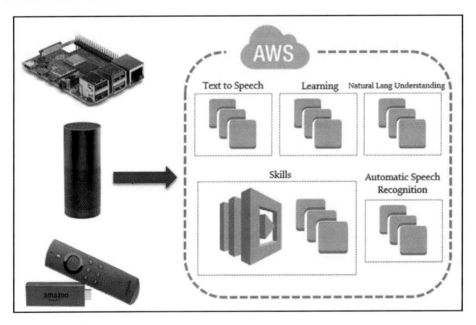

Figure 10-13: Uses of Alexa Service

Note: To use an Alexa skill, first, you need to have a developer account; go to ***developer.amazon.com*** and sign up with the same email address you use for ***alexa.amazon.com.***

How to Build Skill

To build skills, you will always need to start with the skilled service, which is the Lambda function. The next step is to build a skilled interface. The skill interface consists of the invocation name to enable the skill, intent schema, slot types, and utterances.

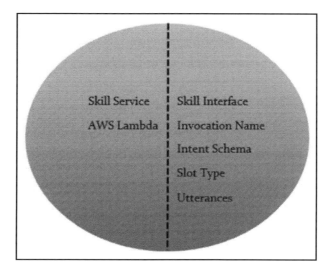

Figure 10-14: Base of Skill Building

Alexa Skill

Amazon Alexa is a cloud-based voice service that lets you create voice interactions for users who use your apps.

In the following section, we will use Amazon Polly service instead of building a serverless website. The Polly service will encode your Mp3 files straight to an S3 bucket. Then, Alexa skills will be used, and the Lambda function will also be built in terms of the Serverless Application Repository. It will be achieved by pointing the Lambda function to the S3 bucket, and then you can build Alexa Skills.

Lab 10-03: Build an Alexa Skill

In this lab, we will create an Alexa Skill of the application that was created in the previous lab, so that students can keep audible study notes with them. To create an Alexa skill, you will need to follow the defined steps to learn how you can use Alexa skill development.

1. Log in to AWS Management Console.
2. Go to Services.

3. Click on **S3**, which is present under **Storage**.

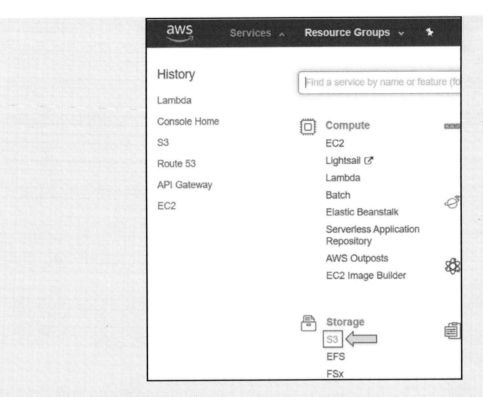

4. Click on the **ips-labs.co.uk** bucket.

5. Click on **Permissions**.

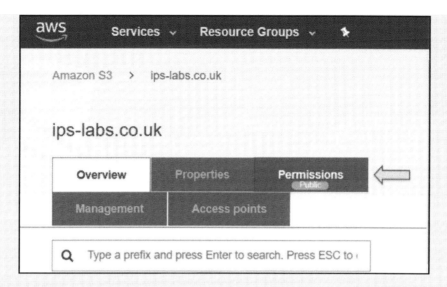

6. Go to Bucket Policy.

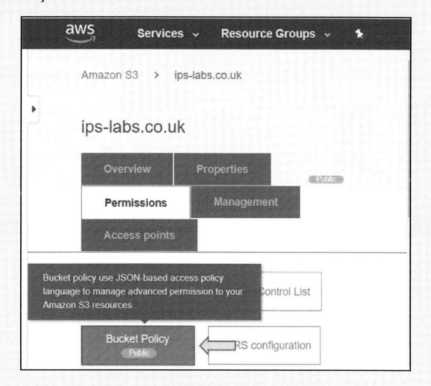

7. Copy the script, which is present in the resources section.

{

  "Version": "2012-10-17",

  "Statement": [

     {

       "Sid": "PublicReadGetObject",

```
        "Effect": "Allow",

        "Principal": "*",

        "Action": "s3:GetObject",

        "Resource": "arn:aws:s3:::ips-labs.co.uk/*"

      }

 ]

}
```

8. Paste the whole script in the bucket policy.
9. Change the name of the bucket.

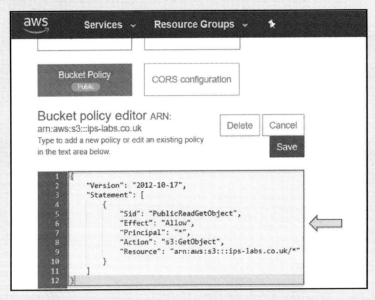

10. Click on **Save**.

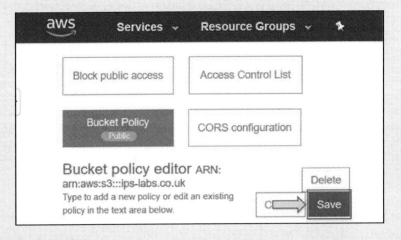

11. Copy the name of the bucket.

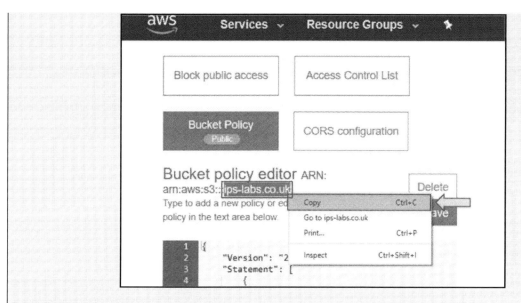

12. The bucket policy has now "Public".
13. Now, this bucket will be used to store MP3 files.
14. This MP3 file will be generated by using "Polly Service".
15. Go to "Services".
16. Click on **Amazon Polly**, which is present under **Machine Learning**.

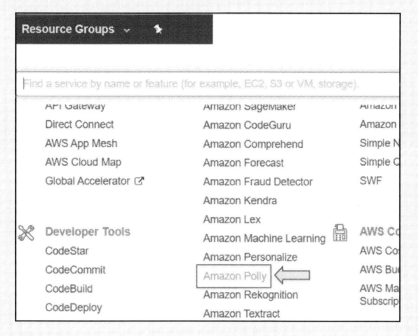

17. Click on **Get started**.

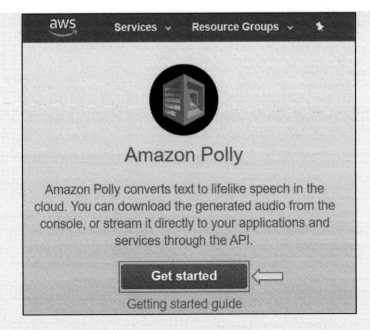

18. Write Welcome To IPSpecialist! It's a great publisher platform in plain text.

19. Choose the voice of your choice.
20. Click on Synthesize to S3.

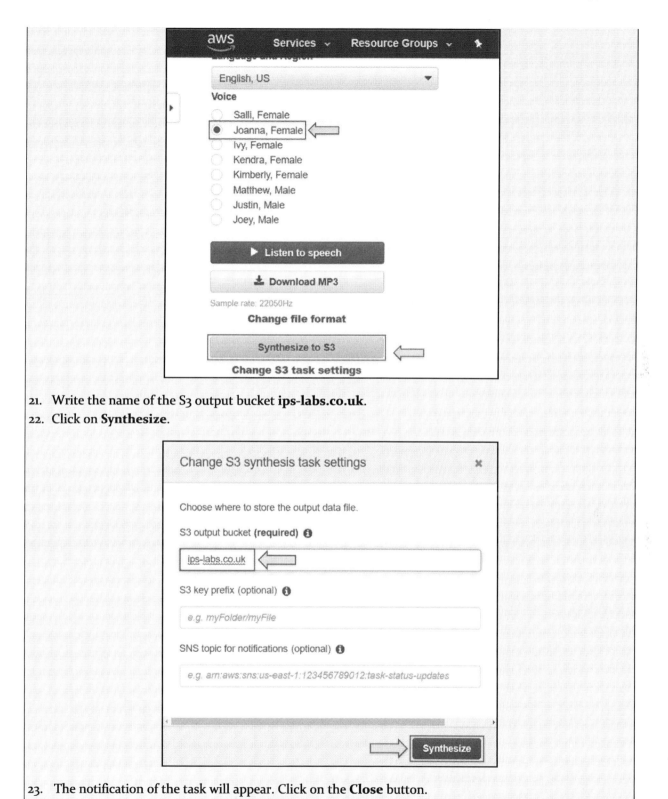

21. Write the name of the S3 output bucket **ips-labs.co.uk**.
22. Click on **Synthesize**.

23. The notification of the task will appear. Click on the **Close** button.

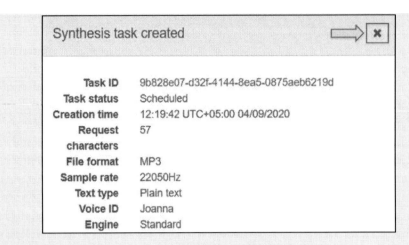

Note: The notification shows that a task is created to synthesize typed text into the MP3 file.

24. Click on **S3 synthesis tasks**, present on the left side menu.

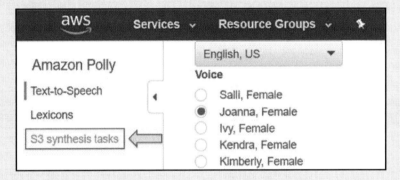

25. You will see that the task has been completed.

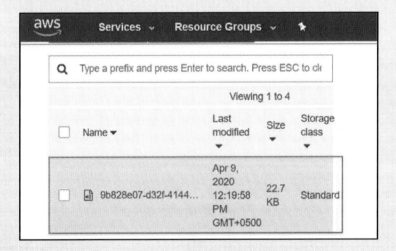

26. Go to **Service** and click on **S3**.
27. Click on ips-lab.co.uk.

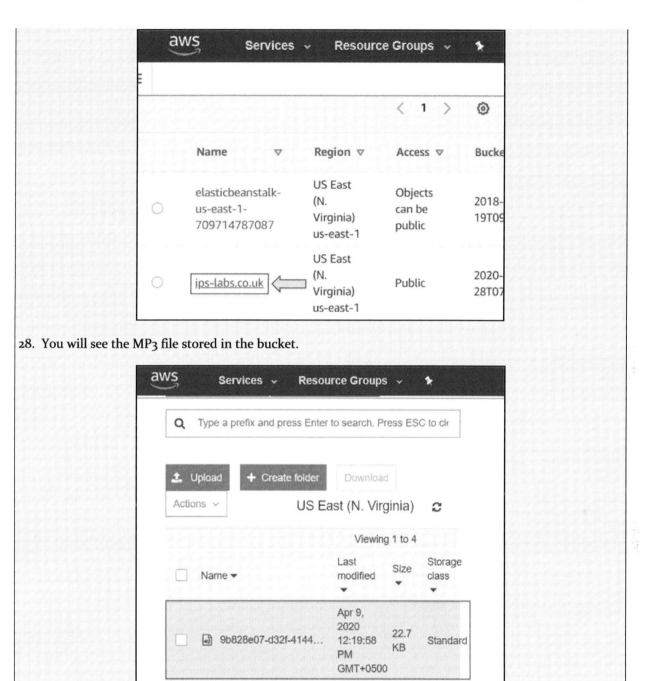

28. You will see the MP3 file stored in the bucket.

29. To create an **Alexa skill**, go to **Services**.
30. Click on **Lambda**.

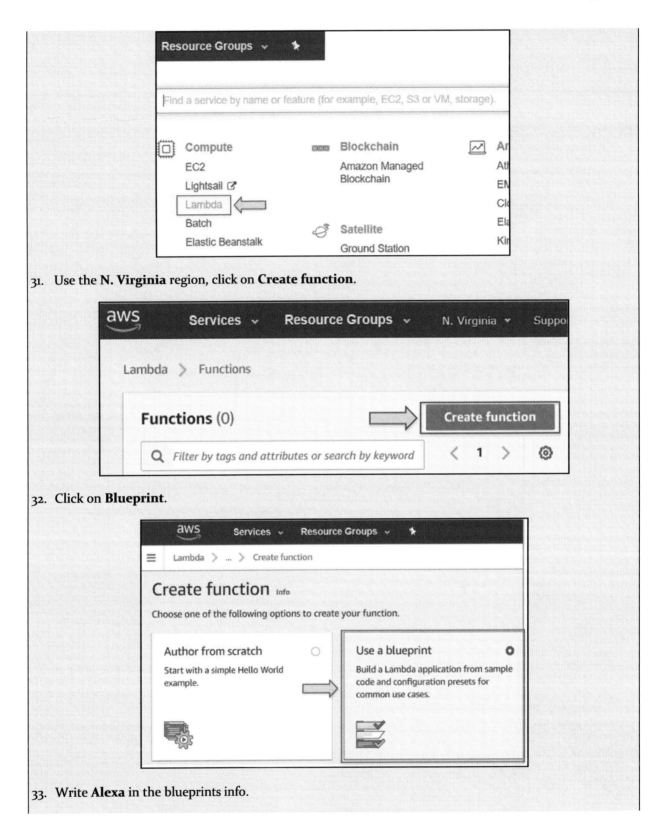

31. Use the **N. Virginia** region, click on **Create function**.

32. Click on **Blueprint**.

33. Write **Alexa** in the blueprints info.

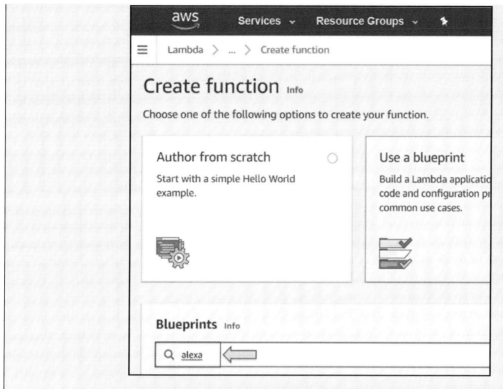

34. Click on Browse serverless application repository.

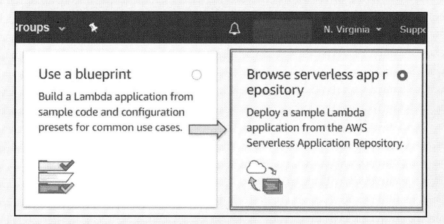

Note: The serverless applications are published by AWS, as well as AWS partners and other developers.

35. Select alexa-skills-kit-nodejs-factskill.

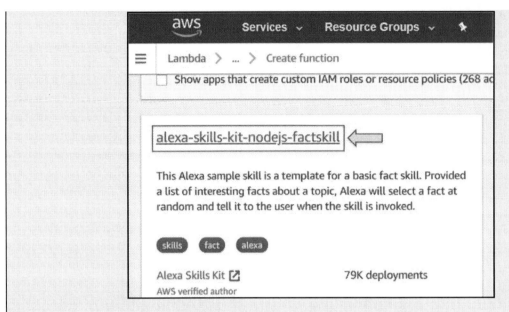

Note: Alexa-skills-kit-nodejs-factskill is the basic template that is used with the serverless applications repository.

36. Leave all the options as default. Click on **Deploy**.

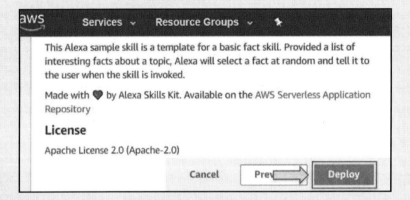

Note: This will deploy an Alexa skill to Lambda.

37. Go to **Services**.

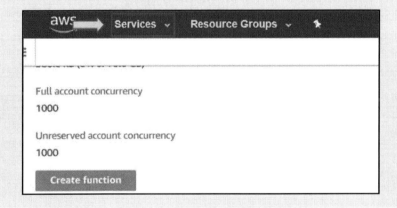

38. Click on **Lambda** to see your deployed skill.

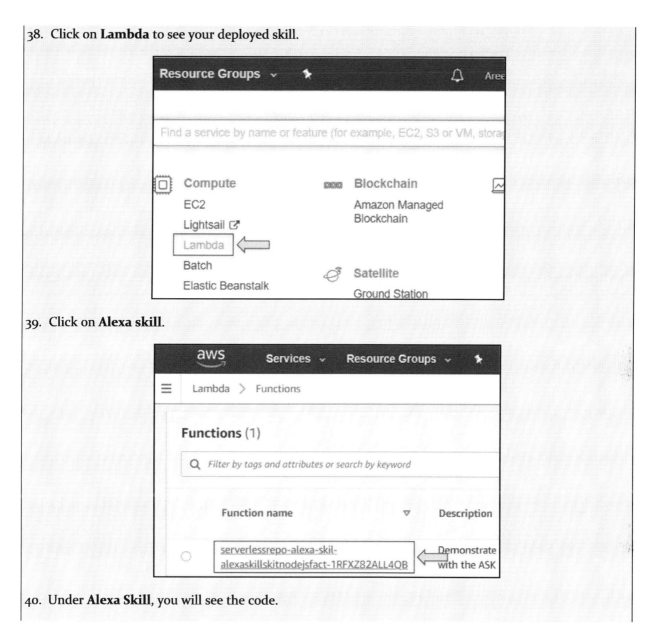

39. Click on **Alexa skill**.

40. Under **Alexa Skill**, you will see the code.

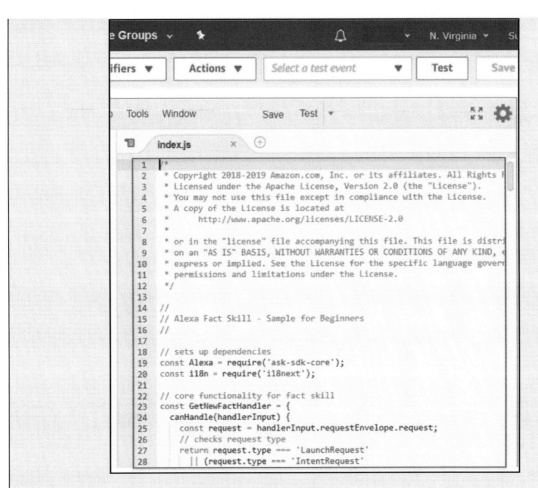

Note: This code will be read out during the function call.

41. Copy **ARN**.

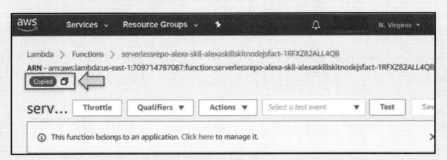

Note: You will need the ARN when you create a skill.

42. To create an Alexa skill, go to **developer.amazon.com**.
43. Click on **Alexa**.

44. Go to Alexa Console.
45. Click on **Skills**.

46. Alexa developer console will open.
47. Click on Create Skill.

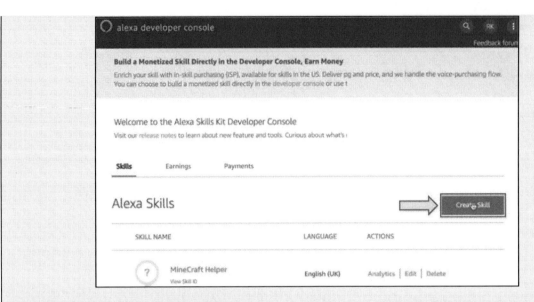

48. Write the skill name **MyStudyBuddy**.
49. Choose the default language as **English(US)**.

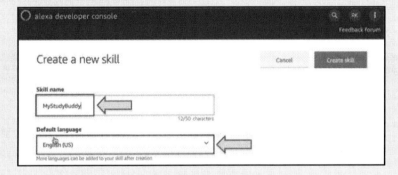

Note: Make sure you choose the default language that matches the Alexa device.

50. Click on Create skill.

51. Select the **Fact Skill** template and click on **Choose**.

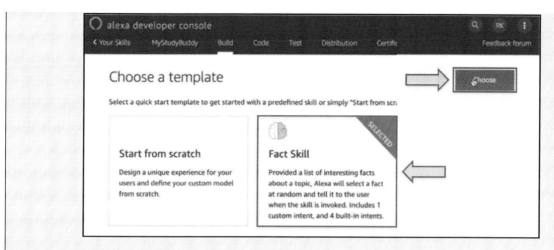

Note: The fact skill template will be used for serverless application repositories.

52. Click on **Invocation**.

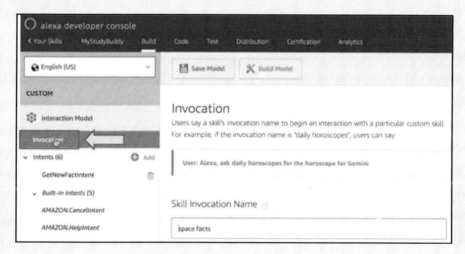

53. Write the invocation name **cloud facts**.
54. Click on **Save Model**.

55. Click on **Endpoint** before going to build the model.

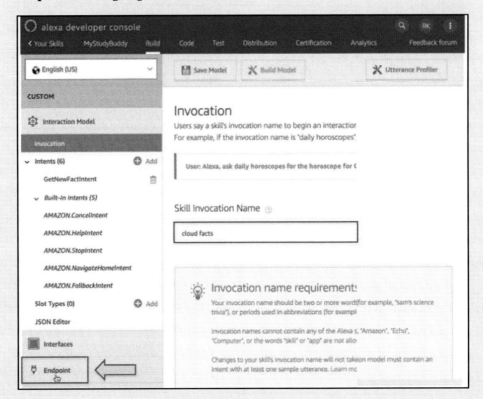

56. Paste the copied ARN in the default region space.

Note: This ARN points the skill to the Lambda function.

57. After entering the ARN, click on **Save Endpoints**.

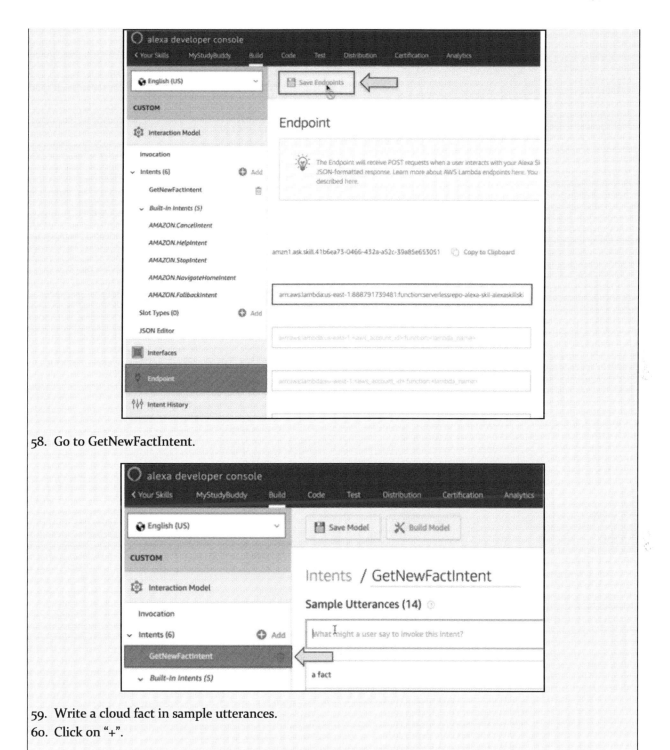

58. Go to GetNewFactIntent.

59. Write a cloud fact in sample utterances.
60. Click on "+".

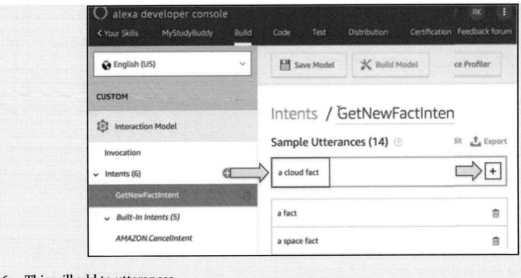

61. This will add to utterances.
62. Click on **Save Model**.

63. Click on **Build Model**.
64. After a while, the notification of **Build Successfully** will appear.

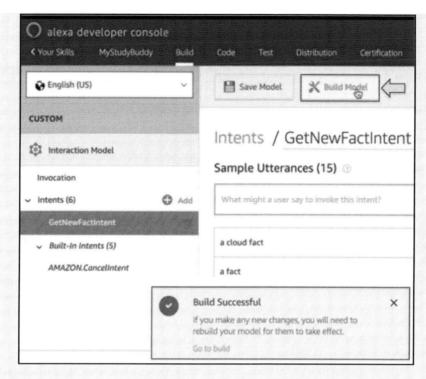

65. Click on **Test**.

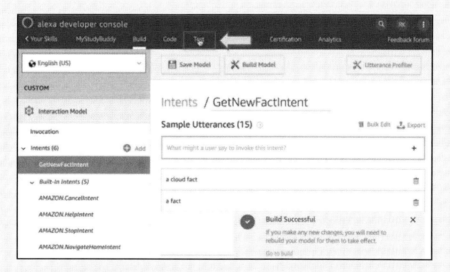

66. Turn the test on to **Development** to test the skill.

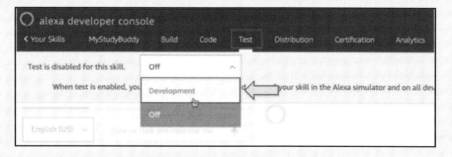

67. Write "open cloud facts" in the given space.

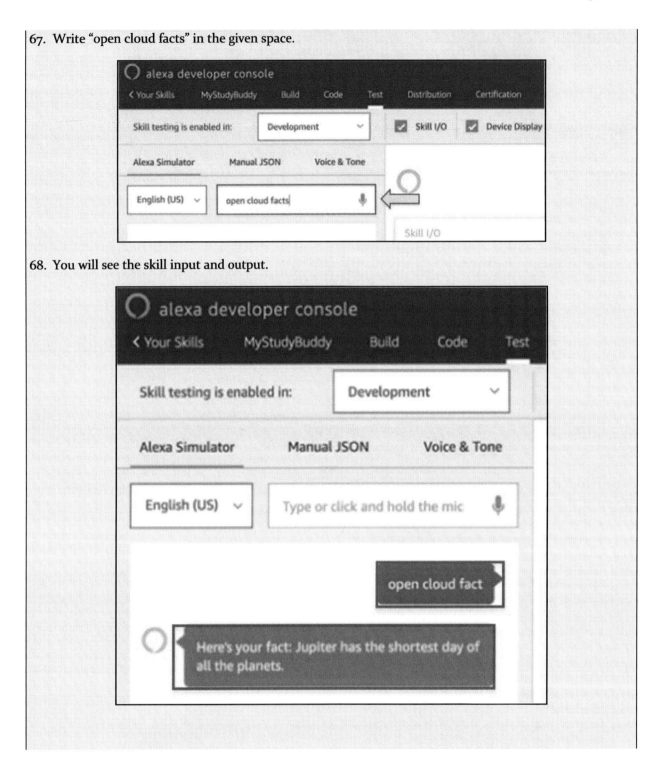

68. You will see the skill input and output.

Skill I/O

JSON Input

```
1 ▾ {
2       "version": "1.0",
3 ▾     "session": {
4           "new": true,
5           "sessionId": "amzn1.echo-api.session.e3b04efa-1123-4556-b65,
6 ▾         "application": {
7               "applicationId": "amzn1.ask.skill.41b6ea73-0466-432a-a5,
8           },
9 ▾         "user": {
10              "userId": "amzn1.ask.account.AFJQW5SSNDXDBF4XOXYTYDUJYV,
11          }
12      },
13 ▾    "context": {
14 ▾        "System": {
15 ▾            "application": {
16                  "applicationId": "amzn1.ask.skill.41b6ea73-0466-432(
17              },
18 ▾            "user": {
19                  "userId": "amzn1.ask.account.AFJQW5SSNDXDBF4XOXYTYD(
20              },
21 ▾            "device": {
22                  "deviceId": "amzn1.ask.device.AFOZSUCDPNERGUDJTPI3R)
23                  "supportedInterfaces": {}
24              },
25              "apiEndpoint": "https://api.eu.amazonalexa.com",
26              "apiAccessToken": "eyJ0eXAiOiJKV1QiLCJhbGciOiJSUzI1NiIs]
27          },
28 ▾        "Viewport": {
29 ▾            "experiences": [
30 ▾                {
31                      "arcMinuteWidth": 246,
```

Skill I/O

JSON Output

```
1 ▾
2 ▾   "body": {
3         "version": "1.0",
4 ▾       "response": {
5 ▾           "outputSpeech": {
6                 "type": "SSML",
7                 "ssml": "<speak>Here's your fact: Jupiter has the shor
8             },
9 ▾           "card": {
10                "type": "Simple",
11                "title": "Space Facts",
12                "content": "Jupiter has the shortest day of all the pl
13            },
14            "type": "_DEFAULT_RESPONSE"
15        },
16        "sessionAttributes": {},
17        "userAgent": "ask-node/2.0.0 Node/v8.10.0"
18    }
19
```

Note: The output shows that the lambda function talks back to you in the form of html.

69. Go back to the Lambda function.

70. Go to **IDE** and change the code to **Welcome To IPSpecialist**.

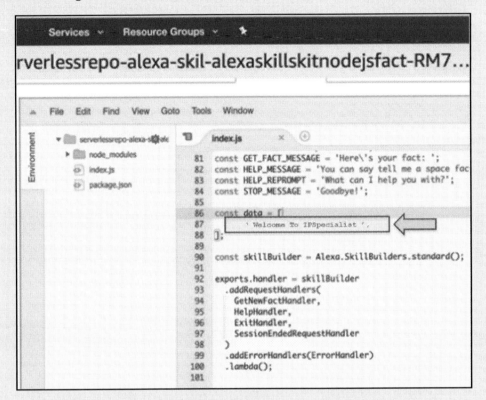

71. Go to **Alexa developer console** and write "open cloud fact" to check the output.

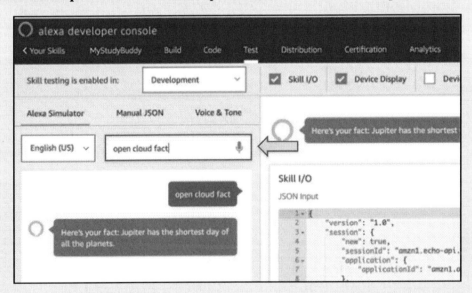

72. You will see the skill input and output.

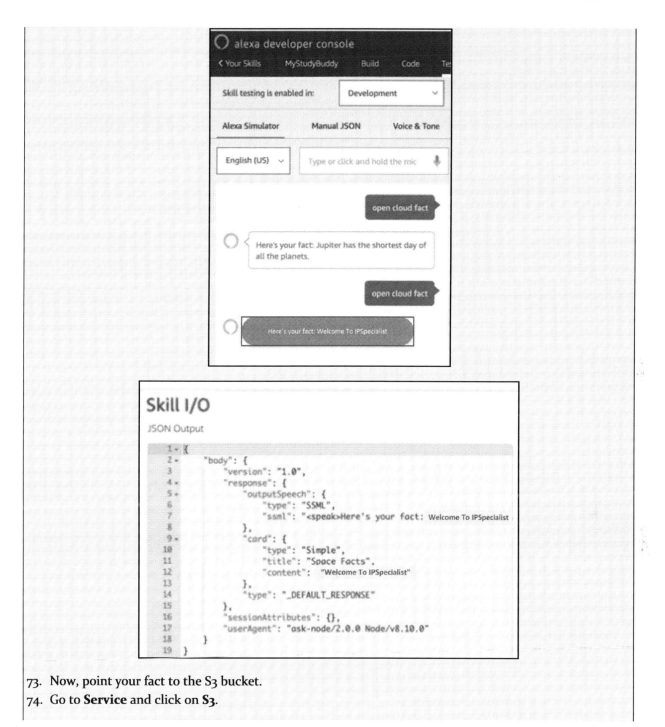

73. Now, point your fact to the S3 bucket.
74. Go to **Service** and click on **S3**.

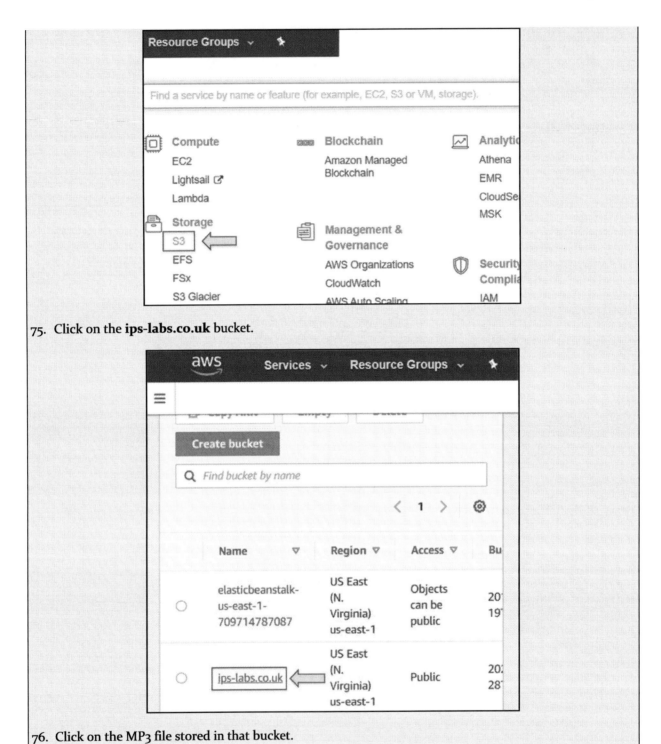

75. Click on the **ips-labs.co.uk** bucket.

76. Click on the MP3 file stored in that bucket.

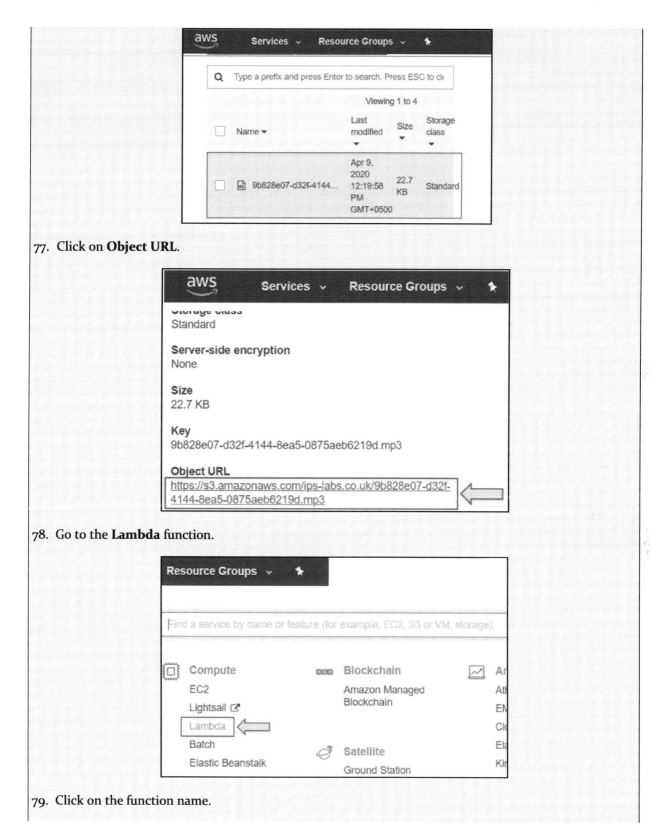

77. Click on **Object URL**.

78. Go to the **Lambda** function.

79. Click on the function name.

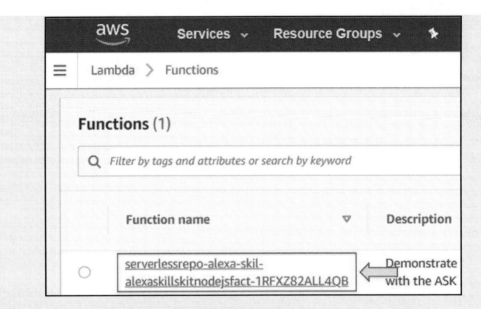

80. Paste the bucket link in the script.

Note: Change the script according to the audio source.

81. Go to the **Alexa** console and write "open cloud fact."

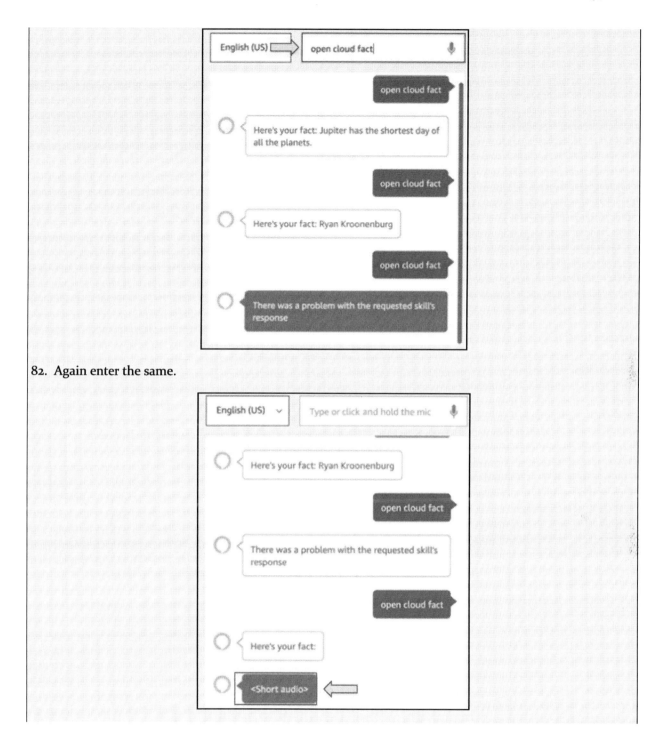

82. Again enter the same.

```
Skill I/O
JSON Output

1 ▾ {
2 ▾     "body": {
3           "version": "1.0",
4 ▾         "response": {
5 ▾             "outputSpeech": {
6                   "type": "SSML",
7                   "ssml": "<speak>Here's your fact: <audio src = \"ht|
8               },
9 ▾             "card": {
10                  "type": "Simple",
11                  "title": "Space Facts",
12                  "content": "<audio src = \"https://s3.amazonaws.com|
13              },
14              "type": "_DEFAULT_RESPONSE"
15          },
16          "sessionAttributes": {},
17          "userAgent": "ask-node/2.0.0 Node/v8.10.0"
18      }
19 }
```

Note: You will need to listen to the audio stored in the bucket.

Mind Map

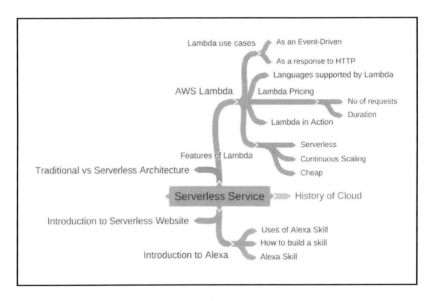

Figure 10-15: Mind Map of Serverless Service

Elastic Container Service (ECS)

Introduction

The SAA- C03 certification expects knowledge of architecting and deploying secure and robust applications on AWS technologies. The course includes a deep understanding of solutions using architectural design principles and provides implementation guidance.

Containers and Docker

Container

A standard way to package your configurations, application's code, and dependencies into a single object is provided by containers. Containers run as resource-isolated processes, ensuring quick, reliable, and consistent deployments, regardless of the environment, and share an Operating System (OS) installed on the server.

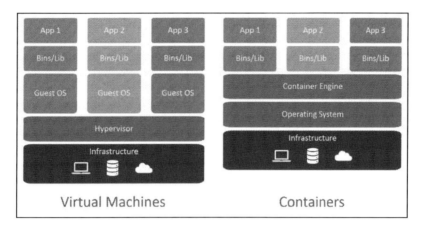

Figure 10-16: ECS

Physical or Virtual Machines

The infrastructure layer can be our physical machine in our data center, a virtual machine running in VMware, or even EC2 instances. Above that, we have a Hypervisor that controls how our virtual machines are allocated and operated. Within each virtual machine, we have layers such as our operating system application libraries, our application runtimes, and then our applications themselves sitting on top of those layers, containerized applications.

Container

Containers have the same infrastructure layers as physical or virtual machines. Above that, we host the operating system and your container engine; this would be Docker, for example.

Your container engine manages your Containers, and they will allocate memory and CPU on a per-container basis.

Dockers

Docker is a software-based platform that allows you to deploy, test, and build applications rapidly. Docker packages software into **containers** with everything that software needs to run, including system tools, runtime, libraries, and code. By using Docker, you can quickly scale applications, deploy them into any environment, and know the code will run.

Elastic Container Service

According to Amazon, Elastic Container Service (ECS) is a fast and highly scalable container management service that makes it trouble-free to stop, run, and manage Docker containers on a cluster.

- Manage container orchestration service
- Create clusters

- Manage fleets of container deployments
- ECS manages EC2 or Fargate instances
- Schedules containers for optimal placement
- Defines rules for CPU and memory requirements
- Monitors resources utilizations
- Deploy, update, rollback

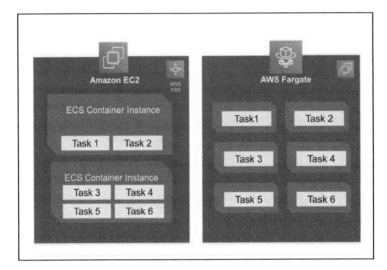

Figure 10-17: Amazon EC2 vs. AWS Fargate

ECS Components

Task Definitions

Task definition is a JSON format text file that describes one or more containers (up to a maximum of 10) that form our application.

Tasks

A task is the instant implementation of a task definition within a cluster.

Clusters

The logical grouping of services or tasks is termed an Amazon ECS cluster. You can list one or more Amazon EC2 instances with your cluster to run tasks on them. Or, you can use the serverless infrastructure Fargate provides to run tasks.

Container Agent

The container agent is the one that runs on each container instance inside an Amazon ECS cluster. The container agent sends information about the resource utilization and the resource's current running tasks to Amazon ECS. It stops and starts tasks whenever it receives a request from Amazon ECS.

Container and Images

A container is a systematic software development unit containing everything a software application needs to run, including relevant runtime, code, system libraries tools, and system tools. A read-only template creates containers called an image.

Fargate

A serverless compute engine that works with both Amazon Elastic Kubernetes Service (EKS) and Amazon Elastic Container Service (ECS) is AWS Fargate. Fargate makes it simple to focus on building applications. Fargate eliminates the need to provision and manage servers, lets you specify and pay for resources per application, and improves security through application isolation by design.

Elastic Kubernetes Service (EKS)

- Also known as K8S, it is open-source software that lets you deploy and manage containerized applications at scale
- Same toolset on-premises and in the cloud
- Containers are grouped in pods
- Like ECS, EKS supports both EC2 and Fargate deployment models

Why EKS?

- Already using Kubernetes
- Migrates your application workloads to AWS

Elastic Container Registry (ECR)

- Managed Docker container registry in AWS
- Stores, manages, and deploys container images
- Integrated with both ECS and EKS
- Works with premises deployments, just like Docker hub can
- Highly available
- Integrated with IAM
- Pay for storage and data transfer similar to S3

ECS + ELB

- Distribute traffic evenly across the tasks in your service
- Support the application load balancer, network load balancer, and classic load balancer load
- Use NLB or CLB to route TCP (layer four) traffic
- Both EC2 and Fargate launch types support them
- Application Load Balancer (ALB) allows
  o Dynamic host port mapping
  o Path-based routing
  o Priority rules
- ALB is recommended over the network or classic load balancers

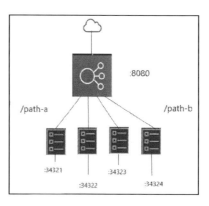

ECS Security

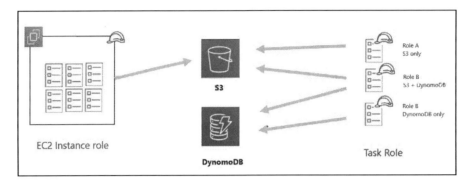

Figure 10-18-: ECS Security Test a Bot

Demo 10-01: Get Started with Amazon Elastic Container Service Using Fargate

Follow the given steps to Get Started

1. Navigate to console.aws.amazon.com.

2. Log in to the AWS Management Console.

3. From All Service, click and open Amazon Elastic Container Service (ECS).

4. Click on **Get started**.

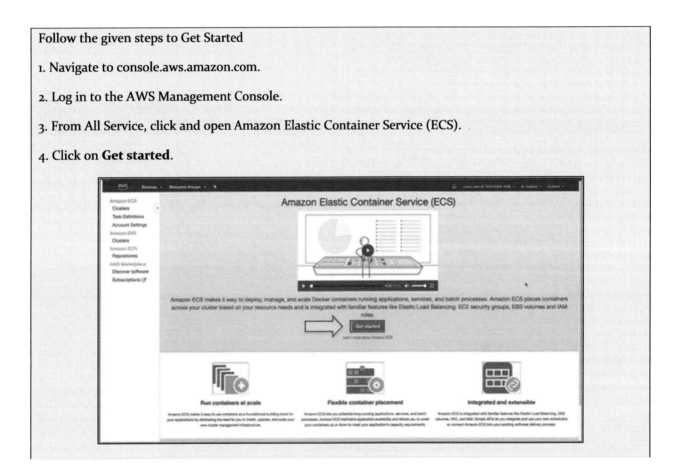

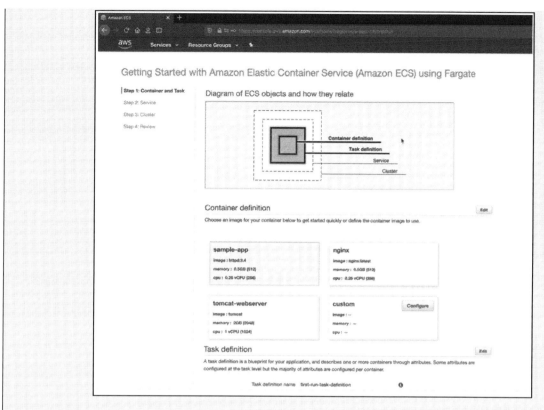

5. The overview page of the Amazon Elastic Container Service will appear.

6. You can start running quickly using one of these examples here. We will be selecting a sample app running **httpd 2.4. 3**. This is the Apache webserver.

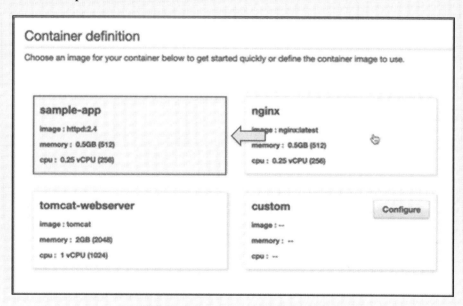

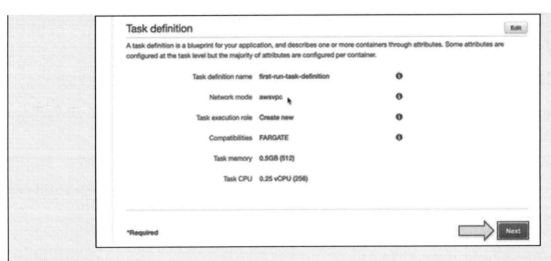

7. We need to define our service. This is going to maintain a specified number of simultaneous instances of our task.

8. Select the number of desired tasks '1'.

9. Click on **Next**.

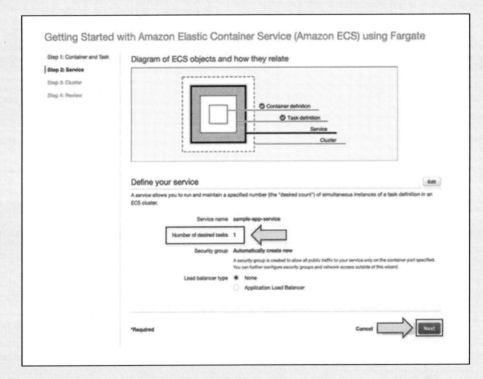

10. We will configure our cluster. Write a cluster name.

11. Click on **Next**.

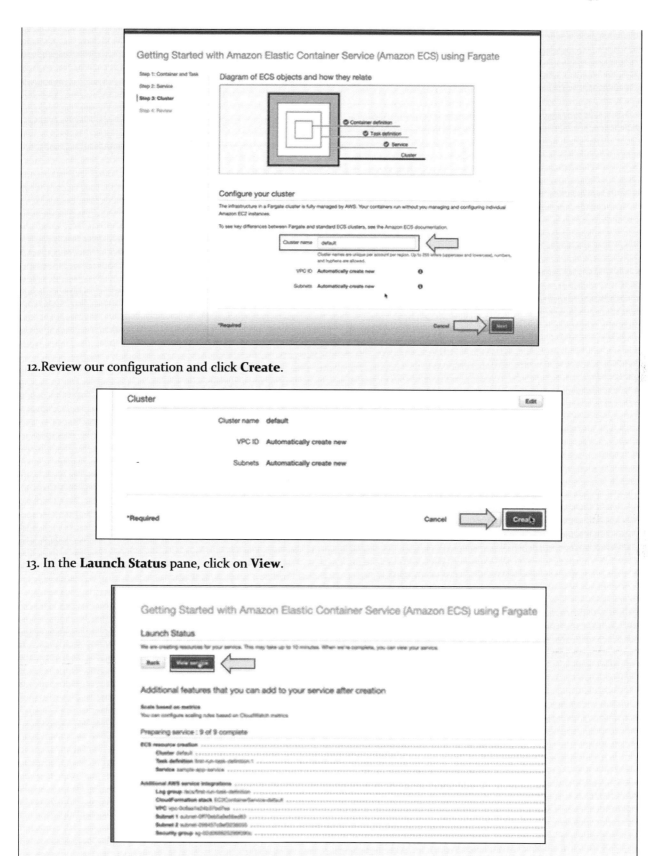

12. Review our configuration and click **Create**.

13. In the **Launch Status** pane, click on **View**.

14. Our ECS services are now complete.

15. Click on **Task** to see that it is now in the running state and our pending count is zero. Our running count is one.

16. Click on **Yes** to connect to the remote computer.

17. Now, go to **Task**.

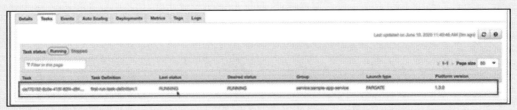

18. You will see it gets both a private and a public IP. Copy out this public IP and open that in a new tab in the browser.

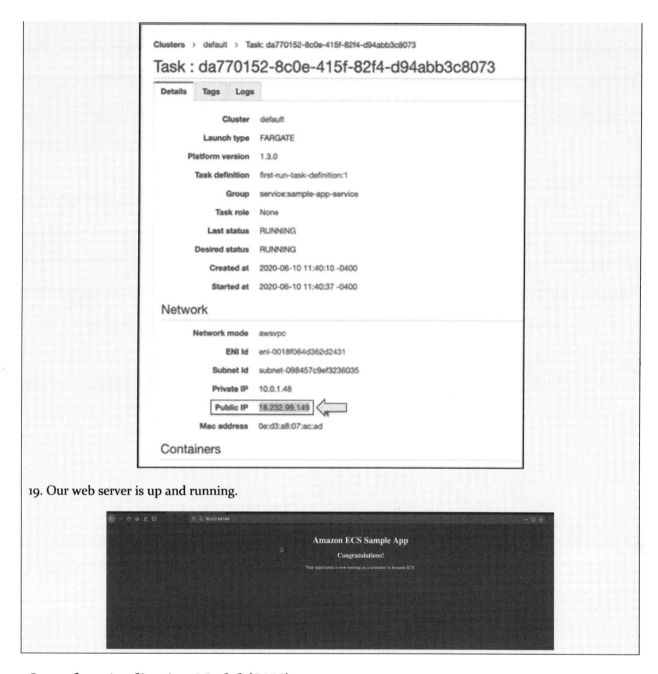

19. Our web server is up and running.

Serverless Application Model (SAM)

SAM is an open-source framework allowing you to build serverless applications easily. This is a Cloud Formation extension optimized for serverless applications. On top of the Cloud Formation, SAM defines the number of new resource types. The new resource can be functions, APIs, tables in Dynamo DB, etc. With a few configuration lines, you can easily define the application of your choice and the model using SAM.

The SAM supports all the things that Cloud Formation supports. You can also run your serverless applications locally using documents. This will help test the applications without activating any AWS resources.

SAM can also be used to package and deploy your applications using CodeDeploy. The following figure shows the anatomy of the SAM template.

The first section informs the Cloud Formation that this is a SAM template. When you deploy the SAM template, Cloud Formation recognizes and transforms it internally with something to a little more level.

The second section of the template is called global. It applies the same properties to all random functions defined in the SAM template. All functions have the same attributes, such as function timing. The function timing is not required to repeat in every single resource.

The third section of the SAM template is called the resources section. This section creates a Lambda Function from the local code. Also, it creates an API Gateway mapping and permissions for you automatically. It is much simpler than defining to do in the simple Cloud Formation.

The last section is called the output section. It gives some relevant information in terms of the output gateway endpoint URL that is automatically generated for you, along with the Lambda Functions ARN and the IAM role that are also created automatically.

```
AWSTemplateFormatVersion: '2010-09-09'
Transform: AWS::Serverless-2016-10-31
Description: Hello World SAM Template

Globals:
  Function:
    Timeout: 3

Resources:
  HelloWorldFunction:
    Type: AWS::Serverless::Function
    Properties:
      CodeUri: hello_world/
      Handler: app.lambda_handler
      Runtime: python3.8
      Events:
        HelloWorld:
          Type: Api
          Properties:
            Path: /hello
            Method: get

Outputs:
  HelloWorldApi:
    Description: "API Gateway endpoint URL for Prod stage for Hello World function"
    Value: !Sub "https://${ServerlessRestApi}.execute-api.${AWS::Region}.amazonaws.com/Prod/hello/"
  HelloWorldFunction:
    Description: "Hello World Lambda Function ARN"
    Value: !GetAtt HelloWorldFunction.Arn
  HelloWorldFunctionIamRole:
    Description: "Implicit IAM Role created for Hello World function"
    Value: !GetAtt HelloWorldFunctionRole.Arn
```

Figure 10-19: Example

Mind Map

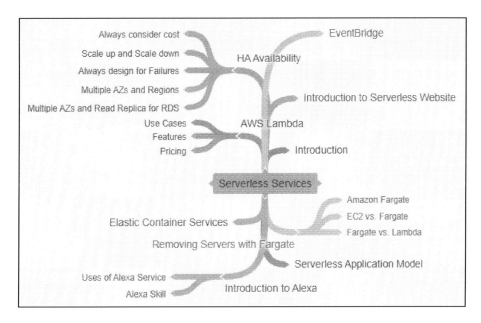

Figure 10-20: Mind Map

Practice Questions

1. Serverless Architecture can be defined as _____ and _____. (Choose two)
a) On-premises management and provision of services
b) Applications that you are required to maintain
c) It is a cloud-based execution model where the cloud service providers act as the server and manage the allocation of resources dynamically
d) Applications that do not require you to provision and manage services

2. AWS Lambda is a _____ service.
a) Compute
b) Storage
c) Machine Learning
d) Migration

3. Lambda is event-driven, so it can be described as _____.
a) PaaS
b) SaaS
c) FaaS
d) IaaS

4. Alexa is an Amazon service that is used to _____.
a) Create distribution networks
b) Distribute the workloads
c) Import code files to Lambda
d) Create voice experiences

5. Which of the following services is an abstraction layer focusing only on the code?

a) Amazon S3
b) Amazon Polly
c) Amazon EC2
d) AWS Lambda

6. AWS Lambda can be used as compute service in response to _____.

a) HTTP request
b) UDP
c) SMTP
d) All of the above

7. Which AWS service allows you to debug the serverless application?

a) Amazon S3
b) AWS X-Ray
c) Amazon AMI
d) Amazon Route 53

8. In serverless architecture, which AWS service is present at the front-end to serve the request?

a) AWS Lambda
b) Dynamo DB
c) API Gateway
d) Elastic Load Balancer

9. Lambda pricing depends on _____ and _____. (Choose two)

a) Number of Requests
b) Only one user
c) Number of SNS
d) Duration

10. Which of the following services is used to build skill architecture?

a) Alexa
b) Outposts
c) CodeBuild
d) CodeDeploy

11. In which direction does AWS Lambda scale automatically?

a) Scale up
b) Scale down
c) Scale-out
d) Scale-in

12. In serverless architecture, which of the following databases would normally be used?

a) RDS

b) MySQL

c) PostgreSQL

d) Dynamo DB

13. Which Alexa skill is used for "Serverless Applications Repository"?

a) alexa-skill-kit-sdk-factskill

b) alexa-skill-kit-color-expert

c) alexa-skill-kit-sdk-howtoskill

d) alexa-skill-kit-color-expert-python

14. Which service can be used to convert text into audio speech?

a) Amazon Lex

b) Amazon Kendra

c) Amazon Polly

d) None of the above

15. Which of the following Lambda functions is used for the deployment of AWS applications?

a) Author from scratch

b) Serverless Application Repository

c) Blueprints

d) All of the above

16. Which software platform allows you to build, test, and deploy applications quickly?

a) Docker

b) Container

c) Both of them

d) None of the above

17. Which serverless compute engine for containers works with both Amazon Elastic Container Service (ECS) and Amazon Elastic Kubernetes Service (EKS)?

a) EKS

b) ELB

c) ECR

d) Fargate

18. Which service migrates your application workloads to AWS?

a) ECR

b) ELB

c) EKS

d) None of the above

19. What are grouped in pods?

a) Docker

b) Containers

c) Both of them

d) None of the above

20. What removes the need to provision and manage servers?

a) Fargate

b) ECR

c) ELB

d) None of the above

Chapter 11: Advanced IAM

AWS Directory Service

AWS Directory Service allows you to manage Microsoft Active Directory (AD). It is a collection of managed services rather than a single service. In the AWS Cloud, AWS Directory Service makes creating and managing directories simple. This cloud-based standalone directory allows users to utilize their existing corporate credentials to access AWS services and apps. The AWS Directory service also provides a single sign-on for any EC2 instance that is part of a domain. If your fleet is connected to an Active Directory domain, you do not need to manage the credentials on any individual EC2 instances.

What is Active Directory?
Active Directory is an on-premises directory service used by most enterprises. It is a hierarchical database of users, groups, and computers organized in a pattern of trees and forests. You can apply group policies to help you manage users and devices on a network. Active Directory is built on the LDAP (Lightweight Directory Access Protocol) and DNS (Domain Name System) technologies (Domain Name Service). Kerberos, LDAP, and NTLM authentication protocols are all supported. Active Directory is designed to be set up in a highly available manner, necessitating many servers.

Microsoft Compatible Services

AWS Managed Microsoft AD
Microsoft AD provides AWS Managed Services AD domain controllers running on real Windows servers. For high availability, you get two domain controllers by default. Each of them has its availability zone. Applications in your VPCs can connect to these domain controllers. Additional domain controllers can be added to boost availability or transaction rates, and you have unique access to them. Those domain controllers will not be shared with any other AWS users. As a result, it is quite safe. An AD trust can also be used to expand your existing Active Directory to your on-premises architecture.

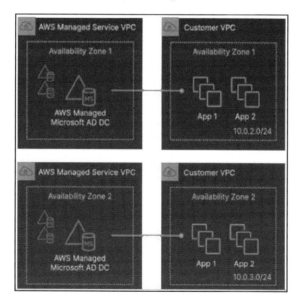

Figure 11-01: AWS Managed Microsoft AD

Responsibilities of AWS and Customer

AWS manages some aspects of the service for you while you, as the customer, are responsible for some other elements.

Responsibilities of AWS:

1. AWS performs a multi-AZ deployment for you and provides high availability.

2. AWS is responsible for patching, monitoring, and recovering your domain controllers.

3. AWS performs instance rotation for the customers, ensuring they are always on the latest software version.

4. AWS also performs backup operations like snapshotting and restoring for the customers.

Responsibilities of the Customer:

1. The customer is concerned with users, groups, and group policy objects.

2. The customer can use standard AD tools they are already familiar with.

3. If the customer wants to scale out the domain controllers, it is their responsibility.

4. The customer can employ AD trusts to form a resource forest.

5. Customer is also responsible for the management of any certificate authorities using LDAP.

6. Customer is responsible for creating AD Federation as well.

Simple AD

Simple AD can be utilized in the cloud as a standalone directory to support Windows applications that require minimal AD functionalities. Your Simple AD can be deployed in two different sizes. Small is for less than 500 people, while large is for up to 5,000 members. It will make it easier to handle services like EC2 instances if you want to connect to those EC2 instances using your existing corporate credentials rather than having to provision usernames and passwords for all of them or manage any kind of keys. Any Linux workload that requires LDAP is an excellent candidate for implementing basic AD.

> **EXAM TIP:** Simple AD cannot manage AD. In other words, you cannot join Simple AD to your on-premises AD infrastructure.

AD Connector

AD Connector can be used when using your existing on-premises directory with compatible AWS services. AD Connector is an on-premises directory gateway or proxy. It prevents the information from being cached in the cloud and allows on-premises users to log into AWS using Active Directory. You can connect your AWS EC2 instances to your existing on-premises AD domain and scale across many AD connectors as your needs grow.

> **EXAM TIP:** Other AWS accounts cannot use the AD Connector. Consider using AWS Managed Microsoft AD to Share your directory if needed.

Cloud Directory

Amazon Cloud Directory is a highly available multi-tenant directory-based store in AWS. With Cloud Directory, you can organize directory objects into multiple hierarchies to support many organizational pivots and relationships across directory information. You can utilize Cloud Directory to build directories for various purposes, including organizational charts, course catalogs, and device registries. The Cloud Directory service is fully managed. It removes time-consuming and costly administrative duties like infrastructure scaling and server management.

Amazon Cognito User Pools

Cognito user pools are a SaaS application's managed user directory. In Amazon Cognito, a user pool is a user directory. Users can sign in to your online or mobile app using Amazon Cognito if they have a user pool. To sign in, users can use social identity providers like Google, Facebook, Amazon, and Apple, as well as SAML identity providers. All members of the user pool have a directory profile that you may access through a Software Development Kit (SDK), whether they join up directly or through a third party.

AD Compatible vs. Non-AD Compatible Services

The AD-compatible services are Managed Microsoft AD, also known as directory service for Microsoft Active Directory, AD connector, and Simple AD. These services enable users to sign in to AWS applications like Amazon workspaces and QuickSight with their Active Directory credentials.

However, Cloud Directory and Cognito user pools are non-AD-compatible services. Suppose you are a developer and do not need Active Directory. In that case, you can create a cloud directory that organizes and manages hierarchical information, and Cognito user pools work with mobile and web applications.

IAM Policies

Amazon Resource Name (ARN)
AWS resources are identified by their Amazon Resource Names (ARNs). When you need to explicitly specify a resource across AWS, such as in IAM policies, Amazon Relational Database Service (Amazon RDS) tags, and API requests, you will need an ARN.

General Format of ARN

Arn : partition : service : region : account-id

Partition: The location of the resource in the partition. A group of AWS Regions is referred to as a partition. Each AWS account has a single partition assigned to it.

The following partitions are supported:

- ✓ aws -AWS Regions
- ✓ aws-cn - China Regions
- ✓ aws-us-gov - AWS GovCloud (US) Regions

- **Service:** The service namespace that identifies the AWS product. For example, s3 for Amazon S3, EC2 RDS, DynamoDB, etc.
- **Region:** The Region code. For example, us-east-2 for US East (Ohio).
- **Account id:** The account id consists of 12 digits. The AWS account ID owns the resource without the hyphens—for example, 123456789012.
- **Resource id:** This component of the ARN can be either the resource's name, ID, or path. For example, for an IAM user, use user/Bob, or for an EC2 instance, use instance/i-1234567890abcdef0. A parent resource (sub-resource-type/parent-resource/sub-resource) or a qualification such as a version are examples of resource identifiers (resource-type:resource-name:qualifier).
- All ARNs begin with a string that follows this structure and end with a form resource or resource type and a qualifier.

The structure might end with:

- resource
- resource_type/resource
- resource_type/resource/qualifier
- resource_type/resource: qualifier
- resource_type:resource
- resource_type:resource: qualifier

Some examples of ARN:

1. arn: aws: iam: : 123456789012: user/ mark
   In this example, we have an IAM user. It starts with ARN AWS, the service name IAM and two colons. IAM is a global region, which means it does not exist in a particular region. It is an omitted value. We skip over that value using two consecutive colons. We have our 12-digit account ID followed by a resource type /resource. In this case, the resource type is user, and the resource is Mark.
2. arn: aws: s3: : :my_awesome_bucket/image.png

It is the ARN for a specific object inside a bucket in S3. We have ARN, AWS, the S3 service, and three colons because no specific region or account ID is needed to identify an object within S3 uniquely. All bucket names in S3 are globally unique. You do not need additional qualifiers for uniqueness. We have the bucket name /object name.

3. arn: aws: dynamodb: us-east-1 : 123456789012: table/orders

This is a single table within DynamoDB. We have ARN, AWS, DynamoDB, colon the region name because DynamoDB is a regional service, our 12-digit account ID, and then our resource type, i.e., table and resource name, i.e., orders.

4. arn: aws: ec2: us-east-1: 123456789012: instance/*

We use ARNs to specify not just a single resource but all resources of a particular type. If we want to refer to all EC2 instances within a single account in a region, we would have ARN, AWS, EC2, US East1 because EC2

is a regional service, our 12-digit account ID, and our resource type, i.e., instance followed by a star. We use a star as a wild card. This represents all EC2 instances in that account in that region.

IAM Policies

When coupled with an identity or resource, a policy is an object in AWS that determines its rights. When creating a permissions policy to restrict access to a resource, you can pick between an Identity-based policy and a Resource-based policy.

- **Identity-based policies**: These policies associate links to a specific IAM user, group, or role. You can determine what that identity can do with these policies (its permissions). You can, for example, attach the policy to the IAM user John, granting him access to the Amazon EC2 RunInstances action. According to the policy, John can receive items from an Amazon DynamoDB table named MyCompany. You can also give John complete control over his IAM security credentials. Policies based on identity can be managed or applied in real-time.
- **Resource-based policies** are policies that are linked to a specific resource. Resource-based policies can be applied to Amazon S3 buckets, Amazon SQS queues, and AWS Key Management Service encryption keys. You can specify who has access to a resource and what activities they can execute using resource-based policies.

An IAM policy does not affect the role unless it is attached. You must attach that policy to an identity or a resource. Unless the policies are attached, they are simply structured as a list of statements.

Basic Format of an IAM Policy

```
{
    "Version" : "2012-10-17",
    "Statement" : [
        {
            .....
        },
        {
            .....
        },
        {
            .....
        }
    ]
}
```

This is a JSON statement; it starts with a version number. The version number helps AWS identify the structure of the document. A policy document is a list of statements. The square brackets represent an array or a list. Each statement is enclosed in curly braces. Here we have three statements in our policy. Each statement matches an AWS API request.

An API request is any action that you could perform against AWS. For example, when we start an EC2 instance, create a table in DynamoDB, or get an object from S3 that is an API request.

Example of an IAM Policy

```
{
    "Version" : "2012-10-17",
    "Statement" : [
        {
            "Sid" : "SpecificTable",
            "Effect" : "Allow",
            "Action" : [
                "dynamodb: BatchGet*",
                "dynamodb: DescribeStream",
                "dynamodb: DescribeTable",
                "dynamodb: Get*",
                "dynamodb: Query",
                "dynamodb: Scan",
                "dynamodb: BatchWrite*",
                "dynamodb: CreateTable",
                "dynamodb: Delete*",
                "dynamodb: Update*",
                "dynamodb: PutItem"
            ],
            "Resource" : "arn: aws: dynamodb: *: *: table/MyTable"
        }
    ]
}
```

```
}
```

Our IAM policy, in this case, starts with SID. It is a string that humans can read. We have an effect, and we can either accept or disallow it. Our IAM policy can accept or disallow particular operations on a given resource. This IAM policy works with DynamoDB, and the policy is matched based on these actions. Actions are of the form, service name, colon action name, and (some of them) wild cards at the end in the form of a star. Any API request that begins with that string is referred to as such. We also have the resource that is being targeted by this action. This IAM policy grants access to this resource for all of these actions. In this example, it is a table known as "my table."

Lab 11-01: Creating and Applying an IAM Policy

1. Log into AWS Console.

2. Go to **Services** and click on **IAM**. Select **Policies**.

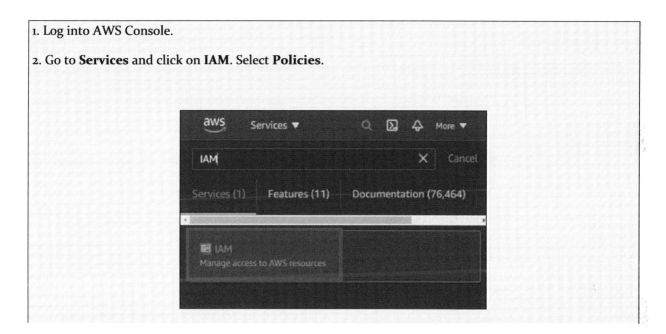

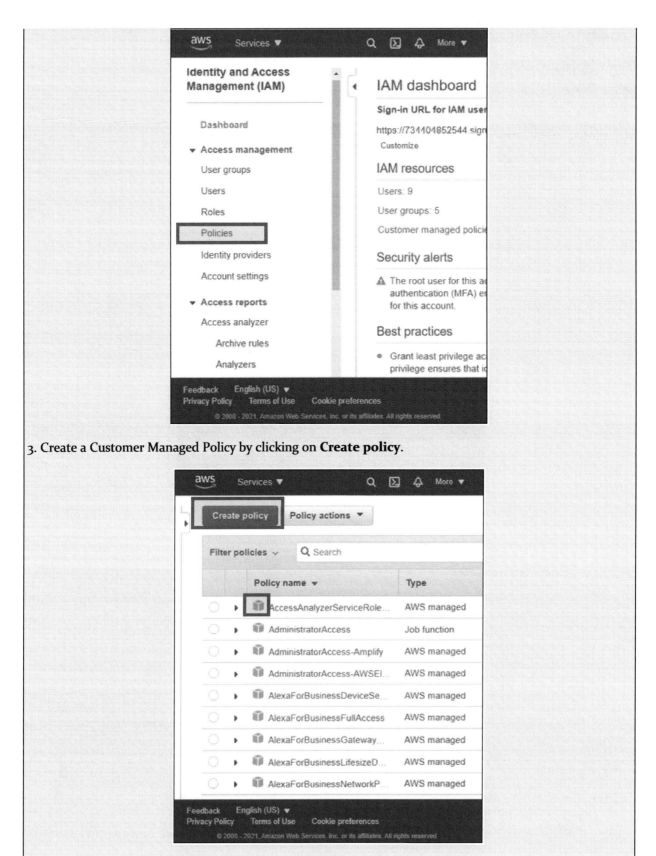

3. Create a Customer Managed Policy by clicking on **Create policy**.

4. You can either use the visual editor or directly input them using JSON.

5. Click on **JSON** and paste the statement given below.

```
{
  "Version": "2012-10-17",
  "Statement" : [
    {
      "Effect": "Allow",
      "Action": ["s3:ListBucket"],
      "Resource":["arn:aws:s3:::test"]
    },
    {
      "Effect": "Allow",
      "Action": [
        "s3:PutObject",
        "s3:GetObject",
        "s3:DeleteObject"
      ],
      "Resource": ["arn:aws:s3:::test/*"]
    }
  ]
```

}

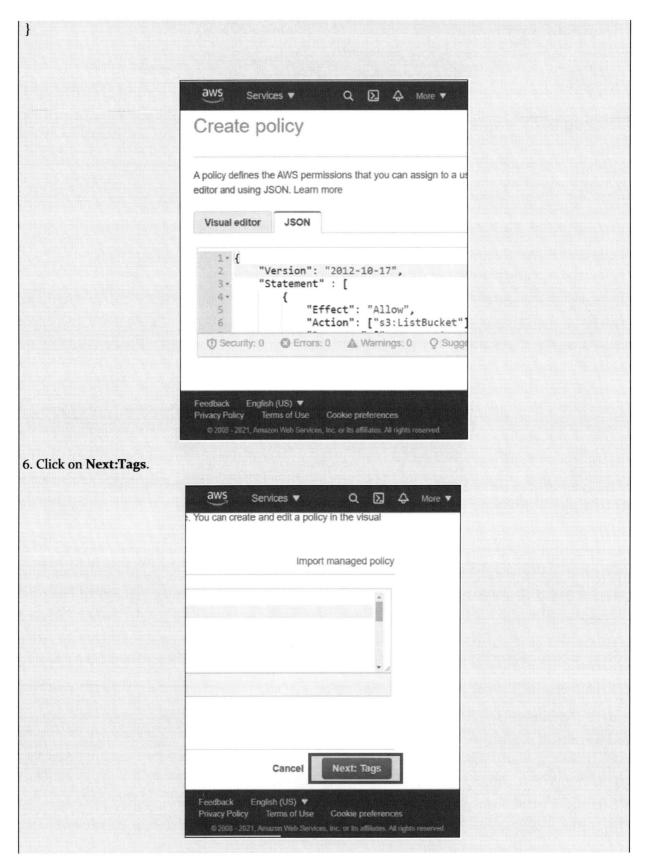

6. Click on **Next:Tags**.

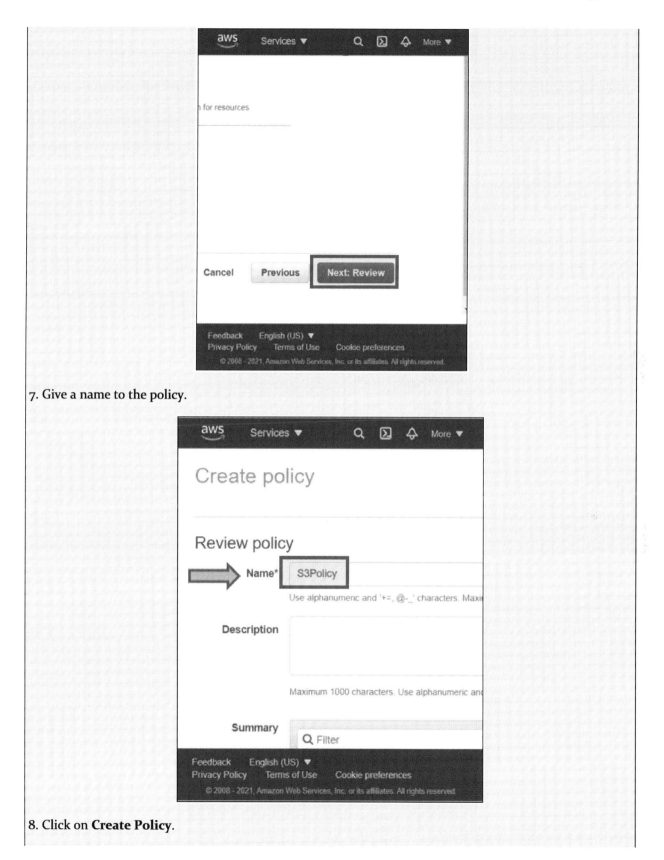

7. Give a name to the policy.

8. Click on **Create Policy**.

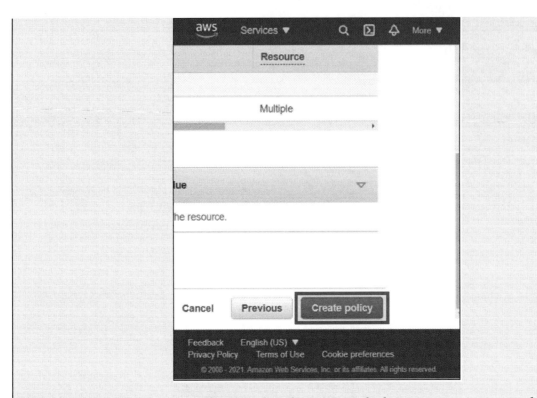

We know that a policy does not affect the role unless it is attached. So, we are going to attach the policy to a role.

9. Go to **Roles**.

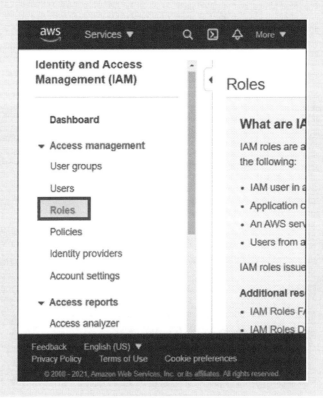

10. Click on **Create role**.

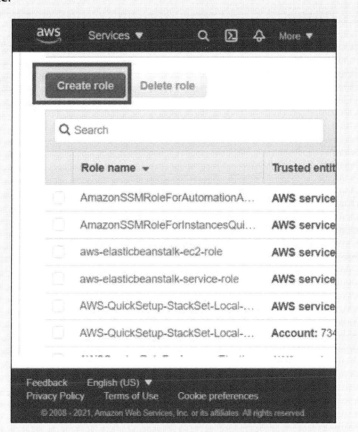

11. If we want to allow EC2 instances access to the S3 test bucket and the three API calls in our policy, we must select **AWS service** and **EC2**.

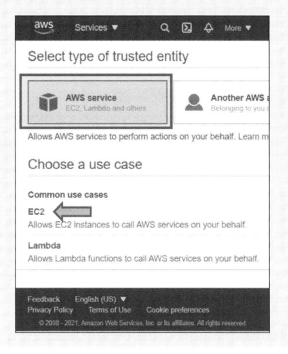

12. Click on Next: Permissions.

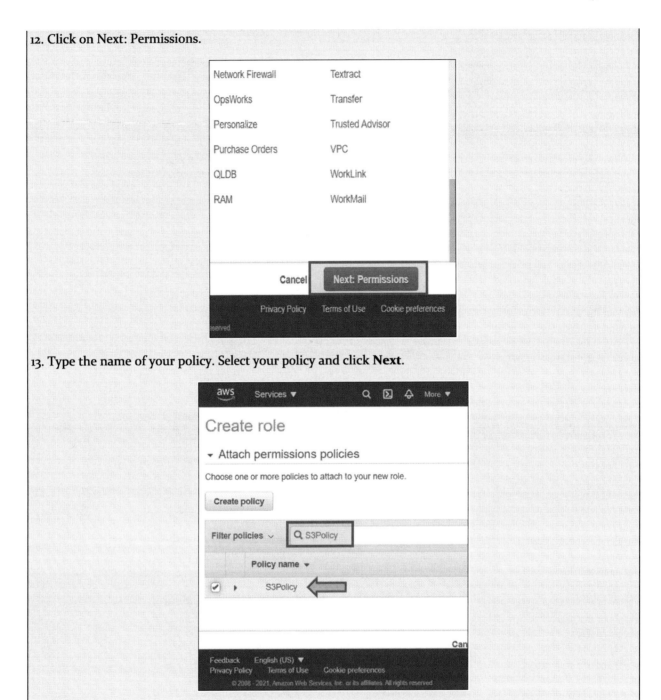

13. Type the name of your policy. Select your policy and click **Next**.

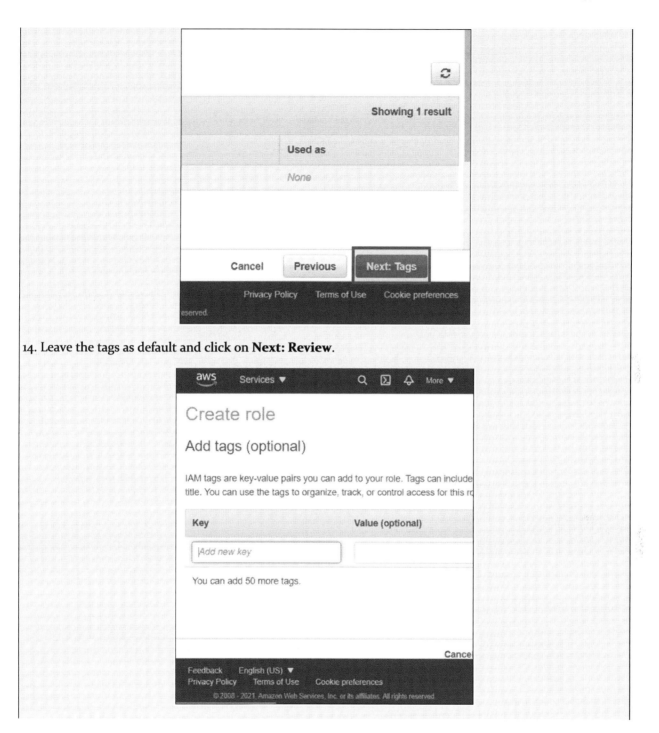

14. Leave the tags as default and click on **Next: Review**.

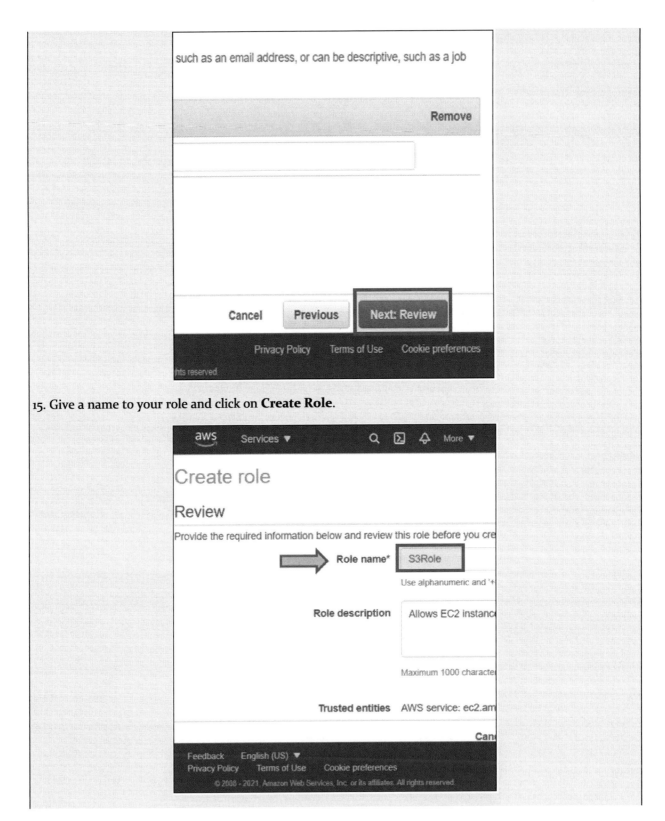

15. Give a name to your role and click on **Create Role**.

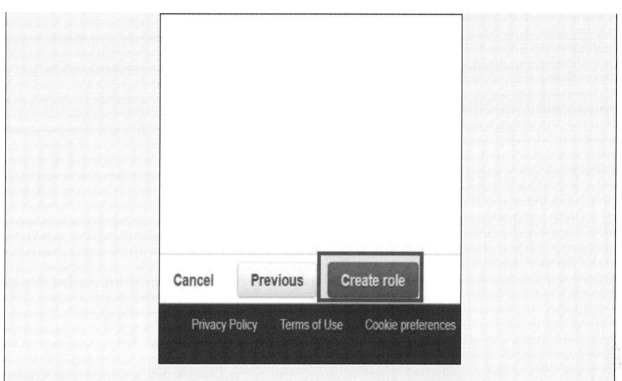

16. Go to the role. Click on **Attach policy** and attach a managed policy. For example, the EC2 instance needs more than just accessing that S3 bucket. It needs full access to all of DynamoDB.

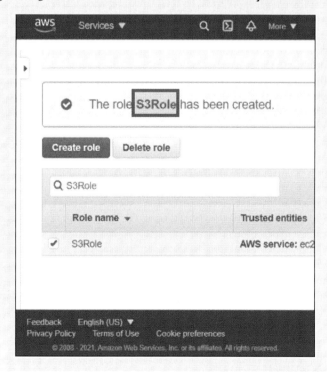

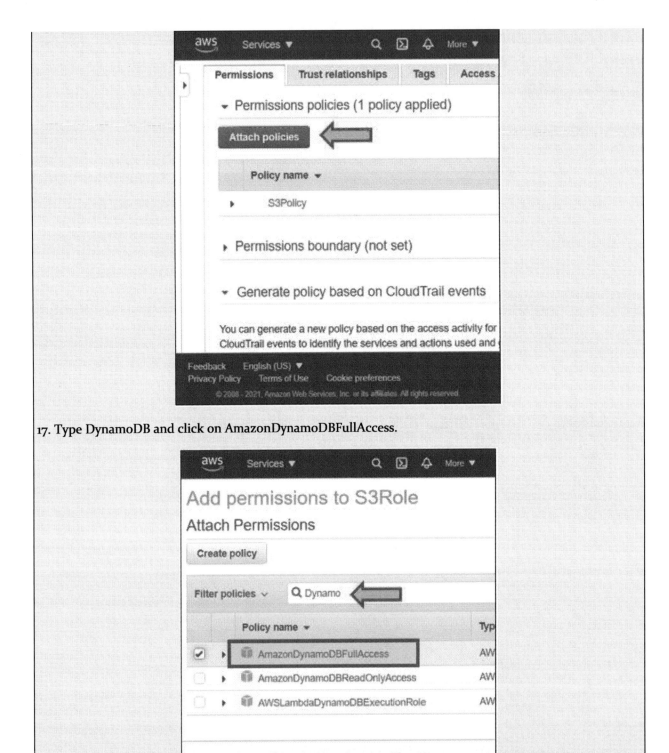

17. Type DynamoDB and click on AmazonDynamoDBFullAccess.

Instead of creating a full IAM policy specifying all the different permissions needed, we can simply choose an AWS-managed policy. This predefined set of permissions will perform everything we need without having to manage that policy.

18. Click on **Attach Policy**.

19. You can see that we have managed the policy alongside our customer-defined policy.

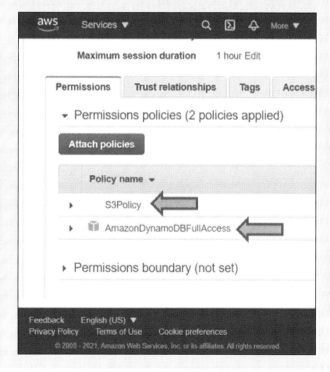

20. If we want to grant some special permission to this role and do not want to define a policy that lives outside the scope of this role, we must use inline policies. Inline policies work just like any other policy, except the scope is limited to just this role. You cannot use this inline policy with any other role.

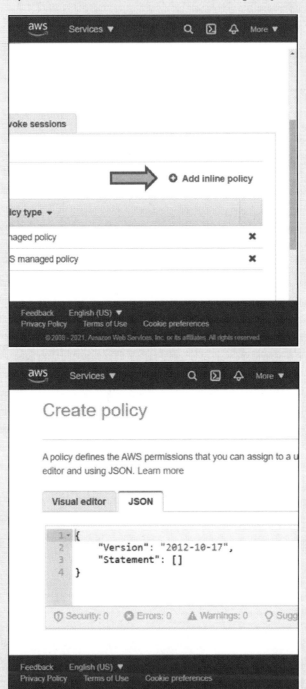

> **EXAM TIP:** 1. Any permissions that are not explicitly allowed are implicitly denied. E.g., if your identity or resource does not have a policy that explicitly allows an AWS API action, it is implicitly rejected.
>
> 2. If you have a policy that is an explicit deny, it overrides anything else in any other policy. E.g., if you have a policy that allows access to an S3 bucket but another policy that explicitly denies access to that same or all S3 buckets, the explicit deny will always override.
>
> 3. Only attached policies affect. Just because you have defined a policy does not mean you can do anything unless connected to a user, group, or role.
>
> 4. When you have multiple policies attached to either identity or resource, AWS will join them to perform its evaluation. If an action is allowed by an identity-based policy, a resource-based policy, or both, AWS enables the action and explicitly denies that these policies override the allow.

Permission Boundaries

Permissions boundaries allow admins to delegate permissions to users so they can create new AWS service roles (for use with services like Amazon EC2 and AWS Lambda) without elevating their permissions. AWS supports permission boundaries for IAM entities.

Permissions boundaries are a sophisticated feature for setting the maximum permissions that an identity-based policy can issue to an IAM object using a managed policy. These are used to prevent privilege escalation or permissions that are overly broad. The entity's permissions boundary authorizes only the acts permitted by its identity-based rules and permission limits. It controls the maximum permissions an IAM policy can grant.

Use Cases of Permission Boundaries

- Developers that create roles for Lambda functions
- Application owners making roles for EC2 instances
- Administrators creating ad hoc users

Lab 11-02: Setting Up Permission Boundaries

1. Go to **IAM**. Click on **Users**.

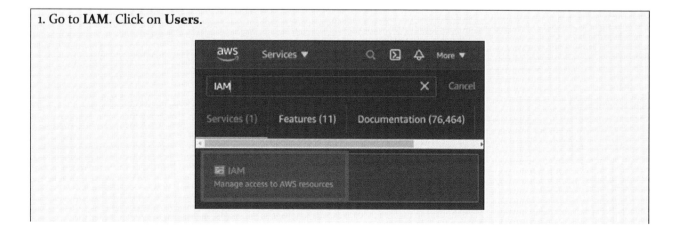

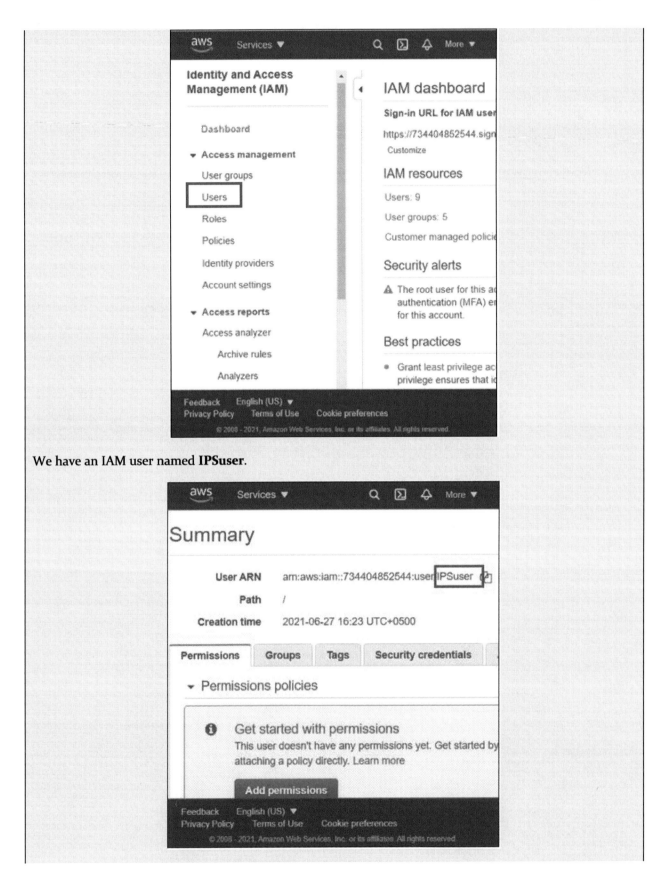

We have an IAM user named **IPSuser**.

2. IPSuser has the directly attached AWS-managed policy administrator access. This IPSuser has full access to all features within this AWS account, but we want to limit their access to DynamoDB. We can apply a permissions boundary.

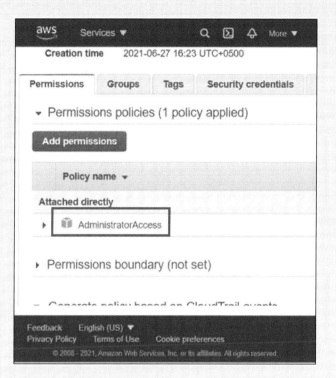

3. Click on Permissions boundary. Select Set boundary.

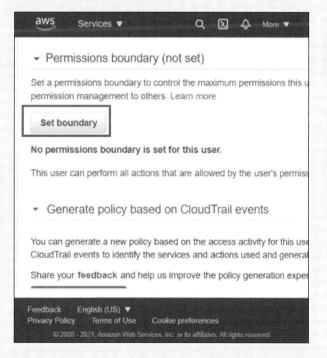

4. Type DynamoDB and select AmazonDynamoDBFullAccess. Click on Set boundary.

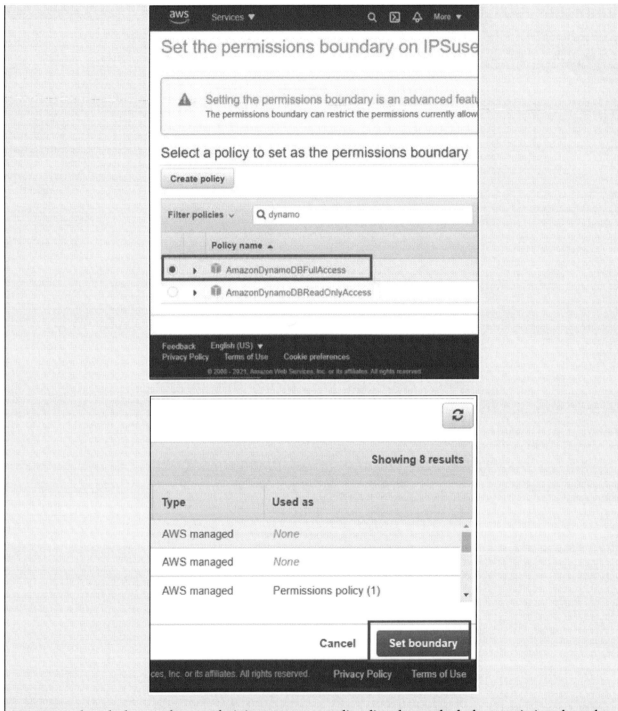

Now, even though the user has an administrator access policy directly attached, the permissions boundary will govern this user's maximum permissions. Hence, even though the user is an administrator, they can only work within DynamoDB while this permissions boundary is set.

AWS Resource Access Manager (RAM)

A multi-account strategy in AWS means using different AWS accounts to separate concerns like administration, billing, or minimizing the blast radius around any mistakes or security vulnerabilities. Using

a multi-account strategy is excellent, but it could be a challenge when you need to create and share resources across accounts. For this purpose, we use Resource Access Manager (RAM).

Resource Access Manager helps you securely share your resources across AWS accounts, within your organization or Organizational Units (OUs) in AWS Organizations, and with IAM roles and IAM users for supported resource types. You can use AWS RAM to share transit gateways, subnets, AWS License Manager License configurations, Amazon Route 53 Resolver rules, and more resource types.

You cannot share every type of resource in AWS using RAM. The services listed below have resource types that you can share out.

- o AWS App Mesh
- o Amazon Aurora
- o AWS Certificate Manager Private Certificate Authority
- o AWS CodeBuild
- o Amazon EC2
- o EC2 Image Builder
- o AWS Glue
- o AWS License Manager
- o AWS Network Firewall
- o AWS Outposts
- o AWS Resource Groups
- o Amazon Route 53
- o AWS Systems Manager Incident Manager
- o Amazon VPC

Example: Launch EC2 Instances in a Shared Subnet

Suppose we want to launch EC2 instances in a shared subnet across accounts. We have two AWS accounts, account one and account two, and a private subnet in account one that we want to share. Then, account two can see this private subnet in account one.

It allows account two to create resources in one's private subnet, like EC2 instances.

Account two has no control over account one's private subnet, so it can not alter the subnet in any way except by adding tags. In other words, the subnet is not copied from account one to account two. It is just shared.

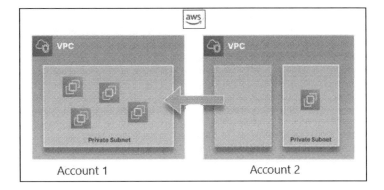

Figure 11-02: Launch EC2 Instances in a Shared Subnet

299

Lab 11-03: Sharing Database Using RAM

Now, we are going to share a database from one account to another using RAM.

1. Log in to the AWS console

2. Go to **RDS** and click on **Databases**.

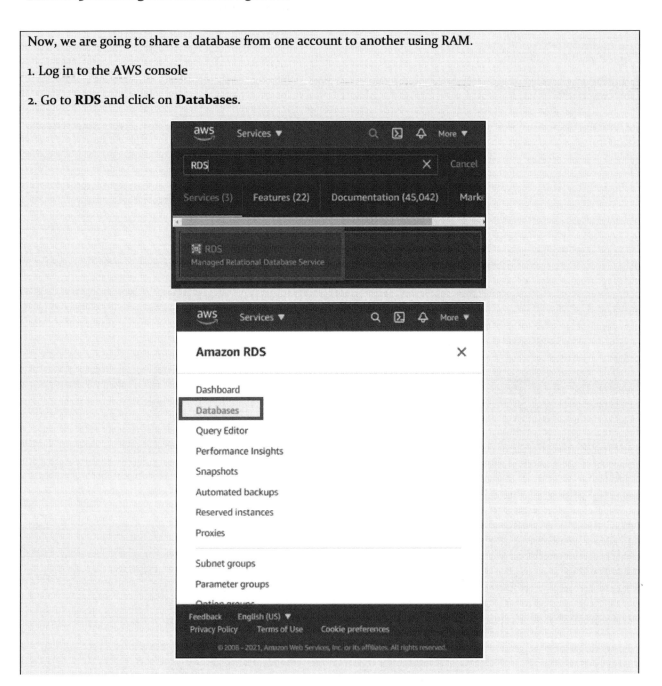

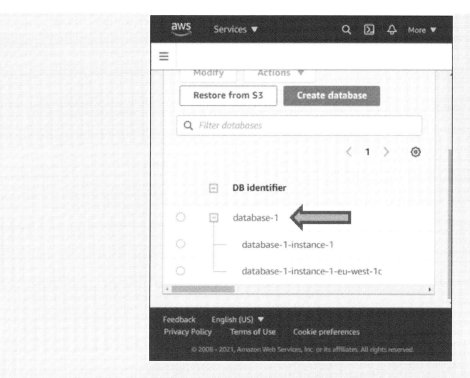

We have two accounts; account one and account two. In account one, we have an Aurora database cluster. We are going to share this database cluster with account two. But since we do not have access to account two, we can grant access using RAM.

3. In account one, go to **Services** and click on **RAM**.

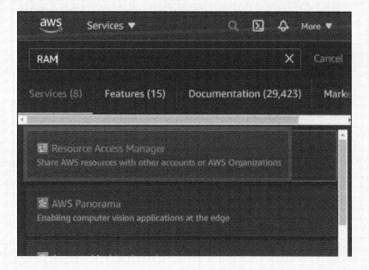

4. Click on Create a resource share.

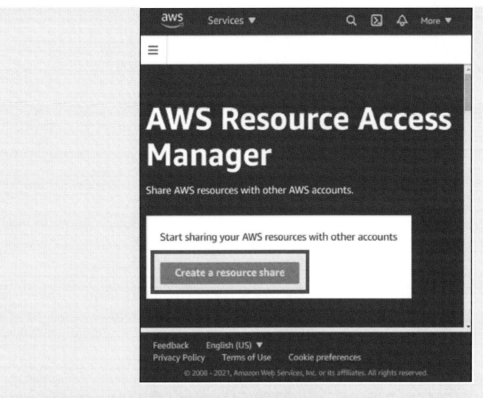

5. Give a name to the resource you want to share, and under resource type, select **Aurora DB Clusters**. You will notice that your database cluster is available for sharing.

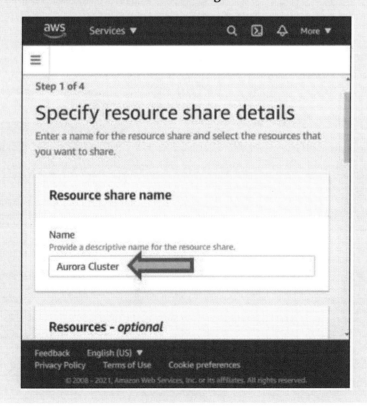

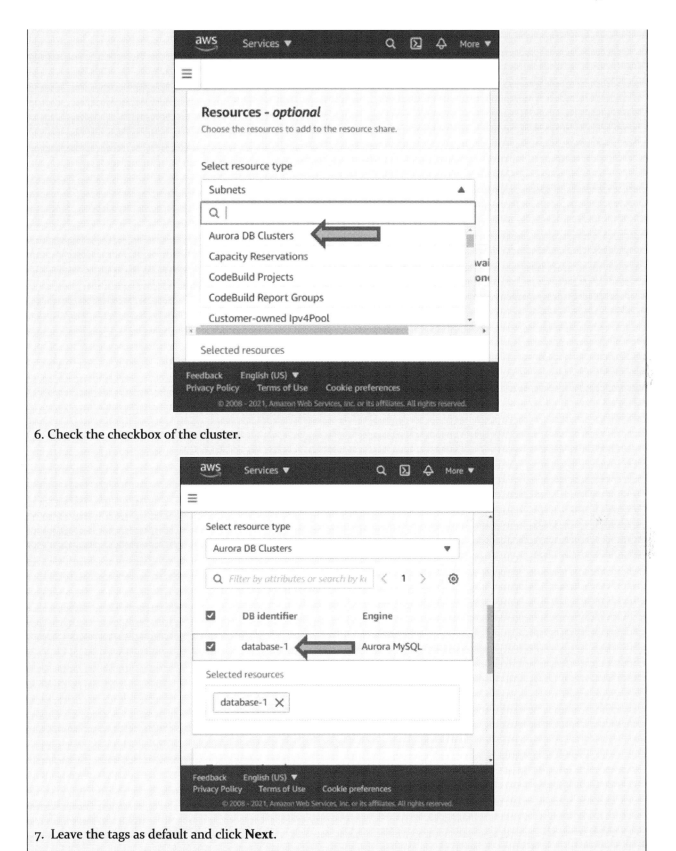

6. Check the checkbox of the cluster.

7. Leave the tags as default and click **Next**.

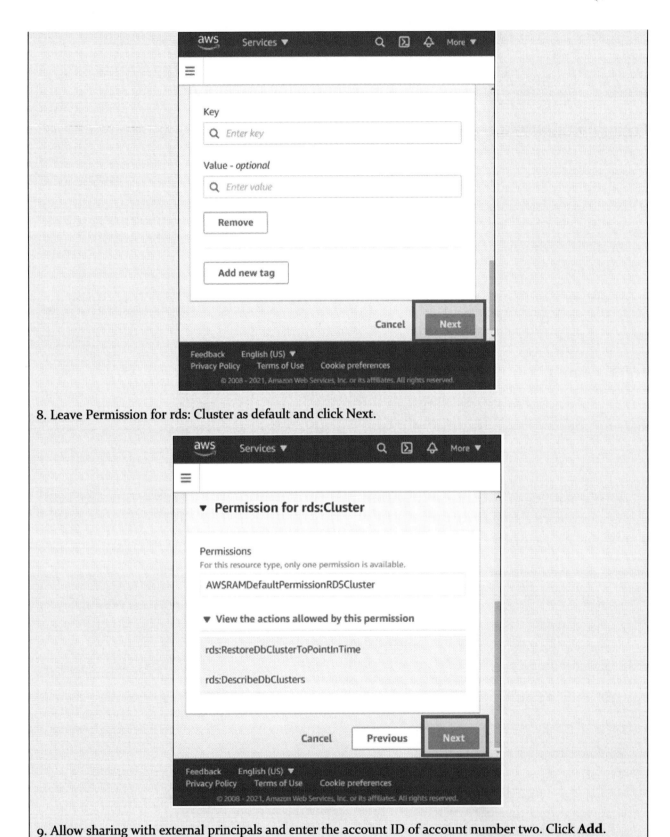

8. Leave Permission for rds: Cluster as default and click Next.

9. Allow sharing with external principals and enter the account ID of account number two. Click **Add**.

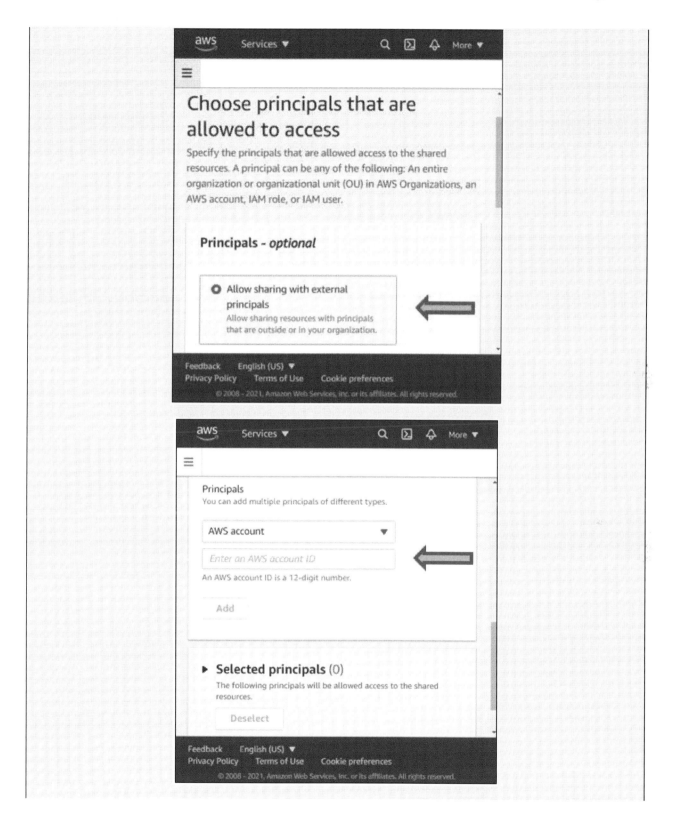

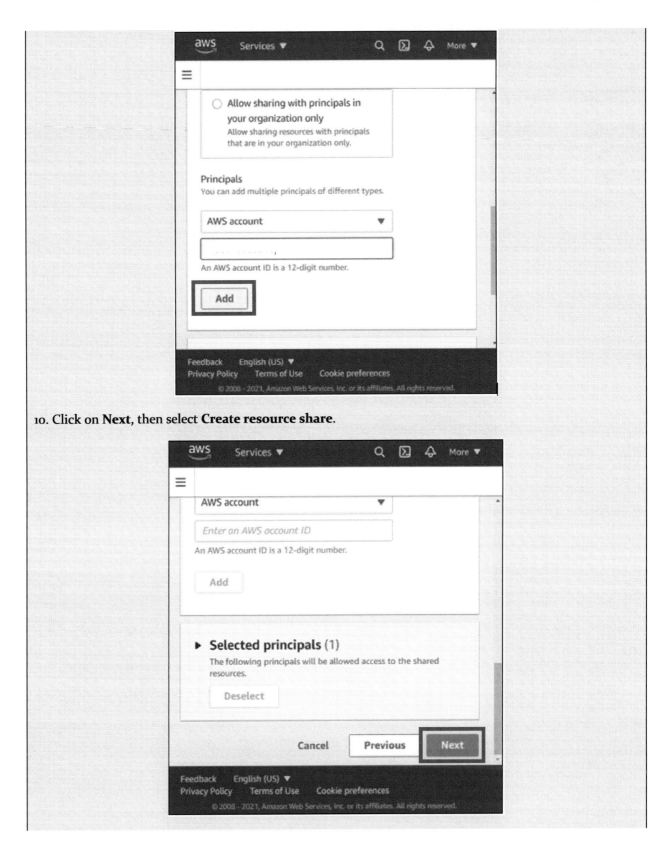

10. Click on **Next**, then select **Create resource share**.

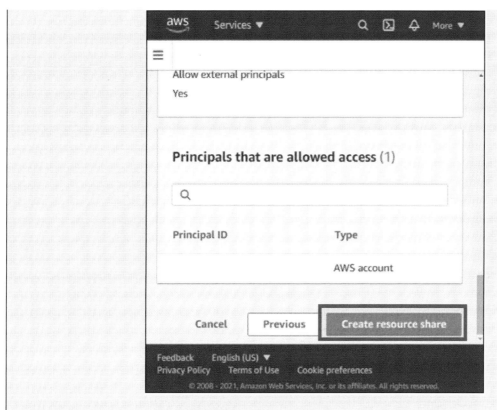

11. Go to the cluster that is shared. Here, you will see that the shared resource is in the **Associated** status, but the shared principals are in the "Associating" state.

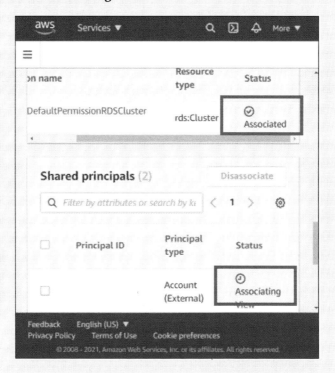

RAM works by sending an invitation from account one to account two that you have first to accept.

12. Go to **RAM** in account two, and under **Shared with me,** click on **Resource shares**.

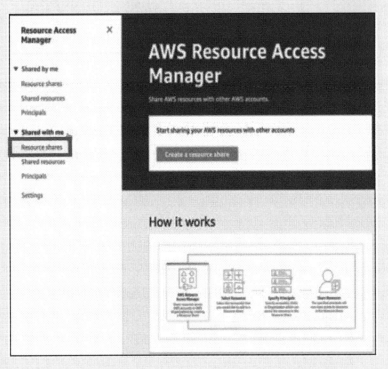

13. Here, you will see a pending invitation. Click on the invitation and select **Accept Resource share**. Click **Ok**.

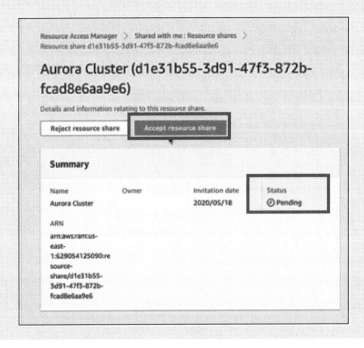

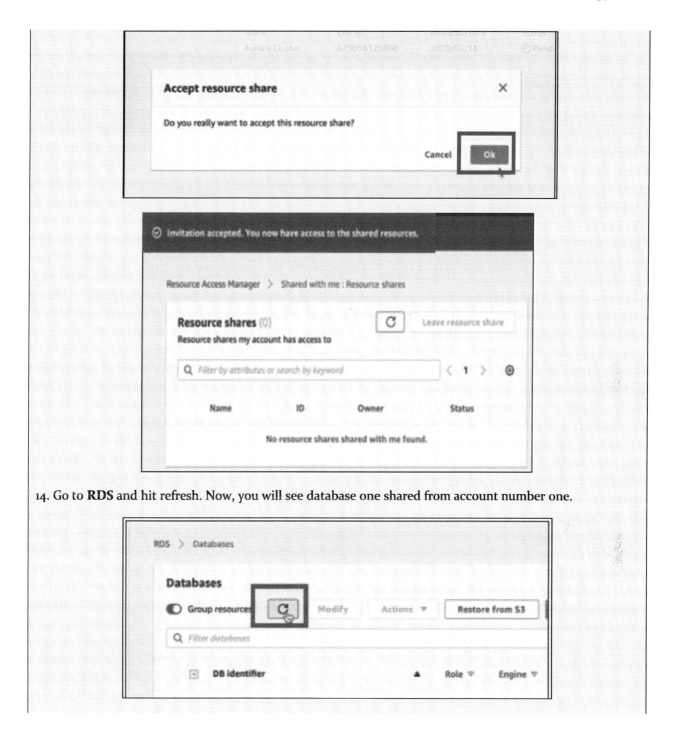

14. Go to **RDS** and hit refresh. Now, you will see database one shared from account number one.

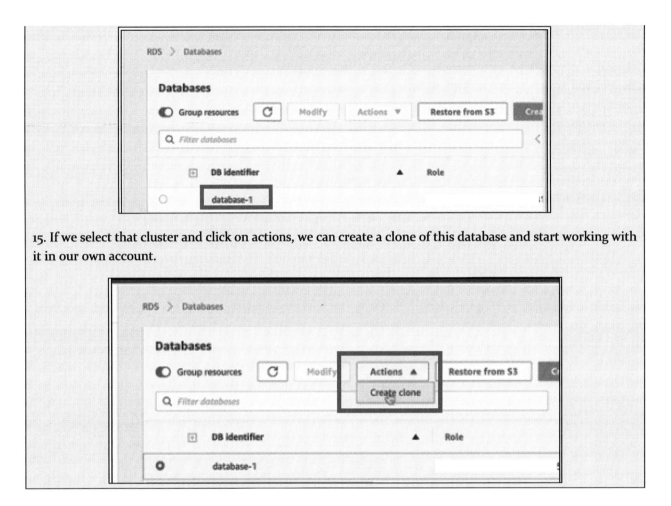

15. If we select that cluster and click on actions, we can create a clone of this database and start working with it in our own account.

AWS Single Sign-On

SSO (Single Sign-On) is a service that allows you to manage access to your AWS accounts and business apps from a single location. You can easily manage access and user rights to all of your AWS Organization accounts using AWS SSO. AWS SSO automatically configures and maintains the essential rights for your accounts, with no additional configuration required in the individual accounts. AWS SSO also includes built-in integrations to many business applications, such as Salesforce, Box, and Microsoft 365.

You may use your existing corporate identities to log in to AWS accounts and third-party accounts in one place using the AWS SSO site and centrally manage your accounts. You can regulate user permissions for your AWS resources across your accounts with AWS Organizations with SSO.

Example using Granular Account-Level Permissions

Let's assume you want to grant your security team administrative access to only the AWS accounts running your security tools, but you only want to grant them auditor-level permissions to other AWS accounts. For this, we will use SSO.

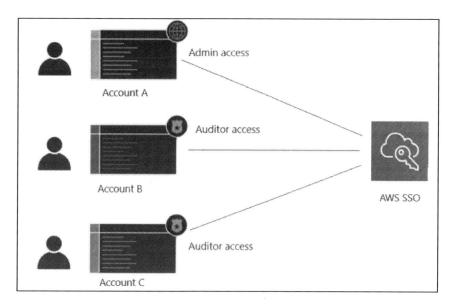

Figure 11-03: Granular Account-Level Permissions

Active Directory and SAML Integration With SSO

SSO enables you to access business applications such as G Suite and Office 365. SSO also works with an active directory or any SAML 2.0 identity provider, such as Azure AD, allowing users to access the AWS SSO portal using their active directory credentials. This can also grant access to AWS Organizations and structures like OUs for development and production environments. It can also gain access to any SAML 2.0-enabled applications. SAML is a standard for logging users into applications based on their sessions in another context. For example, one context is the Microsoft AD environment, and another is business applications like G Suite. All sign-on events are recorded in AWS CloudTrail, and SAML allows you to log into the G Suite application using your AD context. This aids you in meeting your audit and compliance obligations.

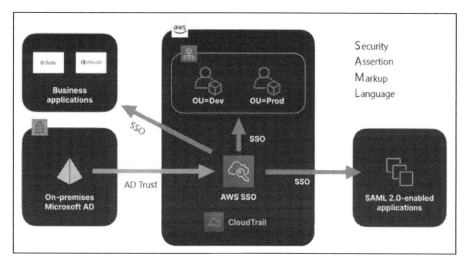

Figure 11-04: Active Directory and SAML Integration

Mind Map

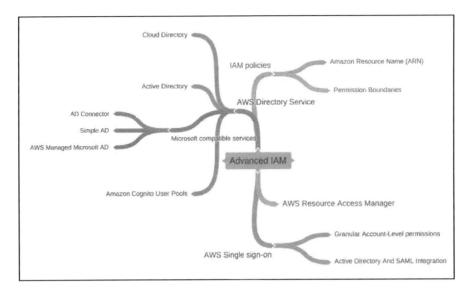

Figure 11-05: Mind Map

Practice Questions

1. AWS Directory Service is a single service. True or false?

a) True

b) False

2. _____ is a standalone directory in the cloud, and it allows users to access AWS resources and applications with their existing corporate credentials.

a) Managed Microsoft AD

b) AWS Directory Service

c) Simple AD

3. _____ is a hierarchical database of users, groups, and computers organized in a pattern of trees and forests.

a) Active Directory

b) Simple AD

c) Managed Microsoft AD

4. AD Connector cannot be shared with other AWS accounts. True or false?

a) True

b) False

5. Which of the following services are Non-AD Compatible services? (Choose 2)

a) Simple AD

b) Cloud Directory

c) Cognito User Pool

d) AD Connector

6. Which of the following services are AD Compatible services? (Choose 2)

a) Simple AD

b) Cloud Directory

c) Cognito User Pool

d) AD Connector

7. Which of the following is the correct format of ARN?

a) Arn : account-id : region : partition : service

b) Arn: service : region : partition : account-id

c) Arn : partition : service : region : account-id

d) Arn : partition : region : service : account-id

8. _____ are attached to an IAM user, group, or role.

a) Identity-based Policies

b) Resource-based Policies

9. Any permissions that are not explicitly allowed are implicitly denied. True or false?

a) True

b) False

10. Policies can affect only when they are unattached to roles. True or false?

a) True

b) False

11. AWS Managed policies are editable by customers. True or false?

a) True

b) False

12. _____ is a service that helps centrally manage access to AWS accounts and business applications.

a) Active Directory

b) RAM

c) AWS Single Sign-On

13. Resource Access Manager (RAM) helps you securely share your resources across AWS accounts. True or false?

a) True

b) False

14. _____ uniquely identify AWS resources.

a) RAM

b) Amazon Resource Names (ARNs)

c) Single Sign-On

15. Cloud Directory is a _____.

a) Fully Managed Service

b) Self-Managed Service

Chapter 12: Security

DDoS Overview

DDoS Attack

A distributed denial of service attack (DDoS) effort occurs when it tries to prevent users from accessing your website or application.

It can be done using a variety of ways, including enormous packet floods, techniques that combine reflection and amplification, and the use of massive botnets.

Layer 4 DDoS Attack

A Layer 4 DDoS attack is often referred to as an SYN flood. It works at the transport layer (TCP).

Using a 3-way handshake, a TCP connection is established. The client sends an SYN packet to a server, the server replies with a SYN-ACK, and the client then responds to that with an ACK.

After the "3-way handshake" is complete, the TCP connection is established after this, applications begin sending data using layer 7 (application layer protocol), such as HTTP etc.

SYN Floods

An SYN flood sends many SYN packets and ignores the server's SYN-ACK responses to overload it by using the TCP stack's built-in patience.

As a result, the server utilizes resources while waiting for the anticipated ACK, which should arrive from a reliable client for a certain period of time.

There are only so many concurrent TCP connections that a web or application server can have open, so if an attacker sends enough SYN packets to a server, it can easily eat through the allowed number of TCP connections. This then prevents legitimate requests from being answered by the server.

Amlification Attack

NTP, SSDP, DNS, CharGEN, SNMP assaults, and other types of attacks can be considered amplification/reflection attacks.

This is where an attacker may send a third-party server (such as NTP server) a request using a spoofed IP address.

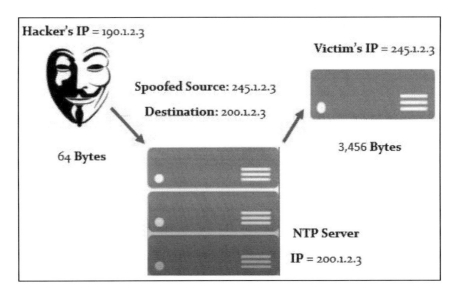

Figure 12-01: Amplification Attack

The server will then reply to that request with a payload larger than the first request (about 28–54 times larger than the request) and send it to the fake IP address. This means that the NTP server might send back up to 3,456 bytes of bandwidth in response to an attacker sending a packet with a fake 64-byte IP address.

Layer 7 Attack

A Layer 7 attack occurs when a web server receives a flood of GET or POST requests, usually from a botnet or a large number of compromised computers.

Exam TIP:
- A Distributed Denial of Service (DDoS) attack attempts to make your website or application unavailable to your end users.
- Common DDoS attacks include Layer 4 attacks such as SYN floods or NTP amplification attacks.
- Common Layer 7 attacks include floods of GET/POST requests.

Reducing Security Threats

Bad Actors

Bad actors are a sort of malicious software. Every internet firms must have faith in polite customers. Some customers are bad performers, but you should know who accesses your information accurately, identifies themselves, or makes use of your services as you anticipate.

The majority of bad actors are automated procedures. Some may attempt to scrape your content for personal gain, while others may misrepresent themselves to circumvent limits; these are known as bad bots. They may, for example, imitate a browser's user agent. A Denial-of-Service (DoS) attack, in which the target is made unavailable owing to a deluge of traffic, could likewise be used against an insecure system.

Benefits of blocking bad actors

- You can reduce security concerns to your systems by blocking bad actors
- You can lower your total costs by not having to deliver traffic to undesired audiences

Network Access Control List (NACL)

You can use network access control lists, or NACLs, to allow or deny specific IP addresses or ranges of IP addresses access to your subnet.

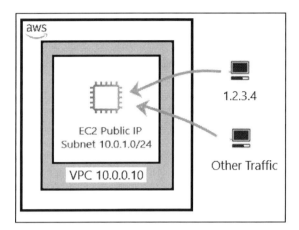

Figure 12-02: Subnet without Network Access Control List (NACL)

It can be accomplished using both inbound and outgoing rules. For example, we want to ban all traffic from IP 1.2.3.4, a known bad actor. As illustrated in the diagram, we establish a new inbound NACL rule, rule 100. All traffic from IP 1.2.3.4 will be blocked. You can use a host-based firewall in addition to an NACL. It runs directly on your EC2 instance and can serve as another layer of defense against bad actors. If you are running Linux, there are software packages like Firewalld, iptables, or UFW. If you are running Windows, you will use Windows Firewall.

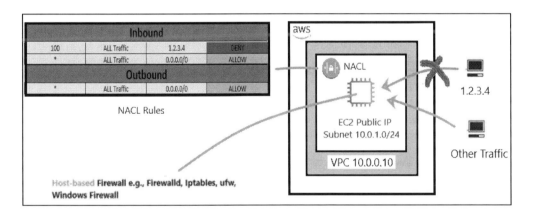

Figure 12-03: Network Access Control List (NACL)

Application Load Balancer (ALB)

The malicious actor's incoming connection will be terminated at the Application Load Balancer (ALB). The EC2 instance will have no idea what the origin IP is. A host-based firewall would be useless in this situation. You could add an extra layer of security by only allowing the ALB security group access to the EC2 security group. However, this will not completely block traffic to the ALB originating from that bad actor, 1.2.3.4. We still have to use an NACL in this case. When using an ALB, the connection from that bad actor will terminate at the ALB, not at the EC2 instance.

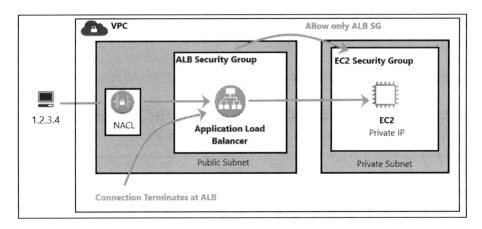

Figure 12-04: Application Load Balancer

Network Load Balancer

The traffic does not end at the Network Load Balancer (NLB), unlike an ALB. It goes straight to your EC2 instance through it. From beginning to conclusion, the client IP, or the bad actor's IP address, is visible. Because the client IP is visible from beginning to end, a firewall block on the EC2 instance is possible, but blocking at the NACL is preferable. A WAF rule might also be utilized.

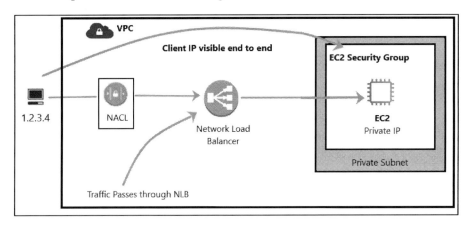

Figure 12-05: Network Load Balancer

Web Application Firewall

In ALB, one additional countermeasure you can employ is to use a web application firewall attached to your load balancer. This is called AWS WAF. A web application firewall service allows you to keep track of web requests and safeguard your web applications against fraudulent queries. WAF is used to restrict or allow requests depending on criteria such as the origin IP address. WAF's pre-configured defenses is used to prevent typical attacks such as sequel, injection assaults, and cross-site scripting attacks.

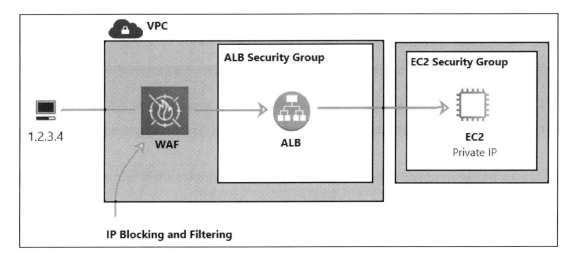

Figure 12-06: Web Application Firewall

💡 EXAM TIP: If you want to block common exploits like sequel injection or cross-site scripting attacks, you must use WAF. WAF operates on layer seven and can inspect that level of traffic for these types of exploits.

If you want to block an IP or range of IPs, you use an NACL that operates on layer four.

You can use WAF in these instances if you are operating a public web application.

WAF + CloudFront

In public web applications, you can have a configuration that involves CloudFront. As with the ALB, you can also attach the wire to your CloudFront distribution. With CloudFront, similar to ALB, the client's connection terminates at CloudFront. The client IP is not visible to your NACL. Only the CloudFront IP is passed along to the NACL. So, blocking your bad actor's IP in an NACL when sitting behind a CloudFront distribution will be ineffective. In these cases, you can attach a WAF to your CloudFront distribution and use the IP blocking and filtering options. Additionally, find that you are getting abuse from a particular country. You can use CloudFront's geo match feature to block that country's traffic altogether.

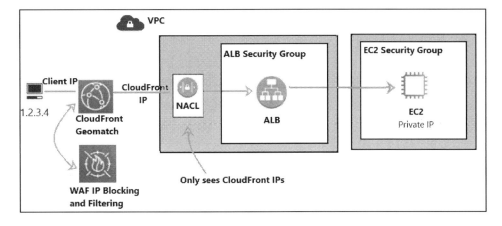

Figure 12-07: WAF + CloudFront

Key Management Service (KMS)

 KMS is a regionally managed service that allows you to easily create and manage the encryption keys that secure your data. Customer master keys, or CMKs, are managed by KMS. A logical representation of a key is a CMK. It is a pointer or reference to some underlying cryptographic material. The CMKs exist in the AWS region and never leave that region or KMS.

KMS is ideal for encrypting S3 objects, database passwords, and API keys stored in the systems manager parameter store. Data up to 4 kilobytes can be encrypted and decrypted using CMKs. Most AWS services are connected with KMS. You pay per API call with KMS. API calls such as listing your keys, encrypting data, decrypting data, and re-encrypting data will cost you money. KMS uses CloudTrail to support auditing. These audit records are sent to Amazon S3. It makes it easy to meet your compliance requirements. KMS is a FIPs 140-2 level two service. FIPS is a US government computer security standard used to approve cryptographic modules. Level two means you have to show evidence of tampering.

Types of CMKs

Type	Can View	Can Manage	Dedicated to My Account
Customer Managed	Yes	Yes	Yes
AWS Managed CMK	Yes	No	Yes
AWS Owned CMK	No	Yes	No

Table 12-01: Types of CMK

AWS Managed CMK: AWS Managed CMKs are available for free. CMK are created automatically when you initially create an encrypted resource in an AWS service. Although you can track the usage of an AWS-managed CMK, KMS manages the key's lifecycle and permissions on your behalf.

Customer Managed CMK: Only you can develop Customer Managed CMKs. Customer-managed CMKs allow you complete control over the key's lifecycle and permissions, including who can use it and under what circumstances. Because encryption key reuse is discouraged by cryptographic best practices, key rotation is required.

AWS Owned CMK: AWS Owned CMKs is a collection of CMKs owned and managed by an AWS service for use across various AWS accounts. Although your AWS account does not contain AWS-owned CMKs, an AWS service can use its AWS-owned CMKs to safeguard your account's resources. The AWS-owned CMKs do not need you to establish or administer them. You cannot. However, view, utilize, track, or audit them.

Symmetric vs. Asymmetric CMKs

Two types of encryptions are applied to CMKs, symmetric and asymmetric.

Symmetric CMKs: A symmetric CMK is created by default when you make a customer master key in KMS. Symmetric encryption employs symmetric keys, which are used for both encryption and decryption. You

must use AWS KMS to use asymmetric CMK. Symmetric CMKs are used by all AWS services that are connected with KMS. Asymmetric CMKs can be used in AWS KMS to encrypt, decrypt, and re-encrypt data and generate data keys, key pairs, and random byte strings. You can also import your own key material using symmetric CMKs.

Asymmetric CMKs: In AWS KMS, you can make an asymmetric CMK. An asymmetric CMK is a pair of public and private keys that are mathematically connected. The public key can be given to anyone, even if they are untrustworthy, but the private key must be kept confidential.

Asymmetric CMKs are based on the RSA and Elliptic Curve Cryptography ECC algorithms. The ECC algorithm is newer and more secure than the RSA algorithm. With asymmetric CMKs, the private key never leaves AWS unencrypted. You must call the KMS APIs to use the private key. You can use the public key outside of AWS by downloading it. Users unable to contact KMS APIs frequently use them outside of AWS. Asymmetric CMKs are not supported by AWS services that are linked with KMS. The symmetric CMKs must be used. The most common use of asymmetric CMKs is to sign communications and verify signatures.

Key Policies
You can provide the key policy for the new CMK when you build a CMK programmatically with the KMS API, including through the AWS SDKs and command-line tools. KMS produces one for you if you do not give one.

```
1 {
2     "Sid": "Enable IAM User Permissions",
3     "Effect": "Allow",
4     "Principal": {"AWS": "arn:aws:iam::111122223333:root"},
5     "Action": "kms:*",
6     "Resource": "*"
7 }
```

Figure 12-08: Default Key Policy

This default key policy has one policy statement that grants complete access to the CMK to the AWS account that owns it and enables IAM policies in the account to allow access to the CMK. The key policies related to your keys must be carefully observed.

Suppose you accidentally delete this statement or change its permissions, such that the account, the root user, cannot access the key. In that case, you will have to contact AWS support to regain access.

Example Policy:

In this policy statement, we are granting a role called "EncryptionApp" access to several actions on this key, principles that can assume this role are allowed to perform the actions listed in the policy statement, which are the cryptographic actions for encrypting and decrypting data with a CMK.

```
1 {
2   "Sid": "Allow use of the key",
3   "Effect": "Allow",
4   "Principal": {"AWS": "arn:aws:iam::111122223333:role/EncryptionApp"},
5   "Action": [
6     "kms:DescribeKey",
7     "kms:GenerateDataKey*",
8     "kms:Encrypt",
9     "kms:ReEncrypt*",
10    "kms:Decrypt"
11  ],
12  "Resource": "*"
13 }
```

Figure 12-09: Grants IAM Role Access to Crypto Actions for Encrypting and Decrypting Data

Lab 12-01: Interaction with KMS using the Command Line:

1. Log in to the **AWS console**.

2. Go to Services and click Key Management Service.

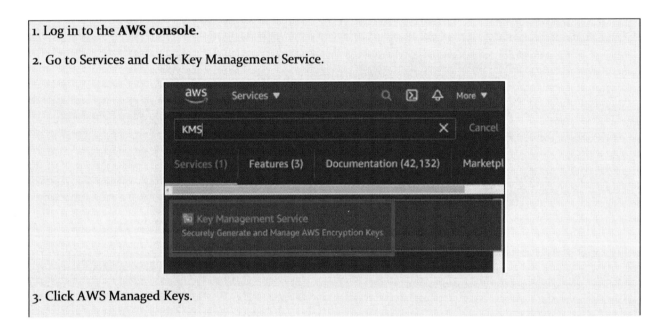

3. Click AWS Managed Keys.

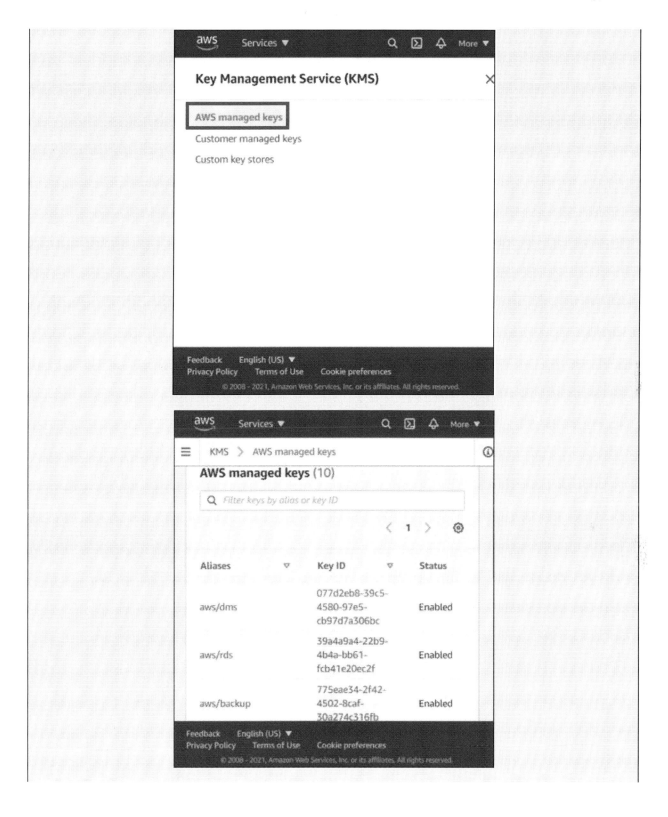

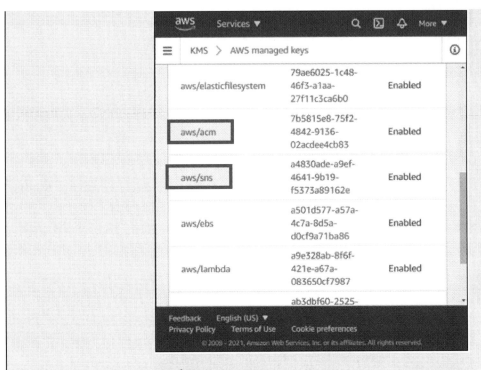

4. Click on Customer Managed Keys.

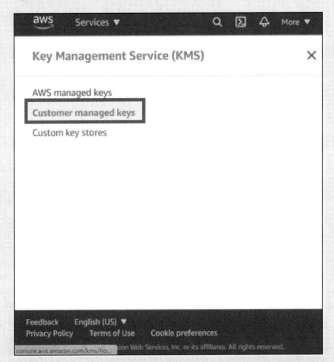

5. Since we do not have any customer-managed keys, we will go to the command line and create a key.

6. We have a terminal with an EC2 instance configured with the AWS configured command. This EC2 instance has full administrative access to the AWS account.

7. The first command is: **aws kms create-key --description "IPS Demo CMK."** This command returns a number of values. Copy the "KeyId" into a clipboard.

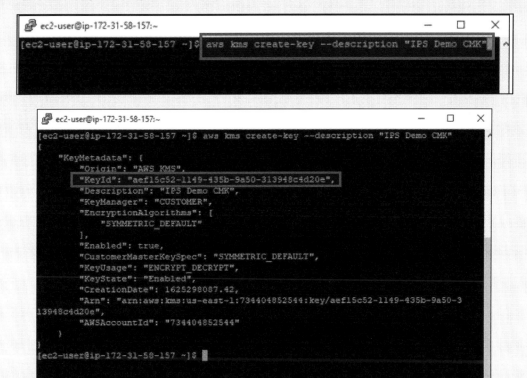

8. The command to create an alias is: aws kms create-alias --target-key-id [KeyId] --alias-name "alias/IPSdemo."

We need to specify a target key ID. This is the key ID returned by the previous command. This command also gives a name to the alias created.

9. Next command is **aws kms list-keys.** This will list the keys and also the key we created.

10. Go back to the AWS console. You can see the "IPSdemo" alias created here.

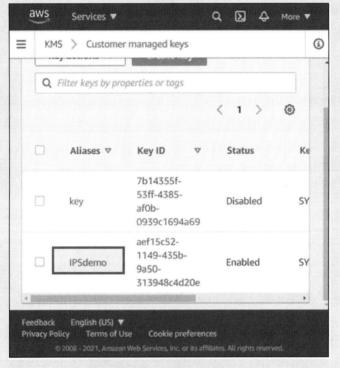

11. Click on the IPSdemo alias to view the **Key Policy**.

12. If you click on **key rotation**, you can also specify a rotation policy. If you check the box, this will automatically rotate the CMK yearly. For AWS-managed keys, they are turned in by AWS every three years.

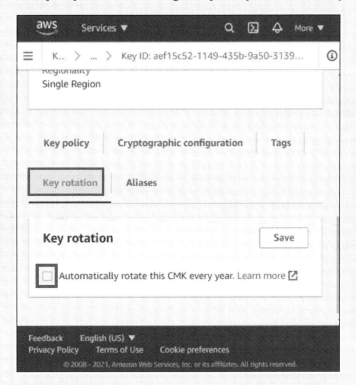

13. Go back to the command line. We will start using the key we have created. We will write out the string to encrypt a text file: "this is a secret message" to a file called top "secret.txt."

The command to do this is: echo "this is a secret message" > topsecret.txt

To view the contents of the file: **cat topsecret.txt**

14. Next command is: aws kms encrypt --key-id "alias/IPSdemo" --plaintext file://topsecret.txt --output text --query CiphertextBlob

In this command, we specify plain text because we are using a local plain text file. We want our output in text format and to get back the value called ciphertext blog. This command will encrypt the topsecret.txt file using the IPSdemo CMK we created in the previous step, and it will output the ciphertext blob in base 64 encoded form.

15. Now, we will decode this encrypted blob base 64 and save the raw encrypted binary data to a local file.

The command to decode is: aws kms encrypt --key-id "alias/IPSdemo" --plaintext file://topsecret.txt --output text --query CiphertextBlob | base64 --decode > topsecret.txt. encrypted

To view the contents of this file: **cat topsecret.txt. encrypted**

16. Next, we are going to decrypt this file using our CMK.

aws kms decrypt --ciphertext-blob fileb://topsecret.txt.encrypted --output text --query Plaintext

In this command, we are using "fileb" instead of a file.

Since every time we work with KMS at the command line, we will be working with base 64 encoded data. Therefore, we need to decode it.

17. The command to decode is:

aws kms decrypt --ciphertext-blob fileb://topsecret.txt.encrypted --output text --query Plaintext | base64 --decode

This gives us decrypted data.

CMKs are used to encrypt and decrypt data up to four kilobytes in size. If you want to encrypt a larger data file than four kilobytes, you can use a data encryption key or DEK.

aws kms generate-data-key --key-id "alias/IPSdemo" --key-spec AES_256

This returns the plain text data key and an encrypted one with the specified CMK version of the data key. The encrypted version is referred to as a ciphertext blob.

The ciphertext blob has metadata that tells KMS which CMK was used to generate it.

While KMS supports sending data up to four kilobytes to be encrypted directly by KMS, envelope encryption can offer significant performance benefits.

EXAM TIP: A Customer Master Key is the primary resource in AWS KMS. You can use a CMK to encrypt, decrypt, and re-encrypt data. It can also generate data keys that you can use outside AWS KMS. Typically, you will use symmetric CMKs, but you can create and use asymmetric CMKs for encryption or signing.

CloudHSM

 AWS CloudHSM is a cloud-based Hardware Security Module (HSM) that lets you create and use your encryption keys on the AWS Cloud. To handle your encryption keys, you can use FIPS 140-2 Level 3 verified HSMs with CloudHSM.

FIPS is a computer security standard developed by the United States government. It has a variety of distinct compliance levels and is used to validate cryptographic modules. Compliance level three is where physical security mechanisms might include the use of strong enclosures and tamper detection or response circuitry that zeroes out all of your plain text cryptographic security providers when the removable doors or covers of the cryptographic module inside open up.

CloudHSM allows you to use industry-standard APIs like PKCS#11, Java Cryptography Extensions (JCE), and Microsoft CryptoNG (CNG) libraries to interface with your apps.

KMS is level 2 compliant, which needs to show evidence of tampering. The difference between KMS and CloudHSM is that you manage your keys with CloudHSM. CloudHSM offers a single-tenant, multi-AZ cluster. It is dedicated to you. KMS is multitenant. It uses HSMs internally, but those are shared across customer accounts. Since CloudHSM is a managed service, you do not have access to the AWS-managed component of CloudHSM. Only the HSM users you specify can access to the encryption keys you produce and use with CloudHSM. Your encryption keys are not visible or accessible to AWS. CloudHSM is housed on a Virtual Private Cloud (VPC) in your account. With CloudHSM, you must keep your keys secure. If you lose your keys, you will not be able to get them back.

CloudHSM Architecture

First, you must create a cluster in either an existing VPC or a new VPC. CloudHSM will operate inside its VPC, being dedicated to CloudHSM from a security isolation standpoint. CloudHSM will then project Elastic Network Interfaces (ENIs) into your chosen VPC. It is how your applications communicate with the CloudHSM cluster. Inside the cluster, you have to create specific instances of HSMs. CloudHSM is not highly available by default. You have to provision HSMs across availability zones explicitly. If any of these HSMs fail or AZ becomes unavailable, you will still have the other HSM instances. Ideally, you can place one HSM per subnet in each availability zone with a minimum of two AZs, as shown in the diagram, which AWS also recommends.

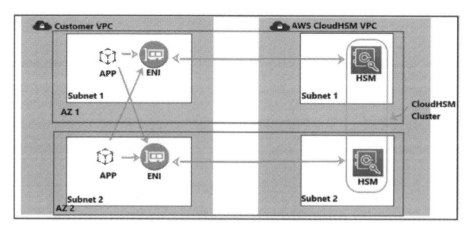

Figure 12-10: CloudHSM Architecture

> EXAM TIP: The AWS CloudHSM is a cloud-based Hardware Security Module (HSM) that helps you meet corporate, contractual, and regulatory compliance requirements for data security by enabling you to generate and use your encryption keys on a FIPS 140-2 Level 3 validated hardware.

Managing Encryption Keys with KMS and CloudHSM

KMS
You may easily generate and manage the encryption keys that are used to encrypt your data with the help of the managed service known as Key Management Service.

Integration
AWS KMS is integrated with other AWS services, such as EBS, S3, RDS, as well as other services to make it simple to encrypt your data with the encryption keys you manage.

Controlling Your Keys
You have centralized control over the lifespan with AWS KMS and permission of your keys. You can create new keys whenever you want and control who can manage keys separately from who can use them.

CMK
The customer master key is a logical representation of a master key. The CMK includes things like metadata, such as the key ID, the creation date, the description, and the key state.

The CMK also contains the key material that is used to encrypt and decrypt your data.

You start using the service by requesting the creation of a CMK. You control the lifecycle of the CMK, as well as who can use or manage it.

HSM
A hardware security module is a physical computing device that safeguards and manages digital keys and performs encryption and decryption functions.

An HSM contains one or more secure crypto processor chips.

Generating A CMK
There are 3 ways to generate a CMK, which are as follows;

- AWS creates the CMK for you. The key material for a CMK is generated within HSMs or hardware security modules managed by AWS KMS.
- Import key material from your own key management infrastructure and associate it with the customer master key.
- Have the key material generated and used in an AWS CloudHSM cluster as part of the custom key store feature in AWS KMS.

Key Rotation
You can choose to have AWS KMS automatically rotate customer master keys every year, provided that those keys were generated within AWS KMS HSMs.

Automatic key rotation is not supported for imported keys, asymmetric keys, or keys generated in AWS CloudHSM clusters using the AWS KMS custom key store feature.

Policies

The primary way to manage access to your AWS KMS CMKs is with policies. Policies are documents that describe who has access to what.

Policies attached to an IAM identity are called identity-based policies or IAM policies, and policies attached to other kinds of resources are called resource-based policies.

Key policies

In AWS KMS, you must attach resource-based policies to your customer master keys. These are called key policies. All KMS CMKs have a key policy.

Ways to control permission

There are 3 ways to control permission which are as follows;

- Use the key policy - Controlling access this way means the full scope of access to the CMK is defined in a single document and this is called the key policy.
- Use IAM policies in combination with the key policy - Controlling access this way enables you to manage all the permissions for your IAM identities in IAM.
- Use grants in combination with the key policies - Controlling access this way enables you to access the CMK in the key policy and allow users to delegate their access to others.

CloudHSM

AWS CloudHSM is a cloud-based HSM that enables you to easily generate and use your own encryption keys on the AWS Cloud.

It is a physical device dedicated to you that can be deployed quickly in a highly available fashion.

KMS vs. CloudHSM

KMS	CloudHSM
Shared tenancy of underlying hardware	Full control of the underlying hardware
Automatic key rotation	No automatic key rotation.
Automatic key generation	Complete control of users, groups, keys, etc

Systems Manager Parameter Store

A parameter store is essential for caching and securely distributing secrets to AWS resources. It is a component of AWS systems manager, abbreviated as SSM.

The parameter store is a serverless, scalable, high-performance system for storing data and secrets, like passwords, database connection strings, license codes, API keys, etc. The values stored in the parameter store can be encrypted using KMS keys, or they can also be plain text. Using parameter stores, you can separate data from source control to avoid leaking access keys into GitHub repositories. In the parameter store, you can also track versions of values. You can also set a TTL (time to live) to expire certain values, such as passwords. It enables you to enforce password rotation. Parameter Store provides secure, hierarchical storage for configuration data management and secrets management.

Organizing Parameters into Hierarchies

With parameter store, data can be stored hierarchically, so you can build tree-like structures.

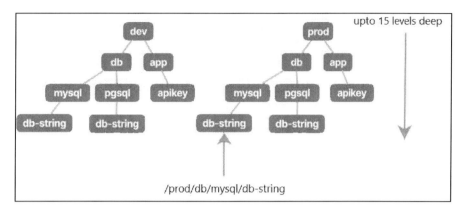

Figure 12-11: Organizing Parameters into Hierarchies

We have two hierarchies in this example: dev and prod. Each level of this hierarchical structure can represent development or production environments. Based on that level, we can access data. You can get all the data for the full prod tree and data for dev, DB, MySQL, and other databases. You can represent a position in the hierarchy using a path /prod/db/mySQL/db-string. Since it is hierarchical, we can grant permissions at any point in this tree structure. Therefore, you can give administrators access to a single piece of information, it can be a single configuration item, or you can grant them access to an entire area for their application, teams access to whole environments, or prod dev or test. There can be up to 15 levels in these systems. The GetParametersByPath API method can retrieve all parameters in the hierarchy. You can specify a path of "/dev" to retrieve the full dev hierarchy, for example. You can use "/dev/db" to retrieve the parameters under the "db" branch of that tree, and if you want to retrieve all the parameters under the app branch of the prod tree, you can specify "/prod/app," etc.

Launching Latest Amazon Linux AMI in CloudFormation

```
1  Parameters:
2    LatestAmiId:
3      Type: 'AWS::SSM::Parameter::Value<AWS::EC2::Image::Id>'
4      Default: '/aws/service/ami-amazon-linux-latest/amzn2-ami-hvm-x86_64-gp2'
5
6  Resources:
7    Instance:
8      Type: 'AWS::EC2::Instance'
9      Properties:
10       ImageId: !Ref LatestAmiId
```

Figure 12-12: Example

AWS makes available the latest AMI IDs in any region via the path and parameter store they manage. This path is given on line 4 in the above example. We can get the latest AMI ID for Amazon Linux 2 in our region and reference that in our EC2 instance resource, as shown in the illustration on line 10. Therefore, there is no need to create and manage any complex mappings.

Lab 12-02: Lambda Function Accessing Parameter Store

1. Log into the **AWS console**.

Note: We are going to create an execution role in IAM. This execution role is going to define permissions that the Lambda function has.

2. Go to **Services** and select **IAM**; click on **Policies** to create a policy.

3. Switch to JSON view and paste the IAM Policy given below:

{

"Version": "2012-10-17",

```
"Statement": [{

"Effect": "Allow",

"Action": [

"logs: CreateLogGroup",

"logs: CreateLogStream",

"logs: PutLogEvents",

"ssm: GetParameter*",

"ssm: GetParametersByPath"

],

"Resource": "*"

}]

}
```

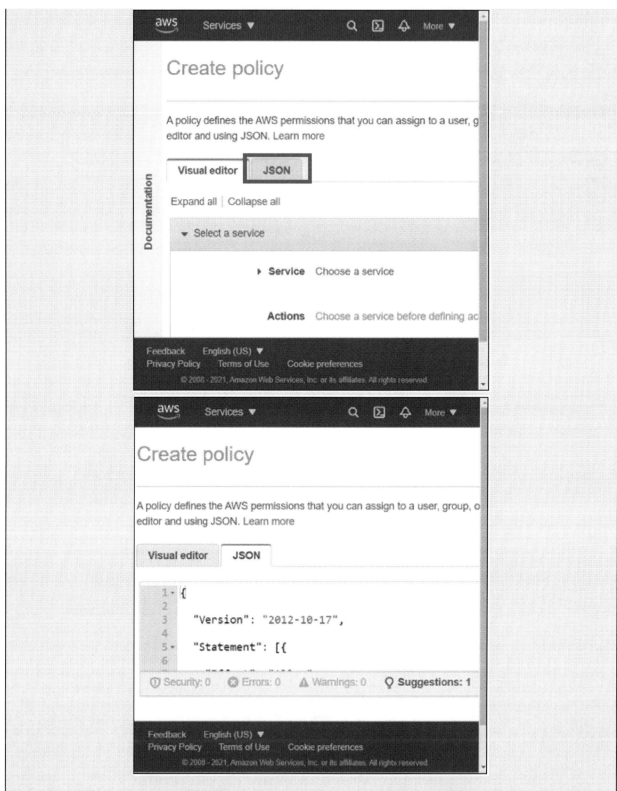

This policy allows access to CloudWatch logs, all of the parameter store API calls that start with get parameter, and GetParametersByPath.

4. Click **Next**. Leave the tags as default.

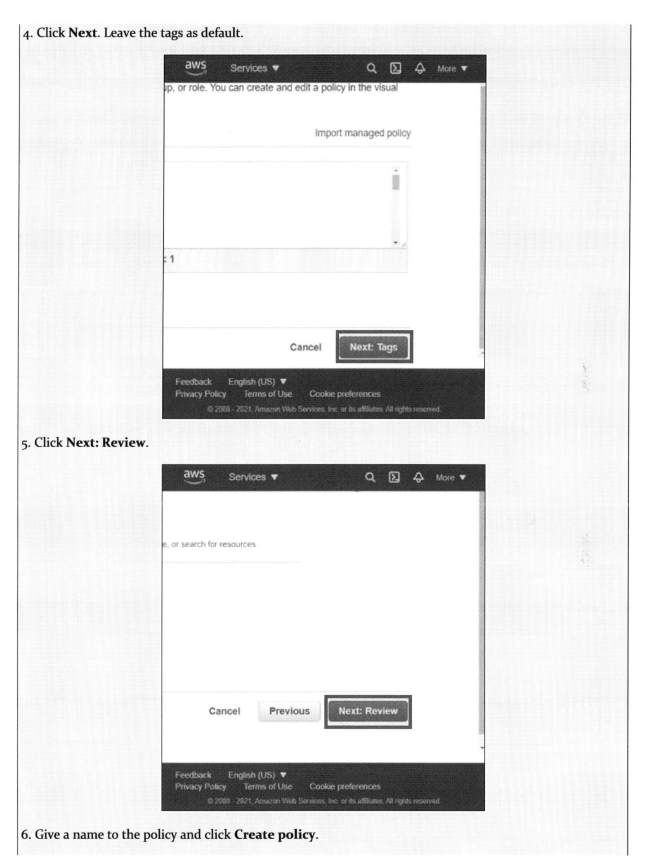

5. Click **Next: Review**.

6. Give a name to the policy and click **Create policy**.

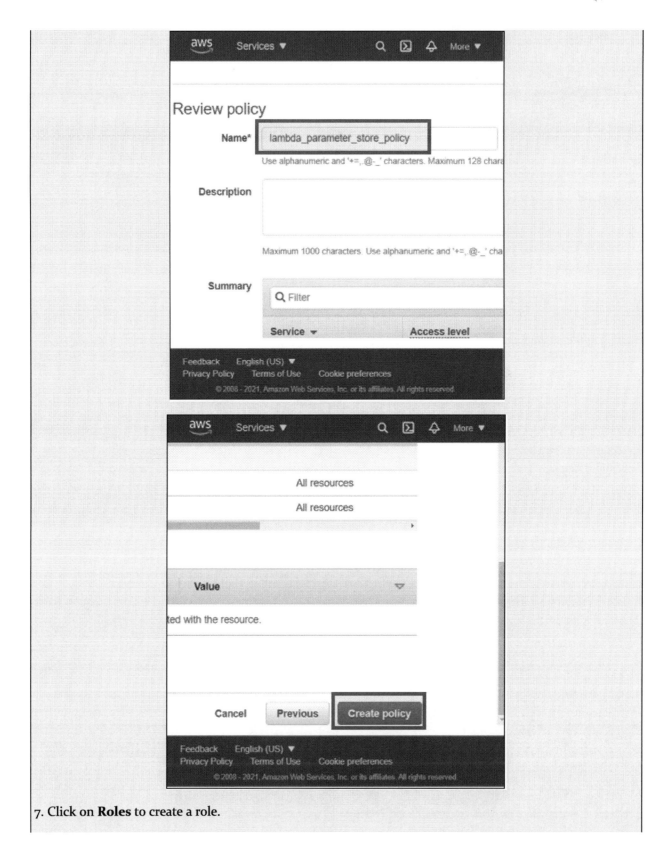

7. Click on **Roles** to create a role.

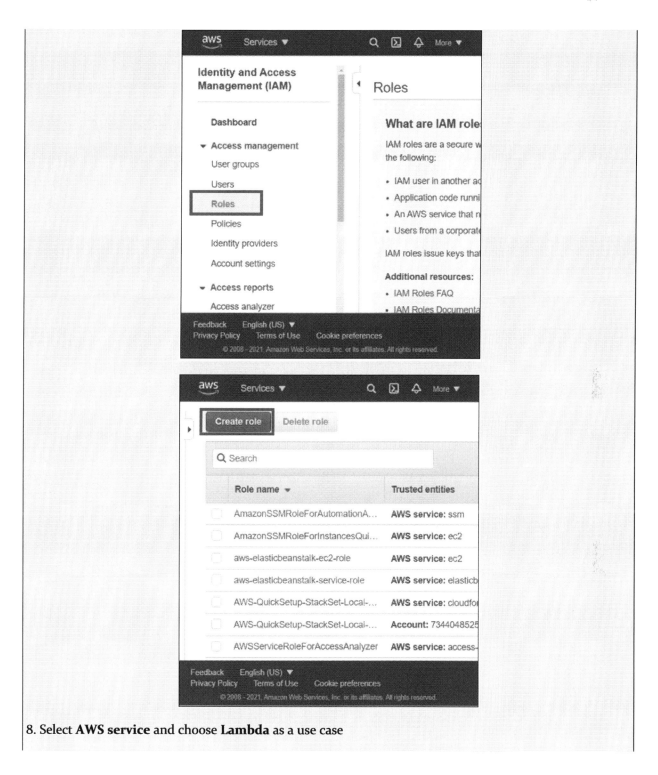

8. Select **AWS service** and choose **Lambda** as a use case

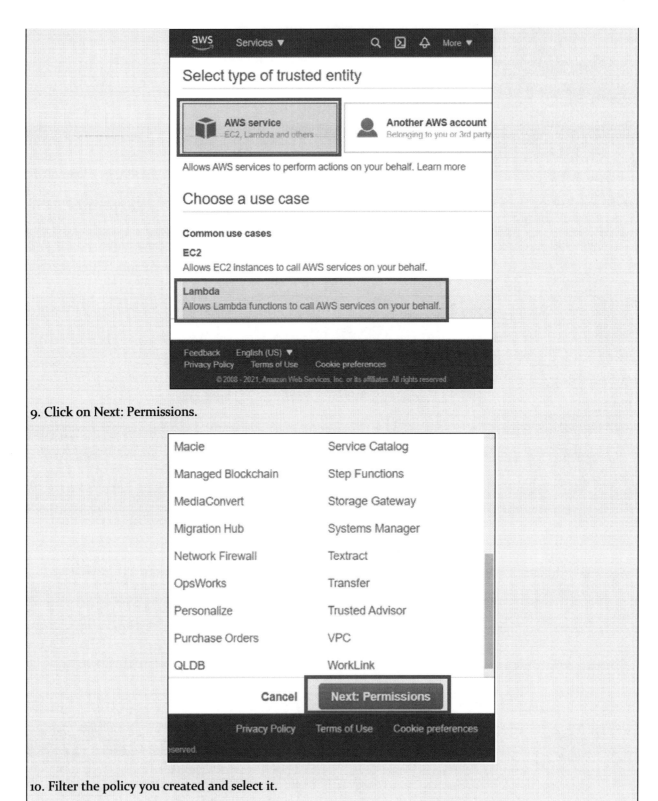

9. Click on Next: Permissions.

10. Filter the policy you created and select it.

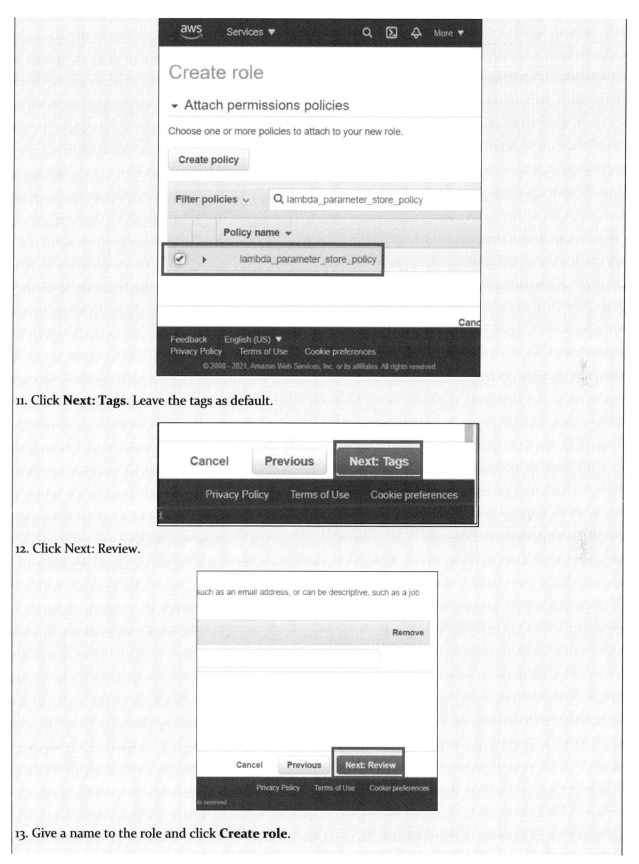

11. Click **Next: Tags**. Leave the tags as default.

12. Click Next: Review.

13. Give a name to the role and click **Create role**.

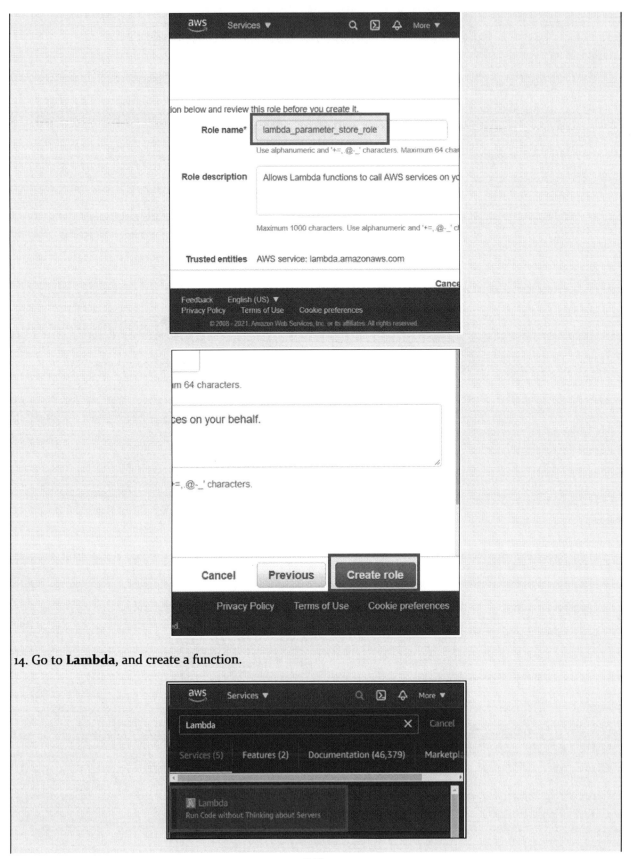

14. Go to **Lambda**, and create a function.

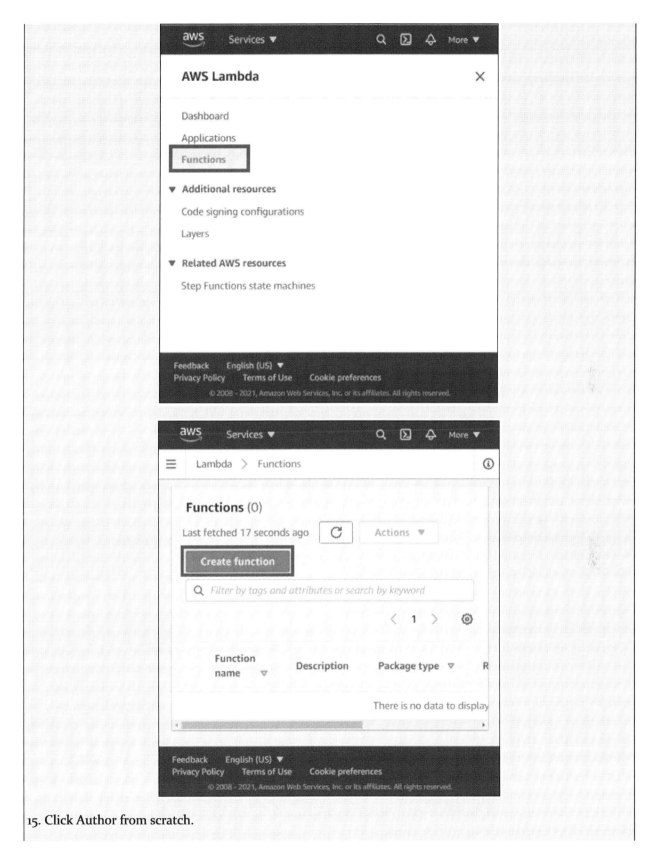

15. Click Author from scratch.

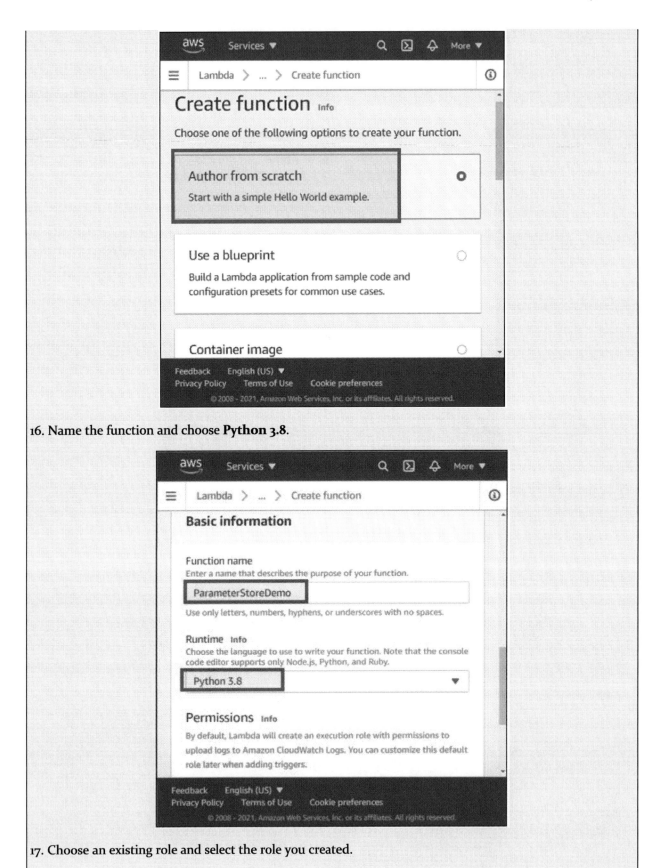

16. Name the function and choose **Python 3.8**.

17. Choose an existing role and select the role you created.

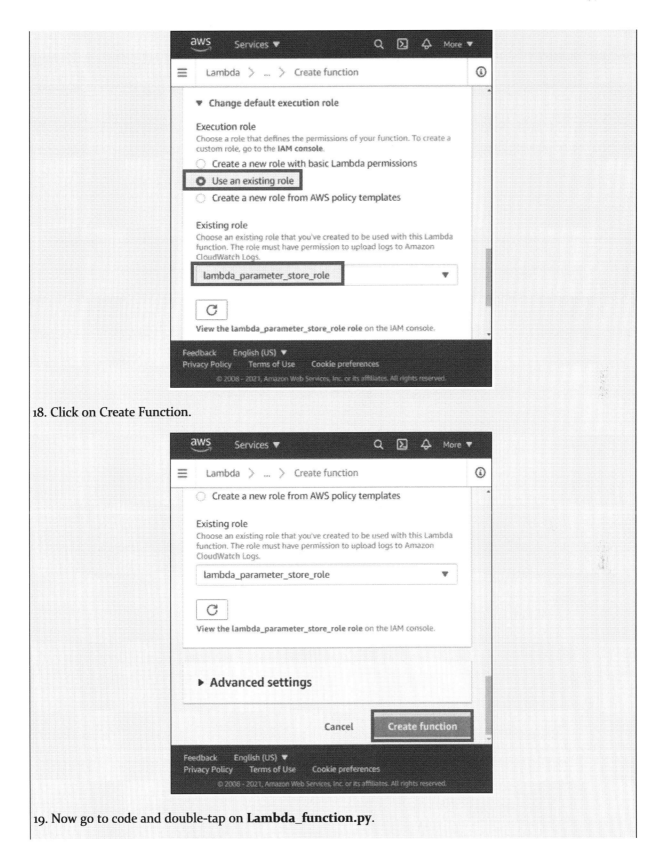

18. Click on Create Function.

19. Now go to code and double-tap on **Lambda_function.py**.

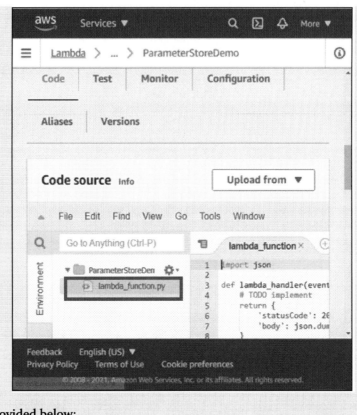

20. Paste the code provided below:

```
import json

import os

import boto3


client = boto3.client("ssm")

env = os.environ["ENV"]

app_config_path = os.environ["APP_CONFIG_PATH"]

full_config_path = "/" + env + "/" + app_config_path


def lambda_handler (event, context):

   print ("Config Path: " + full_config_path)


   param_details = client.get_parameters_by_path (

      Path=full_config_path, Recursive=True, WithDecryption=True
```

)

print (json. dumps (param_details, default=str))

21. Now, go to Configuration and click on Environment variables.

22. Click on Edit and select Add Environment variable.

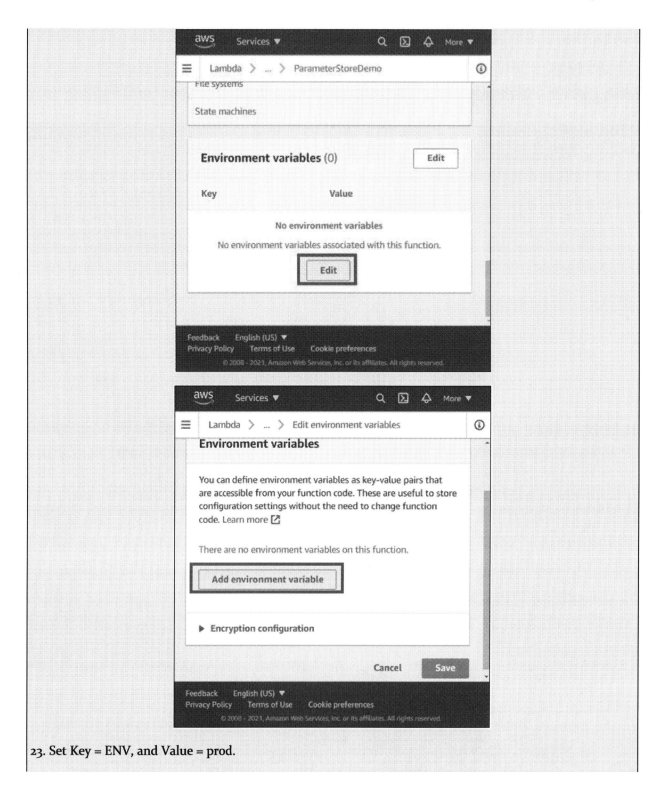

23. Set Key = ENV, and Value = prod.

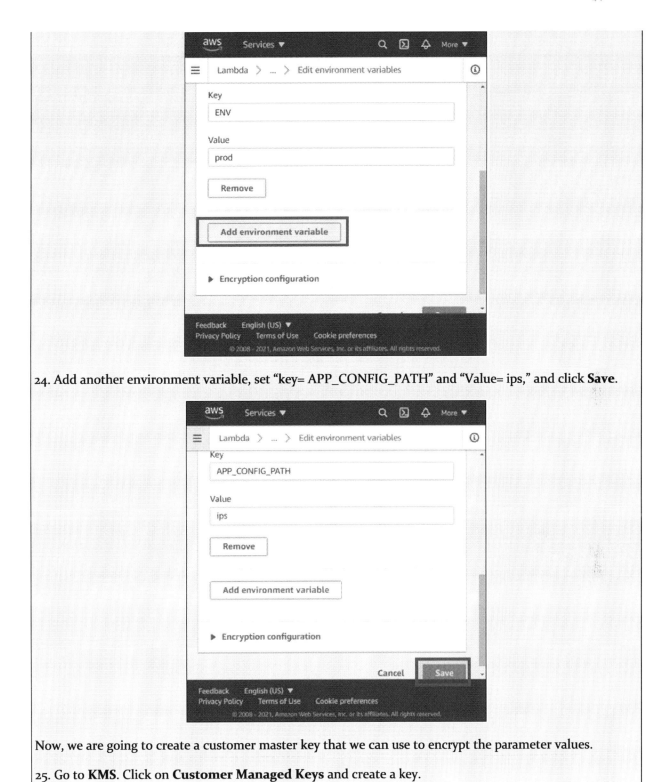

24. Add another environment variable, set "key= APP_CONFIG_PATH" and "Value= ips," and click **Save**.

Now, we are going to create a customer master key that we can use to encrypt the parameter values.

25. Go to **KMS**. Click on **Customer Managed Keys** and create a key.

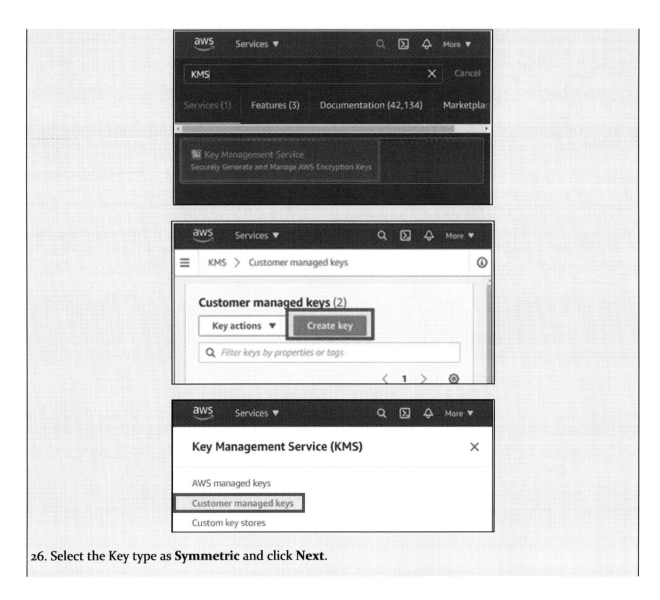

26. Select the Key type as **Symmetric** and click **Next**.

27. Now, give a name to the key and click **Next**.

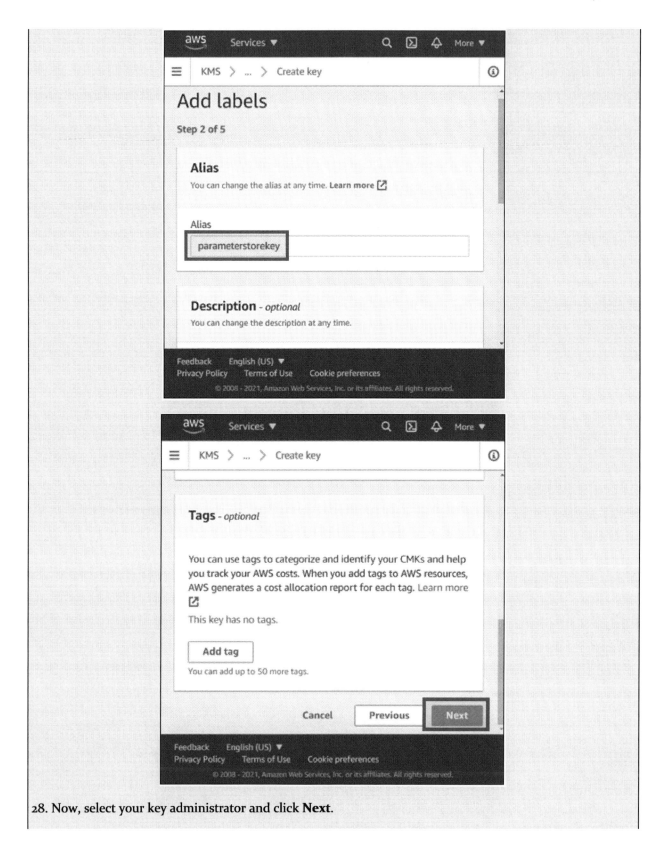

28. Now, select your key administrator and click **Next**.

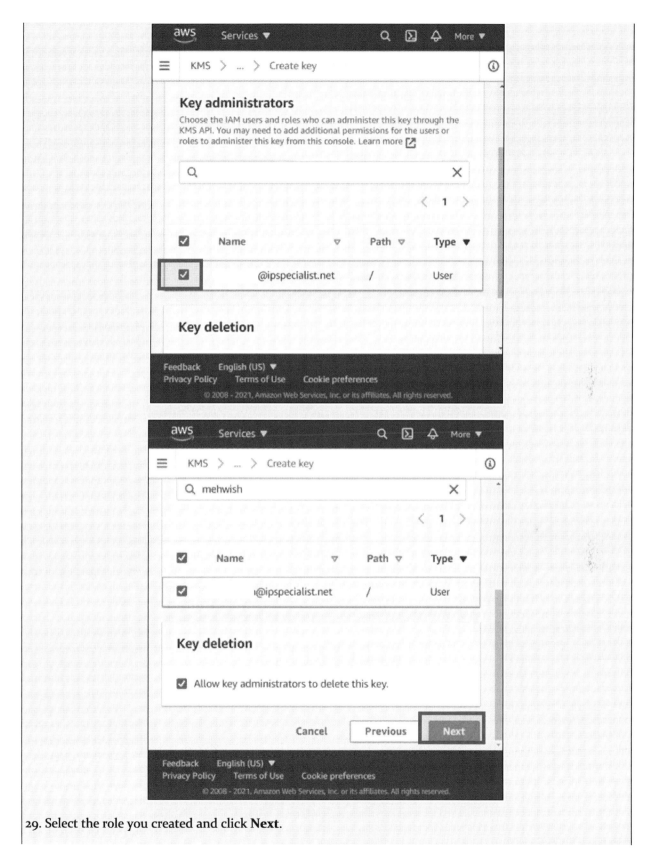

29. Select the role you created and click **Next**.

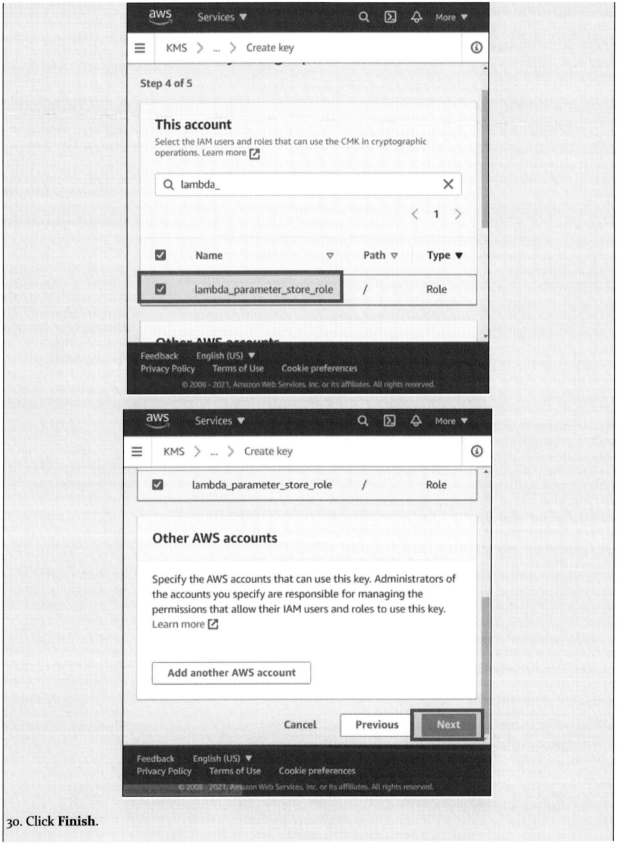

30. Click **Finish**.

31. Go to **SSM** and click on **Parameter store**.

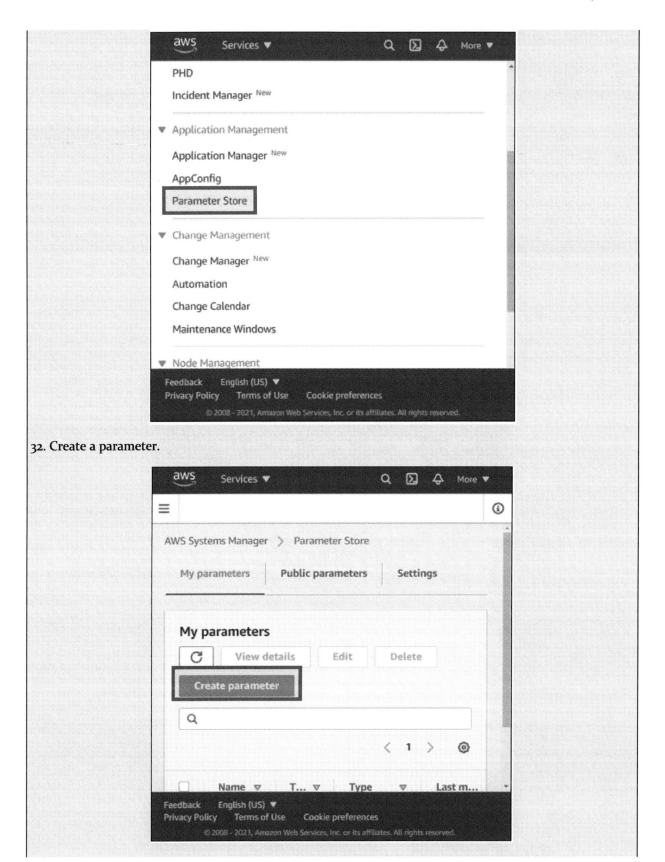

32. Create a parameter.

33. Give a name to the parameter and select **Standard** tier.

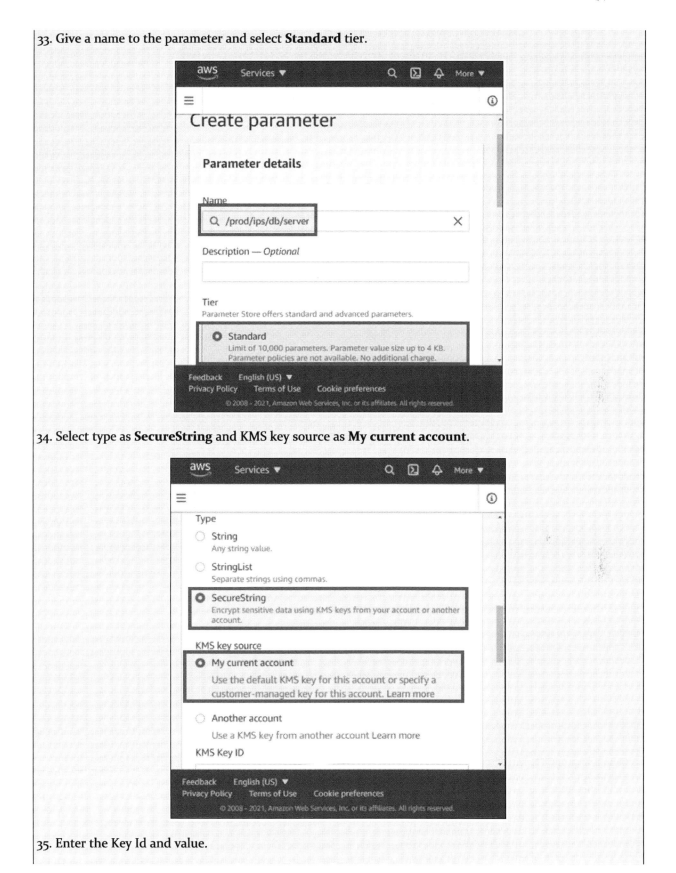

34. Select type as **SecureString** and KMS key source as **My current account**.

35. Enter the Key Id and value.

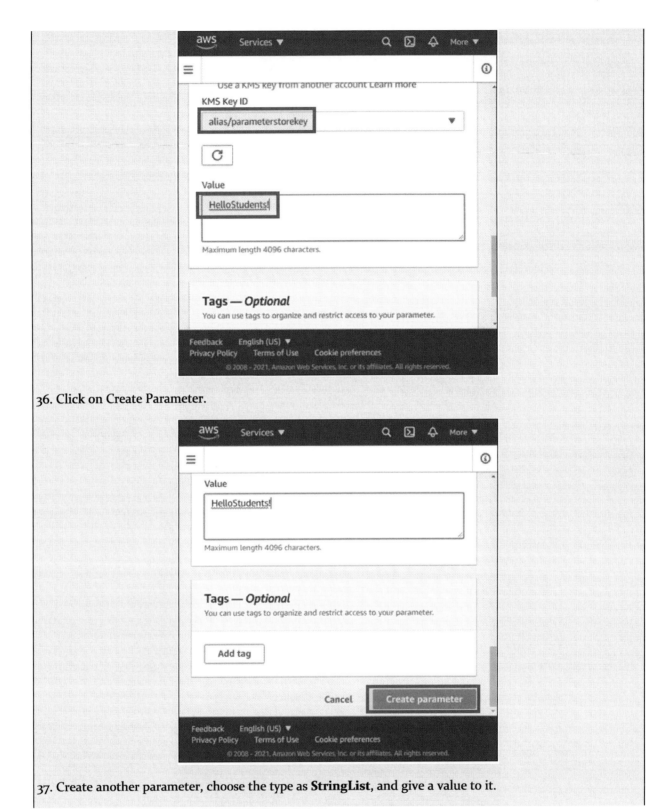

36. Click on Create Parameter.

37. Create another parameter, choose the type as **StringList**, and give a value to it.

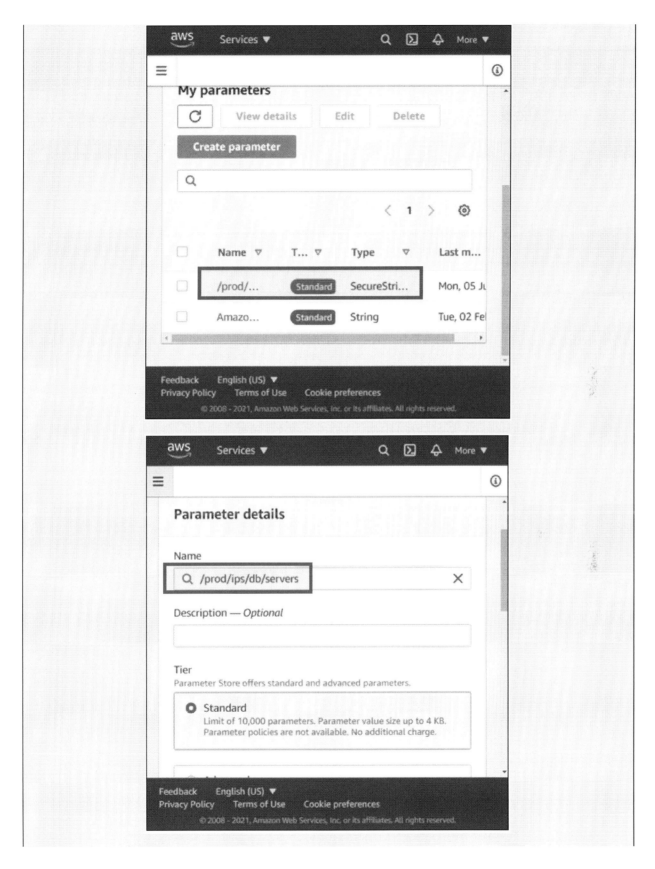

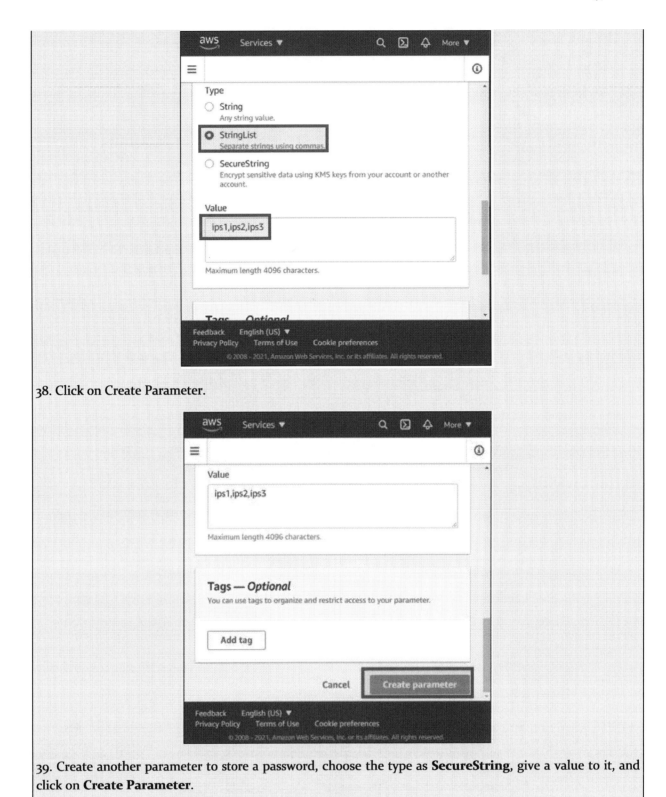

38. Click on Create Parameter.

39. Create another parameter to store a password, choose the type as **SecureString**, give a value to it, and click on **Create Parameter**.

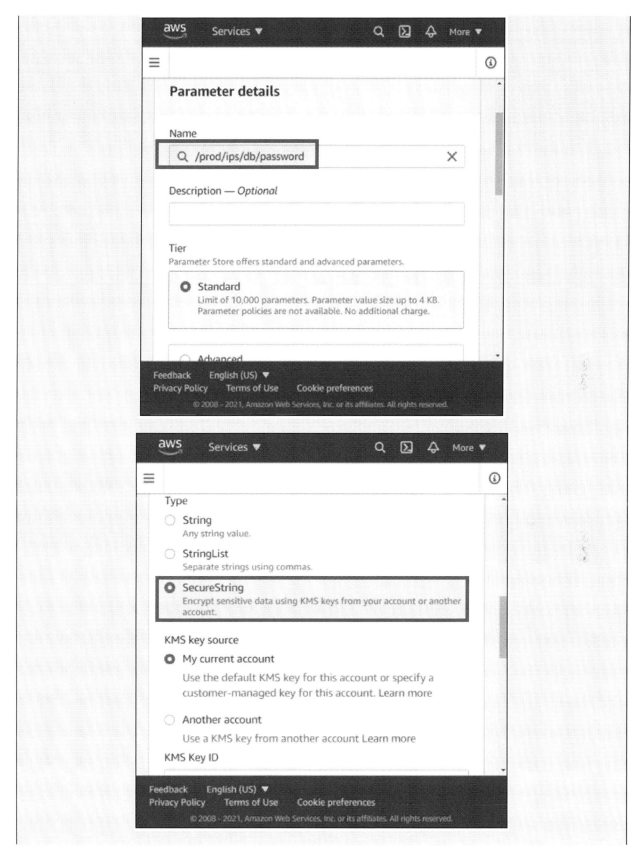

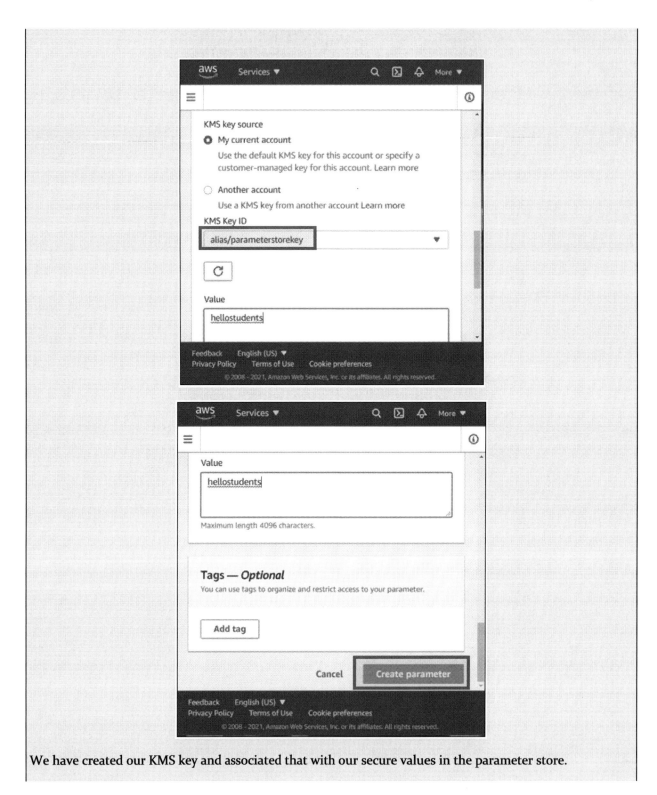

We have created our KMS key and associated that with our secure values in the parameter store.

40. Go to **Lambda** and select the function created.

41. Select **Test**, create a new event, name it, and click on **Save changes**.

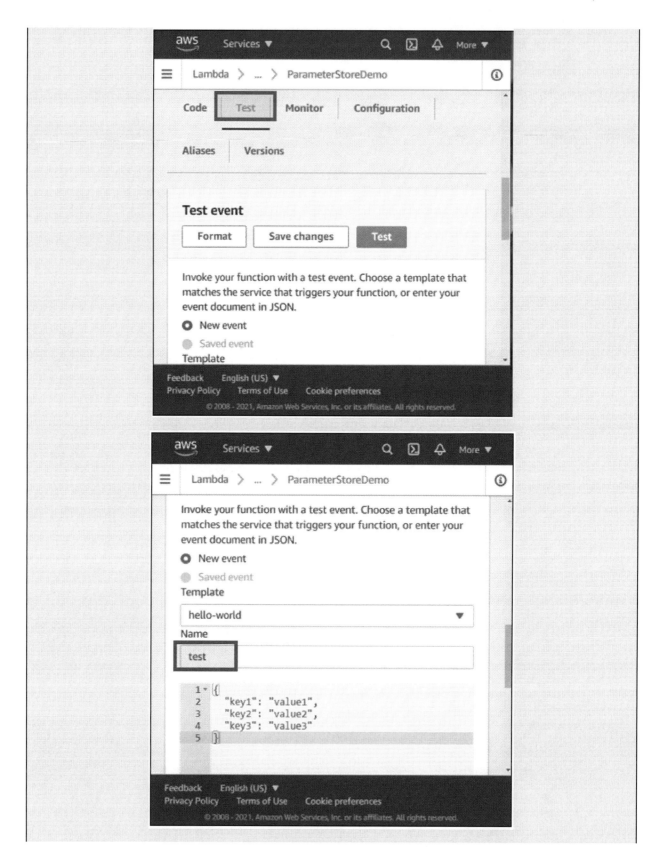

42. Click on **Test**.

43. When the execution is completed, click on **Details**.

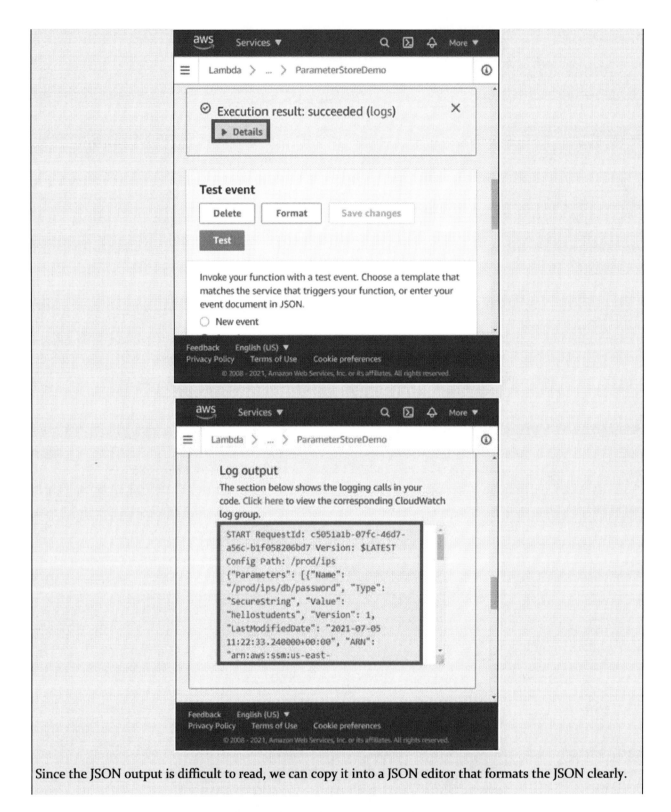

Since the JSON output is difficult to read, we can copy it into a JSON editor that formats the JSON clearly.

```
{
    "Parameters": [{
        "Name": "/prod/ips/db/password",
        "Type": "SecureString",
        "Value": "hellostudents",
        "Version": 1,
        "LastModifiedDate": "2021-07-05 11:22:33.240000+00:00",
        "ARN": "arn:aws:ssm:us-east-1:734404852544:parameter/prod/ips/db/password"
        "DataType": "text"
    },
    {
        "Name": "/prod/ips/db/server",
        "Type": "SecureString",
        "Value": "HelloStudents!",
        "Version": 1,
        "LastModifiedDate": "2021-07-05 11:14:21.082000+00:00",
        "ARN": "arn:aws:ssm:us-east-1:734404852544:parameter/prod/ips/db/server",
        "DataType": "text"},
    {
        "Name": "/prod/ips/db/servers",
        "Type": "StringList",
        "Value": "ips1,ips2,ips3",
        "Version": 1,
        "LastModifiedDate": "2021-07-05 11:20:24.629000+00:00",
        "ARN": "arn:aws:ssm:us-east-1:734404852544:parameter/prod/ips/db/server,
        "DataType": "text"
    }],
```

Here, we can see our parameters have been retrieved.

Secrets Manager

 AWS Secrets Manager protects the secrets needed to access your apps, services, and IT resources. The service allows you to easily rotate, maintain, and retrieve database credentials, API keys, and other secrets during their existence. Secrets Manager APIs allow users and programmers to retrieve secrets, avoiding the need to hardcode sensitive information in plain text. Secrets Manager enables you to access secrets using fine-grained permissions and audit secret rotation centrally for resources in the AWS Cloud, third-party services, and on-premises.

Secrets Manager vs. Parameter Store

Secrets Manager is similar to the Parameter Store in Systems Manager. However, there are some distinctions. There are no additional fees when using the parameter store. There is a limit to how many parameters you can store, which is currently set at 10,000. Secrets manager does have a cost, which is now $.40 for each secret stored. Also, there is an additional $.05 for every 10,000 API calls. This extra cost can be pennies, but these pennies can add up for a large organization and should be considered if you store large amounts of secrets.

Where the secrets manager wins over the parameter store is the ability to rotate secrets automatically. Secrets Manager has built-in support for Amazon RDS, Amazon Redshift, and Amazon DocumentDB, as well as secret rotation. The secrets manager can rotate the keys and automatically apply the new credentials in RDS for you. You can use Lambda to write a function to rotate your keys integrated directly into the secrets manager console. Secrets Manager can generate random secrets. You can randomly generate passwords in CloudFormation and store the passwords in the secrets manager. It is not just functionality for cloud formation. The AWS SDKs can be used in your application code, and the secrets manager can also be shared across accounts.

> **EXAM TIP:** Parameter Store can store data unencrypted or encrypt the data with a KMS key. With Secrets Manager, the secrets are stored encrypted, and there is no option to store unencrypted data.

Lab 12-03: Using Secrets Manager to Authenticate with an RDS Database Using Lambda

Problem

The goal of the software firm Circle of Life is to enhance data-based decision making in the healthcare industry. ZEVAC, its flagship programme, reviews 7 million patient records every day to reveal how antibiotics are dispensed in hospitals.

Circle of Life's engineers had to manually monitor and check whether its container orchestration tool was updated when Kubernetes configurations changed.

Solution

Circle of Life's engineers uses Amazon Elastic Kubernetes Service (Amazon EKS) for container orchestration and Amazon Relational Database Service (Amazon RDS) to manage PostgreSQL and MySQL databases. With Amazon EKS, the company benefits from automatic updates and version control.

Step 1: Create Lambda Function

1. Navigate to Lambda > Functions.

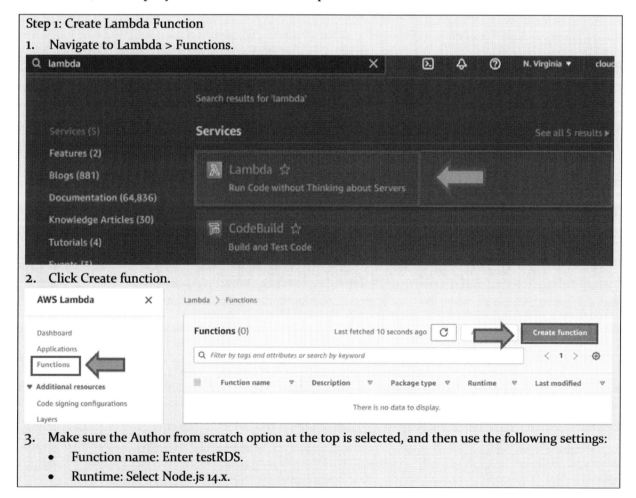

2. Click Create function.

3. Make sure the Author from scratch option at the top is selected, and then use the following settings:
   - Function name: Enter testRDS.
   - Runtime: Select Node.js 14.x.

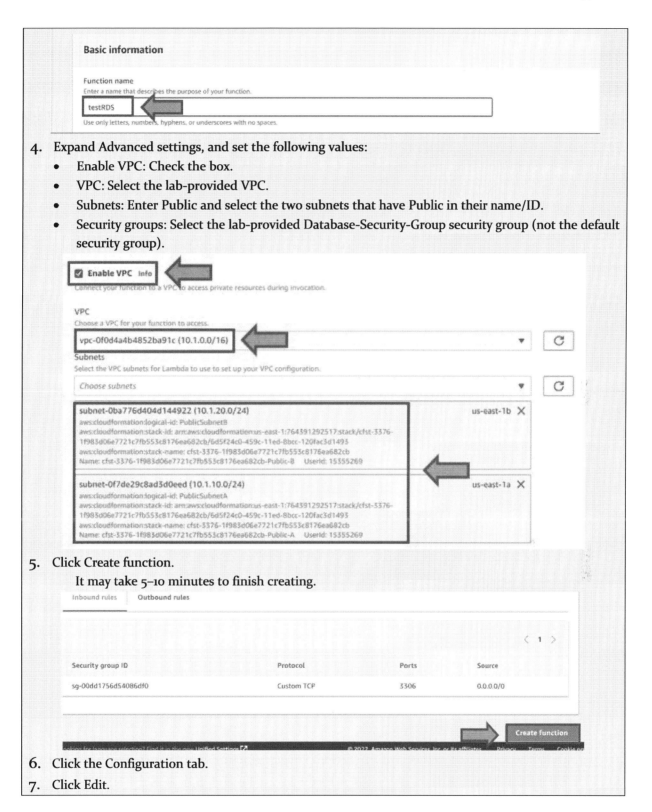

4. Expand Advanced settings, and set the following values:
   - Enable VPC: Check the box.
   - VPC: Select the lab-provided VPC.
   - Subnets: Enter Public and select the two subnets that have Public in their name/ID.
   - Security groups: Select the lab-provided Database-Security-Group security group (not the default security group).

5. Click Create function.

   It may take 5–10 minutes to finish creating.

6. Click the Configuration tab.
7. Click Edit.

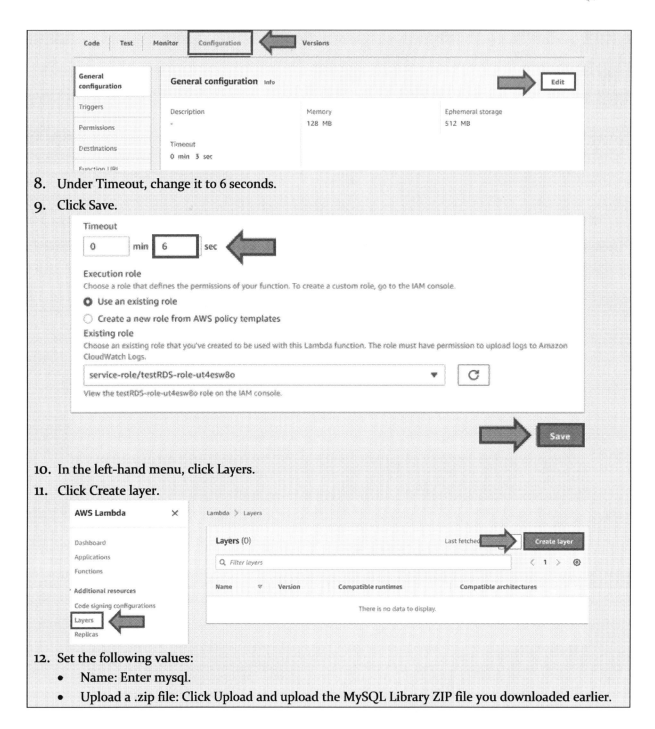

8. Under Timeout, change it to 6 seconds.

9. Click Save.

10. In the left-hand menu, click Layers.

11. Click Create layer.

12. Set the following values:
    - Name: Enter mysql.
    - Upload a .zip file: Click Upload and upload the MySQL Library ZIP file you downloaded earlier.

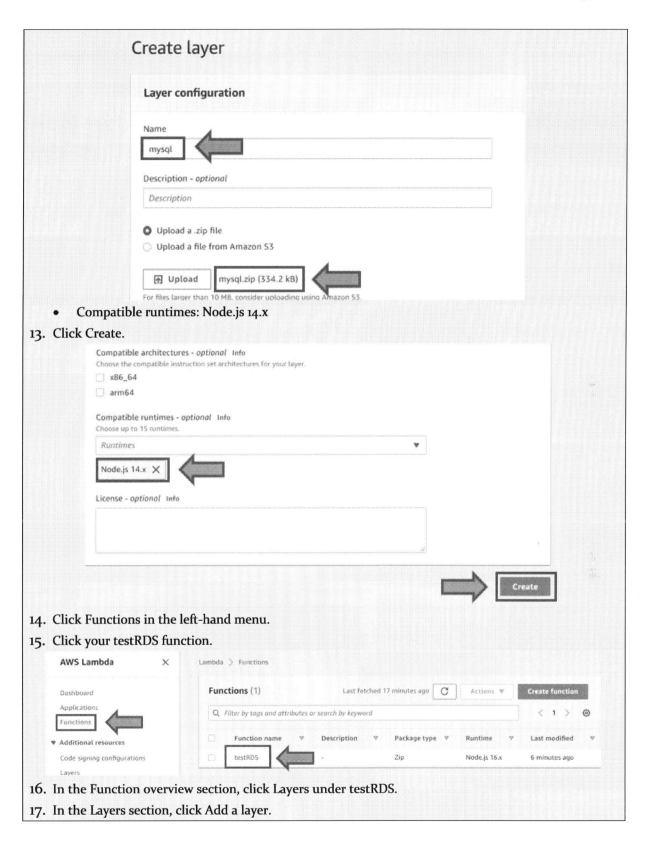

- Compatible runtimes: Node.js 14.x

13. Click Create.

14. Click Functions in the left-hand menu.

15. Click your testRDS function.

16. In the Function overview section, click Layers under testRDS.

17. In the Layers section, click Add a layer.

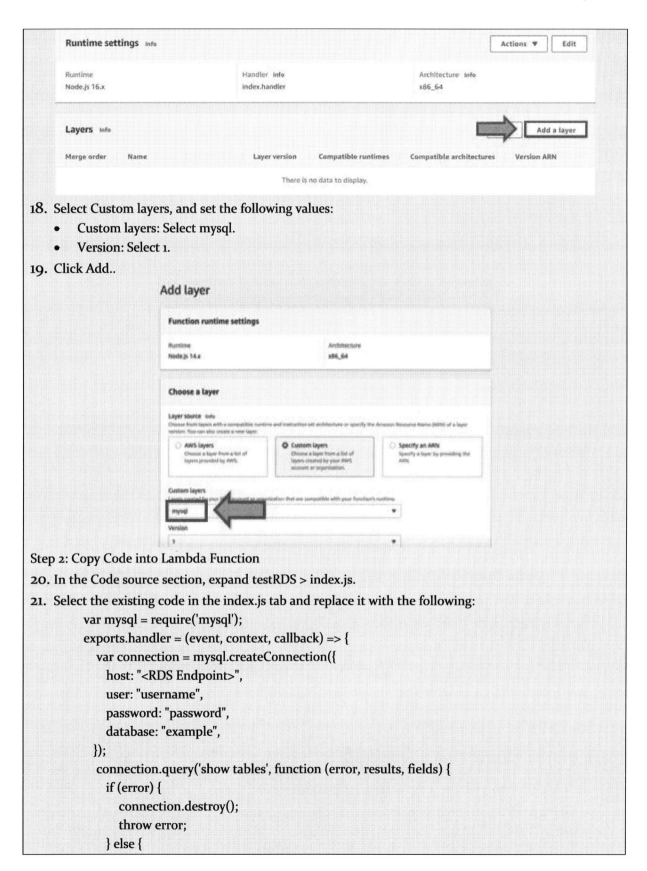

18. Select Custom layers, and set the following values:

    • Custom layers: Select mysql.

    • Version: Select 1.

19. Click Add..

Step 2: Copy Code into Lambda Function

20. In the Code source section, expand testRDS > index.js.

21. Select the existing code in the index.js tab and replace it with the following:

```
var mysql = require('mysql');
exports.handler = (event, context, callback) => {
  var connection = mysql.createConnection({
    host: "<RDS Endpoint>",
    user: "username",
    password: "password",
    database: "example",
  });
  connection.query('show tables', function (error, results, fields) {
    if (error) {
      connection.destroy();
      throw error;
    } else {
```

```
                // connected!
                console.log("Query result:");
                console.log(results);
                callback(error, results);
                connection.end(function (err) { callback(err, results);});
            }
        });
    };
```

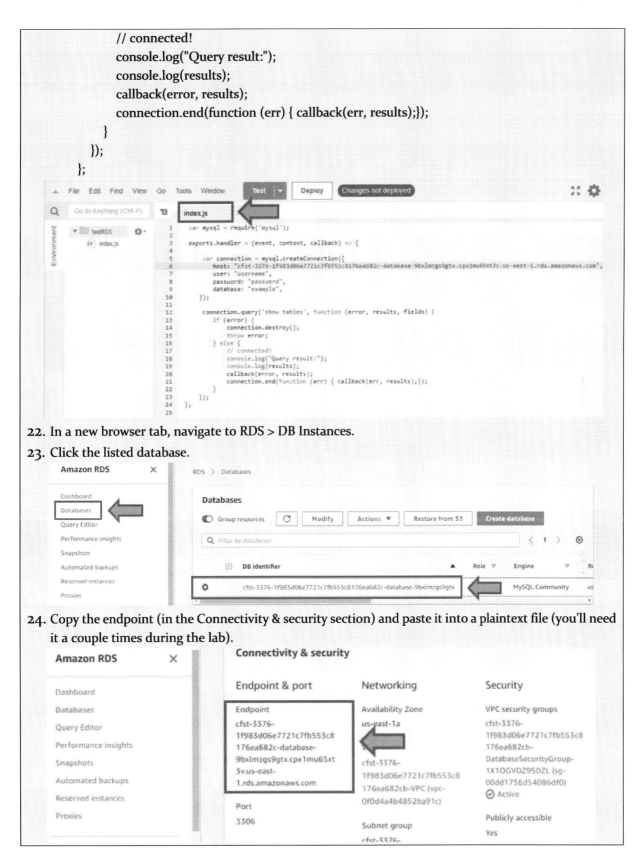

22. In a new browser tab, navigate to RDS > DB Instances.

23. Click the listed database.

24. Copy the endpoint (in the Connectivity & security section) and paste it into a plaintext file (you'll need it a couple times during the lab).

25. Back in the Lambda function code, replace <RDS Endpoint> on line 6 with the endpoint you just copied.
26. Click Deploy.
27. Click Test.

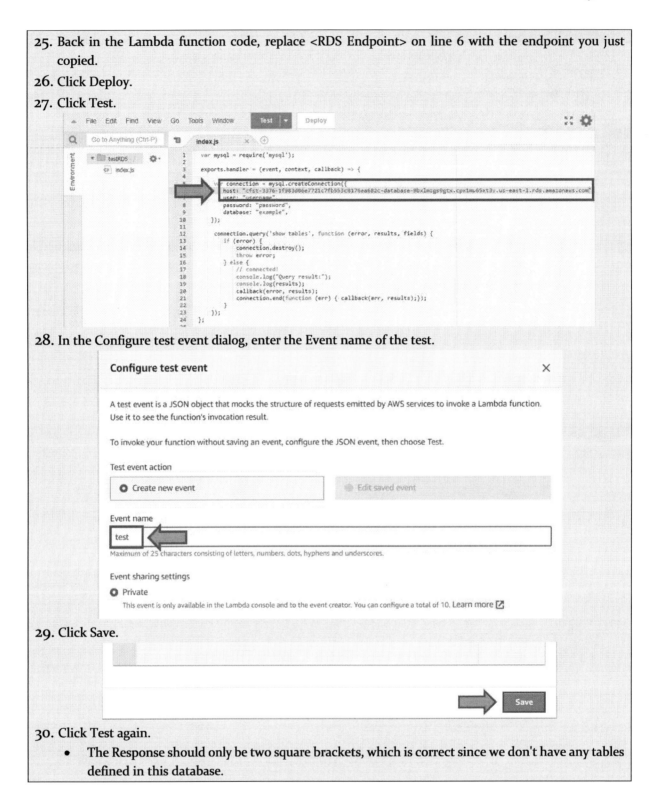

28. In the Configure test event dialog, enter the Event name of the test.

29. Click Save.

30. Click Test again.
    - The Response should only be two square brackets, which is correct since we don't have any tables defined in this database.

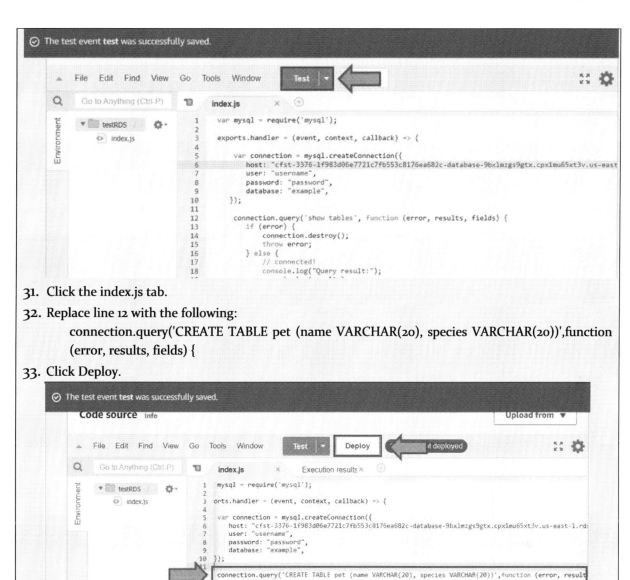

31. Click the index.js tab.
32. Replace line 12 with the following:

    connection.query('CREATE TABLE pet (name VARCHAR(20), species VARCHAR(20))',function (error, results, fields) {

33. Click Deploy.

34. Click Test.
    - This time, the Response should have information within curly brackets.

```
Go   Tools   Window        Test  ▼

  🗐   index.js        ×    Execution results ×   ⊕

  1   mysql = require('mysql');
  2
  3   orts.handler = (event, context, callback) => {
  4
  5   var connection = mysql.createConnection({
  6       host: "cfst-3376-1f983d06e7721c7fb553c8176ea682c-database-9bxlmzgs9gtx.cpx1mu65xt3v.us-east-1.rd:
  7       user: "username",
  8       password: "password",
  9       database: "example",
 10   });
 11
 12   connection.query('CREATE TABLE pet (name VARCHAR(20), species VARCHAR(20))',function (error, result:
 13       if (error) {
 14           connection.destroy();
 15           throw error;
 16       } else {
```

35. Click the index.js tab.

36. Undo the code change (Ctrl+Z or Cmd+Z) to get it back to the original code we pasted in.

37. Click Deploy.

```
Go   Tools   Window        Test  ▼      Deploy         ot deployed

  🗐   index.js        ×    Execution results ×   ⊕

  1   mysql = require('mysql');
  2
  3   orts.handler = (event, context, callback) => {
  4
  5   var connection = mysql.createConnection({
  6       host: "cfst-3376-1f983d06e7721c7fb553c8176ea682c-database-9bxlmzgs9gtx.cpx1mu65xt3v.us-east-1.rd:
  7       user: "username",
  8       password: "password",
  9       database: "example",
 10   });
 11
 12   connection.query('show tables', function (error, results, fields) {
 13       if (error) {
 14           connection.destroy();
 15           throw error;
 16       } else {
 17           // connected!
 18           console.log("Query result:");
```

38. Click Test.

- This time, we should see the pet table listed in the Response.

```
Go   Tools   Window        Test  ▼

  🗐   index.js        ×    Execution results ×   ⊕

  1   mysql = require('mysql');
  2
  3   orts.handler = (event, context, callback) => {
  4
  5   var connection = mysql.createConnection({
  6       host: "cfst-3376-1f983d06e7721c7fb553c8176ea682c-database-9bxlmzgs9gtx.cpx1mu65xt3v.us-east-1.rd:
  7       user: "username",
  8       password: "password",
  9       database: "example",
 10   });
 11
 12   connection.query('show tables', function (error, results, fields) {
 13       if (error) {
 14           connection.destroy();
 15           throw error;
 16       } else {
 17           // connected!
 18           console.log("Query result:");
```

Step 3: Create a Secret in Secrets Manager

39. In a new browser tab, navigate to Secrets Manager.

40. Click Store a new secret.

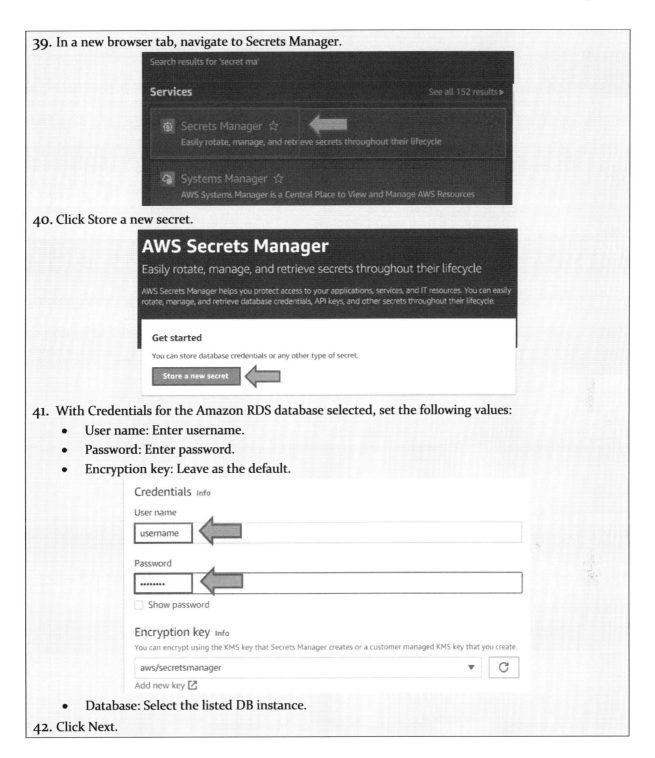

41. With Credentials for the Amazon RDS database selected, set the following values:
    - User name: Enter username.
    - Password: Enter password.
    - Encryption key: Leave as the default.
    - Database: Select the listed DB instance.

42. Click Next.

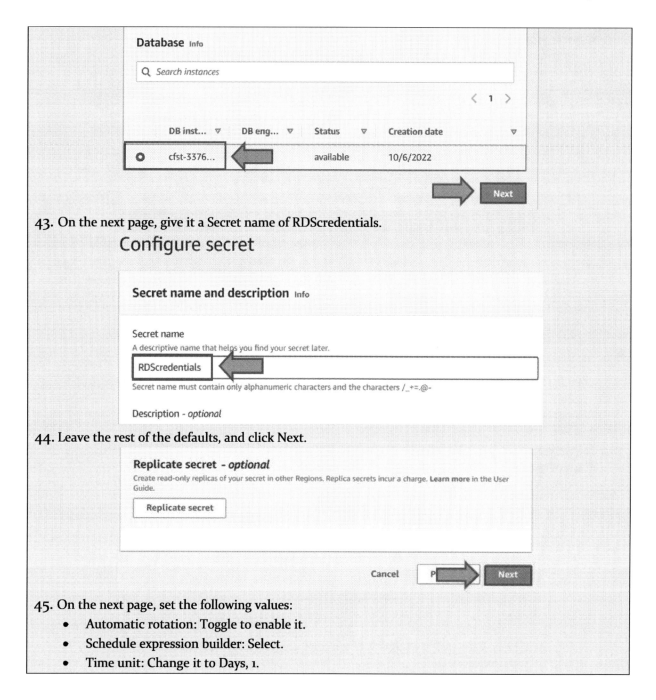

43. On the next page, give it a Secret name of RDScredentials.

44. Leave the rest of the defaults, and click Next.

45. On the next page, set the following values:
   - Automatic rotation: Toggle to enable it.
   - Schedule expression builder: Select.
   - Time unit: Change it to Days, 1.

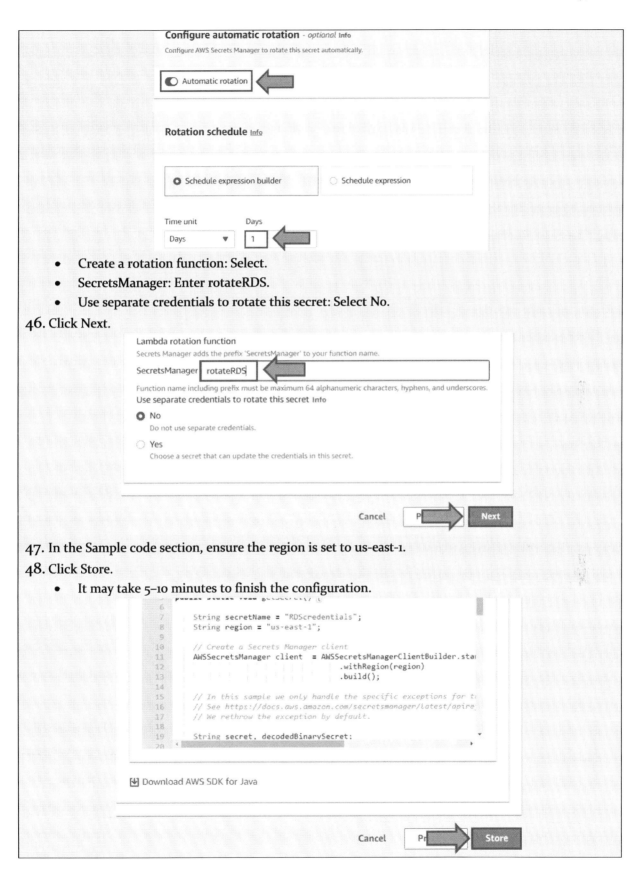

- Create a rotation function: Select.
- SecretsManager: Enter rotateRDS.
- Use separate credentials to rotate this secret: Select No.

46. Click Next.

47. In the Sample code section, ensure the region is set to us-east-1.

48. Click Store.

- It may take 5–10 minutes to finish the configuration.

49. Once it's done, click RDScredentials.

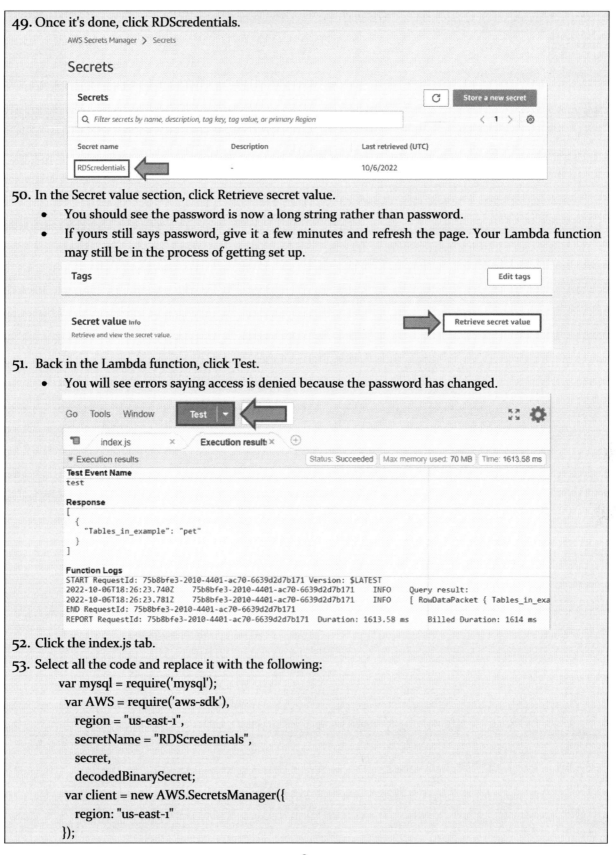

50. In the Secret value section, click Retrieve secret value.
    - You should see the password is now a long string rather than password.
    - If yours still says password, give it a few minutes and refresh the page. Your Lambda function may still be in the process of getting set up.

51. Back in the Lambda function, click Test.
    - You will see errors saying access is denied because the password has changed.

52. Click the index.js tab.

53. Select all the code and replace it with the following:

```
var mysql = require('mysql');
var AWS = require('aws-sdk'),
  region = "us-east-1",
  secretName = "RDScredentials",
  secret,
  decodedBinarySecret;
var client = new AWS.SecretsManager({
  region: "us-east-1"
});
```

```
exports.handler = (event, context, callback) => {
    client.getSecretValue({SecretId: secretName}, function(err, data) {
      if (err) {
        console.log(err);
      }
      else {
        // Decrypts secret using the associated KMS CMK.
        // Depending on whether the secret is a string or binary, one of these fields will be
populated.
          if ('SecretString' in data) {
            secret = data.SecretString;
          } else {
            let buff = new Buffer(data.SecretBinary, 'base64');
            decodedBinarySecret = buff.toString('ascii');
          }
      }
      var parse = JSON.parse(secret);
      var password = parse.password;
      var connection = mysql.createConnection({
        host: "<RDS Endpoint>",
        user: "username",
        password: password,
        database: "example",
      });
      connection.query('show tables', function (error, results, fields) {
        if (error) {
          connection.destroy();
          throw error;
        } else {
          // connected!
          console.log("Query result:");
          console.log(results);
          callback(error, results);
          connection.end(function (err) { callback(err, results);});
        }
      });
    });
};
```

54. Replace <RDS Endpoint> with the value you copied earlier.

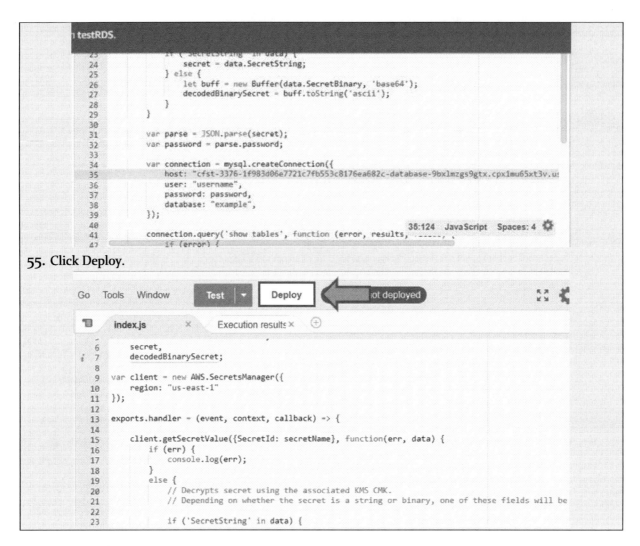

55. Click Deploy.

AWS Shield

AWS Shield is an Amazon Web Services (AWS)-managed Distributed Denial-of-Service (DDoS) protection service. AWS Shield delivers always-on monitoring and automatic inline mitigations that minimize application downtime and latency, so there is no need to contact AWS Support to get DDoS protection. AWS Shield is divided into two categories: Standard and Advanced.

AWS Shield Standard

AWS Shield Standard automatically protects your web applications running on AWS against the most common, frequently occurring DDoS attacks.

When you use WAF with CloudFront or an application load balancer, you get Shield standard at no additional cost. It helps protect you against standard layer three and layer four attacks. Some of these attacks are called SYN or UDP floods. The most common method is when you have UDP packets that flood your servers. Every packet sent to the targeted server needs to be replied to; those are the rules for UDP.

SYN floods work similarly to UDP floods, but they work on TCP rather than UDP. They make your servers wait for an answer. It is done by leaving many connections half-open, waiting for handshakes that are never complete. AWS Shield can also protect against reflection attacks. These are other kinds of UDP attacks where the source IP address of packets is spoofed, and the victim will receive a large volume of response packets it never requested.

AWS Shield has proven to be very effective. In February 2020, AWS was hit with a DDOS attack of 2.3 terabits per second for three days. That was double the attack that took down GitHub in 2018. No AWS services were negatively impacted or went offline by this attack.

AWS Shield Advanced

AWS Shield Advanced delivers stronger defenses against more complex and broad threats for your applications running on protected Amazon EC2, Elastic Load Balancing (ELB), Amazon CloudFront, AWS Global Accelerator, and Route 53 resources. AWS Shield Advanced uses advanced attack mitigation and routing techniques to mitigate threats automatically. Customers with Business or Enterprise support can also use the DDoS Response Team (DRT) to handle and mitigate application-layer DDoS attacks 24 hours a day, seven days a week. During a DDoS assault, the DDoS cost protection for scaling shields your AWS bill from higher prices caused by use spikes from protected Amazon EC2, Elastic Load Balancing (ELB), Amazon CloudFront, AWS Global Accelerator, and Amazon Route 53. Using AWS Shield Advanced, you pay a monthly charge of $3,000 per company.

EXAM TIP: AWS provides two levels of protection against DDoS attacks: AWS Shield Standard and AWS Shield Advanced. AWS Shield Standard is offered at no additional charge over and above what you already pay for AWS WAF and other AWS services. AWS Shield Advanced provides further protection against DDoS attacks. AWS Shield Advanced protects your Amazon EC2 instances, Elastic Load Balancing load balancers, Amazon CloudFront distributions, and Amazon Route 53 hosted zones from DDoS attacks.

Web Application Firewall

WAF (Web Application Firewall) is a web application firewall that lets you monitor HTTP and HTTPS traffic to CloudFront, an application load balancer, or an API gateway. WAF allows you to restrict material access depending on the criteria you define. WAF tells your service whether to respond to requests with the required content or with an error message. It is accomplished by setting up filtering rules that allow or disallow traffic.

WAF supports several different filtering rules. You can filter on:

- The IP address of the incoming request
- Any query string parameters

URLs like http://example.com/page?foo=bar&abc=xyz&baz=123 have question marks, equal signs, and ampersands; these are name-value pairs. You can configure WAF to inspect these values for anything you want to allow or deny. WAF can also protect you against SQL query injection attacks. Attackers sometimes

insert malicious SQL code into web requests to extract data from your database; in cases where your WAF rules block traffic, that blocked traffic returns an HTTP 403 error code, which is the forbidden code.

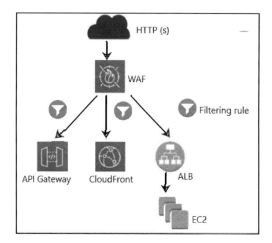

Figure 12-13: WAF

How does WAF Work?
WAF allows three different behaviors:

1. Allow all requests except for those you define in your rules.

2. Filter off all requests except those you specify.

3. Count how many requests match the properties you specified.

Some of those properties are:

- You can look at the originating IP address of the request.
- You can look at the originating country.
- You can examine the request size. You can enforce an upper or lower bound on the size of the request coming into your application.
- You can inspect the string values in HTTP request headers. For example, you can block HTTP requests that do not contain a user agent header.
- You can inspect the strings in requests that match regular expressions or Regex patterns. For example, you can use regex to block known bad bots by looking for ways in the user agent header.
- WAF can be used to block SQL code injection. We can use WAF's built-in SQL injection condition in conjunction with a regex-based condition to look for SQL injection attempts only on URLs ending with .PHP while ignoring URLs ending with .JPEG.
- WAF can also block cross-site scripting or XSS attacks. Cross-site scripting attacks are those where the attacker uses vulnerabilities in an otherwise benign website as a vehicle to inject malicious client-side scripts like JavaScript into other legitimate users and web browsers. This cross-site scripting feature prevents these vulnerabilities in your web applications by inspecting different elements of the incoming request.

 AWS Firewall Manager

AWS Firewall Manager is a security management solution that lets you centrally set up and administer firewall rules across your AWS accounts. You can use firewall management to set up WAF rules for your:

- Application Load Balancer (ALB)
- API Gateway
- CloudFront Distributions

You can also create AWS Shield advanced protection policies to automatically discover resources like:

- Application Load Balancers
- ELB Classic Load Balancers
- Elastic IPS (EIP)
- CloudFront Distributions

You can also consistently apply DDoS protection to all those resources or use tags to specify a subset of resources. You can use the AWS firewall to configure security groups across multiple accounts in your organization and continuously audit them to detect overly permissive or misconfigured rules that apply to EC2 instances and elastic network interfaces.

> **EXAM TIP:** AWS WAF is a web application firewall that lets you monitor the HTTP and HTTPS requests forwarded to Amazon CloudFront or an Application Load Balancer. At the same time, AWS Firewall Manager simplifies your AWS WAF administration and helps you enforce WAF rules on the resources across all the accounts in an AWS Organization by using AWS Config in the background. AWS Firewall Manager also enables you to selectively apply the rules to specific resources.

Guarding Your Network with GuardDuty

Amazon GuardDuty
GuardDuty is a threat detection service that continuously scans for harmful behavior using machine learning.

- Unusual API calls calls from a known malicious IP.
- Attempts to disable CloudTrail logging.
- Unauthorized deployments.
- Compromised instances
- Reconnaissance by would be attackers
- Port scanning failed logins

Features

- Alerts appear in the GuardDuty console and CLoudWatch Events.
- Receives feeds from third parties like Proofpoint and CrowdStrikes, as well as AWS Security, about known malicious domains and IP addresses, etc.
- Monitors CloudTrail Logs, VPC Flow Logs, and DNS logs.
- Centralize threat detection across multiple AWS accounts.

- Automated response using CloudWatch Events and Lambda.
- Machine Learning and anomaly detection.

Threat Detection With AI

7-14 days to set a baseline. Once active, you will see findings on the GuardDuty console and in CloudWatch Events only if GuardDuty detects behavior it considers a threat.

 Exam TIP:

- GuardDuty uses AI to learn what normal behavior looks like in your account and to alert you of any abnormal or malicious behavior
- GuardDuty updates a database of known malicious domains using external feeds from third parties.
- GuardDuty monitors CloudTrail logs, VPC Flow Logs, and DNS logs.
- Findings appear in GuardDuty dashboard. CLoudWatch Events can be used to trigger functions to address a threat.

Monitoring S3 Buckets with Macie

Macie

With the use of machine learning and pattern matching, Amazon Macie, a fully managed data security and privacy solution, can find and guard your sensitive AWS data.

Personally Identifiable Information

Any data that might be used to identify a specific person is considered personally identifiable information (PII). PII refers to any information that might be utilized to identify a specific individual or to deanonymize previously anonymous data.

Some of the features of PII are as follows;

- Information about an individual's identity that is personal
- Criminals might utilize this information for financial fraud and identity theft.
- Home address, email address, Social Security number
- Passport number, or driver's license number
- Date of birth, your phone number, your bank account, and even your credit card numbers.

Automated Analysis Of Data

Macie searches S3 for sensitive data using machine learning and pattern matching.

- Uses artificial intelligence to identify sensitive data in your S3 items, such as personally identifiable information.
- Alerts you to unencrypted buckets
- Alerts you about your public buckets
- Alerts you about buckets that are shared with AWS accounts that are outside of those defined in your AWS organizations.
- Great for frameworks like HIPAA and GDPR

Macie Alerts

- You can filter and search Macie alerts in the AWS console.
- Alerts sent to Amazon EventBridge can be integrated with your security incident and event management (SIEM) systems.
- Can be integrated with AWS Security Hub for a broader analysis of your organization's security posture.
- It is compatible with other AWS services, such as step functions, to automatically take remediation actions.

Exam TIP:

- Macie uses AI to analyze data in S3 and helps identify PII, PHI, and financial data.
- It is great for HIPAA and GDPR compliance and preventing identity theft.
- Macie alerts can be sent to Amazon EventBridge and integrated with your event management systems.
- You can automate remediation actions using other AWS services

Securing Operating Systems with Inspector

Amazon Inspector

An automated security evaluation programme called Amazon Inspector aids in enhancing the safety and legal compliance of apps running on AWS.

Amazon Inspector automatically evaluates applications for flaws or departures from recommended practices.

Assessment Findings

Following an evaluation, Amazon Inspector generates a thorough list of security findings that are ranked according to their seriousness.

These results can be examined alone or as part of comprehensive assessment reports that are accessible through the console or API of Amazon Inspector.

Types of Assessment

Network Assessment

Network configuration analysis to check for ports reachable from outside the VPC. An Inspector agent is not required.

Host Assessment

Vulnerable software (CVE), host hardening (CIS Benchmarks); and security best practices. An Inspector agent is required.

Working

Steps of a working of Inspector are as follows;

- Create assessment target
- Install agents on EC2 instances. AWS will automatically install the agent for instance, that allows the System Manager Run Command.

- Create assessment techniques.
- Perform assessment run
- Review findings against the rules.

Exam TIP:
- Inspector is used to performing vulnerability scans on both EC2 instances and VPCs.
- These are also called host assessments and network assessments. You can run these assessments once or alternatively, run them weekly.

AWS Certificate Manager

AWS Certificate Manager allows you to create, manage, and deploy public and private SSL certificates for use with other AWS services.

It integrates with other services such as Elastic Load Balancing, CloudFront distributions, and API Gateway allowing you to easily manage and deploy SSL certificates in your AWS environment.

Benefits of AWS Certificate Manager

Cost

No more paying for SSL certificates. AWS Certificate Manager provisions both public and private certificates for free. You will still pay for the resources that utilize your certificates (such as Elastic Load Balancing).

Automated Renewals and Deployment

AWS Certificate Manager can automate the renewal of your SSL certificate and then automatically update the new certificate with ACM-integrated services, such as Elastic Load Balancing, CloudFront. And API Gateway.

Easier to Set Up

Removes a lot of the manual process, such as generating a key pair or creating a certificate signing request (CSR). You can create your own SSL certificate with just a few clicks in the AWS Management Console.

Exam TIP:
- Supported Services - AWS Certificate Manager integrates with Elastic Load Balancing, CLoudFront, and API Gateway.
- Benefits - AWS Certificate Manager is a free service that saves time and money. Automatically renew your SSL certificates and rotate the old certificates with new certificates with the supported AWS service.

Global Caching with CloudFront

CloudFront

CloudFront is a fast content delivery network (CDN) service that securely delivers global data, videos, applications, and APIs to customers. It helps reduce latency and provide higher transfer speeds using AWS edge locations.

CloudFront Settings

Security

Defaults to HTTPS connection with the ability to add a custom SSL certificate.

Endpoint Support

It can be used to front AWS endpoints along with non-AWS applications.

Global Distribution

You cannot pick specific countries, just general areas of the globe.

Expiring Content

You can force expiration of content from the cache if you cannot wait for the TTL.

 Exam TIP:
- CloudFront's main purpose is to cache content at the edge locations to speed up the delivery of data.
- CLoudFron can be used to block individual countries, but the WAF is a better tool for it.

Caching Your Data with ElastiCache and DAX

ElastiCache

ElastiCache is an AWS managed version of 2 open-source technologies: Memcached and Redis. Neither of these tools is specific to AWS, but by using ElastiCache you avoid a lot of common issues you might encounter.

Memcached vs. Redis

Memcached	Redis
• Simple database caching solution	• Supported as a caching solution
• Not a database by itself	• Functions as a standalone database
• No failover or Multi-AZ support	• Failover and Multi-AZ support
• No backups	• Supports backups

Mind Map

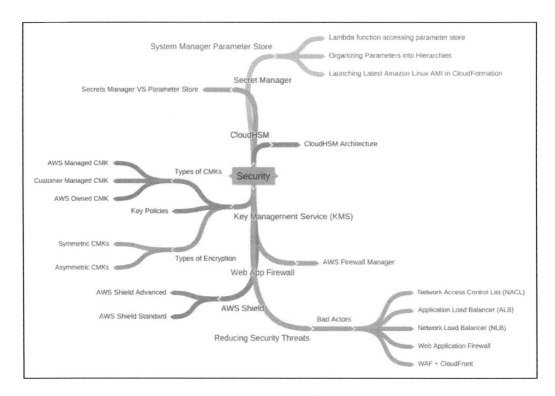

Figure 12-14: Mind Map

Practice Questions

1. If you want to block common exploits like sequel injection or cross-site scripting attacks, then you have to use _____.

a) NACL

b) WAF

c) AWS Shield

2. If you want to block an IP or range of IPs, then you must use _____.

a) NACL

b) WAF

c) NLB

3. _____ is ideal for encrypting S3 objects, database passwords, and API keys stored in the systems manager parameter store.

a) CloudHSM

b) KMS

c) Secret Manager

4. CMKs can encrypt and decrypt data up to _____ kilobytes in size.

a) 5

b) 6

c) 4

5. KMS is a FIPs 140-2 level two service. True or false?

a) True

b) False

6. Which of the following statement is incorrect about AWS Managed CMK?

a) You can view AWS Managed CMK

b) You can manage AWS Managed CMK

c) AWS Managed CMKs are created automatically when you first create an encrypted resource in an AWS service

7. You cannot view AWS-owned CMKs. True or false?

a) True
b) False

8. With CloudHSM, you can manage your own encryption keys using FIPS 140-2 Level 2 validated HSMs. True or false?

a) True

b) False

9. _____ is an essential tool for caching and distributing secrets securely to AWS resources.

a) Parameter Store

b) KMS

c) CloudHSM

10. _____ enables you to control access to secrets using fine-grained permissions and audit secret rotation centrally for resources in the AWS Cloud, third-party services, and on-premises.

a) Parameter Store

b) KMS

c) Secrets Manager

11. _____ can automatically rotate secrets.

a) KMS

b) Secrets Manager

c) Parameter Store

12. Secrets Manager has the ability to generate random secrets. True or false?

a) True

b) False

13. Parameter Store provides the option to store data unencrypted or to encrypt the data with a KMS key. True or false?

a) True

b) False

14. _____ is a managed Distributed-Denial-of-Service (DDoS) protection service that safeguards applications running on AWS.

a) AWS Shield

b) AWS Inspector

c) AWS WAF

15. _____ lets you monitor HTTP or HTTPS requests to CloudFront, application load balancer, or API gateway.

a) AWS Shield

b) AWS Inspector

c) AWS WAF

Answers

Chapter 08: High Availability (HA) Architecture

1. Answer: a

Explanation: Network Load Balancer is best suited for Load Balancing of Transfer Control Protocol (TCP) traffic where extreme performance is required.

2. Answer: b

Explanation: Internal load balancer is often used in a multi-tier application to load balance between tiers of the application such as an Internet-facing load balancer might receive and balance traffic to the web or presentation tier whose Amazon EC2 instances and send its request to the load balancer of the application tier.

3. Answer: a and c

Explanation: Following protocols are supported by Elastic Load Balancing;

- HTTP
- HTTPS
- TCP
- SSL

4. Answer: b

Explanation: You can also modify configuration settings using either Command Line Interface (CLI) or AWS Management Console.

5. Answer: b

Explanation: The load balancer manages an idle timeout for each connection that is triggered when data is not sent over the connection for a specified period. When the idle timeout period has elapsed, if data has not been sent or received, the connection closes by the load balancer.

6. Answer: c

Explanation: You can use sticky session feature, which is also known as session affinity that enables the load balancer to bind the user's session to the specific instance.

7. Answer: a

Explanation: Health checks are supported by Elastic Load Balancing to test the status of Amazon EC2 instances behind an Elastic Load Balancing load balancer.

8. Answer: b

Explanation: A configuration template is used by ASGs to launch EC2 instances. In a configuration template, you can specify information such as the AMI ID, key pair, security groups, and block device mapping for your instance.

9. Answer: a

Explanation: A really good example of planning for failure is Netflix simian army, it is a way of injecting failure into their production systems so that they can be sure about the working of the system during the disaster.

10. Answer: a

Explanation: Keep in mind the differences between RDS Multi-AZ and Read Replicas. Multi AZ is for disaster recovery while read replicas improve performance.

11. Answer: b

Explanation: Developers may abstract away the intricacies of specific resource APIs by using a declarative approach to deploy and change compute, database, and other resources. AWS CloudFormation is a service that allows you to manage resource lifecycles regularly, predictably, and safely while also providing for automatic rollbacks, automated state management, and resource management across accounts and regions. Multiple ways to create resources have recently been added, including using the AWS CDK to code in higher-level languages, importing existing resources, detecting configuration drift, and a new Registry that makes it easier to create custom types that inherit many of the core CloudFormation benefits.

12. Answer: a

Explanation: AWS Quick Starts are automated AWS Cloud reference deployments for important workloads. Each Quick Start starts, configures, and operates the AWS compute, network, storage, and other services needed to deploy a given workload on AWS, all while adhering to AWS security and availability best practices. Quick Starts are shortcuts that reduce hundreds of manual tasks into a few simple steps. They are fast, low-cost, and customizable. They are fully functional and designed for production.

13. Answer: d

Explanation: AWS Elastic Beanstalk enables developers to swiftly install and manage applications in the AWS Cloud. Developers simply upload their apps, and Elastic Beanstalk takes care of the rest, including capacity provisioning, load balancing, auto scaling, and application health monitoring.

14. Answer: c

Explanation: Migrate data from one Oracle database to another Oracle database across endpoints that use the same database engine. Also, migrate data between multiple database engines, such as Oracle and PostgreSQL, at the source and target ends. The only requirement for using AWS DMS is that at least one of your endpoints is hosted on an AWS service. It is not possible to move from one on-premises database to another using AWS DMS.

15. Answer: a

Explanation: The AWS Server Migration Service automates the migration of VMware vSphere, Microsoft Hyper-V/SCVMM, and Azure virtual machines from your on-premises environment to the AWS Cloud. AWS SMS replicates your server VMs in the cloud as Amazon Machine Images (AMIs) that may be deployed on Amazon EC2. You can quickly test and update your cloud-based images using AMIs before deploying them in production. It can be used as a backup tool, as part of a multi-site plan on-premises and off-premises, and as part of a Disaster Recovery (DR) strategy.

16. Answer: d

Explanation: The AWS Application Discovery Service gathers and provides data to help enterprise clients better understand the configuration, usage, and behavior of servers in their IT systems. Server data is saved in the Application Discovery Service, where it may be classified and categorized into apps to aid with AWS migration planning. Collected data can be exported for analysis in Excel or other cloud migration analysis tools.

17. Answer: b

> **Explanation:** Templates are JSON or YAML formatted text files. AWS CloudFormation uses JSON or YAML format files to describe the collection of AWS resources (known as a stack), their associated dependencies, and any required runtime parameters are called CloudFormation Template.
>
> **18. Answer: b**
>
> **Explanation:** You can achieve fault tolerance by introducing redundancy into your system and by decoupling the parts of your architecture such that one side does not rely on the uptime of the other.
>
> **19. Answer: a**
>
> **Explanation:** A single EC2 instance can fail for many reasons: hardware failure, network problems, availability-zone outage, and so on. To achieve high availability or fault-tolerance, use auto scaling groups to set up a fleet of EC2 instances that serve requests redundantly.
>
> **20. Answer: d**
>
> **Explanation:** AWS Elastic Beanstalk supports Java, .NET, PHP, Node.js, Python, Ruby, Go, and Docker and is ideal for web applications. However, due to Elastic Beanstalk's open architecture, non-web applications can also be deployed using Elastic Beanstalk.

Chapter 09: Applications Introduction

> 1.   **Answer:** b
>
> **Explanation:** SQS is a queuing system. It is a way of storing messages independently from your EC2 instances. You can use Amazon's simple queue services to transfer any volume of data, at any level of throughput, without misplacing messages or requiring other services to be continuously available.
>
> 2.   **Answer:** d
>
> **Explanation:** Messages are 256KB in size or less. Message can be kept in the queue from 1 minute to 14 days; the default retention period is four days. If you want to store a message that contains above 256KB of text, then this message cannot be stored in SQS. The message will be stored in the S3 bucket.
>
> 3.   **Answer:** b
>
> **Explanation:** FIFO queues also support message groups that allow multiple ordered message groups within a single queue. FIFO queues are not as fast as standard queues. These queues are limited to 300 Transactions Per Second (TPS); however, it has all the capabilities of the standard queue.
>
> 4.   **Answer:** c
>
> **Explanation:** Amazon Simple Workflow Service is a web service that makes coordinating work across distributed application components easy. Amazon SWF enables an application for a wide range of use cases, including media processing, web application back-ends, business process workflow, and analytics pipelines, to be designed as coordination of tasks. A task represents the invocation of various processing steps in an application that can be performed by executable code, web service calls, human action, and scripts.
>
> 5.   **Answer:** a
>
> **Explanation:** The decider controls the flow of the activity task in the workflow execution. A decider decides what to do next if something has finished or failed in a workflow.
>
> 6.   **Answer:** a
>
> Explanation:
>
> **SQS** – With SQS, you need to implement your application-level tracking, especially when applications use multiple queues.

SWF – It ensures that the task is assigned only once and is never duplicated. It keeps track of all the tasks and events in an application.

7. **Answer:** d

Explanation: Amazon Simple Notification Service (SNS) is a web service that makes it simple to set up, operate, and grant notifications from the cloud. It gives developers a highly scalable, flexible, and cost-effective efficiency in sending messages from an application and instantly delivering them to subscribers or other applications.

8. **Answer:** b

Explanation: SNS allows us to group multiple recipients using topics. A topic is an "access point" allowing recipients to dynamically subscribe for identical copies of the same notifications.

9. **Answer:** c

Explanation:

SQS – Simple Queue Service is a pull-based service. It is a way of storing messages independently from your EC2 instances.

SNS – Simple Notification Service is a push service. You can push messages out to different devices via text messages, notifications, etc.

10. **Answer:** b

Explanation: The elastic transcoder is a cloud-based media transcoder. It enables the conversion of media files from their original format to formats that can be played on smartphones, tablets, PCs, and other devices.

11. **Answer:** c

Explanation: Amazon API Gateway is a fully managed service that enables publishing, maintaining, monitoring, and secure APIs at any size simple for developers. Using the AWS Management Console, you can develop an API that works as a front door for applications to access data, business logic, or functionality from your back-end services.

12. **Answer:** a and b

Explanation: Using Amazon API Gateway, you can track and control usage using the API key and connect CloudWatch to log requests for monitoring.

13. **Answer:** c

Explanation: API Gateway caching is a way to cache your endpoint's response. With caching, you can reduce the number of calls made to your endpoint and improve the latency of the requests to your API. When enabling caching for the stage, API Gateway caches responses from your endpoint for the specific Time-To-Live (TTL) period in seconds.

14. **Answer:** a

Explanation: The Same Origin Policy is done to stop malicious websites from attacking other websites, sometimes called Cross-Site Scripting (XSS) attacks. The two things that are done to prevent Cross-Site scripting are:

- Enforced by web browsers
- Ignored by tools like PostMan and curl

15. **Answer:** c

Explanation: Amazon Kinesis is a platform on AWS to send your streaming data. Amazon Kinesis makes it easy to load and analyze streaming data and allows you to build custom applications for your business needs.

16. **Answer:** b

Explanation: Cross-Origin Resource Sharing (CORS) is a way for a web page in one domain to talk to a web page in another domain and request resources from it.

17. **Answer:** d

Explanation: There are three services for real-time streaming of data provided by Amazon Kinesis:

- Amazon Kinesis Streams
- Amazon Kinesis Firehose
- Amazon Kinesis Analytics

18. **Answer:** c

Explanation: Amazon Kinesis Analytics allows you to run SQL Queries of data in Kinesis Firehose and Kinesis Streams. Then it uses those SQL queries to store data in Amazon S3, Amazon Redshift, and ElastiCache. It is used when using standard SQL to build the streaming application.

19. **Answer:** a

Explanation: Amazon Kinesis Streams allows us to persistently store data for 24 hours to seven days. Data consumers go through that data, and after analyzation, they can store analytics in the place where EC2 instance can access.

20. **Answer:** b

Explanation: Shards are uniquely identified groups of a data record within a stream. A Stream is made up of one or more than one shards, each of which provides a fixed amount of capacity. Each shard is capable of supporting up to 5 transactions per second for reading, up to a maximum data read rate of 2 MB per second, and up to 1,000 records per second for writes, which includes a maximum total data write rate of 1 MB per second (including partition keys). The capacity of the single shard is 1MB per second of data input.

21. **Answer:** b

Explanation: Amazon Kinesis Firehose is a fully managed service for collecting and loading streaming data into S3, Redshift, and Elasticsearch Cluster in near real-time. Kinesis Firehose is a versatile and long-lasting product. The information is duplicated across multiple AWS regions. Firehose is a fully managed solution that can scale automatically to match your throughput needs and does not require any administration. This service also handles sharding and monitoring.

22. **Answer:** a

Explanation: Web Identity Federation provides access to your users over AWS resources after they have been successfully authenticated from a web-based identity provider such as Google, Facebook, Amazon, etc.

23. **Answer:** b

Explanation: Amazon Cognito is an AWS service that acts as Identity Broker, which handles interaction between applications and Web ID providers (there is no need to write your code to do this).

24. **Answer:** c

Explanation: Cognito User Pools are user directories, and they are used to manage sign-up and sign-in functionality for mobile and web applications. Users can sign in directly to the User Pool, which means username and password are stored within Cognito, or they can use a third-party identity broker like Facebook, Amazon, or Google. Cognito acts as an Identity Broker between the identity provider and AWS. A successful authentication generates a JSON Web Token (JWT).

25. **Answer:** b

Explanation: Cognito Identity Pools are enabled to provide temporary AWS credentials to access AWS services like S3 or Dynamo DB. Identity Pools are all about authorization access to AWS resources.

26. **Answer:** a

Explanation: Publish/Subscribe or PUB/SUB messaging provides instant event notifications for distributed applications. The pub/sub model allows messages to be broadcast asynchronously to different parts of a system.

27. **Answer:** d

Explanation: SNS message provides a mechanism to broadcast asynchronous event notifications and endpoints that allow other AWS services to connect to the topic to send and receive those messages.

28. **Answer:** a

Explanation: The S3 event notification feature enables you to receive notifications when certain events happen in your bucket; notifications can be delivered to SQS queues, SNS topics, or Lambda functions.

29. **Answer:** c

Explanation: To broadcast a message, a publisher's component simply pushes a message to the topic. The publisher can be your own application or one of many AWS services to publish messages to SNS topics.

30. **Answer:** b

Explanation: The dead-letter queue is an SQS queue to which messages published to a topic can be sent in case those messages cannot be delivered to a subscribed endpoint messages they cannot be delivered due to client errors or server errors are held in the dead-letter queue for further analysis or reprocessing.

Chapter 10: Serverless Services

1. **Answer:** c and d

Explanation: You are free of provisioning and maintenance burdens in the serverless architecture. The cloud service provider is responsible for the allocation of resources and maintenance.

2. **Answer:** a

Explanation: AWS Lambda service comes under the compute category of the AWS management console.

3. **Answer:** c

Explanation: You can use AWS Lambda to run code reacting to events such as data updates, system state alterations, or user activities. AWS services such as S3, Dynamo DB, Kinesis, SNS, and CloudWatch can directly trigger Lambda, or AWS Step Functions can arrange it into workflows. This enables you to create a variety of serverless real-time data processing systems. Custom code is run in ephemeral containers that a third party fully manages in a serverless architecture. Custom code is usually only a minor portion of a larger application. It's also known as a function. Function as a Service is another name for serverless architecture (FaaS).

4. **Answer:** d

Explanation: Alexa is Amazon's cloud-based voice service that builds natural voice experiences.

5. **Answer:** d

Explanation: AWS Lambda is the ultimate abstraction layer. Lambda is a Function as a Service (FaaS) product, which means you have a function provided with code, and AWS executes that code.

6. **Answer:** a

Explanation: AWS Lambda can also be used as a compute service to run your code in response to HTTP requests using Amazon API Gateway, or API calls made using AWS SDKs.

7. **Answer:** b

Explanation: Architectures can get extremely complicated with AWS Lambda, making debugging difficult. Therefore, the AWS service " X-Ray " allows you to debug serverless applications.

8. Answer: c

Explanation: In serverless architecture, the user sends a request to API Gateway, which then responds to AWS Lambda. AWS Lambda communicates with databases like Dynamo DB, Amazon Aurora, or serverless Aurora. It will then send a response back to the user.

9. Answer: a and d

Explanation: Lambda pricing depends on the following:

Number of Requests – The first one million requests are free. Then, $0.20 per 1 million requests is charged. AWS Lambda is very cheap; it allows startups to scale very quickly.

Duration is estimated from the start of your code until it returns or finishes, rounded up to the nearest 100 milliseconds. The cost is determined by how much memory you allocate to your function. For each GB-second consumed, you will be charged $0.00001667.

10. Answer: a

Explanation: The Alexa feature can be used by constructing a skilled architecture. In skill architecture, a user first asks questions, and skill matches what that question would intend. The skill will then send the intent to the AWS Lambda function. The Lambda function will take the data and return a relevant response. The last step is echo speak back the response to the user.

11. Answer: c

Explanation: AWS Lambda function can scale out automatically. When the Lambda function is triggered, it creates a new instance, and when several requests go down, it automatically adjusts.

12. Answer: d

Explanation: In serverless architecture, AWS Lambda can communicate with databases like Dynamo DB or Amazon Aurora, or serverless Aurora.

13. Answer: a

Explanation: Alexa-skill-kit-nodejs-factskill is the basic template that is used with serverless applications repositories.

14. Answer: c

Explanation: Amazon Polly is an AWS service that converts text into speech and creates applications that build new speech-enabled products.

15. Answer: b

Explanation: Serverless Application Repository allows us to deploy serverless applications. These serverless applications are published by AWS, as well as AWS partners and other developers.

16. Answer: a

Explanation: Docker bundles software into containers, which include everything the software requires to operate, including libraries, system tools, code, and runtime.

17. Answer: d

Explanation: Fargate allows you to concentrate on developing your applications. Fargate eliminates the need to deploy and manage servers, allows you to select and pay for resources per application, and increases security by design.

18. Answer: c

Explanation: EKS migrates your application workloads to AWS.

19. Answer: b

Explanation: A standard way to package your configurations, application's code, and dependencies into a single object is provided by containers. Containers run as resource-isolated processes, ensuring

quick, reliable, and consistent deployments, regardless of the environment, and share an Operating System (OS) installed on the server.

20. Answer: a

Explanation: Fargate allows you to concentrate on developing your applications. Fargate eliminates the need to deploy and manage servers, allows you to select and pay for resources per application, and increases security by design.

Chapter 11: Advanced IAM

1. Answer: b

Explanation: AWS Directory Service lets you run Microsoft Active Directory (AD) as a managed service. It is not a single service but a family of managed services. AWS Directory Service makes it easy to set up and run directories in the AWS Cloud.

2. Answer: b

Explanation: AWS Directory Service is a standalone directory in the cloud, and it allows users to access AWS resources and applications with their existing corporate credentials.

3. Answer: a

Explanation: Active Directory is an on-premises directory service used by most enterprises. It is a hierarchical database of users, groups, and computers organized in a pattern of trees and forests.

4. Answer: a

Explanation: AD Connector cannot be shared with other AWS accounts. Consider using AWS Managed Microsoft AD to share your directory if this is a requirement.

5. Answer: b and c

Explanation: Cloud Directory and Cognito user pools are non-AD-compatible services. Suppose you are a developer and do not need Active Directory. In that case, you can create a cloud directory that organizes and manages hierarchical information, and Cognito user pools work with mobile and web applications.

6. Answer: a and d

Explanation: The services that are AD compatible are Managed Microsoft AD, also known as directory service for Microsoft Active Directory, AD connector, and Simple AD. These services enable users to sign in to AWS applications like Amazon workspaces and QuickSight with their Active Directory credentials.

7. Answer: c

Explanation: The general format of ARN is Arn: partition : service : region : account-id.

8. Answer: a

Explanation: Identity-based policies are attached to an IAM user, group, or role. These policies let you specify what that identity can do (its permissions).

9. Answer: a

Explanation: Any permissions that are not explicitly allowed are implicitly denied. E.g., if your identity or resource does not have a policy that explicitly allows an AWS API action, it is implicitly denied.

10. Answer: b

Explanation: Only the attached policies affect. Just because you have defined a policy does not mean you can do anything unless connected to a user, group, or role.

11. Answer: b

Explanation: AWS-managed policies are created by AWS for the customer's convenience and are denoted with an orange box icon. These policies are not editable by customers, but you can use as many as you like.

---

12. **Answer:** c

Explanation: SSO (Single Sign-On) is a solution that allows you to manage access to your AWS accounts and business apps from a single location. You can easily manage access and user rights to all of your AWS Organization accounts using AWS SSO.

13. **Answer:** a

Explanation: For supported resource types, Resource Access Manager (RAM) allows you to securely share resources between AWS accounts, within your organization or Organizational Units (OUs) in AWS Organizations, and with IAM roles and IAM users. You may share transit gateways, subnets, AWS Licensing Manager license configurations, Amazon Route 53 Resolver rules, and other resource types using AWS RAM.

14. **Answer:** b

Explanation: AWS resources are identified by their Amazon Resource Names (ARNs). When you need to explicitly identify a resource across AWS, such as in IAM policies, Amazon Relational Database Service (Amazon RDS) tags, and API requests, you'll need an ARN.

15. **Answer:** a

Explanation: The Cloud Directory service is fully managed. It removes time-consuming and costly administrative duties like infrastructure scaling and server management.

Chapter 12: Security

---

1. **Answer:** b

Explanation: If you want to block common exploits like sequel injection or cross-site scripting attacks, you must use WAF. WAF operates on layer seven and can inspect that level of traffic for these types of exploits.

2. **Answer:** a

Explanation: If you want to block an IP or range of IPs, you use an NACL that operates on layer four.

3. **Answer:** b

Explanation: KMS is ideal for encrypting S3 objects, database passwords, and API keys stored in the systems manager parameter store.

4. **Answer:** c

Explanation: CMKs can encrypt and decrypt data up to 4 kilobytes in size.

5. **Answer:** a

Explanation: KMS is a level two FIPs 140-2 service. FIPS is a computer security standard used by the US government to approve cryptography modules. You must provide evidence of tampering at level two.

6. **Answer:** b

Explanation: AWS Managed CMKs are available for free. These are created automatically when you initially create an encrypted resource in an AWS service. Although you can track the usage of an AWS-managed CMK, KMS manages the key's lifecycle and permissions on your behalf.

7. **Answer:** a

Explanation: You do not need to create or manage the AWS-owned CMKs. However, you cannot view, use, track, or audit them.

8. **Answer:** b

Explanation: With CloudHSM, you can manage your own encryption keys using FIPS 140-2 Level 3 validated HSMs. FIPS is a US Government computer security standard. It is used to approve

---

cryptographic modules and has several different compliance levels. Compliance level three is where physical security mechanisms might include the use of strong enclosures and tamper detection or response circuitry that zeroes out all of your plain text cryptographic security providers when the removable doors or covers of the cryptographic module inside open up.

9. **Answer:** a

Explanation: Parameter store is an essential tool for caching and distributing secrets securely to AWS resources. It is a component of AWS systems manager, abbreviated as SSM.

10. **Answer:** c

Explanation: Secrets Manager enables you to control secret access using fine-grained permissions and centrally audit secret rotation for resources in the AWS Cloud, third-party services, and on-premises.

11. **Answer:** b

Explanation: Secrets Manager can rotate secrets for you automatically. Secrets Manager has built-in support for Amazon RDS, Amazon Redshift, and Amazon DocumentDB, as well as secret rotation.

12. **Answer:** a

Explanation: The Secrets Manager can generate random secrets. In CloudFormation, you can generate passwords at random and save them in the secrets manager

13. **Answer:** a

Explanation: Parameter Store provides the option to store data unencrypted or to encrypt the data with a KMS key. But with Secrets Manager, the secrets are stored encrypted, and there is no option to store unencrypted data.

14. **Answer:** a

Explanation: AWS Shield is a managed Distributed-Denial-of-Service (DDoS) protection service that safeguards applications running on AWS.

15. **Answer:** c

Explanation: WAF is a web application firewall that lets you monitor HTTP or HTTPS requests to CloudFront, application load balancer, or API gateway. WAF lets you control access to content based on the rules you specify.

Acronyms

AAD	Additional Authenticated Data
ACL	Access Control List
ACM PCA	AWS Certificate Manager Private Certificate Authority
ACM	AWS Certificate Manager
ACU	Aurora Capacity Unit
AMI	Amazon Machine Image
API	Application Programming Interface
APN	AWS Partner Network
ARN	Amazon Resource Name
ASN	Autonomous System Number
AUC	Area Under the Curve
AWS	Amazon Web Services
BGP	Border Gateway Protocol
CapEx	Capital Expenditure
CDN	Content Delivery Network
CIDR	Classless Inter-Domain Routing
CLI	Command Line Interface
CMK	Customer Master Key
CNAME	Canonical Name
DB	Database
DKIM	DomainKeys Identified Mail
DNS	Domain Name System
DX	Direct Connect
EBS	Elastic Block Store
EC2	Elastic Cloud Compute
ECR	Elastic Container Registry

ECS	Elastic Container Service
EFS	Elastic File System
EIP	Elastic IP
ELB	Elastic Load Balancer
EMR	Elastic Map Reduce
ENI	Elastic Network Interface
ES	Elasticsearch Service
ETL	Extract, Transform, and Load
FBL	Feedback Loop
FIM	Federated Identity Management
HMAC	Hash-based Message Authentication Code
HPC	High Performance Compute
HSM	Hardware Security Module
HTTP	Hypertext Transfer Protocol
HTTPS	Hypertext Transfer Protocol Secure
IaaS	Infrastructure as a Service
IAM	Identity and Access Management
IdP	Identity Provider
IGW	Internet Gateway
ISP	Internet Service Provider
JSON	JavaScript Object Notation
KMS	Key Management Service
MFA	Multi-Factor Authentication
MIME	Multipurpose Internet Mail Extensions
MTA	Mail Transfer Agent
NACL	Network Access Control List
NAT	Network Address Translation
NS	Name Server
PaaS	Platform as a Service

OpEx	Operational Expenditure
ORC	Optimized Row Columnar
OU	Organizational Unit
RAM	Resource Access Manager
RDS	Relational Database Service
S3	Simple Storage Service
SaaS	Software as a Service
SCP	Service Control Policy
SDK	Software Development Kit
SES	Simple Email Service
SMTP	Simple Mail Transfer Protocol
SNS	Simple Notification Service
SOAP	Simple Object Access Protocol
SQS	Simple Queue Service
SSE	Server-Side Encryption
SSH	Secure Shell
SSL	Secure Sockets Layer
SSO	Single Sign-On
STS	Security Token Service
SWF	Simple Workflow Service
TCP	Transmission Control Protocol
TGW	Transit Gateway
TLD	Top Level Domain
TLS	Transport Layer Security
TTL	Time to Live
VERP	Variable Envelope Return Path
VPC	Virtual Private Cloud
VPG	Virtual Private Gateway
VPN	Virtual Private Network

Appendix B: Acronyms

WAF	Web Application Firewall
WAM	WorkSpaces Application Manager
WSDL	Web Services Description Language

References

o https://aws.amazon.com/
o https://medium.com/techloop/a-10-000-feet-overview-of-aws-and-its-resources-part-1-cdccb56ff9bd
o https://aws.amazon.com/about-aws/global-infrastructure/
o https://console.aws.amazon.com/console/home?nc2=h_ct&region=us-east-1&src=header-signin
o https://aws.amazon.com/about-aws/whats-new/2015/
o https://aws.amazon.com/about-aws/whats-new/2016/
o https://aws.amazon.com/about-aws/whats-new/2017/
o https://aws.amazon.com/about-aws/global-infrastructure/
o https://docs.aws.amazon.com/AmazonRDS/latest/UserGuide/Concepts.RegionsAndAvailabilityZones.html
o https://docs.aws.amazon.com/whitepapers/latest/aws-overview/ar-and-vr.html
o https://aws.amazon.com/pinpoint/customer-engagement/
o https://aws.amazon.com/appstream2/
o https://aws.amazon.com/gaming/mobile-backend-services/
o https://docs.aws.amazon.com/whitepapers/latest/aws-overview/global-infrastructure.html
o https://aws.amazon.com/about-aws/global-infrastructure/regions_az/
o https://aws.amazon.com/iam/
o https://docs.aws.amazon.com/storagegateway/latest/userguide/StorageGatewayConcepts.html#storage-gateway-vtl-concepts
o https://docs.aws.amazon.com/storagegateway/latest/userguide/WhatIsStorageGateway.html
o https://aws.amazon.com/storagegateway/volume/
o https://docs.aws.amazon.com/IAM/latest/UserGuide/introduction.html
o https://aws.amazon.com/blogs/security/tag/iam/
o https://docs.aws.amazon.com/AmazonS3/latest/gsg/GetStartedWithS3.html
o https://docs.aws.amazon.com/AmazonS3/latest/gsg/CreatingABucket.html
o https://docs.aws.amazon.com/s3/index.html
o https://docs.aws.amazon.com/AmazonS3/latest/dev/Welcome.html
o https://docs.aws.amazon.com/AmazonS3/latest/dev/UsingBucket.html
o https://docs.aws.amazon.com/AmazonS3/latest/dev/storage-class-intro.html
o https://docs.aws.amazon.com/AmazonS3/latest/dev/bucket-encryption.html
o https://docs.aws.amazon.com/AmazonS3/latest/dev/UsingEncryption.html
o https://docs.aws.amazon.com/AmazonS3/latest/dev/UsingClientSideEncryption.html
o https://docs.aws.amazon.com/AmazonS3/latest/dev/ObjectVersioning.html
o https://docs.aws.amazon.com/AmazonS3/latest/dev/object-lifecycle-mgmt.html
o https://docs.aws.amazon.com/AmazonS3/latest/dev/transfer-acceleration.html
o https://www.amazonaws.cn/en/snowball/faq/
o https://aws.amazon.com/snowball/
o https://docs.aws.amazon.com/organizations/latest/userguide/orgs_introduction.html
o https://aws.amazon.com/organizations/features/
o https://docs.aws.amazon.com/AmazonS3/latest/dev/replication.html
o https://docs.aws.amazon.com/AWSEC2/latest/UserGuide/concepts.html
o https://aws.amazon.com/ec2/

o https://do.awsstatic.com/whitepapers/aws_pricing_overview.pdf
o https://aws.amazon.com/pricing/
o https://docs.aws.amazon.com/AWSEC2/latest/UserGuide/ebs-volume-types.html
o https://docs.aws.amazon.com/AWSEC2/latest/UserGuide/ebs-volumes.html
o https://docs.microsoft.com/en-us/windows-hardware/drivers/network/overview-of-single-root-i-o-virtualization--sr-iov-
o https://aws.amazon.com/cloudwatch/
o https://aws.amazon.com/efs/
o https://aws.amazon.com/fsx/lustre/
o https://aws.amazon.com/fsx/windows/
o https://aws.amazon.com/waf/
o https://aws.amazon.com/nosql/
o https://aws.amazon.com/nosql/key-value/
o https://aws.amazon.com/rds/
o https://aws.amazon.com/products/databases/
o https://aws.amazon.com/products/databases/open-source-databases/
o https://www.slideshare.net/AmazonWebServices/building-with-aws-databases-match-your-workload-to-the-right-database-dat301-aws-reinvent-2018
o https://aws.amazon.com/rds/features/
o https://aws.amazon.com/elasticache/
o https://aws.amazon.com/dynamodb/pricing/
o https://docs.aws.amazon.com/AmazonRDS/latest/UserGuide/Overview.DBInstance.Modifying.html
o https://aws.amazon.com/elasticache/memcached/
o https://docs.aws.amazon.com/AmazonElastiCache/latest/red-ug/Clusters.html
o https://docs.aws.amazon.com/AmazonElastiCache/latest/red-ug/CacheNodes.html
o https://docs.aws.amazon.com/AmazonElastiCache/latest/mem-ug/WhatIs.html
o https://docs.aws.amazon.com/AmazonElastiCache/latest/mem-ug/WhatIs.Components.html
o https://docs.aws.amazon.com/whitepapers/latest/aws-overview/database.html
o https://docs.aws.amazon.com/AmazonRDS/latest/UserGuide/CHAP_CommonTasks.BackupRestore.html
o https://docs.aws.amazon.com/AmazonRDS/latest/UserGuide/USER_WorkingWithAutomatedBackups.html
o https://docs.aws.amazon.com/AmazonRDS/latest/UserGuide/UsingWithRDS.html
o https://docs.aws.amazon.com/AmazonRDS/latest/UserGuide/Overview.Encryption.html
o https://aws.amazon.com/dynamodb/features/
o https://docs.aws.amazon.com/redshift/latest/gsg/index.html
o https://docs.aws.amazon.com/redshift/latest/dg/welcome.html
o https://docs.aws.amazon.com/redshift/latest/dg/c_redshift_system_overview.html
o https://docs.aws.amazon.com/redshift/latest/dg/c_Compression_encodings.html
o https://docs.aws.amazon.com/redshift/latest/dg/c_challenges_achieving_high_performance_queries.html
o https://docs.aws.amazon.com/AmazonRDS/latest/AuroraUserGuide/Aurora.Replication.html
o https://aws.amazon.com/rds/aurora/serverless/
o https://aws.amazon.com/blogs/aws/data-compression-improvements-in-amazon-redshift/

o https://docs.aws.amazon.com/AmazonRDS/latest/AuroraUserGuide/AuroraMySQL.Replication.MySQL.html

o https://aws.amazon.com/redshift/pricing/

o https://docs.aws.amazon.com/AmazonRDS/latest/UserGuide/APITroubleshooting.html

o https://acloud.guru/course/aws-certified-solutions-architect-associate/learn/route53/domainname/watch?backUrl=~2Fcourses

o https://docs.aws.amazon.com/Route53/latest/DeveloperGuide/registrar-tld-list.htmlhttps://docs.aws.amazon.com/amazondynamodb/latest/developerguide/TTL.html

o https://docs.aws.amazon.com/vpc/latest/userguide/vpc-ip-addressing.html

o https://aws.amazon.com/getting-started/hands-on/get-a-domain/

o https://docs.aws.amazon.com/Route53/latest/DeveloperGuide/dns-configuring.html

o https://aws.amazon.com/premiumsupport/knowledge-center/multivalue-versus-simple-policies/

o https://docs.aws.amazon.com/Route53/latest/DeveloperGuide/routing-policy.html

o https://en.wikipedia.org/wiki/Bastion_host

o https://aws.amazon.com/global-accelerator/

o https://docs.aws.amazon.com/cli/latest/reference/globalaccelerator/index.html

o https://www.zdnet.com/article/aws-global-accelerator-to-boost-performance-across-regions/

o https://docs.aws.amazon.com/vpc/latest/userguide/vpc-ip-addressing.html#subnet-public-ip

o https://docs.aws.amazon.com/vpc/latest/userguide/amazon-vpc-limits.html

o https://docs.aws.amazon.com/general/latest/gr/global_accelerator.html

o http://www.itcheerup.net/2018/05/aws-vpc-cost/

o https://aws.amazon.com/vpc/pricing/

o https://docs.aws.amazon.com/vpc/latest/userguide/VPC_NAT_Instance.html

o https://docs.aws.amazon.com/vpc/latest/userguide/vpc-nat-comparison.html

o https://docs.aws.amazon.com/directconnect/latest/UserGuide/Welcome.html

o https://docs.aws.amazon.com/vpc/latest/userguide/vpc-nat-gateway.html

o https://docs.aws.amazon.com/vpc/latest/userguide/vpc-endpoints.html

o https://docs.aws.amazon.com/vpc/index.html

o https://docs.aws.amazon.com/vpc/latest/userguide/what-is-amazon-vpc.html

o https://docs.aws.amazon.com/vpc/latest/userguide/vpce-gateway.html

o https://docs.aws.amazon.com/vpc/latest/userguide/vpce-interface.html

o https://docs.aws.amazon.com/vpc/latest/userguide/vpc-network-acls.html#nacl-ephemeral-ports

o https://cloudacademy.com/blog/aws-network-acl-vpc-subnets-network-security/

o https://cloudacademy.com/blog/aws-bastion-host-nat-instances-vpc-Peering-security/

o https://docs.aws.amazon.com/vpc/latest/Peering/what-is-vpc-Peering.html

o https://docs.aws.amazon.com/vpc/latest/userguide/VPC_Subnets.html

o https://www.sumologic.com/aws/vpc/use-aws-vpc-flow-logs/

o https://docs.aws.amazon.com/vpc/latest/userguide/flow-logs.html

o https://aws.amazon.com/blogs/aws/vpc-flow-logs-log-and-view-network-traffic-flows/

o https://aws.amazon.com/blogs/security/securely-connect-to-linux-instances-running-in-a-private-amazon-vpc/

o https://docs.aws.amazon.com/AWSEC2/latest/UserGuide/TroubleshootingInstancesConnecting.html

o https://www.sumologic.com/insight/aws-vpc/

o https://www.sumologic.com/insight/use-aws-vpc-flow-logs/

- https://docs.aws.amazon.com/elasticloadbalancing/latest/application/tutorial-load-balancer-routing.html
- https://docs.aws.amazon.com/autoscaling/ec2/userguide/what-is-amazon-ec2-auto-scaling.html
- https://docs.aws.amazon.com/AWSSimpleQueueService/latest/SQSDeveloperGuide/sqs-how-it-works.html
- https://aws.amazon.com/sqs/
- https://docs.aws.amazon.com/AWSSimpleQueueService/latest/SQSDeveloperGuide/standard-queues.html
- https://aws.amazon.com/swf/
- https://docs.aws.amazon.com/sns/latest/dg/welcome.html
- https://aws.amazon.com/elastictranscoder/
- https://docs.aws.amazon.com/apigateway/latest/developerguide/welcome.html
- https://aws.amazon.com/api-gateway/
- https://docs.aws.amazon.com/apigateway/latest/developerguide/api-gateway-caching.html
- https://docs.aws.amazon.com/AmazonS3/latest/dev/cors.html
- https://aws.amazon.com/kinesis/
- https://aws.amazon.com/kinesis/data-analytics/
- https://docs.aws.amazon.com/IAM/latest/UserGuide/id_roles_providers_oidc.html
- https://aws.amazon.com/cognito/
- https://help.acloud.guru/hc/en-us/articles/115003704634
- https://docs.aws.amazon.com/lambda/latest/dg/welcome.html
- https://docs.aws.amazon.com/lambda/latest/dg/invocation-scaling.html
- https://developer.amazon.com/en-US/docs/alexa/custom-skills/speech-synthesis-markup-language-ssml-reference.html#audio

About Our Products

Other products from IPSpecialist LTD regarding CSP technology are:

 AWS Certified Cloud Practitioner Study guide

 AWS Certified SysOps Admin - Associate Study guide

 AWS Certified Solution Architect - Associate Study guide

 AWS Certified Developer Associate Study guide

 AWS Certified Advanced Networking – Specialty Study guide

 AWS Certified Security – Specialty Study guide

 AWS Certified Big Data – Specialty Study guide

 AWS Certified Database – Specialty Study guide

 AWS Certified Machine Learning – Specialty Study guide

 Microsoft Certified: Azure Fundamentals

 Microsoft Certified: Azure Administrator

 Microsoft Certified: Azure Solution Architect

 Microsoft Certified: Azure DevOps Engineer

 Microsoft Certified: Azure Developer Associate

 Microsoft Certified: Azure Security Engineer

 Microsoft Certified: Azure Data Fundamentals

 Microsoft Certified: Azure AI Fundamentals

 Microsoft Certified: Azure Database Administrator Associate

 Google Certified: Associate Cloud Engineer

 Google Certified: Professional Cloud Developer

 Microsoft Certified: Azure Data Engineer Associate

 Microsoft Certified: Azure Data Scientist

 Ansible Certified: Advanced Automation

 Oracle Certified: OCI Foundations Associate

 Oracle Certified: OCI Developer Associate

 Oracle Certified: OCI Architect Associate

 Oracle Certified: OCI Operations Associate

 Kubernetes Certified: Application Developer

Other Network & Security related products from IPSpecialist LTD are:

- CCNA Routing & Switching Study Guide
- CCNA Security Second Edition Study Guide
- CCNA Service Provider Study Guide
- CCDA Study Guide
- CCDP Study Guide
- CCNP Route Study Guide
- CCNP Switch Study Guide
- CCNP Troubleshoot Study Guide
- CCNP Security SCOR Study Guide
- CCNP Service Provider SPCOR Study Guide
- CCNP Enterprise ENCOR Study Guide
- CCNP Enterprise ENARSI Study Guide
- CompTIA Network+ Study Guide
- CompTIA Security+ Study Guide
- Certified Blockchain Expert (CBEv2) Study Guide
- EC-Council CEH v10 Second Edition Study Guide
- EC-Council CEH v12 First Edition Study Guide
- Certified Blockchain Expert v2 Study Guide

Made in the USA
Las Vegas, NV
09 May 2023

71802944R00227